THE LITERATURE OF DEATH AND DYING

THE LITERATURE OF
DEATH AND DYING

Advisory Editor
Robert Kastenbaum

Editorial Board
Gordon Geddes
Gerald J. Gruman
Michael Andrew Simpson

DEATH, GRIEF AND BEREAVEMENT

A Bibliography
1845-1975

Compiled by
ROBERT FULTON

with the assistance of
Jerry Carlson, Karl Krohn,
Eric Markusen and Greg Owen
Center for Death Education and Research
University of Minnesota

ARNO PRESS

A New York Times Company

New York / 1977

First publication 1977 by Arno Press Inc.

Copyright © 1977 by Robert Fulton

THE LITERATURE OF DEATH AND DYING
ISBN for complete set: 0-405-09550-3
See last pages of this volume for titles.

Manufactured in the United States of America

———————◆———————

Library of Congress Cataloging in Publication Data

Fulton, Robert Lester, 1926-
   Death, grief, and bereavement.

   (The Literature of death and dying)
   Reprint of the 1976 ed. published by Center for Death
Education and Research, University of Minnesota, Minne-
apolis.
    1. Death--Bibliography. 2. Grief--Bibliography.
3. Bereavement--Bibliography. I. Title. II. Series.
Z5725.F855 1977 [BD444] 016.128'5   76-19572
ISBN 0-405-09570-8

INTRODUCTION

This is the first published edition of the bibliography on Death, Grief, and Bereavement prepared by the Center for Death Education and Research at the University of Minnesota. It is offered with the hope that it will aid in acquainting scholars and other interested persons with the scientific research and discussion that has taken place concerning the subject of death since the middle of the last century.

Interest in the topic has been notable, particularly in the past few years. Evidence of this can be found not only in the compilation of this and other bibliographies, but also in the exponential increase in the number of books and articles that have been published. By actual count, more books and articles have been written on the subject of death and dying over the past decade than during the previous 150 years. When the book Death and Identity was being prepared for publication in 1964, few more than 400 scholarly references could be found in the initial bibliographic survey of the field. The present bibliography, it will be noted, contains over 3800 items. The upsurge of interest began with the publication of Herman Feifel's book, The Meaning of Death, in 1959, but the floodgates were opened in 1969 with the appearance of Elisabeth Kubler-Ross' On Death and Dying. From that time, the exponential growth in the level of interest in the field has been a phenomenon of sociological interest itself. The increased volume of publications has been paralleled by a rise in death-related course offerings in high schools, colleges, and universities throughout the country. This trend followed the first course of lectures on death offered at the University of Minnesota in 1963. It has recently been determined that there are now well over 2,000 courses presented at the college and university

level alone. Ninety percent of these courses have been in existence for less
than three years.

There is no question that the issues that presently confront our society
relevant to death are many and that communication dealing with the specific
problems associated with death is extensive. I trust that this bibliography
will serve to illuminate as well as facilitate this communication.

It should be noted that this edition of the bibliography, like the previous
unpublished edition, is arranged alphabetically by author whereas the first two
compilations were arranged chronologically by date of publication. It is my
belief that this format, given the voluminous outpouring of material over the past
five years, serves the researcher and scholar more advantageously. In addition,
a subject index has been compiled to enhance the convenience of the bibliography
to the reader.

Generally, in preparing the bibliography, only references that treat the
subject from an empirical perspective have been considered. Except in those
instances in which a book or article has particular historical significance
or relevance, no journalistic, literary or theological works have been included.
Moreover, given the extensive bibliographies presently available in the area
of suicide, references to this subject have, in the main, been omitted. On
the other hand, the reader will notice that materials dealing with definitions
of death, organ transplantation, terminal care, euthanasia, sudden infant
death syndrome and abortion appear in greater plenitude in this edition. This
reflects the growing attention that is now being given to these increasingly
problematical and controversial subjects.

No special effort has been made to include foreign references. However, books and articles that have come to my attention or that are available in translation have generally been included.

I owe a debt of gratitude to many people for their advice and assistance in the preparation of this bibliography. Particularly I would like to acknowledge my debt to friends and colleagues who have called my attention to new or overlooked references during the past few years. I would also like to recognize the staff of the Center, without whose efforts and forbearance the bibliography could not have been prepared. I extend my sincerest appreciation for a tedious, but I hope not fruitless, task to Marcia Stedman, who bore the brunt of the work in the preparation of the third compilation of the bibliography, and to the other members of the staff who toiled by her side: Ann Moore, Cindi Paulsen, Sonja Fagerberg, Rhonda Knoop, Stephanie Steppe and Diana Tostenrud.

I would like to thank the three Ober Fellows of the Center, Karl Krohn, Eric Markusen and Greg Owen for their unstinting efforts and Lori Taft for her secretarial assistance in the preparation of this edition for publication by the Arno Press. Finally I would especially like to thank Jerry Carlson for his overseeing the editing and the typing of the manuscript.

In a continuing project such as this, there will inevitably be errors of omission and commission. It is hoped that such errors will be brought to the editor's attention.

Robert Fulton
Center for Death Education and Research
University of Minnesota

July 14, 1976

1. Aarons, E.S. _Death Is My Shadow_. New York: MacFadden-Bartell, 1970.

2. Aasterud, Margaret. "Defenses Against Anxiety in the Nurse Patient Relation-ship," _Nursing Forum_, 1 (Summer, 1963), 34-59.

3. Abadi, M. "Psychoanalytic Study of a Basic Fantasy on the Fear of Death," _Revista de Psicoanalisis_, 17 (1960), 431-48.

4. Abely, X., M. Leconte. "Attempt to Interpret Manic Reactions after Sorrow," _American Journal of Medical Psychology_, 96 (1938), 232-40.

5. Ablon, J. "Bereavement in a Samoan Community," _British Journal of Medical Psychology_, 44 (Nov., 1971), 329-37.

6. Abraham, C. "Thought and Fear of Death in Aged with Mental Disorders," _Schweizer Archiv fur Neurologie, Neurochirurgie und Psychiatrie_, 90 (1962), 362-69.

7. Abram, Harry S. "Adaptation to Open Heart Surgery: A Psychiatric Study of Response to the Threat of Death," _American Journal of Psychiatry_, 122 (1965), 659-7.

8. _____. "Death Psychology: Science Fiction and Writings of S.G. Weinbaum," _Suicide_, 5 (1975), 93-7.

9. _____. "Intensive Care Units: Psychological Problems, Management Con-cepts and Research," Nutley, NH: Hoffman-LaRoche, 1975.

10. _____. "The Psychiatrist, the Treatment of Chronic Renal Failure and the Prolongation of Life," _American Journal of Psychiatry_, 124 (1968), 1351-7.

11. _____. "The Psychiatrist, the Treatment of Chronic Renal Failure and the Prolongation of Life: II," _American Journal of Psychiatry_, 126 (1969), 157-67.

12. _____. "The Psychology of Terminal Illness as Portrayed in Solzhenitsyn's _The Cancer Ward_," _Archives of Internal Medicine_, 124 (Dec., 1969), 758-60.

13. Abrams, Ruth D. "The Patient with Cancer--His Changing Pattern of Communi-cation," _New England Journal of Medicine_, 274 (Feb. 10, 1966), 317-22.

14. _____, J.E. Finesinger, "Guilt Reactions in Patients with Cancer," _Cancer_, 6 (May, 1953), 474-82.

15. _____, et al. "Terminal Care in Cancer," _New England Journal of Medicine_, 232 (June 21, 1945), 719-24.

16. Abramson, Jane. "Facing the Other Fact of Life: Death in Recent Children's Fiction," _School Library Journal_, 21 (Dec., 1974), 31-3.

17. Academy of Religion and Mental Health. Religion and Childhood: Religion in the Developing Personality, Proceedings of the Second Academy Symposium, 1958, New York: New York University Press, 1960.

18. Achte, K.A. "Psychological Factors and Death," Nordisk Psykiatrisk Tidsskrift, 19 (1965), 268-73.

19. _____, M.L. Vauhkonen. "Cancer and the Psyche," Omega, 2 (Feb., 1971), 45-56.

20. Ackerknecht, Erwin. "Death in the History of Medicine," Bulletin of the History of Medicine, 42 (Jan.-Feb., 1968), 19-23.

21. Ad Hoc Committee of the Harvard School to Examine the Definition of Brain Death. "A Definition of Irreversible Coma," Journal of the American Medical Association, 205 (Aug. 5, 1968), 337-40.

22. Adamek, Mary Elaine. "Some Observations on Death and a Family," Nursing Science, (Aug., 1965), 258-67.

23. Adamek, Raymond J. "Abortion, Personal Freedom, and Public Policy," The Family Coordinator, 23 (Oct., 1974), 411-19.

24. Adams, J.M. "Unexpected Death in Infants," Forensic Science, 2 (Aug., 1973), 383-4.

25. Adelson, L., E.R. Kenney. "Sudden and Unexpected Death in Infancy and Childhood," Pediatrics, 17 (1956), 663-97.

26. Adelson, S.E. "Dying Patient: An Unspoken Dialogue," New Physician, 20 (Nov., 1971), 706ff.

27. Adelstein, A.M. "Precision in Death Certification," Lancet, 1 (Mar. 29, 1969), 682.

28. Adler, Alfred. "Das Todesproblem in der Neurose," Internationale Zeitschrift, 14 (Jan.-Mar., 1936), 1-6.

29. Adler, C.S. "The Meaning of Death to Children," Arizona Medicine, 26 (Mar., 1969), 266ff.

30. Adlerstein, Arthur M. The Relationship Between Religious Belief and Death Affect, Ann Arbor: University Microfilms, 1963.

31. Agate, John. "Care of the Dying in Geriatric Departments," Lancet, 1 (Mar., 1973), 364-6.

32. Agee, James. A Death in the Family, New York: Avon, 1957.

33. Aginsky, B.W. "The Socio-psychological Significance of Death Among the Pomo Indians," American Imago, 1 (1940), 1-11.

34. Aguilera, D.C. "Crisis: A Moment of Truth," Journal of Psychiatric Nursing, 9 (May-June, 1971), 23.

35. Aherne, W. "The Pathology of Sudden Unexpected Death in Childhood," Journal of the Forensic Science Society, 12 (Oct., 1972), 585-6.

36. Ainsworth, Mary D. et al. Deprivation of Maternal Care, New York: Schocken, 1966.

37. Aitken, P.Q. "The Right to Live and the Right to Die," Medical Times, 95 (Nov., 1967), 1184-7.

38. Aitken-Swan, Jean. "Nursing the Late Cancer Patient at Home," Practitioner, 183 (1959), 64-9.

39. _____, E.C. Easson. "Reactions of Cancer Patients on Being Told their Diagnosis," British Medical Journal, 1 (Mar. 21, 1959), 779-83.

40. Akaishi, S. "Problems Concerning Death from the Viewpoint of Legal Medicine," Naika, 23 (May, 1969), 861-9.

41. Albertz, M. "Lasst die Toten Ihre Toten Begraben!" Zeichen der Zeit, 8 (1954), 135-8.

42. Aldern, Henry Mills. A Study of Death, New York: Harper and Brothers, 1895.

43. Aldenhoven, H. "Klinischer Beitrag Zur Frage Der Todesahnungen," (Clinical Contribution to the Question of Death Premonitions), Psychotherapie, 2 (1957), 55-9.

44. Alderson, M.R. "Care of the Dying," British Medical Journal, 1 (Jan. 20, 1973), 170.

45. _____. "Relationship Between Month of Birth and Month of Death in Elderly," British Journal of Preventive Science, 29 (1975), 151-6.

46. Aldrich, C., M. Knight. "The Dying Patient's Grief," Journal of the American Medical Association, 184 (May 4, 1963), 329-31.

47. _____. "Personality Factors and Mortality in the Relocation of the Aged," Gerontologist, 4 (1964), 92-3.

48. _____, et al. "Relocation of the Aged and Disabled: A Mortality Study," Journal of the American Geriatric Society, 11 (1963), 185-94.

49. Alexander, Franz. "The Need for Punishment and the Death Instinct," International Journal of Psychoanalysis, 10 (1929), 256-69.

50. Alexander, George H. "An Unexplained Death Coexistent with Death-Wishes," Psychosomatic Medicine, 5 (1943), 188-94.

51. Alexander, I.E., A.M. Adlerstein. "Affective Responses to the Concept of Death in a Population of Children and Early Adolescents," Journal of Genetic Psychology, 93 (Dec., 1958), 167-77.

52. _____, et al. "Is Death a Matter of Indifference?" Journal of Psychology, 43 (1957), 277-83.

53. Alexander, Michael et al. "Fear of Death in Parachute Jumpers," Perceptual and Motor Skills, 34 (Feb., 1972), 338.

54. Alexander, Shana. "They Decide Who Lives, Who Dies," Life, 53 (1962), 102-25.

55. Alk L. et al. "Sudden Infant Death: Normal Cardiac Habituation and Poor Autonomic Control," New England Journal of Medicine, 291 (Aug. 1, 1974), 219-22.

56. Altman, Leon L. "'West' as a Symbol of Death," Psychoanalytic Quarterly, 28 (1959), 236-41.

57. Alsop, Stewart. Stay of Execution: A Sort of Memoir. Philadelphia: J.B. Lippincott, 1973.

58. Alvarez, Alfred. The Savage God. New York: Bantam, 1973.

59. Alvarez, Walter C. "Care of the Dying," Journal of the American Medical Association, 150 (Sep., 1952), 86-91.

60. _____. "Controversy over the Determination of Death," Geriatrics, 27 (Feb. 24, 1972), 48.

61. _____. "Death Often is Not So Difficult or Painful," Geriatrics, 18 (Mar., 1963), 165-6.

62. _____. "Help for the Dying Patient," Geriatrics, 19 (Feb., 1964), 69-71.

63. _____. "Some Aspects of Death," Geriatrics, 19 (Jul., 1964), 465-6.

64. Amelineau, Emile. Histoire de la Sepulture et des Funerailles dans l'Ancienne Egypte. Annales du Musee Guimel, vols. xxviii-xxix. Paris: 1896.

65. American Academy of Pediatrics. Care of Children in Hospitals. Evanston: American Academy of Pediatrics, 1960.

66. _____, Committee on Infant and Preschool Children. "Home Monitoring for Sudden Infant Death," Pediatrics, 55 (Jan., 1975), 144-5.

67. The American Battle Monuments Commission. American Memorials and Overseas Military Cemeteries. Washington: USGPO, 1970.

68. The American Medical Association. "Physician and Dying Patient: Report of Judicial Council," Connecticut Medicine, 39 (1975), 514-5.

69. Anderson, B.G. "Bereavement as a Subject of Cross-Cultural Inquiry: An American Sample," Anthropological Quarterly, 38 (1965), 181-200.

70. Anderson, Charles. "Aspects of Pathological Grief and Mourning," International Journal of Psychoanalysis, 30 (1949), 48-55.

71. Anderson, Fred. "Death and the Doctors: Who Will Decide Who is to Live?" The New Republic, 160 (Apr. 19, 1969), 9-10.

72. Anderson, J. Death and Friends. Pittsburgh: University of Pittsburgh Press, 1970.

73. Anderson, R., J.F. Rosenblith. "Sudden Unexpected Death Syndrome: Early Indicators," Biological Neonate, 18 (1971), 395-406.

74. _____, et al. "Sudden Death in Infancy: A Study of Cardiac Specialized Tissue," British Medical Journal, 2 (Apr. 20, 1974), 135-9.

75. Anderson, Stephen G. "Abortion and the Husband's Consent," Journal of Family Law, 13 (1973), 311-31.

76. Anderson, W.F. "A Death in the Family: A Professional View," British Medical Journal, 1 (Jan. 6, 1973), 31-2.

77. Andree, R.A. et al. "When Death is Inexorable," Science, 169 (Aug., 1970), 717.

78. Andrews, L. "The Last Night," American Journal of Nursing, 74 (Jul., 1974), 1305-6.

79. Andrieux, F. "Image of Death in Protestant Churches' Liturgies," Archives of Social Science and Religion, 20 (1975), 119-26.

80. Angrist, A.A. "A Pathologist's Experience with Attitudes Toward Death," Rhode Island Medical Journal, 43 (Mov., 1960), 693-97.

81. Annas, George J. "Rights of the Terminally Ill Patient," Journal of Nursing Administration, (Mar.-Apr., 1974), 40-4.

82. Anonymous. "Abortion Death," British Medical Journal, 4 (Nov. 4, 1972), 295.

83. _____. "After Sudden Death," Emergency Medicine, 6 (Sep., 1974), 53-60.

84. _____. "Any Man's Death Diminishes Me," New England Journal of Medicine, 278 (June 27, 1968), 1455.

85. _____. "Against Euthanasia," Lancet (Jan. 30, 1971), 220.

86. _____. "Aspects of Death and Dying," Journal of the American Medical Women's Association, 19 (June., 1964).

87. Anonymous. "The Australasian Voluntary Euthanasia Society," Australasian Nurses Journal, 2 (Sep., 1974), 2.

88. _____. "Bereavement," Canadian Medical Assocation Journal, 97 (Nov. 18, 1967), 1296-7.

89. _____. "Between Death and Life," Hibbert Journal, 5 (1906-7), 554-7.

90. _____. "Buffering the Deadly Impact," Journal of the American Medical Association, 205 (Jul. 22, 1968), 238.

91. _____. "Care of the Dying," British Medical Journal, 1 (Jan. 6, 1973), 29-41.

92. _____. "Care for the Dying," Canadian Medical Assocation Journal, 91 (Oct. 24, 1964), 926.

93. _____. "Care of the Dying," Lancet, 1 (Feb. 20, 1965), 424-5.

94. _____. "Care of the Dying," Lancet, 2 (Oct. 2, 1971), 753ff.

95. _____. "Cause of Death," British Medical Journal, 4 (Nov. 20, 1971), 441-2.

96. _____. "The Coffin," Omega, 1 (May, 1970), 143-4.

97. _____. Cohort Mortality and Survivorship: United States Death Registration, States, 1900-1968. Washington: USGPO, 1972.

98. _____. "Comfort for Your Dying Patient," Registered Nurse, 25 (Oct., 1962), 63-5.

99. _____. "Cot Deaths," British Medical Journal, (Oct. 30, 1971), 250-1.

100. _____. "Cot Deaths," Journal of the Royal College of General Practitioners, 22 (Oct., 1972), 651-2.

101. _____. "Court Requires 'Extraordinary' Means to Prolong Life," Hospital, Progress, 52 (Aug., 1971), 19.

102. _____. "Dealing with Death: Thanatology Looks at the Doctor and the Dying Patient," Medical World News, 12 (May 21, 1971), 30-6.

103. _____. "Death . . . A Concept to Reconsider," Journal of the Florida Medical Association, 56 (Oct., 1969), 799.

104. _____. "Death," Nursing Times, 58 (Aug. 17, 1962), 1035.

105. _____. "Death in America," Scientific American, 216 (Feb., 1967), 56.

106. _____. "Death in Childhood," Canadian Medical Association Journal, 98 (May 18, 1968), 967-9.

107. Anonymous. "Death in the Family," Metropolitan Life Insurance Company Statistical Bulletin, 48 (1967), 5-7.

108. _____. "Death in the First Person," American Journal of Nursing, 70 (Feb., 1970), 181-2.

109. _____. "Death of a Human Being," Lancet, 2 (Sep., 1971), 590-1.

110. _____. "Death or Dialysis," Psychiatry in Medicine, 3 (Apr., 1972), 151-61.

111. _____. "Decline in Infant and Child Mortality," World Health Organization Chronicle, 19 (1965), 112-15.

112. _____. "Defining Death," Science News, 94 (Aug. 25, 1968), 177-8.

113. _____. "Definition of Death," Science Digest, 65 (Mar., 1969), 77.

114. _____. "Definitions of Death," Scientific American, 225 (Dec., 1971), 40ff.

115. _____. "Dialogue on Death: Physician and Patient," Geriatric Focus, 5 (Feb., 1966), 1ff.

116. _____. "Distress in Dying," British Medical Journal, 2 (Aug. 17, 1963), 400-1.

117. _____. "Distress of the Dying," Lancet, 1 (Apr., 1963), 927-8.

118. _____. "Disturbed Behavior Caused by Fear of Old Age, Death," Geriatric Focus, 4 (Dec. 1, 1965), 1ff.

119. _____. "Do You Often Lose Touch with a Dying Patient?" Patient Care, 4 (May 31, 1970), 59ff.

120. _____. "Dying and Death," Resuscitation, 1 (Jul., 1972), 85-90.

121. _____. "Dying: Children and Adults," Medical Journal of Australia, 1 (May 22, 1971), 1095-6.

122. _____. "The Dying Patient," Lancet, 2 (Dec. 9, 1972), 1238-9.

123. _____. "Editorial: Brain Damage and Brain Death," Lancet, 1 (Mar. 2, 1974), 341-2.

124. _____. "Editorial: Brain Death," British Medical Journal, 1 (Feb. 15, 1975), 356.

125. _____. "Editorial: Causes of Death--Ancient and Modern," South African Medical Journal, 48 (Feb 9, 1974), 198.

126. _____. "Editorial: Moment of Death--Brain or Heart?" Nursing Mirror, 140 (Feb. 6, 1975), 33.

127. Anonymous. "Effecting 'Death with Dignity'," Hawaii Medical Journal, 30 (Jul.-Aug., 1971), 278.

128. _____. "Effects of Bereavement," Canadian Medical Association Journal, 90 (1964), 668.

129. _____. "Emotional Stress and Sudden Death," Connecticut Medicine, 25 (Sep., 1971), 558-60.

130. _____. "Euthanasia," Journal of the American Medical Association, 218 (Oct. 11, 1971), 249ff.

131. _____. "Euthanasia," Nursing Mirror, 140 (Mar. 6, 1975), 44.

132. _____. "Euthanasia: An Overview for our Time," California Medicine, 118 (Mar., 1973), 55-8.

133. _____. "Euthanasia Weighed," American Journal of Nursing, 71 (Feb., 1971), 359-60.

134. _____. "Experiences with Dying Patients," American Journal of Nursing, 73 (June, 1973), 1058-64.

135. _____. "Fear of Death Linked to Career Decision," United States Medicine, (Oct. 1, 1967), 4.

136. _____. "Helping the Geriatric Staff Face Conflicts about Death," Frontiers of Hospital Psychiatry (Roche Report), 5 (Dec. 1, 1968), 1-2ff.

137. _____. "Hospice for the Dying Patient in Greater New Haven," Hospital Management, (Aug., 1971), 19.

138. _____. "How the Patient Faces Death," Medical World News, 10 (June 6, 1969), 31-4.

139. _____. "How to Die," Medical Journal of Australia, 2 (Sep. 23, 1972), 734-5.

140. _____. "Intercepted Letter: Euthanasia Act," Lancet, 2 (Jul. 3, 1971), 39.

141. _____. "Is Death's Sting Sharper for the Doctor?" Medical World News, 8 (Oct. 6, 1967), 77.

142. _____. "Leading Causes of Death Among Insured Lives," Statistical Bulletin of the Metropolitan Life Insurance Company, 54 (Mar., 1973), 9.

143. _____. "Life-in-Death," New England Journal of Medicine, 256 (Apr. 18, 1957), 760-1.

144. _____. "Man, Medicine and Mercy," Nursing Times, 59 (Mar. 29, 1963), 402-3.

145. Anonymous. Manual of Simple Burial. 2d ed. Burnsville, NC: The Celo Press, 1964.

146. _____. "Medical Examiners and Infant Deaths," New England Journal of Medicine, 287 (Nov. 16, 1972), 1050-2.

147. _____. "The Moment of Death," New Zealand Medical Journal, 75 (Feb., 1972), 97-8.

148. _____. "The Moment of Death," South African Medical Journal, 43 (Jan 18, 1969), 50.

149. _____. "Moratorium Day," American Journal of Nursing, 69 (Dec., 1969), 2645.

150. _____. "Mortality from Home Accidents," Statistical Bulletin of the Metropolitan Life Insurance Company, 54 (Mar., 1973), 2-5.

151. _____. "Mortality Trends in the Western World," Geriatrics, 24 (1969), 64.

152. _____. "The Mystery of Sudden Infant Death," Consumer Reports, (June, 1975), 363-5.

153. _____. "A New Ethic for Medicine and Society," California Medicine, 113 (1970), 67-8.

154. _____. "Notes of a Dying Professor," Nursing Outlook, 20 (1972), 502-6.

155. _____. "Nurses' Attitudes to Death and Related Matters," Nursing Forum, 3 (May-June, 1975), 8-9.

156. _____. "On the Significance of Death in Hospital Practice," Modern Hospital, 78 (Mar., 1962), 86-88.

157. _____. "Passive Death," Lancet, 2 (June 21, 1973), 151-2.

158. _____. "Patients Can Face Hard Truths," Medical World News, 6 (Feb 12, 1965), 64-5.

159. _____. "The Phantom Limb," Trans-Action, 4 (Jul.-Aug., 1967), 5.

160. _____. "Physician as Supergod," Journal of the American Medical Association, 218 (Dec., 1971), 1829.

161. _____. "Preventing Sudden Infant Deaths," Science News, (Sep. 28, 1974), 199.

162. _____. "Problem of the Dying Patient," New York State Medical Journal, 65 (Sep. 15, 1965), 2356-66.

163. _____. "Problems of a Physician's Widow," Wisconsin Medical Journal, 67 (Jan, 1968), 50.

164. Anonymous. "Proposed Criteria for the Determination of Death," Journal of Forensic Medicine, 16 (1969), 4-6.

165. _____. "Protocol for the Determination of Death Endorsed by the Allegheny County Ad Hoc Committee on Tissue Transplantation," Pennsylvania Medicine, 72 (Mar., 1969), 17-20.

166. _____. "Race and Education the Most Significant Factors in Attitudes of Aged Toward Death, Study Shows," Geriatric Focus, 4 (Jan 15, 1966), 2-3.

167. _____. "Recent Mortality Trends in the Western World," Metropolitan Life Insurance Company Statistical Bulletin, 46 (Aug., 1965), 1-4.

168. _____. "Refinements in Criteria for the Determination of Death: An Appraisal," Journal of the American Medical Association, 221 (Jul. 3, 1972), 48-52.

169. _____. "Research into Problems of Terminal Care: Report from Westminster," Nursing Mirror, 132 (May 7, 1971), 8ff.

170. _____. "Research into Sudden Cardiac Death," Nursing Mirror, 22 (Jan, 1971), 32-3.

171. _____. "The Right to Abortion: A Psychiatric View," Group for the Advancement of Psychology, Report, 7 (Oct., 1969), 197-230.

172. _____. "Right to Die in Peace: Mentally Competent Adult in Florida May Refuse Further Life-Sustaining Treatment," Newsletter of the Society of Hospital Attorneys, 4 (Aug., 1971), 1.

173. _____. "The Role of the Law of Homicide in Fetal Destruction," Iowa Law Review, 56 (Feb., 1971), 658-674.

174. _____. "Scared to Death?" British Medical Journal, 5463 (Sep. 18, 1965), 700-2.

175. _____. "The Sensation of Death," British Medical Journal, 1 (Apr. 7, 1906), 818.

176. _____. "Study of Maternal Mortality," Journal of the Kentucky Medical Association, 71 (June, 1973), passim.

177. _____. "Sudden Death in Infants," Lancet, (Nov. 13, 1971), 1070-1.

178. _____. "Sudden Death in Young Adults," Journal of the American Medical Association, 203 (Jan 8, 1968), 1358.

179. _____. "The Sudden Infant Death Syndrome," Medical Journal of Australia, 2 (May 27, 1972), 1217-8.

180. _____. "The Sudden Infant Death Syndrome," Pediatrics 50 (Dec., 1972), 964-5.

181. Anonymous. Sudden Infant Death Syndrome. Washington: USGPO, 1974.

182. _____. "Sudden, Unexpected Death," Journal of the American Medical Association, 209 (Sep. 1, 1969), 1358.

183. _____. "Survey Finds Determinants of Attitudes Toward Abortion," American Journal of Nursing, 71 (Oct., 1971), 1900.

184. _____. "Symposium on Death and Attitudes Toward Death," Geriatrics, 27 (Aug., 1972), 52-60.

185. _____. "Telling the Relatives," Hospital Medicine, 1 (Apr., 1967), np.

186. _____. "Termination of Life," British Medical Journal, 1 (Jan 23, 1971), 187ff.

187. _____. "A Time to Die: Further Reflections," Medical Journal of Australia, 1 (Jan. 18, 1969), 127-8.

188. _____. "Unexpected Deaths of Babies," British Medical Journal, 1 (Feb. 19, 1973), 308-10.

189. _____. "What and When Is Death?" Journal of the American Medical Association. 204 (May 6, 1968), 539-40.

190. _____. "What Is the Physician's Responsibility Toward the Hopelessly Ill Patient Whose Death is Inevitable?" Symposium, Physician's Management, (May, 1971), 45ff.

191. _____. "What Man Shall Live and Not See Death?" Nursing Outlook, 12 (Jan., 1964), 23.

192. _____. "When Death Strikes the Child," Nursing Update, 2 (Aug., 1971), 1ff.

193. _____. "When Do We Let the Patient Die?" Annals of Internal Medicine, 68 (Mar., 1968), 695.

194. _____. "When You Have to Break the Bad News," Physician's Management, 1 (June, 1961), 56-52.

195. _____. "Yale Plans 'Hospice' Like St. Christopher's," American Journal of Nursing, 71 (Dec., 1971), 2296.

196. Ansohn, E. "The Physician and the End of Life," Wiener Medizinische Wochenschrift, 118 (Nov. 30, 1968), 1025-9.

197. Anthony, Sylvia. The Child's Discovery of Death. New York: Harcourt, Brace, 1940.

198. _____. The Discovery of Death in Childhood and After. Baltimore: Penguin, 1973.

199. Anthony, Sylvia. "A Study of the Development of the Concept of Death," British Journal of Educational Psychology, 9 (1939), 276-7.

200. Apfeldorf, Max. "Religious Belief, Emotional Adjustment, and Constructive Ward Behavior in the Elderly Patient During the Period of Reduced Life Expectancy: Research Plans," Journal of Thanatology, 3 (1975), 113-141.

201. Appel, J.A. "Ethical and Legal Questions Posed by Recent Advances in Medicine," Journal of the American Medical Association, 205 (Aug. 12, 1968), 513-6.

202. Apseloff, Marilyn. Death in Current Children's Fiction: Sociology of Literature. St. Louis: Midwest Modern Language Association, 1974.

203. Archibald, Herbert C. et al. "Bereavement in Childhood and Adult Psychiatric Disturbances," Psychosomatic Medicine, 24 (1962), 343-51.

204. Arehart, J.L. "Right to Life: Who is to Decide?" Science News, 100 (Oct., 1971), 293.

205. Aries, Philippe. "Major Stages and Meaning of Evolution of our Attitudes Toward Death," Archives of Social Science and Religion, 20 (1975), 159-67.

206. _____. "La Vie et la Mort Chez les Francais d'Aujourd'Hui (Life and Death Among the French Today)," Ethno-Psychologie, 27 (Mar., 1972), 39-44.

207. _____. Western Attitudes Toward Death. Baltimore: Johns Hopkins University Press, 1974.

208. Aring, C.D. "An Appreciation of Death and Dying," Hospital Tribune, (June 26, 1967), 6.

209. _____. "Intimations of Mortality: An Appreciation of Death and Dying," Annals of Internal Medicine, 69 (July, 1968), 137-152.

210. Armiger, Bernadette. "About Questioning the Right to Die: Reprise and Dialogue," Nursing Outlook, 16 (Oct., 1968), 26-28.

211. Armstrong, M.E. "Dying and Death--and Life Experiences of Loss and Gain: A Proposed Theory," Nursing Forum, 14 (1975), 95-104.

212. Arnold, John et al. "Public Attitudes and the Diagnosis of Death," Journal of the American Medical Association, 206 (Nov. 25, 1968), 1949-54.

213. Arnstein, Helene S. What to Tell Your Child about Birth, Illness, Death, Divorce and Other Family Crises. Indianapolis: Bobbs-Merrill, 1962.

214. Arnstein, R.L. "The Threat of Death as a Factor in Psychological Reaction to Illness," Journal of the American College Health Association, 23 (Dec., 1974), 154-6.

215. Aronson, Marvin et al. "The Impact of the Death of a Leader on a Group Process," American Journal of Psychotherapy, 16 (July, 1962), 460-8.

216. Arthur, Bettie, Mary L. Kemme. "Bereavement in Childhood," Journal of Child Psychology and Psychiatry, 5 (June, 1964), 37-49.

217. Arvio, Raymond R. The Cost of Dying and What You Can Do about It. New York: Harper and Row, 1974.

218. Asch, S.S. "Sudden Unexpected Deaths May Be Infanticides," Pediatric Herald, (Mar., 1968), 7.

219. Ashbrook, J.B. Responding to Human Pain. Valley Forge: Judson Press, 1975.

220. Asquith, G.H. Death is All Right. Nashville: Abingdon Press, 1970.

221. Assell, R. "An Existential Approach to Death," Nursing Forum, 8 (1969), 200-11.

222. Atchley, R.C. "Dimensions of Widowhood in Later Life," Gerontologist, 15 (Apr., 1975), 176-8.

223. Augustin, Demetrio R. "Ceremonies in Connection with the Dead in Malolos, Bulacan," Philippine Sociological Review, 4 (Apr.-June, 1956), 32-8.

224. Austin, Mary. Experiences Facing Death. Indianapolis: Bobbs-Merrill, 1931.

225. Autton, N. "A Study of Bereavement, 2 . . . To Comfort All That Mourn," Nursing Times, 58 (Dec. 7, 1962), 1551-2.

226. Averill, James R. "Grief: Its Nature and Significance," Psychological Bulletin, 6 (1968), 721-48.

227. Ayd, Frank J., Jr. "The Hopeless Case--Medical and Moral Considerations," Journal of the American Medical Association, 181 (Sep. 29, 1962), 1099-1102.

228. _____. "Voluntary Euthanasia: The Right to be Killed," Medical Counterpoint, (June, 1970), 12-24.

229. Bachman, C. Charles. *Ministering to the Grief Sufferer*. Englewood Cliffs: Prentice-Hall, 1964.

230. Bacon, Francis. *A History Natural and Experimental of Life and Death*. In Sylvarum, Sylva, ed. 6, London, Printed by J.F. for William Lee, 1651.

231. _____. "On Death," in S.H. Reynolds, ed., *Bacon's Essays*, Vol. 11. Oxford: Clarendon Press, 1890. 12-18.

232. Bahrmann, E. et al. "Problems of Determination of Death," *Deutsche Gesundheit- swesen*, 23 (Dec. 19, 1968), 2403-7.

233. Bailey, Orville T. "Death in Life," *Scientific Monthly*, 58 (Feb., 1944), 117-28.

234. Bakan, David. *Disease, Pain and Sacrifice: Toward a Psychology of Suffering*. Chicago: University of Chicago Press, 1968.

235. Baker, G.W., D.W. Chapman, eds. *Man and Society in Disaster*. New York: Basic Books, 1962.

236. Baker, J.M., K.C. Sorensen. "A Patient's Concern with Death," *American Journal of Nursing*, 63 (July, 1963), 90-2.

237. Bakke, John L. "Managing the Fatal Illness," *Northwest Medicine*, 59 (July, 1960), 901-4.

238. Balduzzi, P.C., R.M. Greendyke. "Sudden Unexpected Death in Infancy and Viral Infection," *Pediatrics*, 38 (1966), 201-6.

239. Baler, Lenin A., Peggy J. Golde. "Conjugal Bereavement: A Strategic Area of Research in Preventive Psychiatry," in *Working Papers in Community Mental Health*, Harvard School of Public Health, 2 (Spring), 1974.

240. Balint, Michael. *The Doctor, His Patient and the Illness*. London: Pitman Medical Publishing Company, 1956.

241. Bane, J. Donald, ed. *Death and Ministry*. New York: Seabury Press, 1975.

242. Banks, Sam A. "Dialogue on Death: Freudian and Christian Views," *Pastoral Psychology*, 14 (June, 1963), 41-9.

243. Banowsky, L.H. et al. "The Medical and Legal Determination of Death: Its Effect on Cadaveric Organ Procurement," *Journal of Legal Medicine*, 2 (Nov.-Dec., 1974), 44-8.

244. Barbarin, Georges. *Le Livre de la Mort Douce*. Paris: Editions Adyar, 1937.

245. Barber, Hugh. "The Act of Dying," *Practitioner*, 161 (Aug., 1948), 76-9.

246. Barber, Theodore X. "Death by Suggestion," *Psychosomatic Medicine*, 23 (1961), 153-5.

247. Barcal, R., J. Matousek. "Der Tod und Kosmische Einflusse (Death and Cosmic Influences)," Zeitschrift fur die Gesamte Innere Medizin und Ihre Grenz-gebiete, 15 (Feb. 1, 1960), 126-30.

248. Barckley, Virginia. "What Can I Say to the Cancer Patient?" Nursing Outlook, 6 (June, 1958), 316-8.

249. Bard, Bernard, Joseph Fletcher. "The Right to Die," The Atlantic Monthly, (April, 1958), 59-64.

250. Barker, J.C. Scared to Death. Letchworth, Hertfordshire: Garden City Press, 1968.

251. Barlow, J.M. "Loss and Mourning: Some Implications for Psychotherapy," Journal of the Tennessee Medical Association, 67 (Oct., 1974), 834-6.

252. Barnacle, Clarke H. "Grief Reactions and their Treatment," Diseases of the Nervous System, 10 (1949), 173-6.

253. Barnard, Charles N. "A Good Death," Family Health, (April, 1975), 41-2, 60-2.

254. Barnard, M. "Sudden Infant Death Syndrome," Medico-Legal Bulletin, 224 (Dec., 1971), 1-12.

255. Barnes, B.O. et al. "The Role of Natural Consequences in the Changing Death Patterns," Journal of the American Geriatric Association, 22 (Apr., 1974), 176-9.

256. Barnes, Earl. "Punishment as Seen by Children," Pedagogical Seminary and Journal of Genetic Psychology, 3 (Oct., 1894), 235-45.

257. Barnes, M. "Reactions to the Death of a Mother," Psychoanalytic Study of the Child, 19 (1964), 334.

258. Barnouw, V. "Chippewa Social Atomism: Feast of the Dead," American Anthro-pologist, 63 (Oct., 1961), 1006-13.

259. Barnum, Marilyn Clark. "An Occupational Therpist's Observations Concerning President Kennedy's Assassination; With Ramifications for Understanding Loss," American Journal of Occupational Therapy, 20 (Nov.-Dec., 1966), 280-5.

260. Barrett, G.V., R.H. Franke. "Psychogenic Death," Science, 167 (Jan 16, 1970), 304-6.

261. Barry, Herbert, Jr. "Orphanhood as a Factor in Psychoses," Journal of Abnormal and Social Psychology, 30 (1936), 431-8.

262. _____. "Significance of Maternal Bereavement Before the Age Eight in Psychi-atric Patients," Archives of Neurological Psychiatry, 62 (1949), 630-7.

263. Barry, Herbert, Jr. "A Study of Bereavement: An Approach to Problems in Mental Disease," American Journal of Orthopsychiatry, 9 (1939), 355-9.

264. _____, W.A. Bousfield. "Incidence of Orphanhood Among Fifteen Hundred Psychotic Patients," Journal of Genetic Psychology, 50 (1937), 198-202.

265. _____, et al. "Dependency in Adult Patients Following Early Maternal Bereavement," The Journal of Nervous and Mental Disease, 140 (Mar., 1955), 196-206.

266. _____, Erich Lindemann. "Critical Ages for Maternal Bereavement in Psychoneurosis," Psychosomatic Medicine, 22 (1960), 166-81.

267. Barry, M.J., Jr. "The Prolonged Grief Reaction," Mayo Clinic Proceedings, 48 (May, 1973), 329-35.

268. Barton, David. "Death and Dying: A Psychiatrist's Perspective," Soundings, 55 (1972), 459-71.

269. _____. "The Dying Patient: Intimations of Your Own Mortality," Medical Dimensions, 2 (1973), 14.

270. _____. "The Need for Including Instruction on Death and Dying in the Medical Curriculum," Journal of Medical Education, 47 (Mar., 1972), 169-75.

271. _____. "Teaching Psychiatry in the Context of Dying and Death," American Journal of Psychiatry, 130 (Nov., 1973), 1290-1.

272. _____, Miles K. Crowder. "The Use of Role Playing Techniques as an Instructional Aid in Teaching about Dying, Death, and Bereavement," Omega 6 (1975), 243-50.

273. _____, et al. "Death and Dying: A Course for Medical Students," Journal of Medical Education, 47 (Dec., 1972), 945-51.

274. _____, et al. "Psychological Death: An Adaptive Response to Life-Threatening Illness," Psychiatry in Medicine, 3 (July, 1972), 227-36.

275. Barton, E.A. "Old Age and Death," Practitioner, 123 (Aug., 1929), 111-19.

276. Baruch, Dorothy W. You . . . Your Children . . . and War. New York: Appleton-Century Company, 1942.

277. Bascue, Loy O. Counselor Responses to Death and Dying: Guidelines for Training. New Orleans: American Personnel and Guidance Association, 1974.

278. Basowitz, Harold, et al. Anxiety and Stress: An Interdisciplinary Study of a Life Situation. New York: McGraw-Hill, 1955.

279. Bassett, S.D. "Death, Dying, and Grief: A Personal View," Texas Report on Biological Medicine, 32 (Apr., 1972), 347-50.

280. Bataille, Georges. Death and Sensuality: A Study of Eroticism and the Taboo. New York: Walker, 1962.

281. Bauman, Harold. Grief's Slow Work. Scottdale, PA: Herald Press, 1960.

282. Bayless, Raymond. The Other Side of Death. New Hyde Park, NY: University Books, 1971.

283. Bayley, Joseph. The View from the Hearse. Elgin, IL: David D. Cooke, 1969.

284. Beach, H.D., R.A. Lucas, eds. Individual and Group Behavior in a Coal Mine Disaster. Disaster study #13. Washington: National Academy of Sciences, National Research Council, 1960.

285. Beachy, W.N. "Assisting the Family in Time of Grief," Journal of the American Medical Association, 202 (Nov. 6, 1967), 559-60.

286. Beal, S. "Simultaneous Sudden Death in Infancy in Identical Twins," Medical Journal of Australia, 1 (June 9, 1973), 1146-8.

287. _____. "Sudden Infant Death Syndrome," Medical Journal of Australia, 2 (May 25, 1972), 1123-9.

288. Bean, William B. "On Death," Archives of Internal Medicine, 101 (Feb., 1958), 199-202.

289. Beatty, D. "Shall We Talk about Death?" Pastoral Psychology, 6 (1955), 11-4.

290. Beauchamp, J.M. "Euthanasia and the Nurse Practitioner," Nursing Forum, 14 (1975), 56-73.

291. Beck, Aaron T. et al. "Childhood Bereavement and Adult Depression," Archives of General Psychiatry, 9 (1963), 295-302.

292. Beck, Frances. The Diary of a Widow: Rebuilding a Family after the Funeral. Boston: Beacon Press, 1965.

293. Becker, Diane, Faith Margolin. "How Surviving Parents Handled Their Young Children's Adaptation to the Crisis of Loss," American Journal of Ortho-psychiatry, 37 (July, 1967), 753-7.

294. Becker, Ernest. The Denial of Death. New York: The Free Press, 1975.

295. Becker, Howard P. et al. Boys in White. Chicago: University of Chicago Press, 1961.

296. Becker, Howard S. "Some Forms of Sympathy: A Phenomenological Analysis," Journal of Abnormal and Social Psychology, 26 (Apr., 1951), 56-8.

297. _____. "The Sorrow of Bereavement," Journal of Abnormal and Social Psy-chology, 27 (1933), 391-410.

298. Becker, Howard S., David K. Bruner. "Attitudes Toward Death and the Dead and Some Possible Causes of Ghost Fear," Mental Hygiene, 15 (1931), 828-37.

299. Beckley, J.S. "Problems which Pertain to the Welfare Aspect of Sudden Death in Infancy," Public Health, 89 (May, 1975), 147-51.

300. Beckwith, J. Bruce. The Sudden Infant Death Syndrome. Chicago: Year Book Medical Publishers, 1973.

301. _____. "The Sudden Infant Death Syndrome," Current Problems in Pediatrics, 3 (June, 1973), 1-36.

302. _____. "The Sudden Infant Death Syndrome: A New Theory," Pediatrics, 55 (May, 1974), 583-4.

303. _____, A.B. Bergman. "The Sudden Death Syndrome of Infancy," Hospital Practice, 2 (Nob., 1967), 44-52.

304. Bedau, Hugo Adam, ed. The Death Penalty in America. New York: Doubleday, 1964.

305. Bedell, J.W. "Role Reorganization in the One-Parent Family: Mother Absent Due to Death," Sociological Focus, 5 (1971), 84.

306. Beecher, Henry K. "After the 'Definition of Irreversible Coma," New England Journal of Medicine, 281 (Nov. 6, 1969), 1071-2.

307. _____. "Definitions of 'Life' and 'Death' for Medical Science and Practice," Annals of the New York Academy of Sciences, 169 (Jan 21, 1970), 471-4.

308. _____. "Ethical Problems Created by the Hopelessly Unconscious Patient," New England Journal of Medicine, 278 (June 27, 1968), 1245-30.

309. _____, et al. "The New Definition of Death: Some Opposing Views," Internationale Zeitscrift fur Klinische Pharmakologie, Therapie und Toxikologie, 5 (Oct., 1971), 120-4.

310. Behnke, J.A., S. Bok, eds. The Dilemmas of Euthanasia. New York: Anchor Press/ Doubleday, 1975.

311. Beidelman, T.O. "Three Tales of the Living and the Dead: The Ideology of Kaguru Ancestral Propitiation," Journal of the Royal Anthropological Institute of Great Britain and Ireland, 94 (July-Dec., 1964), 109-37.

312. Beigler, Jerome S. "Anxiety as an Aid in the Prognostication of Impending Death," Archives of Neurological Psychiatry, 77 (Feb., 1957), 171-7.

313. Bell, Bill D. "The Experimental Manipulation of Death Attitudes: A Preliminary Investigation," Omega, 6 (1975), 199-205.

314. Bell, Leland V. "Death in a Technocracy," Journal of Human Relations, 18 (1970), 833-9.

315. Bell, Thomas. In the Midst of Life. New York: Atheneum, 1961.

316. Bellak, Leopold, ed. Psychology of Physical Illness. New York: Grune and Stratton, 1952.

317. Benda, C.E. "Bereavement and Grief Work," Journal of Pastoral Care, 16 (Spring, 1962), 1-13.

318. Bendann, Effie. Death Customs: An Analytical Study of Burial Rites. New York: Knopf, 1930.

319. Bender, David L., ed. Problems of Death: Opposing Viewpoints. Anoka, MN: Greenhaven, 1974.

320. Bender, Lauretta. Aggression, Hostility and Anxiety in Children. Springfield: C.C. Thomas, 1953.

321. _____. Dynamic Psychopathology of Childhood. (Children's Reaction to Death in the Family.) Springfield: C.C. Thomas, 1954.

322. _____, ed. Contributions to Developmental Neurophsychiatry. New York: International Universities Press, 1964.

323. Bendiksen, Robert, Robert Fulton. "Death and the Child: An Anterospective Test of the Childhood Bereavement and Later Behavior Disorder Hypothesis," Omega, 6 (1975), 45-9.

324. Bendowski, B. "Sudden Unexpected Death in the Elderly," Journal of the American Geriatric Society, 21 (Sep., 1973), 405-8.

325. Benedek, Therese. "Todestrieb und Angst (Death Drive and Anxiety)," International Zeitschrift fur Psychoanalyse, 17 (1931), 333-43.

326. Bengston, V., et al. "Attitudes Toward Death and Dying: Contrasts by Age, Sex, Ethnicity, and SES," Gerontology, 15 (1975), 63.

327. Bennett, Roger V. Death and the Curriculum. Chicago: American Educational Research Association, 1974.

328. Bennholdt-Thomsen, C. "Sterben und Tod des Kindes (Dying and the Death of the Child)," Deutsche Medizinische Wochenschrift, 84 (Aug. 14, 1959), 1437-42.

329. Benoleil, Jeanne Q. "Assessments of Loss and Grief," Journal of Thanatology, 1 (May-June, 1971), 182.

330. _____. "Comment: Some Thoughts about the Complexities of Education for Humanistic Care in the Face of Death," Omega, 2 (Aug., 1971), 215-6.

331. Beloliel, Jeanne Quint. "The Concept of Care for a Child with Leukemia," Nursing Forum, 11, (1972), 194-204.

332. _____. "Death and Bereavement: The Nurse's Role," Alberta Association of Registered Nurses, 26 (Sep.-Oct., 1970), 4-6.

333. _____. "The Dying Patient: A Nursing Dilemma," Washington State Journal of Nursing, 43 (Jan.-Feb., 1971), 3-4.

334. _____. "Talking to Patients about Death," Nursing Forum, 9 (1970), 254-68.

335. Benson, G., Jr. "Death and Dying: A Psychoanalytic Perspective," Hospital Progress, 53 (Mar., 1972), 52-9.

336. Berardi, R.S. "Deaths in a Small Community Hospital," Journal of the Kentucky Medical Association, 67 (Oct., 1969), 749-51.

337. Berardo, Felix M. "Social Adaptation to Widowhood Among a Rural-Urban Aged Population," Washington Agricultural Experiment Station, College of Agriculture, Washington State University, Bulletin 689 (Dec., 1967), 1-31.

338. _____. "Survivorship and Social Isolation: The Case of the Aged Widower," The Family Coordinator, 19 (1970), 11-25.

339. _____. "Widowhood Status in the United States: Perspectives on a Neglected Aspect of the Family Life Cycle," The Family Coordinator, 17 (1968), 191-203.

340. Beres, David, Samuel J. Obers. "The Effects of Extreme Deprivation in Infancy on Psychic Structures in Adolescence," The Psychoanalytic Study of the Child, 5 (1950), 212-35.

341. Berezin, M.A. "The Psychiatrist and the Geriatric Patient: Partial Grief in Family Members and Others who Care for the Elderly Patient," Journal of Geriatric Psychiatry, 4 (Fall, 1970), 53-70.

342. Berg, Constance Demuth. "Cognizance of the Death Taboo in Counseling Children," School Counselor, 21 (Sep., 1973), 28-33.

343. Berg, David W., George C. Daugherty. "Teaching about Death," Today's Education, 62 (Mar., 1973), 46-7.

344. _____, et al. "On Death and Dying," Journal of Medical Education, 47 (July, 1972), 587-8.

345. Berg, M., B. Cohen. "Early Separation from the Mother," Journal of Nervous and Mental Disorders, 128 (1959), 365-9.

346. Bergen, R.P. "Management of Terminal Illness," Journal of the American Medical Association, 229 (Sep. 2, 1974), 1352-3.

347. Bergersen, Betty S., ed. Distance and the Dying Patient. St. Louis: C.V. Mosby, 1967.

348. Bergler, Edmund. "Psychopathology and Duration of Mourning and Neurotics," Journal of Clinical Psychopathology, 3 (1948), 478-82.

349. Bergman, A.B. "Crib Deaths Exact Needless Toll of Grief in Infants' Families," Hospital Topics, 47 (Feb., 1969), 69-73.

350. _____. "Psychological Aspects of Sudden Unexpected Death in Infants and Children. Review and Commentary," Pediatric Clinics of North America, 21 (Feb., 1974), 115-21.

351. _____. "A Shared Experience," International Nursing Review, 14 (Oct., 1967), 39-42.

352. _____. "Sudden Infant Death," Nursing Outlook, 20 (Dec., 1972), 775-7.

353. _____. "Sudden Infant Death Syndrome," American Family Physician, 8 (July, 1973), 95-100.

354. _____, et al. "The Apnea Monitor Business," Pediatrics, 56 (July, 1975), 1-3.

355. _____, et al. "The Psychiatric Toll of the Sudden Infant Death Syndrome," General Practitioner, 40 (Dec., 1969), 99-105.

356. _____, et al. "Studies of the Sudden Infant Death Syndrome in King County, Washington, III: Epidemiology," Pediatrics, 49 (1972), 860-70.

357. _____, et al. "Sudden Death Syndrome: The Physician's Role," Clinical Pediatrics, 5 (Dec., 1966), 711-7.

358. _____, et al. Sudden Infant Death Syndrome. Seattle: University of Washington Press, 1970.

359. _____, C. Schulte, eds. "Care of the Child with Cancer," Pediatrics, 4 (Sep., 1967), 492-546.

360. Bergman, Paul, Sibylle K. Escalona. "Unusual Sensitivities in Very Young Children," Psychoanalytic Study of the Child, 3 (1947), 333-52.

361. Bergmann, Thesi, Anna Freud. Children in the Hospital. New York: International Universities Press, 1965.

362. Bergson, Henri. La Pensee et le Mourant. Paris: Felix Alcan, 1934.

363. Berlin, Joyce E., Carl L. Erhardt, eds. Mortality and Morbidity in the U.S. Cambridge: Harvard University Press, 1974.

364. Berman, M.I. "The Todeserwartung Syndrome," Geriatrics, 21 (May, 1966), 187-92.

365. Berman, Alan L., James E. Hays. "Relation Between Death Anxiety, Belief in Afterlife, and Locus of Control," Journal of Consulting and Clinical Psychology, 41 (Oct., 1973), 318.

366. Bergman, Abraham B., et al. Sudden Unexpected Death in Infants: Papers by Abraham B. Bergman, John W. Melton, Robert E. Baker, et al. New York: MSS Information, 1974.

367. Bermann, Eric. Scapegoat: The Impact of Death-Fear on an American Family. Ann Arbor: University of Michigan Press, 1973.

368. Bernard, Hugh Y. The Law of Death and Disposal of the Dead. New York: Oceana Publications, 1966.

369. Bernstein, A.H. "The Law of the Dead," Hospitals, 48 (Oct. 1, 1974), 62, 64, 75.

370. Bernstein, Norman R., Caroline B. Tinkham. "Group Therapy Following Abortion," Journal of Nervous and Mental Disease, 152 (May, 1971), 303-14.

371. Berry, F.B. "Life, Death, Dignity and Doctors," Resident and Staff Physician, 17 (Oct., 1971), 14.

372. Berry, R. "An Easy Way to Die," Journal of Practical Nursing, 24 (Oct., 1974), 18, 39.

373. _____. "Is Death Our Failure?" Journal of Practical Nursing, 24 (Nov., 1974), 30, 37.

374. Best, Pauline. "An Experience in Interpreting Death to Children," Journal of Pastoral Care, 2 (1948), 29-34.

375. Beswick, David G., "Attitudes to Taking Human Life," Australian and New Zealand Journal of Sociology, 6 (Oct., 1970), 120-30.

376. Better Business Bureau. Alerting Bereaved Families: A Special Bulletin. New York: Better Business Bureau, 1961.

377. _____. Facts Every Family Should Know about Funerals and Interments. New York: Better Business Bureau, 1961.

378. _____. The Pre-arrangement and Pre-financing of Funerals. New York: Better Business Bureau, 1960.

379. Beverly, B.I. "Medical Scaring of Children," Transactions of the Central States Pediatric Society, 8 (Oct., 1933), 29-30.

380. Bhardwaj, K.S., Saroj Mullick. "Attitudes of Indian Women Towards Abortion," The Indian Journal of Social Work, 33 (Jan., 1973), 317-22.

381. Bhatia, J.C. "Abortionists and Abortion Seekers," The Indian Journal of Social Work, 34 (Oct., 1973), 275-85.

382. Bibring, Grete L. "The Death of an Infant: A Psychiatric Study," The New England Journal of Medicine, 283 (Aug. 13, 1970), 370-1.

383. Bichat, Xavier. Physiological Researches upon Life and Death. Philadelphia: Smith and Maxwell, 1809.

384. Bierer, J. "Death: Unacceptable Problem or Acceptable Fact," International Journal of Social Psychiatry, 21 (Winter-Spring, 1974-5), 11-3.

385. Bierman, Howard R. "Parent Participation Program in Pediatric Oncology, A Preliminary Report," Journal of Chronic Diseases, 3 (June, 1956), 632-9.

386. Binger, C.M., et al. "Childhood Leukemia: Emotional Impact on Patient and Family," New England Journal of Medicine, 280 (1969), 414-8.

387. Biorck, Gunnar. "How Do You Want to Die? Answers to a Questionnaire and their Implications for Medicine," Archives of Internal Medicine, 132 (Oct., 1973), 605-6.

388. _____. "On the Definitions of Death," World Medical Journal, 14 (Sep.-Oct., 1967), 137-9.

389. _____. "Thoughts on Life and Death," Perspectives in Biology and Medicine, 11 (Summer, 1968), 527-43.

390. Biran, S. "Attempt at the Psychological Analysis of the Fear of Death," Confinia Psychiatrica, 11 (1968), 154-76.

391. Birk, Alma. "The Bereaved Child," Mental Health, 25 (1966), 9-11.

392. Birnbaum, F., et al. "Crisis Intervention after a Natural Disaster," Social Casework, 54 (1973), 545-51.

393. Birrell, F., F.L. Lucas, eds. The Art of Dying: An Anthology of Last Words. London: L. and V. Woolf, 1930.

394. Birtchnell, John. "Case-register Study of Bereavement," Proceedings of the Royal Society of Medicine, 64 (Mar., 1971), 279-82.

395. _____. "Depression in Relation to Early and Recent Parent Death," British Journal of Psychiatry, 116 (1970), 299-306.

396. _____. "Early Parent Death and Mental Illness," British Journal of Psychiatry, 116 (1970), 281-88.

397. Birtchnell, John. "Early Parent Death and Psychiatric Diagnosis," Social
      Psychiatry, 7 (1972), 202-10.

398. _____. "Early Parent Death in Relation to Size and Constitution of Sibship
      in Psychiatric Patients and General Population Controls," Acta Psychiatrica
      Scandanavica, 47 (1971), 250-70.

399. _____. Effects of Early Parent Death. New York: MSS Information, 1973.

400. _____. "Parent Death in Relation to Age and Parental Age at Birth in
      Psychiatric Patients and General Population Controls," British Journal
      of Preventive and Social Medicine, 23 (1969), 244-50.

401. _____. "The Personality Characteristics of Early-Bereaved Psychiatrics
      Patients," Social Psychiatry, 10 (Apr., 1975), 97-103.

402. _____. "The Possible Consequences of Early Parent Death," British Journal
      of Medical Psychology, 42 (Mar., 1969), 1-12.

403. _____. "Psychiatric Sequelae of Childhood Bereavement," British Journal
      of Psychiatry, 116 (1970), 572-3.

404. _____. "Recent Parent Death and Mental Illness," British Journal of Psy-
      chiatry, 116 (1970, 289-97.

405. _____. "The Relationship Between Attempted Suicide, Depression, and Parent
      Death," British Journal of Psychiatry, 116 (1970), 307-13.

406. _____. "Some Psychiatric Sequelae of Childhood Bereavement," British Journal
      of Psychiatry, 116 (Mar., 1970), 346-7.

407. Bishop, John P, Edmund Wilson. The Undertaker's Garland. New York: Haskell
      House, 1974.

408. Bjerre, I., G. Ostberg. "Infant Mortality: Causes of Death During the First
      Year of Life in a Five-Year Series," ACTA Paediatrica Scandanavia, 63
      (Jan., 1974), 49-58.

409. Black, P.M. "Criteria of Brain Death: Review and Comparison," Canadian Medical
      Association Journal, 112 (Feb. 8, 1975), 69-74.

410. Blacker, C.P. "Life and Death Instincts," British Journal of Medical Psychology,
      9 (1929), 277-302.

411. Blackman, Margaret B. "Totems to Tombstones: Culture Change as Viewed through
      the Haida Mortuary Complex, 1877-1971," Ethnology, 12 (Jan, 1973), 47-56.

412. Blackwood, Andrew Watterson. The Funeral. Philadelphia: Westminister Press,
      1942.

413. Blaine, Graham, "Some Emotional Problems of Adolescents," Medical Clinics of
      North America, 49 (Mar., 1965), 387-404.

414. Blake, J. "Abortion and Public Opinion: 1960-70 Decade," Science, 171
      (Oct. 30, 1971), 5409-9.

415. Blake, Robert Richmond. "Attitudes Toward Death as a Function of Develop-
      mental Stages," Dissertation Abstracts, 30 (Jan., 1970), 3380-B.

416. Blauner, Robert. "Death and Social Structure," Psychiatry, 29 (Nov., 1966),
      378-94.

417. Bloch, A. "Sudden Infant Death Syndrome in the Ashkelon District: A Ten-Year
      Survey," Israel Journal of Medical Science, 9 (Apr., 1973), 452-8.

418. Bloch, Dorothy. "Feelings that Kill: The Effect of the Wish for Infanticide
      in Neurotic Depression," Psychoanalytic Review, 52 (Spring, 1965), 51-66.

419. _____, et al. "Some Factors in Emotional Reactions of Children to Disaster,"
      American Journal of Psychiatry, 113 (1956), 416-22.

420. Bloch, Maurice. Placing the Dead: Tombs, Ancestral Villages and Kinship Organ-
      ization in Madagascar. London: Academic Press, 1971.

421. Bloch, Oscar. Om Døden (Concerning Death). Kjøbenhaun: Lund, 1903.

422. _____. Vom Tode (On Death). German translation by Dr. Peter Misch.
      Stuttgart: Axel Juncker, 1909.

423. Bloch, S. "A Clinical Course on Death and Dying for Medical Students," Journal
      of Medical Education, 50 (June, 1975), 630-2.

424. Bloom, Harold. "Death and the Native Strain in American Poetry," Social
      Research, 39 (Autumn, 1972), 449-62.

425. Bloom, Sholom. "On Teaching an Undergraduate Course on Death and Dying,"
      Omega, 6 (1975), 223-6.

426. Bluestein, Venus W. "Death-Related Experiences, Attitudes, and Feelings Reported
      by Thanatology Students and a National Sample," Omega, 6 (1975), 207-18.

427. Bluestone, E.M. "On the Significance of Death in Hospital Practice," Modern
      Hospital, 78 (Mar., 1952), 86-88.

428. Bluestone, H., C.C. McGahee. "Reaction to Extreme Stress: Impending Death
      by Execution," American Journal of Psychiatry, 119 (Nov., 1962), 393-6.

429. Blum, G.S., S. Rosenzweig. "The Incidence of Sibling and Parental Deaths in
      the Anamnesis of Female Schizophrenics," Journal of General Psychology
      31 (1944), 3-13.

430. Boas, Franz. "The Idea of Future Life Among Primitive Tribes," in Boas,
      Race, Language and Culture. New York: MacMillan, 1940.

431. Boase, Thomas Sherrer Ross. Death in the Middle Ages: Mortality, Judgment, and Remembrance. New York: McGraw-Hill, 1972.

432. Boba, Antonio. Death in the Operating Room. Springfield, IL: C.C. Thomas, 1965.

433. Bohannan, Paul, ed. African Homicide and Suicide. Princeton, NJ: Princeton University Press, 1960.

434. Bolduc, Jeannette. "A Developmental Study of the Relationship Between Experiences of Death and Age and Development of the Concept of Death," Dissertation Abstracts International, 33 (Dec., 1972), 2758.

435. Bonaparte, Marie. "De la Mort et des Fleurs," Revue Francaise de Psychanalyse, 2 (1928), 541-65.

436. _____. "L'Identification d'une Fille a sa Mere Morte," Revue Francaise de Psychanalyse, 2 (1928), 541-65.

437. _____. "Masturbation and Death or a Compulsive Confession of Masturbation," Psychoanalytic Study of the Child, 7 (1952), 170-2.

438. _____. "Time and the Unconscious," International Journal of Psychoanalysis, 21 (1949), 427-68.

439. Bonine, B.N. "Student's Reactions to Children's Death," American Journal of Nursing, 67 (July, 1967), 1439-40.

440. Bonnar, Alphonsus. Medicine and Men. London: Burns and Oates, 1962.

441. Bonnard, A. "Truancy and Pilfering Associated with Bereavement," in S. Lorand and H.I. Schneer, eds., Adolescents. New York: Haeber, 1961.

442. Bonnell, George C. "The Pastor's Role in Counselling the Bereaved," Pastoral Psychology, 22 (Feb., 1971), 27-36.

443. Bonnet, J.D. "Bill of Rights of Dying Patients," Baylor Law Review, 27 (1975), 27-30.

444. Booth, G. "Three Psychobiological Paths Toward Death: Cardiovascular Disease, Tuberculosis, and Cancer," Bulletin of the New York Academy of Medicine, 51 (Mar., 1975), 415-31.

445. Booth, H. "The Christian Nurse: A Nurse's Special Problems, 2: Care for the Dying," Nursing Times, 60 (Dec. 4, 1964), 1615.

446. Boots, Doloris D., "Helping the Cancer Patient: The Minister and the Social Worker," Pastoral Psychology, 22 (Jan, 1971), 35-40.

447. Borel, David M. "Defining Death," General Practitioner, 39 (Jan., 1969), 171-8.

448. Borhani, N.O. et al. "Post-Neonatal Sudden Unexplained Death in a California Community," California Medicine, 118 (May, 1973), 12-6.

449. Borkenau, Franz. "The Concept of Death," The Twentieth Century, 157 (1955), 313-29.

450. Bornstein, P.E., P.J. Clayton. "The Anniversary Reaction," Diseases of the Nervous System, 33 (July, 1972), 470-2.

451. _____, et al. "The Depression of Widowhood after Thirteen Months," British Journal of Psychiatry, 122 (May, 1973), 561-6.

452. Boros, Ladislaus. Mystery of Death. New York: Seabury, 1973.

453. Bose, A.B., M.L.A. Sen. "Some Characteristics of the Widow in Rural Society," Man in India, 46 (1966), 226-32.

454. Boshes, B. "A Definition of Cerebral Death," Annual Review of Medicine, 26 (1975), 465-70.

455. Bossard, James H., Elanor S. Boll. Ritual in Family Living: A Contemporary Study. Philadelphia: University of Pennsylvania Press, 1950.

456. Bouchard, Rosemary. Nursing Care of the Cancer Patient. St. Louis: C.V. Mosby, 1967.

457. Boulanger, J.B. "Depression in Childhood," Canadian Psychiatric Association Journal, 11 (1966), 309-12.

458. Bourguignon, A. "La Mort et le Medecin (Death and the Physician)," Semaine des Hopitaux de Paris, 22 (May 14, 1963), supplement 25/5, 2-3.

459. Boutonier, Juliette. L'Angoisse (Anxiety). Paris: Presses Universitaires de France, 1945.

460. Bowen, A. "The Psychiatric Aspects of Bereavement," Practitioner, 210 (Jan., 1973), 127-34.

461. Bowers, Edgar. The Form of Loss. New York: AMS Press, 1956.

462. Bowers, M.K. et al. Counselling the Dying. New York: Nelson, 1964.

463. Bowlby, John. Attachment and Loss. New York: Basic Books, 1969.

464. _____. "Childhood Mourning and Its Implications for Psychiatry," American Journal of Psychiatry, 118 (Dec., 1961), 481-98.

465. _____. "Grief and Mourning in Infancy and Early Childhood," The Psycho-analytic Study of the Child, 15 (1960), 9-52.

466. Bowlby, John. Maternal Care and Mental Health. New York: Schocken Books, 1966.

467. _____. "The Nature of the Child's Tie to His Mother," The International Journal of Psychoanalysis, 39 (1958), 1-23.

468. _____. "Pathological Mourning and Childhood Mourning," Journal of the American Psychoanalytic Assocation, 11 (1963), 500-41.

469. _____. "Processes of Mourning," The International Journal of Psychoanalysis, 42 (1961), 317-40.

470. _____. "Separation Anxiety," International Journal of Psychanalysis, 41 (1960), 89-113.

471. _____. "Separation Anxiety: A Critical Review of the Literature," Journal of Child Psychology and Psychiatry, 1 (Feb., 1961), 251-69.

472. _____. "Some Pathological Processes Engendered by Early Mother-Child Separation," British Journal of Psychiatry, 99 (1953), 265-72.

473. Bowman, LeRoy Edward. The American Funeral: A Study in Guilt, Extravagance and Sublimity. Washington: Public Affairs Press, 1959.

474. Boyar, J.I. "The Construction and Partial Validation of a Scale for the Measurement of the Fear of Death," Dissertation Abstracts, 25 (Sep., 1964), 2041.

475. Bozeman, Mary F. et al. "Psychological Impact of Cancer and Its Treatment, III: The Adaption of Mothers to the Threatened Loss of Their Children Through Leukemia, Part I," Cancer, 8 (Jan.-Feb., 1955), 1-19.

476. Bradley, N.C. "The Growth of the Knowledge of Time in Children of School Age," British Journal of Psychology, 38 (1947), 67-78.

477. Brady, E. "Grief and Amputation," American Nursing Association Convention Clinical Sessions, (1968), 297-301.

478. Brainard, F. "Rather than Scream: What's It LIke to Have a Terminal Disease?" Today's Health, 49 (June, 1971), 32-7.

479. Branch, C.H.H. "Psychiatric Approach to Patients with Malignant Disease," Rocky Mountain Medical Journal, 49 (1962) 749-53.

480. Brandon, S.G.F. "Grief," Practitioner, 212 (June., 1974), 867-75.

481. _____. The Judgment of the Dead: The Idea of Life after Death in the Major Religions. New York: Charles Scribner's Sons, 1967.

482. _____. "Origin of Death in Some Ancient Near Eastern Religions," Religious Studies, 1 (1966), 217-28.

483. Branson, H.K. "The Terminal Patient and His Family," Bedside Nurse, 3 (June, 1970), 21-3.

484. Brauer, Paul. "Should the Patient Be Told the Truth," Nursing Outlook, 8 (Dec., 1960), 672-76.

485. Braun, Heinrich. Das Geheimnis vom Leben und Sterben: Eine Darstellung der Abhamgigkeit der Labensvorgange von den Umwelteinflussen (The Mystery of Living and Dying: An Illustration of the Dependence of Life Processes Upon Environmental Influence). Tubingen: Mohr, 1949.

486. Breed, J.E. "Mangement of the Patient with Terminal Illness," Illinois Medical Journal, 139 (May, 1971), 503.

487. _____. "New Questions in Medical Morality," Illinois Medical Journal, 135 (Apr., 1969), 504ff.

488. Breen, J.L. "Thoughts Concerning the Care of the Terminal Patient," Journal of the Medical Society of New Jersey, 72 (May, 1975), 448-50.

489. Breen, Paula. "Who Is to Say?" American Journal of Nursing, 67 (Aug., 1967), 1689-90.

490. Brennan, M.J. "The Cancer Gestalt," Geriatrics, 25 (Oct., 1970), 96-101.

491. Brenner, Charles. "An Addendum to Freud's Theory of Anxiety," International Journal of Psychoanalysis, 34 (1953), 18-24.

492. _____. "The Concept and Phenomenology of Depression, with Special Reference to the Aged, Some Observations on Depression, on Nosology, on Affects, and on Mourning," Journal of Geriatric Psychiatry, 7 (1974), 6-20.

493. Brenner, M.H. "Fetal, Infant, and Maternal Mortality During Periods of Economic Instability," International Journal of Health Services, 3 (Spring, 1973), 145-69.

494. Brewster, Henry H. "Grief: A Disrupted Human Relationship," Human Organization, 9 (1950), 19-22.

495. _____. "Separation Reaction in Psychosomatic Disease and Neurosis," Psychosomatic Medicine, 14 (1952), 154-60.

496. Bright, Florence, M.L. France. "The Nurse and the Terminally Ill Child," Nursing Outlook, 15 (Sep., 1967), 39-42.

497. Brill, A.A. "Necrophilia," Journal of Criminal Psychopathology, 2 (1941), 433-43.

498. _____. "Thoughts on Life and Death; or, Vidonian All Souls' Eve," Psychiatric Quarterly, 21 (Apr., 1947), 199-211.

499. Brill, Norman Q., Edward H. Liston, Jr. "Parental Loss in Adults with Emotional Disorders," Archives of General Psychiatry, 14 (Mar., 1966), 307-13.

500. Brim, Orville G., Jr. et al. Death and Medical Conduct. New York: Russell Sage Foundation, 1969.

501. _____, et al, eds. The Dying Patient. New York: Russell Sage Foundation, 1975.

502. Brimblecombe, F. "Discussion of Papers on the Inner London Survey on Sudden Death in Infancy," Public Health, 89 (May, 1975), 163.

503. Briscoe, C.W., J.B. Smith. "Depression in Bereavement and Divorce. Relationship to Primary Depressive Illness: A Study of 128 Subjects," Archives of General Psychiatry, 32 (Apr., 1975), 439-43.

504. Brodsky, B. "Liebestod Fantasies in a Patient Faced with a Fatal Illness," International Journal of Psychoanalysis, 40 (1959), 13-16.

505. _____. "The Self-Representation, Anality and the Fear of Dying," Journal of the American Psychoanalytic Association, 7 (1959), 95-108.

506. Brody, B.A. "Abortion and the Law," Journal of Philosophy, 63 (June 17, 1971), 357.

507. Brokhoff. If Your Dearest Should Die. Lima, OH: CSS Publishing, 1975.

508. Bromberg, Walter, Paul Schilder. "The Attitudes of Psychoneurotics Toward Death," Psychoanalytic Review, 23 (1936), 1-25.

509. _____. "Death and Dying," Psychoanalytic Review, 20 (1933), 133-85.

510. Bromley, Dennis Basil. The Psychology of Human Aging. Baltimore: Penguin Books, 1966.

511. Brooke, B.N. "The Styx," Lancet, 2 (July 13, 1974), 96-7.

512. Brookes, P. "Increasing Death Rate Among Women," Nursing Times, 70 (June 6, 1974), 881.

513. Brown, Arthur E. "Grief in the Chimpanzee," American Naturalist, 13 (1879), 173-5.

514. Brown, Felix. "Childhood Bereavement and Subsequent Crime," British Journal of Psychiatry, 112 (1966), 1043-48.

515. _____. "Childhood Bereavement and Subsequent Psychiatric Disorder," British Journal of Psychiatry, 112 (1966), 1035-41.

516. _____. "Depression and Childhood Bereavement," Journal of Mental Science, 107 (1961), 754-77.

517. Brown, J.P. "Terminal Nursing Care," Nursing Times, 61 (Nov., 1965), 1562.

518. Brown, N.D. et al. "The Preservation of Life," Journal of the American
        Medical Association, 211 (Jan 5, 1970), 76-82.

519. Brown, N.K. et al. "How Do Nurses Feel about Euthanasia and Abortion,"
        American Journal of Nursing, 71 (July, 1971), 1413-16.

520. Brown, Norman O. Life Against Death. London: Routledge and Kegan Paul, 1959.

521. Brown, Paula. "Chimbu Death Payment," Journal of the Royal Anthropological
        Institute of Great Britain and Ireland, 91 (Jan.-June., 1961), 77-96.

522. Browne, I.W., T.P. Hackett. "Emotional Reactions to the Threat of Impending
        Death," Irish Journal of Medical Science, 6 (Apr. 6, 1967), 177-87.

523. Browne, Thomas. Religio Medici. Boston: Ticknor and Fields, 1862.

524. _____. "The Shame of Death," in Dawson, William, and Coningsby, eds.,
        The Great English Essayists. New York: Harper, 1909.

525. Browning, Mary H., Edith Patton Lewis. The Dying Patient: A Nursing Perspective.
        New York: American Journal of Nursing Company, 1972.

526. Bruce, Sylvia J. "Reactions of Nurses and Mothers to Stillbirths," Nursing
        Outlook, 10 (Feb., 1962), 88-91.

527. Bruhn, John G. et al. "Psychological Predictors of Sudden Death in Myocardial
        Infarction," Journal of Psychosomatic Research, 18 (June, 1974), 187-191.

528. Brun, R. "Uber Freuds Hypothese vom Todestrieb," Psyche, 7 (1953), 81-111.

529. Bucher, Rue. "Blame and Hostility in Disaster," American Journal of Sociology,
        62 (1957), 465-75.

530. Buck, Rodger. "Sociocultural Stresses and the Physician-Patient Relationship,"
        Journal of the American Medical Association, 170 (Aug., 1959), 1648-51.

531. Bucove, A.D. "Death and Confidentiality," American Journal of Psychiatry,
        127 (Dec., 1970), 845.

532. Budge, E.A.T.W. The Book of the Dead. New Hyde Park, NY: University Books,
        1960.

533. Bugenthal, J.F. "A Critique of Peter Koestenbaum's 'The Vitality of Death',"
        Journal of Existentialism, 5 (Summer, 1965), 433-9.

534. Buhrmann, M.V. "Death--Its Psychological Significance in the Lives of Children,"
        South African Medical Journal, 44 (May, 1970), 586-9.

535. Buhrmann, M.V. "The Dying Child," South African Medical Journal, 47 (June 30, 1973), 1114-56.

536. Bulger, Roger J. "Doctors and Dying," Archives of Internal Medicine, 112 (Sep., 1963), 327-32.

537. _____. "The Dying Patient and His Doctor," Harvard Medical Alumni Bulletin, 34 (1960), 23ff.

538. Bulka, Reuben P. "Death in Life: Talmudic and Logotherapeutic Affirmations," Humanitas, 10 (Feb., 1974), 33-41.

539. Bullough, Vern L. "The Banal and Costly Funeral," The Humanist, 4 (1960), 213-18.

540. Bultmann, Randolph et al. Life and Death. New York: Fernhill, 1965.

541. Bunch, J. "The Influence of Parental Death Anniversaries Upon Suicide Dates," British Journal of Psychiatry, 118 (1971), 621-6.

542. _____. "Recent Bereavement in Relation to Suicide," Journal of Psychosomatic Research, 16 (Aug., 1972), 361-6.

543. _____, et al. "Early Parental Bereavement and Suicide," Social Psychiatry, 6 (1971), 200.

544. _____, et al. "Suicide Following Bereavement of Parents," Social Psychiatry, 6 (1971), 192-9.

545. Burgert, Omer E., Jr. "Emotional Impact of Childhood Acute Leukemia," Mayo Clinic Proceedings, 47 (Apr., 1972), 273-7.

546. Burkhalter, P.K. "Fostering Staff Sensitivity to the Dying Patient," Registered Nurse, 6 (Apr., 1975), 55-9.

547. Burland, C.A. Myths of Life and Death. New York: Crown Publishers, 1974.

548. Burnell, George M. "Maternal Reaction to the Loss of Multiple Births: A Case of Septuplets," Archives of General Psychiatry, 30 (Feb., 1974), 183-4.

549. Burnett, Wanda M. Sudden Death in Infants: Proceedings of the Conference on Causes of Sudden Death in Infants, Seattle, 1963. Washington: USGPO, 1966.

550. Burnside, I.M. "Loss: A Constant Theme in Group Work with the Aged," Hospital and Community Psychiatry, 21 (June, 1970), 73ff.

551. _____. "You Will Cope, Of Course . . . . ," American Journal of Nursing, 71 (Dec., 1971), 2354-7.

552. Burrell, R.M.W. "Spells, Sorcery and the Will to Die," Medical World News, 25 (1961), 33-4.

553. Burrows, Grace. "The Man Who Died Laughing," Registered Nurse, 26 (Apr, 1963), 87-98.

554. Burton, Arthur, "Death as a Countertransference," Psychoanalysis and the Psychoanalytic Review, 49 (Winter, 1962), 3-20.

555. _____. "Fear of Death as Countertransference," Omega, 2 (Nov., 1971), 287-98.

556. Burton, Lindy, ed. Care of the Child Facing Death. Boston: Routledge and Kegan Paul, 1974.

557. Busse, Ewald W., Eric Pfeiffer. Behavior and Adaptation in Late Life. Boston: Little, Brown, and Comapny, 1970.

558. Butler, Robert N. "Attitudes Toward Death (An Interview)," Geriatrics, 19 (Feb., 1964), 58Aff.

559. Buxbaum, Robert E. "Grief Begins Not with Death, but with Knowing It Is Near," Texas Medicine, 62 (Oct., 1966), 44-5.

560. Bynum, Jack. "Social Status and Rites of Passage: The Social Context of Death," Omega, 4 (Winter, 1973), 323-332.

561. Byrn, Robert M. "An American Tragedy: The Supreme Court on Abortion," Fordham Law Review, 41 (May, 1973), 807-62.

562. Byrne, P.M., M.J. Stogre. "Agathanasia and the Care of the Dying," Canadian Medical Association Journal, 112 (June 21, 1975), 1396-7.

563. Cabot, Richard C., Russell L. Dicks. The Art of Ministering to the Sick. New York: Macmillan, 1936.

564. Cain, Albert C. "The Legacy of Suicide: Observations on the Pathogenic Impact of Suicide upon Marital Partners," Psychiatry, 29 (Nov., 1966), 873-80.

565. _____, Barbara S. Cain. "On Replacing a Child," Journal of the American Academy of Child Psychiatry, 3 (July, 1964), 443-56.

566. _____, Irene Fast. "Children's Disturbed Reactions to Parent Suicide," American Journal of Orthophsyciatry, 5 (Oct., 1966), 873-80.

567. _____, et al. "Children's Disturbed Reactions to the Death of a Sibling," American Journal of Orthophsyciatry, 34 (July, 1964), 741-52.

568. _____, et al. "Children's Disturbed Reactions to their Mother's Miscarriage," Psychosomatic Medicine, 24 (1964), 58-66.

569. Caine, Lynn. Widow. New York: William Morrow, 1974.

570. Caldwell, Diane, Brian L. Mishara. "Research on Attitudes of Medical Doctors Toward the Dying Patient: A Methodological Problem," Omega, 3 (Nov., 1972), 341-46.

571. Caldwell, J.R. "One Hundred Deaths in Practice: A Study of Terminal Care," Journal of the Royal College of General Practice, 21 (Aug., 1971), 460-3.

572. Calkins, Kathy. "Shouldering a Burden," Omega, 3 (Feb., 1972), 23-36.

573. Callaway, Enoch. "The Psychological Care of the Cancer Patient," Journal of the Medical Association of Georgia, 41 (Nov., 1952), 503-4.

574. Callaway, Joseph A. "Burials in Ancient Palestine; From the Stone Age to Abraham," The Biblical Archaeologist, 26 (Sep., 1963), 74-91.

575. Calloway, N.O. "Patterns of Senile Death," Journal of the American Geriatric Society, 14 (Feb., 1966), 156-66.

576. Cameron, A.H., P. Asher. "Cot Deaths in Birmingham," 1958-61," Medical Science Law, 5 (Oct., 1965), 187-99.

577. Cameron, Charles. "Professional Attitudes and Terminal Care," Public Health Reports, 67 (Oct., 1952), 955-9.

578. Cameron, J.M. "Sudden Death in Infancy," Public Health, 89 (May, 1975), 161-2.

579. Cameron, P. "The Imminency of Death," Journal of Consulting Clinical Psychology, 32 (Aug., 1968), 479-81.

580. Campbell, H. "Changes in Mortality Trends: England and Wales," Vital Health Statistics, 3 (Nov., 1965), 1-49.

581. Campbell, K. "Sudden Infant Death Syndrome," American Journal of Diseases of Children, 124 (Nov., 1972), 788.

582. Camps, Francis E. "When Infant Death Occurs," Nursing Mirror, 133 (Nov. 12, 1971), 14-5.

583. _____, Robert Gordon Carpenter, eds. Sudden and Unexpected Deaths in Infancy (Cot Deaths). Baltimore: Williams and Wilkins, 1972.

584. Canning, Ray R. "Mormon Return from the Dead Stories: Fact or Folklore," Utah Academy Proceedings, 42 (1965), 29-37.

585. Cannon, Walter B. "'Voodoo' Death," American Anthropologist, 44 (1942), 169-81.

586. Cantu, R.C. "Brain Death as Determined by Cerebral Arteriography," Lancet, 1 (June 16, 1973), 1391-2.

587. Caplan, Gerald. Emotional Problems of Early Childhood. New York: Basic Books, 1955.

588. _____, et al. "Four Studies of Crisis in Parents of Prematures," The Community Mental Health Journal, 1 (Summer, 1965), 149-61.

589. Cappon, Daniel, "Attitudes of and Towards the Dying," Canadian Medical Association Journal, 87 (Sep., 1972), 693-700.

590. _____. "Attitudes on Death," Omega, 1 (May, 1970), 103-8.

591. _____. "Attitudes Toward Death," Postgraduate Medical Journal, 47 (Feb., 1970), 257.

592. _____. "The Dying," Psychiatric Quarterly, 33 (1959), 466-89.

593. _____. "The Psychology of Dying," Pastoral Psychology, 12 (1961), 35-44.

594. Caprio, Frank S. "Ethnological Attitudes Toward Death: A Psychoanalytic Evaluation," Journal of Clinical and Experimental Psychopathology, 7 (1946), 737-52.

595. _____. "Morbid Fears," Medical Annals of Washington, D.C. 13 (Mar., 1944), 98-101.

596. _____. "A Psycho-Social Study of Primitive Conception of Death," Journal of Criminal Psychopathology, 5 (1943), 303-17.

597. _____. "A Study of Some Psychological Reactions During Prepubescence to the Idea of Death," Psychiatric Quarterly, 24 (1950), 405-505.

598. Capron, A. "Determining Death: Do We Need Statute?" Hastings Center Reports, 3 (Feb., 1973), 6-7.

599. Carabeur, M. "Ethical and Religious Problems Raised by Removal of Organs in Cerebral Death," Annals of Anesthesia, 15 (1974), 151-75.

600. Carey, Raymond G. "Emotional Adjustment in Terminal Patients: A Quantitative Approach," Journal of Counseling Psychology, 21 (1974), 433-9.

601. _____. "Living until Death," Hospital Progress, 55 (Feb., 1974), 82-7.

602. Cargas, H.J., A. White, eds. Death and Hope. Washington: Corpus Books, 1970.

603. Carlozzi, Carl G. Death and Contemporary Man: The Crisis of Terminal Illness. Grand Rapids: Wm. B. Eerdmans, 1968.

604. Carmichael, B. "The Death Wish in Daily Life," Psychoanalytic Review, 30 (1943), 59-66.

605. Carpenter, Edmund S. "Eternal Life and Self-Definition among the Aivilik Eskimos," American Journal of Psychiatry, 110 (1954), 840-3.

606. Carpenter, Edward. The Drama of Love and Death. New York: Mitchell Kennerly, 1912.

607. Carpenter, J.O., C.M. Wylie. "On Aging, Dying, and Denying: Delivering Care to Older Dying Patients," Public Health Reports, 89 (Sep., Oct., 1974), 403-7.

608. Carpenter, Kathryn, Marion J. Stewart. "Parents Take Heart at City of Hope," American Journal of Nursing, 62 (Oct., 1962), 82-5.

609. Carpenter, R.G., J.L. Emery. "Identification and Follow-up of Infants at Risk of Sudden Death in Infancy," Nature, 250 (Aug. 30, 1974), 729.

610. Carr, A.C. et al., eds. Grief: Selected Readings. New York: Health Sciences Publishing, 1975.

611. Carr, J.L. "The Coroner and the Common Law, III: Death and its Medical Imputations," California Medicine, 93 (1960), 32-4.

612. Carr, Robin L. "Death as Presented in Children's Books," Elementary English, 50 (May, 1973), 701-5.

613. Carr, W. "Theological Reflections on Death," North Carolina Medical Journal, 28 (Nov., 1967), 461-4.

614. Carrel, Alexis. "The Mystery of Death," in I. Galdston, ed., Medicine and Mankind. New York: Appleton-Century, 1936. 197-217.

615. Carrere, J. et al. "Apropos of a Case Report: Reflection on Death and Paranoia," Annals of Medicopsychology (Paris), 122 (Oct., 1964), 408-10.

616. Carrigan, Robert L. "The Hospital, Chaplain, Research and Pastoral Care," Pastoral Psychology, 17 (June, 1966), 39-48.

617. Carrington, Hereward, John R. Meader. Death, Its Causes and Pehnomena. New York: Dodd, Mead and Co., 1921.

618. Carroll, Charles. "Medicine Without an Ethic," Journal of the Louisiana State Medical Society, 124 (1972), 313-20.

619. Carson, J. "Learning from a Dying Patient," American Journal of Nursing, 71 (Feb., 1971), 333-4.

620. Carstairs, G.M. "Attitudes to Death and Suicide in an Indian Cultural Setting," International Journal of Social Psychiatry, 1 (1955), 33-41.

621. Carter, John R., Dale L. Martin. "A Pathology Assistant Program: The Role of Licensed Morticians," American Journal of Clinical Pathology, 53 (Jan., 1970), 26-31.

622. Carter, N. Death Strain. Lincoln, NE: University Publishing Company, 1970.

623. Cartwright, Ann et al. Life Before Death. London: Routledge and Kegan Paul, 1973.

624. Casler, L. "Death as a Psychosomatic Condition: Prolegomena to a Longitudinal Study," Psychological Reports, 27 (Dec., 1970), 953-4.

625. Cassady, June R., John Fall Altrocchi. "Patients' Concerns about Surgery," Nursing Research, 9 (1960), 219-21.

626. Cassell, Eric J. "Being and Becoming Dead," Social Research, 39 (Autumn, 1972), 528-42.

627. _____. "Death and the Physician," Commentary, 47 (June, 1969), 73-4.

628. _____. "Learning to Die," Bulletin of the New York Academy of Medicine, 49 (Dec., 1973), 1110-8.

629. Cassem, N.H. "Can Loss Be Gain?" Journal of Geriatric Psychiatry, 7 (1974), 116-20.

630. _____. "Care of the Dying Person," in E.A. Grollman, ed., Concerning Death: A Practical Guide for the Living. Boston: Beacon Press, 1974. 13-48.

631. _____. "Confronting the Decision to Let Death Come," Critical Care Medicine, 2 (Aug., 1974), 113-7.

632. _____. "Controversies Surrounding the Hopelessly Ill Patient," Catholic Mind, 73 (1975), 40-8.

633. _____. "Pastoral Care of the Dying Patient," Pastoral Psychology, 23 (1972), 52-61.

634. _____. "The Simultaneous Confrontation with Death and the Hereafter," Archives of Foundations of Thanatology, 1 (1970), 149-50.

635. _____. "What You Can Do for Dying Patients," Medical Dimensions, 2 (1973), 29-34.

636. _____, M. Shubow. "Counseling the Dying Patient," Pulse, 2 (1972), 114-7, 122, 124.

637. _____, R.S. Stewart. "Management and Care of the Dying Patient," International Journal of Psychiatry in Medicine, 6 (1975), 293-304.

638. _____, et al. "How Coronary Patients Respond to Last Rites," Postgraduate Medicine, 45 (1969), 147-52.

639. Cather, Willa. Death Comes for the Archbishop. New York: Knopf, 1929.

640. Cavan, Ruth S. The Family. New York: Crowell, 1942. Chapter 10.

641. _____, et al. Personal Adjustment in Old Age. Chicago: Science Research Associates, Inc., 1949.

642. Cavanagh, J.R. "The Chaplain and the Dying Patient," Hospital Progress, 52 (Nov., 1971), 34-40.

643. _____. "The Right of the Patient to Die with Dignity," The Catholic Nurse, 11 (Dec., 1963), 24-33.

644. Cavins, A.W. "Thanatology Resurrected," Journal of the Indiana Medical Association, 61 (Aug., 1968), 1159.

645. Chadwick, Edwin. Report . . . On the Results of a Special Inquiry into the Practice of Interment in Towns. Philadelphia: C. Sherman, 1845.

646. Chadwick, Mary. "Die furcht vor Dem Tode," International Zeitschrift fur Psychoanalyse, 15 (1929), 271-84.

647. _____. "Die Gott-Phantasie bei Kindern," Imago, 13 (1927), 383-94.

648. _____. "Notes on the Fear of Death," Psychoanalytic Review, 15 (1928), 102-3.

649. Chambers, D. "The Pattern of Sudden Infant Death in Inner North London in 1973," Public Health, 89 (May, 1975), 145-6.

650. Champagne, Marian. Facing Life Alone. New York: Bobbs-Merrill, 1964.

651. Champigy, R. "Suffering and Death," Symposium, 24 (Fall, 1970), 197-205.

652. Chandler, Kenneth A. "Three Processes of Dying and Their Behavioral Effects," Journal of Counsulting Psychology, 29 (1965), 296-301.

653. Chandra, R.K. "A Child Dies," Indian Journal of Pediatrics, 35 (July, 1968), 363-4.

654. Chapman, A.H. "Obsessions of Infanticide," Archives of General Psychiatry (Chicago), 1 (1959), 12-6.

655. Chapman, Earle M. "He Was in the Prime of Life," Journal of Pastoral Care, 14 (Summer, 1960), 98-103.

656. Charmaz, K.C. "Coroners Strategies for Announcing Death," Urban Life, 4 (1975), 296-317.

657. Charyk, W. "The Physician as Witness: The Problem of Dying Declarations," Medical Annals of Washington, D.C., 41 (Oct., 1972), 641-2.

658. Chase, H.C. "A Study of Infant Mortality from Linked Records: Comparison of Neo-Natal Mortality from Two Cohort Studies: United States, January-March, 1950 and 1960," Vital Health Statistics, 20 (June, 1972), 1-99.

659. Chase, Peter, Irving Beck. "Making a Graceful Exit," Rhode Island Medical Journal, 39 (Sep., 1956), 497-9ff.

660. Chasin, Barbara Helen. "Neglected Variables in the Study of Death Attitudes," The Sociological Quarterly, 12 (Winter, 1971), 107-13.

661. _____. "Value Orientations and Attitudes Toward Death," Dissertation Abstracts, 29 (Dec., 1968), 1963-A.

662. Chellam, Grace. "The Disengagement Theory: Awareness of Death and Self-Engagement," Dissertation Abstracts, 25 (May, 1965), 6806.

663. Cherico, D.J. et al., eds. Thanatology Course. New York: MSS Information, 1975.

664. Chesterton, G.K. Eugenics and Other Evils. London: Cassell and Company, 1922.

665. Chethik, M. "The Impact of Object Loss on a Six Year Old," Journal of the American Academy of Child Psychiatry, 9 (Oct., 1970), 624-43.

666. Chevan, A., J.H. Korson. "The Widowed Who Live Alone: An Examination of Social and Demographic Factors," Social Forces, 51 (1972), 45-53.

667. Childers, P. et al. "The Concept of Death in Early Childhood," Child Development, 42 (Oct., 1971), 1299-1301.

668. Chiles, Robert E. "The Rights of Patients," New England Journal of Medicine, 277 (Aug., 1967), 409-11.

669. Chodoff, Paul. "The Dying Patient," Medical Annals of Washington, D.C., 29 (Aug., 1960), 447-50.

670. _____. "A Psychiatric Approach to the Dying Patient," CA Bulletin of Cancer Progress, 10 (Jan.-Feb., 1960), 29-32.

671. Chodoff, Paul, et al. "Stress, Defenses and Coping Behavior: Observations in Parents of Children with Malignant Disease," American Journal of Psychiatry, 120, (Feb., 1964), 743-9.

672. Choron, Jacques. Death and Modern Man. New York: Collier Books, 1971. Originally published with title: Modern Man and Mortality. New York: Macmillan, 1964.

673. _____. Death and Western Thought. New York: Macmillan, 1973.

674. Christ, Adolph E. "Attitudes Toward Death Among a Group of Acute Geriatric Psychiatric Patients," Journal of Gerontology, 16 (1961), 56-9.

675. Christenson, L. "The Physician's Role in Terminal Illness and Death," Minnesota Medicine, 46 (1963), 881-3.

676. Christopherson, L.K., T.A. Gonda. "Patterns of Grief: End-Stage Renal Failure and Kidney Transplantation," Transplantation Proceedings, 5 (June, 1973), 1041-7.

677. Christopherson, L.K., D.T. Lunde. "Heart Transplant Donors and Their Families," Seminars in Psychiatry, 3 (Feb., 1971), 26-35.

678. _____. "The Selection of Cardiac Transplant Recipients and Their Subsequent Psychosocial Adjustment," Seminars in Psychiatry, 3 (Feb., 1971), 36-45.

679. Chura, Victoria. "I Was My Father's Nurse," American Journal of Nursing, 68 (Sep., 1968), 1908-9.

680. Church, June S. "The Buffalo Creek Disaster: Extent and Range of Emotional and/or Behavioral Problems," Omega, 5 (1974), 61-3.

681. Clark, Margie B. "Children and Death," Virginia Medical Monthly, 101 (July, 1974), 573-6.

682. _____. "A Therapeutic Approach to Treating a Grieving Two and One-Half Year Old," Journal of the American Academy of Child Psyhciatry, 11 (Oct., 1972), 705-11.

683. Clarke, K.S. "Calculated Risk of Sports Fatalities," Journal of the American Medical Association, 197 (Sep., 1966), 894-6.

684. Clausen, C.R. et al. "Studies of the Sudden Infant Death Syndrome in King County, Washington, IV: Immunologic Studies," Pediatrics, 52 (July, 1973), 45-51.

685. Claypool, J.R. "Family Deals with Death," Baylor Law Review, 27 (1975), 34-8.

686. Clayton, P.J. "The Clinical Morbidity of the First Year of Bereavement: A Review," Comprehensive Psychiatry, 14 (Mar.-Apr., 1973), 151-7.

687. Clayton, Paula J. "The Effect of Living Alone on Bereavement Symptoms," American Journal of Psychiatry, 132 (Feb., 1975), 133-7.

688. _____, et al. "Anticipatory Grief and Widowhood," British Journal of Psychiatry, 122 (Jan., 1973), 47-51.

689. _____. "The Bereavement of the Widowed," Diseases of the Nervous System, 32 (Sep., 1971), 597-604.

690. _____. "The Depression of Widowhood," British Journal of Psychiatry, 120 (Jan., 1972), 71-7.

691. _____. "Mourning and Depression: Their Similarities and Differences," Canadian Psychiatric Association Journal, 19 (June, 1974), 309-12.

692. _____. "A Study of Normal Bereavement," American Journal of Psychiatry, 125 (Aug., 1968), 168-78.

693. Clayton, Richard R., William L. Tolone. "Religiosity and Attitudes Toward Induced Abortion: An Elaboration of the Relationship," Sociological Analysis, 34 (Spring, 1973), 26-39.

694. Cleary, E.G. "Mercy Killing: It's Such a Slippery Slope," Human Life. Melbourne: Human Life Research Foundation, 1971.

695. Cleary, F.X. "Death and Afterlife: Biblical and Theological Interpretation," Hospital Progress, 56 (1975), 40-4.

696. Cleaveland, F.P. "The Dance of Death," Journal of the American Medical Association, 176 (1961), 142-3.

697. _____. "'Masquerades': Homicide, Suicide, Accident or Natural Death," Journal of the Indiana Medical Association, 53 (1960), 2181-4.

698. Cleveland, S.E., D.L. Johnson. "Motivation and Readiness of Potential Human Tissue Donors and Non-Donors," Psychiatric Medicine, 32 (1970), 225-231.

699. Clouse, G.D. "Introduction to Widowhood: The Role of the Family Physician," Ohio Medical Journal, 62 (Dec., 1966), 1281-4.

700. Cobb, Beatrix R. "Psychological Impact of Long Illness and Death of a Child on the Family Circle," Journal of Pediatrics, 49 (1956), 746-51.

701. _____, et al. "A Psychology Program in a Cancer Hospital," Texas Report of Biological Medicine, 12 (1954), 30-8.

702. Cobb, Stanley, Erich Lindemann. "Neuropsychiatric Observations after the Cocoanut Grove Fire," Annals of Surgery, 117 (June, 1943), 814.

703. Cochrane, A.L. "Elie Metschnikoff and his Theory of an 'Instinct de la Mort'," International Journal of Psychoanalysis, 15 (1934), 265-70.

704. Cochrane, A.L. "A Little Widow Is A Dangerous Thing," _International Journal of Psycho-Analysis_, 17 (1936), 494-509.

705. Cockerill, Eleanor E. "The Cancer Patient as a Person," _Public Health Nursing_, 40 (1948), 78-83.

706. Cohen, Kathleen Rogers. _Metamorphosis of a Death Symbol: The Changing Meaning of the Transi Tomb in 15th and 16th Century Europe_. Berkeley: University of California Press, 1974.

707. Cohen, M., L.M. Lipton. "Spontaneous Remission of Schizophrenic Psychoses Following Maternal Death," _Psychiatric Quarterly_, 24 (1950), 716-725.

708. Cohen, R.J., C. Parker. "Fear of Failure and Death," _Psychological Report_, 34 (Feb., 1974), 54.

709. Cohen, Ruth K. _A Boy's Quiet Voice_. New York: Greenberg, 1957.

710. Cohen, Sidney. "Psychiatric Help for the Incurable Patient," _The Physician's Panorama_, 5 (Oct., 1967), 12-20.

711. Cole, Fay-Cooper. "Relations Between the Living and the Dead," _American Journal of Sociology_, 21 (Mar., 1916), 611-2.

712. Collett, Lora Jean, David Lester. "The Fear of Death and the Fear of Dying," _The Journal of Psychology_, 72 (July, 1969), 179-81.

713. Collings, Anne, William E. Sedlacek. "Grief Reactions Among University Students," _Journal of the National Association of Women Deans and Counselors_, 36 (Summer, 1973), 178-83.

714. Collins, Vincent J. "Considerations in Prolonging Life: A Dying and Recovery Score, Part I," _Illinois Medical Journal_, 147 (June, 1975), 543-7.

715. _____. "Considerations in Prolonging Life: A Dying and Recovery Score, Part II," _Illinois Medical Journal_, 148 (June, 1975), 42-6.

716. _____. _Grief, How to Live with Sorrow_. St. Meinrad, IN: Abbey Press, 1966.

717. _____. "Limits of Medical Responsibility in Prolonging Life: Guides to Decisions," _Journal of the American Medical Association_, 206 (Oct. 7, 1968), 389-92.

718. Colomb, Georges, Jean Hamburger. "Psychological and Moral Problems of Renal Transplantation," _International Psychiatry Clinics_, 4 (1967), 157-77.

719. Colton, Arthur E. et al. "A Faculty Workshop on Death Attitudes and Life Affirmation," _Omega_, 4 (1973), 51-6.

720. Combes, John D. "Ethnography, Archaeology, and Burial Practices Among Coastal South Carolina Blacks," _The Conference on Historic Site Archaeology Papers_, 7 (1974), 52-61.

721. Committee on Infant and Preschool Children. "The SIDS," Pediatrics, 50 (Dec. 1972), 964-5.

722. Comparat, S. "Psychology of War: Civilization as Death or Love," Minerva Medicine, 66 (1975), 2962-70.

723. Comper, Frances M., ed. Ars Moriendi: The Book of the Craft of Dying and Other Early English Tracts Concerning Death. London: Longmans, Green and Co., 1917.

724. Comstock, G.W., K.B. Partridge. "Church Attendance and Health," Journal of Chronic Disorders, 25 (Dec., 1972), 665-72.

725. Conley, J.C. "Rights of the Dying Patient," Archives of Otolaryngology, 90 (Oct., 1969), 405.

726. Conley, Sharon. "The Will to Live," Tomorrow's Nurse, 4 (Oct.-Nov., 1963), 20-2.

727. Connell, E.H. "The Significance of the Idea of Death in the Neurotic Mind," British Journal of Medical Psychology, 4 (1924), 115-24.

728. Conrad, B. Famous Last Words. Garden City, NY: Doubleday, 1961.

729. Consultation Clinic. "On Fatal Illness," Pastoral Psychology, 6 (Feb., 1955) 42-53.

730. Cook, Sara Sheets. Children and Dying. New York: Health Sciences Publishing, 1973.

731. _____. "Children's Perceptions of Death," Children and Dying. Health Sciences Publishing, 1973. 1-15.

732. Cooke, Mother M. Gerard. Hallucination and Death as Motifs of Escape in the Novels of Julien Green. Washington: Catholic University of America Press, 1960.

733. Cooke, R.E. "Is There a Right to Die--Quickly?" Journal of Pediatrics, 80 (May, 1972), 906-8.

734. Coolidge, J.C. "Unexpected Death in a Patient Who Wished to Die," Journal of the American Psychoanalytic Association, 17 (Apr., 1969), 413-20.

735. Coombs, R.H., P.S. Powers. "Socialization for Death: Physician's Role," Urban Life, 4 (1975), 25-271.

736. Cooperman, I.G. "Second Careers: War Wives and Widows," Vocational Guidance Quarterly, 20 (1971), 103-111.

737. Corbett, L.P. "The Diagnosis of Cerebral Death in the Community Hospital," Journal of the American Osteopathic Association, 74 (Sep., 1974), 43-55.

738. Corder, M.P., R.L. Anders. "Death and Dying: Oncology Discussion Group," Journal of Psychiatric Nursing, 12 (July-Aug., 1974), 10-14.

739. Corey, Lawrence G. "An Analogue of Resistance to Death Awareness," Journal of Gerontology, 16 (1961), 59-66.

740. Coriolis. Death, Here Is Thy Sting. Toronto: McClelland and Stewart, 1967.

741. Corney, R.T., F.T. Horton, Jr. "Pathological Grief Following Spontaneous Abortion," American Journal of Psychiatry, 131 (July, 1974), 825-7.

742. Cornils, Stanley. Managing Grief Wisely. Grand Rapids: Baker Books, 1967.

743. Corso, Gregory. The Happy Birthday of Death. New York: New Directions, 1960.

744. Coser, Rose Laub. Life in the Ward. East Lansing, MI: Michigan State University Press, 1962.

745. Cosneck, B.J. "Family Patterns of Older Widowed Jewish People," Family Coordinator, 19 (1970), 368-73.

746. Cotter, M.M. "Sudden Death in the Work Situation," Occupational Health, 22 (Feb., 1970), 39-42.

747. Cotter, Z.M. "Institutional Care of the Terminally Ill," Hospital Progress, 52 (June, 1971), 42-8.

748. _____. "On Not Getting Better," Hospital Progress, 53 (Mar., 1972), 60-3.

749. Couch, N.P. "Supply and Demand in Kidney and Liver Transplantation," Transplantation, 4 (Sep., 1966), 587-95.

750. Cousinet, R. "L'Idee de la Mort chez les Enfants," Journal de Psychologie Normale et Pathologique, 36 (1969), 65-75.

751. Covalt, Nila Kirkpatrick. "The Meaning of Religion to Older People," Geriatrics, 15 (Sep., 1960), 658-64.

752. Covill, F.J. "Bereavement--A Public Health Challenge," Canadian Journal of Public Health, 59 (Apr., 1968), 169-70.

753. Cowan, C. "Shalom Means Suicide," Suicide, 5 (1975), 177-82.

754. Cowin, R. "Problems of Impending Death: The Role of the Social Worker," Physical Therapy, 48 (July, 1968), 743-8.

755. Cox, Harvey. Feast of Fools. Cambridge: Harvard University Press, 1969.

756. Cox, Peter R., John R. Ford. "The Mortality of Widows Shortly after Widowhood," Lancet, 1 (Jan. 18, 1964), 163-4.

757. Craddick, Ray A. "Symbolism of Death: Achetypal and Personal Symbols," International Journal of Symbology, 3 (Dec., 1972), 35-44.

758. Crafoord, C.C. "Cerebral Death and the Transplantation Era," Diseases of the Chest, 55 (Feb., 1969), 141-5.

759. Crain, H. "Basic Concepts of Death in Children's Literature," Elementary English, 49 (Jan., 1972), 111-5.

760. Cramond, W.A. "Medical, Moral and Legal Aspects of Organ Transplantation and Long-Term Resuscitative Measures: Psychological, Social and Community Aspects," Medical Journal of Australia, 2 (1968), 522-7.

761. _____. "The Psychological Care of Patients with Terminal Illness," Nursing Times, 69 (Mar. 15, 1973), 339-43.

762. _____. "Renal Homotransplantation--Some Observations on Recipients and Donors," British Journal of Psychiatry, 113 (1967), 1223-30.

763. _____, et al. "The Psychiatric Contribution to a Renal Unit Undertaking Chronic Haemodialysis and Renal Homotransplantation," British Journal of Psychiatry, 113 (1967), 1201-12.

764. _____, et al. "Psychological Screening of Potential Donors in a Renal Homotransplantation Programme," British Journal of Psychiatry, 113 (1967), 1213-21.

765. Crane, Diana. The Sanctity of Social Life: Physicians' Treatment of Critically Ill Patients. New York: Russell Sage Foundation, 1975.

766. _____. "Social Aspects of the Prolongation of Life," in Social Science Frontiers 1. New York: Russell Sage Foundation, 1969.

767. Cranville-Grossman, R. "Early Bereavement and Schizophrenia," British Journal of Psychiatry, 112 (1966), 307-14.

768. Crase, D. "Death and Young Child: Some Practical Suggestions on Support and Counseling," Clinical Pediatrics, 14 (1975), 747-50.

769. Craven, J. "Hospice Care for Dying Patients," American Journal of Nursing, 75 (1975), 1816.

770. Creegan, R.F. "A Symbolic Action During Bereavement," Journal of Abnormal and Social Psychology, 37 (1942), 403-5.

771. Cresswell, P.A. "Factors Associated with Radical Behavior Amongst Students," The International Journal of Social Psychiatry, 18 (Autumn, 1972), 219-24.

772. Crisp, A.H., R.G. Priest. "Psychoneurotic Status During the Year Following Bereavement," Journal of Psychosomatic Research, 16 (Aug., 1972), 351-5.

773. Cross, K.W., S.R. Lewis. "Upper Respiratory Obstruction and Cot Death," _Archives of Diseases in Childhood_, 46 (1971), 211-3.

774. Crown, B. et al. "Attitudes Toward Attitudes Toward Death," _Psychological Reports_, 20 (June, 1967), Supplement, 1181-2.

775. Cryer, Newman S., John Monroe Vayhinger, eds. _Casebook in Pastoral Counseling_. Nashville: Abingdon Press, 1962.

776. Cumming, Elaine, William E. Henry. _Growing Old_. New York: Basic Books, 1961.

777. Cumming, John, Elaine Cumming. _Ego and Milieu_. New York: Atherton Press, 1962.

778. Cumpston, J.H.L. "Life and Death," _Medical Journal of Australia_, 1 (June 1, 1929), 728-40.

779. Cunnick, W.R., Jr., E.A. Lew. "What Kills and Disables People Who Work," _Journal of Occupational Medicine_, 15 (Feb., 1973), 89-91.

780. Cunningham, F.B.J. _Morality of Organic Transplantation_. Washington: Catholic University Press, 1944.

781. Curran, W.J. "Abortion Law in the Supreme Court," _New England Journal of Medicine_, 285 (July, 1971), 30-1.

782. _____. "Legal and Medical Death: Kansas Takes the First Step," _New England Journal of Medicine_, 284 (Feb. 4, 1971), 260-1.

783. Curtin, Sharon R. _Nobody Ever Died of Old Age_. Boston: Little, Brown, and Company, 1973.

784. Custer, H.R. "Nursing Care of the Dying," _Hospital Progress_, 42 (Dec., 1961), 68ff.

785. Cutler, Donald R. "Death and Responsibility: A Minister's View," _Psychiatric Opinion_, 3 (Aug., 1966), 8-12.

786. _____, ed. _Updating Life and Death_. Boston: Beacon, 1968.

787. Cutter, Fred. _Coming to Terms with Death: How to Face the Inevitable with Wisdom and Dignity_. Chicago: Nelson-Hall, 1974.

788. _____. "Letter to My Friends," _Omega_, 1 (Nov., 1970), 349-55.

789. _____. "Robert Seymour: A Psycho-historical Autopsy," _Omega_, 2 (Aug., 1971), 195-214.

790. _____. "Some Psychological Problems in Hemodialysis," _Omega_, 1 (Feb., 1970), 37-47.

791. Cutter, Fred. "Transplants and Psychological Survival in the Treatment of Kidney Disease," Omega, 3 (Feb., 1972), 57-66.

792. Daly, Cahal. Morals, Law and Life. Chicago: Scepter, 1966.

793. Daniel, M.P. "The Social Worker's Role," British Medical Journal, 1 (Jan 6, 1973), 36-8.

794. Danto, Bruce L. "Firearm Homicide in the Home Setting," Omega, 1 (Nov., 1970), 331-47.

795. _____. "Humanistic Aspects of Psychopharmacological Care of the Terminal Cancer Patient," Michigan Medicine, 72 (Dec., 1973), 833-4.

796. Dargeon, Harold. "The Diagnosis and Management of Neoplastic Diseases in Childhood," Medical Clinics of North America, 31 (May, 1947), 498-524.

797. Das, S. Sunder. "Grief and Suffering," Psychotherapy, 8 (Spring, 1971), 8-9.

798. _____. "Grief and the Imminent Threat of Non-Being," British Journal of Psychiatry, 118 (Apr., 1971), 467-8.

799. Dastre, A. Life and Death. Translated by W.I. Greenstreet. London: W. Scott, 1911.

800. Daufer, C. "Criteria of Cerebral Death," Minnesota Medicine, 56 (Apr., 1973), 321-4.

801. Davey, Richard. A History of Mourning. London: Jay's, 1890.

802. David, H.P. "Abortion in Psychological Perspective," American Journal of Orthopsychiatry, 42 (Jan., 1972), 61-8.

803. Davidson, Glen W. "Basic Images of Death in America: An Historical Analysis," Dissertation Abstracts, 27 (Oct., 1966), 1102-A.

804. Davidson, Glen W. Living with Dying. Minneapolis: Augsburg Publishing, 1975.

805. Davidson, Henry A. "Emotional Precipitants of Death," Journal of the Medical Society of New Jersey, 46 (1949), 350-2.

806. Davidson, Ramona Powell. "To Give Care in Terminal Illness," American Journal of Nursing, 66 (Jan., 1966), 74-5.

807. Davidson, Susannah. "Bereavement in Children," Nursing Times, 62 (Dec. 16, 1966), 1650-2.

808. Davies, J. "Sudden Death in Infancy," Public Health, 89 (May, 1975), 143.

809. Davies, Robert K. et al. "Organic Factors and Psychological Adjustment in Advanced Cancer Patients," Psychosomatic Medicine, 35 (Nov., 1973), 464-71.

810. Davis, B.A. "Until Death Ensues," Nursing Clinics of North America, 7 (June, 1972), 303-9.

811. Davis, Charles H.S. The Egyptian Book of the Dead. New York: G.P. Putnam's Sons, 1894.

812. Davis, D. Russell. "The Death of the Artist's Father: Henrik Ibsen," British Journal of Medical Psychology, 46 (June, 1973), 135-141.

813. Davis, J.A. "The Attitude of Parents to the Approaching Death of Their Child," Developmental Medicine and Child Neurology, (London), 6 (June, 1964), 286-8.

814. Davis, Nanette J. "Clergy Abortion Broker: A Transactional Analysis of Social Movement Development," Sociological Focus, 6 (Fall, 1973), 87-109.

815. Davis, R.W. "Psychologic Aspects of Geriatric Nursing," American Journal of Nursing, 68 (Apr., 1968), 802-4.

816. Davis, Richard H., ed. The Doctor and the Dying Patient. Los Angeles: California School of Medicine, 1971.

817. _____, ed. Dealing with Death. Los Angeles: University of Southern California Press, 1973.

818. Davoli, G. "The Child's Request to Die at Home," Pediatrics, 38 (Nov., 1966) 925.

819. Day, Richard Whiteside. "Heroic Death, A Study from a Christian Point of View," Dissertation Abstracts, 14 (1954), 192.

820. Day, Stacey B. "Editorial--A Time to Die," Postgraduate Medicine, 54 (Dec., 1973), 113-4.

821. _____, Thomas Dillon Redshaw. Tuluak and Amaulik: Dialogues on Death and Mourning with the Inuit Eskimo. Minneapolis: University of Minnesota Medical School, Bell Museum of Pathobiology, 1973.

822. _____, ed. Death and Attitudes Towards Death. Minneapolis: University of Minnesota Bell Museum, 1972.

823. Daynes, G. "Intercultural Problems in the Care of the Dying Patient," South African Medical Journal, 48 (Jan. 26, 1974), 139-40.

824. De Bary, R. My Experiments with Death. London: Longmans, Green and Company, 1936.

825. de Bosis, Lauro. The Story of My Death. New York: Oxford University Press, 1933.

826. de Beauvoir, Simone. A Very Easy Death. New York: Warner Paperback Library, 1973.

827. Dedek, John F. Human Life: Some Moral Issues. New York: Sheed and Ward, 1972.

828. DeDellarossa, G.S. "The Concept of Death in Your Self-Development," *Revista de Psicoanalisis*, 22 (1965), 26-44.

829. Defoe, Danial. *Journal of the Plague Year*. New York: New American Library, 1975.

830. Degner, Lesley. "The Relationship Between Some Beliefs Held by Physicians and their Life-Prolonging Decisions," *Omega*, 5 (Fall, 1974), 223-232.

831. DeJarast, S.G. "Mourning in Relation to Learning," *Revista de Psicoanalisis*, 15 (1958), 31-5.

832. Delano, James G. "Separation Anxiety as a Cause of Early Emotional Problems in Children," *Mayo Clinic Proceedings*, 39 (1964), 743-9.

833. Delmonico, F.L., J.G. Randolph. "Death--A Concept in Transition," *Pediatrics*, 51 (Feb., 1973), 234-9.

834. DeMoerloose, J. "Abortion Throughout the World," *Nursing Times*, 67 (July 3, 1971), 678-80.

835. Dempsey, David. *The Way We Die*. New York: Macmillan, 1975

836. Demske, James M. *Being, Man, and Death: A Key to Heidegger*. Lexington: University Press of Kentucky, 1970.

837. Demuth Berg, Constance. "Cognizance of the Death Taboo in Counseling Children," *School Counselor*. 21 (Sep., 1973), 28-33.

838. Denckla, W.D. "A Time to Die," *Life Science*, 16 (Jan. 1, 1975), 31-44.

839. Dennehy, Constance M. "Childhood Bereavement and Psychiatric Illness," *British Journal of Psychiatry*, 112 (1966), 1049-69.

840. Dennis, Wayne. "Historical Notes on Child Animism," *Psychological Reivew*, 45 (1938), 257-66.

841. De-Nour, A. Kaplan, J.W. Czaczkes. "Emotional Problems and Reactions of the Medical Team in a Chronic Haemodialysis Unit," *The Lancet*, 2 (Nov. 9, 1968), 987-91.

842. Dent, M.J. "Should Nurses Diagnose Death?" *Nursing Mirror*, 130 (Dec., 1969), 28-9.

843. de Parvillez, Alphonse. *Joy in the Face of Death*. Translated by Pierre de Fon. New York: Desclee, 1963.

844. DeRopp, Robert S. *Man Against Aging*. New York: St. Martin's Press, 1960.

845. Destouni, N. "Psychology of Dying Patients," *Dynamic Psychology*, 8 (1975), 234-9.

846. Deutsch, Felix. "Euthanasia: A Clinical Study," Psychoanalytic Quarterly, 5 (1936), 347-68.

847. Deutsch, Helene. "Absence of Grief," Psychoanalytic Quarterly, 6 (1937), 12-22.

848. _____. "A Two-Year-Old Boy's First Love Comes to Grief," in L. Jessner and E. Pavenstedt, eds., Dynamics of Psychopathology in Childhood. New York: Grune and Stratton, 1959.

849. Deutsch, J.M. The Development of Children's Concepts of Causal Relationships Minneapolis: University of Minnesota Press, 1937.

850. Devereux, George. "Primitive Psychiatry: Funeral Suicide and the Mohave Social Structure," Bulletin of the History of Medicine, 11 (1942), 522-42.

851. _____. "Social Structure and the Economy of Affective Bonds," Psycho-Analytic Review, 29 (1942), 303-14.

852. DeVos, George, Hiroshi Wagatsuma. "Psycho-Cultural Significance of Concern over Death and Illness among Rural Japanese," International Journal of Social Psychiatry, 5 (Summer, 1959), 5-19.

853. Dewi, Rees W. "The Distress of Dying," British Medical Journal, 3 (July 8, 1972), 105-7.

854. DeWind, E. "Confrontation with Death," International Journal of Psychoanalysis, 49 (1968), 302-5.

855. _____. "Facing Death," Psyche (Stuttgart), 22 (June, 1968), 423-41.

856. Diamond, Israel. "Going Downhill--a Lethal Journey," Journal of the Kentucky Medical Association, 58 (June, 1960), 710-14.

857. Diamond, Milton et al. "Sexuality, Birth Control and Abortion: A Decision-Making Sequence," Journal of Biosocial Science, 5 (July, 1973), 347-61.

858. Diaz, E. "A Death on the Ward," Hospital Topics, 47 (May, 1969), 83-7.

859. Dicks, Russell, Thomas Kepler. And Peace at the Last. Philadelphia: Westminster Press, 1953.

860. Dickstein, Louis S. "Death Concern: Measurement and Correlates," Psychological Reports, 30 (April, 1972), 563-71.

861. _____. "Relationship Between Death Anxiety and Demographic Variables," Psychological Reports, 37 (1975), 262.

862. _____. "Self-Report and Fantasy Correlates of Death Concern," Psychological Reports, 37 (Aug., 1975).

863. Dickstein, Louis S., Sidney J. Blatt. "Death Concern, Futurity, and Anticipation," Journal of Consulting Psychology, 30 (1966), 11-7.

864. Diggory, James C., Doreen Z. Rothman. "Values Destroyed by Death," Journal of Abnormal and Social Psychology, 63 (1961), 205-10.

865. Dimock, Hedley C. The Child in Hospital. Toronto: MacMillan Company, 1959.

866. Dizmang, Larry H. "Loss, Bereavement and Depression in Childhood," International Psychiatry Clinics, 6 (1969), 175-95.

867. Djerassi, C. "Fertility Control Through Abortion: Assessment of the Period 1950-1980," Bulletin of the Atomic Scientists, 28 (Jan., 1972), 9-14.

868. Dobihal, E.F. Jr. "Talk or Terminal Care," Connecticut Medicine, 38 (July, 1974), 364-7.

869. Dobzhansky, Theodosius. "Religion, Death, and Evolutionary Adaptation," in Melford E. Spiro, ed., The Context and Meaning of Cultural Anthropology. New York: The Free Press, 1965.

870. Dodds, E.R. Pagan and Christian in an Age of Anxiety. New York: Cambridge University Press, 1965.

871. _____. "Two Concordant Experiences Coinciding with a Death," Journal for the Society for Psychical Research, 41 (1962), 337-46.

872. Dodge, Joan S. "How Much Should the Patient Be Told--and By Whom?" Hospitals, 37 (Dec., 16, 1963), 66ff.

873. _____. "Nurses' Sense of Adequacy and Attitudes Toward Keeping Patients Informed," Journal of Health and Human Behavior, 2 (1961), 213-16.

874. Dollen, Charles (comp.). Abortion in Context: A Select Bibliography. Metuchen, NJ: Scarecrow Press, 1970.

875. Donaldson, Peter J. "Denying Death: A Note Regarding Some Ambiguities in the Current Discussion," Omega, 3 (Nov., 1972), 285-93.

876. Dondlinger, P. "Was Terry Dead?" Nursing, 5 (June, 1975), 57.

877. Donne, John. Biathanatos, 1644. Reprint of the First Edition. New York: Facsimile Text Society, 1930.

878. Donovan, D.M. "Some Thoughts on Being and Having," International Journal of Social Psychiatry, 21 (Winter-Spring, 1974-5), 12-3.

879. Dorpat, T.L. "Psychiatric Observations on Assassinations," Northwest Medicine, 67 (Oct., 1968), 976-9.

880. Doss, Richard W. The Last Enemy: A Theology of Death. New York: Harper
      and Row, 1974.

881. _____. "Towards a Theology of Death," Pastoral Psychology, 23 (1972),
      15-23.

882. Douglass, Truman B. "On Doing One's Own Dying," Theology and Life, 9 (1966),
      99-105.

883. Douglass, W.A. Death in Murelaga: Funeral Ritual in a Spanish Basque Village.
      Seattle: University of Washington Press, 1969

884. Dovenmuehle, R.H. "Death and Dying: Attitudes of Patient and Doctor," Group
      for the Advancement of Psychiatry, (Symposium #11), 5 (Oct., 1965),
      607-13.

885. Dow, T. "Family Reaction to Crisis," Journal of Marriage and Family, 27 (1965),
      363-7.

886. Dowd, Donald W. Medical, Moral and Legal Implications of Recent Medical Advan-
      ces. New York: DeCapo Press, 1971.

887. Dowd, Q.L. Funeral Management and Costs. Chicago: University of Chicago
      Press, 1921.

888. Downey, Gregg W. "Dying Patients Still Have Human Needs," The Modern Hospi-
      tal, 114 (Mar., 1970), 78-81.

889. Downie, P.A. "Symposium: Care of the Dying: A Personal Commentary on the
      Care of the Dying on the North American Continent," Nursing Mirror,
      139 (Oct. 10, 1974), 68-70.

890. Downing, A.B., ed. Euthanasia and the Right to Death. London: Low and
      Brydone, 1969.

891. Doyle, Nancy. The Dying Person and the Family. New York: Public Affairs
      Committee, 1972.

892. Drake, Cyndi. "And to Die is Different," Tomorrow's Nurse, 4 (Aug.-Sep.,
      1963), 14-7.

893. Drant, Melvin J. Dying and Dignity: The Meaning and Control of a Personal
      Death. Springfield: C.C. Thomas, 1974.

894. Draughon, M. "Step-Mother's Model of Identification in Relation to Mourning
      in the Child," Psychological Reports, 36 (Feb., 1975), 183-9.

895. Drotar, Dennis. "Death in the Pediatric Hospital: Psychological Consultation
      with Medical and Nursing Staff," Journal of Clinical Child Psychology,
      4 (Spring, 1975), 33-5.

896. Drummond, Elenor E. "Communication and Comfort for the Dying Patient," Nursing Clinics of North America, 5 (Mar., 1970), 55-63.

897. _____, Jeanne Blumberg. "Death and the Curriculum," Journal of Nursing Education, 1 (May-June, 1962),21-8.

898. Dublin, Louis I. Factbook on Man from Birth to Death. New York: MacMillan, 1965.

899. Ducasse, C.J. A Critical Examination of the Belief in a Life after Death. Springfield: C.C. Thomas, 1962.

900. _____. Nature, Mind and Death. La Salle, IL: Open Court Publishing Co., 1951.

901. Duckett, Eleanor Shipley. Death and Life in the Tenth Century. Ann Arbor: University of Michigan Press, 1967.

902. Duff, Raymond, A.G.M. Campbell. "Moral and Ethical Dilemmas in the Special-Care Nursery," New England Journal of Medicine, 289 (1973), 890-4.

903. Duke, Phyllis. "Media on Death and Dying," Omega, 6 (1975), 275-87.

904. Dumont, Richard G., Dennis C. Foss. The American View of Death: Acceptance or Denial?. Cambridge: Schenkman, 1972.

905. Dunne, John S. The City of the Gods: A Study in Myth and Mortality. New York: MacMillan, 1973.

906. _____. Time and Myth. Notre Dame: University of Notre Dame Press, 1975.

907. Durkheim, Emile. The Elementary Forms of Religious Life. Translated by J.W. Swaine. London: Allen and Unwin, 1954.

908. Durlak, Joseph A. "Measurement of the Fear of Death: An Examination of Some Existing Scales," Journal of Clinical Psychology, 28 (Oct., 1972), 545-7.

909. Durlak, Joseph A. "Relationship Between Various Measures of Death Concern and Fear of Death," Journal of Consulting and Clinical Psychology, 41 (Aug., 1973), 162.

910. Dusinberre, R.K. et al. "Statutory Definition of Death," New England Journal of Medicine, 286 (Mar., 1972), 549-50.

911. Earle, A.M., B.V. Earle. "Early Maternal Deprivation and Later Psychiatric Illness," American Journal of Orthopsychiatry, 31 (1961), 181-6.

912. Easson, William M. "Care of the Young Patient Who Is Dying," Journal of the American Medical Association, 205 (July 22, 1968), 203-7.

913. _____. Dying Child: The Management of the Child or Adolescent Who Is Dying. Springfield: C.C. Thomas, 1970.

914. _____. "The Family of the Dying Child," Pediatric Clinics of North America, 19 (Nov., 1972), 1157-65.

915. _____. "Management of the Dying Child," Journal of Clinical Child Psychiatry, 3 (Summer, 1974), 25-7.

916. Eaton, Joseph W. "The Art of Aging and Dying," The Gerontologist, 4 (June, 1964), 94-100.

917. Ebert, Max. "Die Anfange europaischen Totenkultus," Praehistorische Zeitschrift, 13-14 (1921-2), 1-19.

918. Echeverria, Jose. Reflexions Metaphysiques sur la Mort et la Probleme du Sujet. Paris: J. Urin, 1957.

919. Eckardt, A. Roy. "Death in the Judaic and Christian Traditions," Social Research, 39 (Autumn, 1972), 489-514.

920. Edelson, Stuart R., Porter H. Warren. "Catatonic Schizophrenia as a Mourning Process," Diseases of the Nervous System, 24 (1963), 2-8.

921. Edelston, H. "Separation Anxiety in Young Children," Genetic Psychology, 28 (June, 1942), 3-95.

922. Edgell, P.G. "Depression the Commonest Disease," Canadian Medical Association Journal, 106 (Jan., 1972), 1759.

923. Edwards, H.A. et al. "Apparent Death with Accidental Hypothermia: A Case Report," British Journal of Anaesthesia, 42 (Oct., 1970), 906-8.

924. Edwards, P. "Heidegger and Death as Possibility," Mind, 84 (1975), 548-66.

925. Egger, Victor, "Le Moi des Mourants," Revue Philosophique, 41 (1896), 26-38.

926. _____. "Le Moi des Mourants, Mouveaux Faits," Revue Philosophiques, 42 (1896), 337-68.

927. Egelson, Jim, Janet Egelson. Parents Without Partners. New York: E.P. Dutton and Co., 1961.

928. Ehrenberg, Rudolf. "Der Ablauffzum Tode (The Running Down Toward Death)," Studium Generale, 4 (Dec., 1951), 559-66.

929. Ehrenwald, J. "Out-of-the Body Experiences and the Denial of Death," Journal of Nervous and Mental Diseases, 159 (Oct., 1974), 227-33.

930. Eigen, M. "Fear of Death: A Symptom with Changing Meanings," Journal of Humanistic Psychology, 14 (Summer, 1974), 29-33.

931. Eisenberg, John A., Paula Bourne. The Right to Live and Die. Toronto: Institute for Studies in Education, 1973.

932. Eisenberg, P.B. "Rest in Peace, Ruthless Roger," American Journal of Nursing, 70 (Jan., 1970), 132.

933. Eisendrath, R. "The Role of Grief and Fear in the Death of Kidney Transplant Patients," American Journal of Psychiatry, 126 (1969), 381-7.

934. Eisman, R. "Why Did Joc Die?" American Journal of Nursing, 71 (Mar., 1971), 501-3.

935. Eissler, Kurt R. "Death Drive, Ambivalence, and Narcissism," Psychoanalytic Study of the Child, 26 (1971), 25-78.

936. _____. The Psychiatrist and the Dying Patient. New York: International University Press, 1970.

937. Eitinger, L. "A Follow-Up Study of the Norwegian Concentration Camp Survivors' Mortality and Morbidity," Israel Annals of Psychiatry, 11 (Sep., 1973), 199-209.

938. Ekblom, B. "On Mortality in Recent Widows and Widowers," Svenska Lakartidningen, 61 (1964), 3343-50.

939. _____. "The Significance of Social Psychological Factors for the Death Risk, Especially in Aged Persons," Nordisk Psychiatrisk Tidsskrift, 18 (1964), 272-81.

940. Elder, Ruth G. "What is the Patient Saying?" Nursing Forum, 2 (1963), 24-37.

941. Elfert, H. "The Nurse and the Grieving Parent," Canadian Nurse, 71 (Feb., 1975), 30-1.

942. Eliade, Mircea. Death, Afterlife and Eschatology. New York: Harper and Row, 1974.

944. Eliot, Thomas D. "The Adjustive Behavior of Bereaved Families: A New Field for Research," Social Forces, 8 (1930), 543-9.

945. _____. "Attitudes Toward Euthanasia," Research Studies of the State College of Washington, 15 (1947), 131-4.

946. Eliot, Thomas D. "The Bereaved Family," Annals of the American Academy of Political and Social Sciences, 160 (1932), 184-90.

947. _____. "Bereavement as a Field of Social Research," Bulletin of the Society for Social Research, 17 (1938), 4.

948. _____. "Bereavement as a Problem for Family Research and Technique," The Family, 11 (1930), 114-5.

949. _____. "Bereavement: Inevitable but Not Insurmountable," in H. Becker and R. Hill, eds., Family, Marriage and Parenthood. Boston: Heath, 1955.

950. _____. ". . . . Of the Shadow of Death," Annals of the American Academy of Political and Social Sciences, 229 (Sep., 1943), 87-99.

951. _____. "A Step Toward the Social Psychology of Bereavement," Journal of Abnormal and Social Psychology, 27 (1933), 380-90.

952. _____. "War Bereavements and Their Recovery," Marriage and Family Living, 8 (Winter, 1946), 1-5.

953. Elkinton, J. Russell. "The Experimental Use of Human Beings," Annals of Internal Medicine, 65 (Aug., 1966), 371-3.

954. _____. "Life and Death and the Physician," Annals of Internal Medicine, 67 (Sep., 1967), 669.

955. _____. "Moral Problems in the Use of Borrowed Organs, Artificial and Transplanted," Annals of Internal Medicine, 60 (Feb., 1964), 309-13.

956. _____. "Scared to Death," Annals of Internal Medicine, 74 (May, 1971), 789-90.

957. _____. "When Do We Let the Patient Die?" Annals of Internal Medicine, 68 (Mar., 1968), 695-700.

958. Ellard, John. "Emotional Reactions Associated with Death," Medical Journal of Australia, 1 (June 8, 1968), 979-83.

959. _____. Normal and Pathological Responses to Bereavement. New York: MSS Information, 1974.

960. Elliot, G. Twentieth Century Book of the Dead. New York: Scribner, 1972.

961. Ellitt, Neil. The Gods of Life. New York: MacMillan, 1974.

962. Ellis, R.S. "The Attitude Toward Death and the Types of Belief in Immortality," Journal of Religious Psychology, 7 (1915), 466-510.

963. Ellison, David L. "Alienation and the Will to Live of Retired Steel Workers," Proceedings of the 7th International Congress on Gerontology, (1966), 167-70.

964. Elspeth, Wallace, Brenda D. Townes. "The Dual Role of Comforter and Bereaved," Mental Hygiene, 53 (1969), 327-32.

965. Emde, Robert et al. "Anaclitic Depression in an Infant Raised in an Institution," Journal of the American Academy of Child Psychiatry, 4 (1965), 545-53.

966. Emery, J.L. "Classifying and Recording Unexpected Deaths of Infants," Journal of Clinical Pathology, 26 (May, 1973), 386.

967. _____. "Unexpected Deaths in Infants," Nursing Times, 69 (Apr. 12, 1973), 474-5.

968. _____. "Welfare of Families of Children Found Unexpectedly Dead," British Medical Journal, 1 (Mar. 5, 1972), 612-5.

969. _____, J.A. Wetherall. "Certification of Cot Deaths," British Medical Journal, 4 (Dec. 16, 1972), 669.

970. _____, et al. "Hypernatraemia and Uraemia in Unexpected Death in Infancy," Archives of Diseases in Childhood, 49 (Sep., 1974), 686-92.

971. Engel, George L. "The Death of a Twin: Mourning and Anniversary Reactions. Fragments of 10 Years of Self-Analysis," International Journal of Psychoanalysis, 56 (1975), 23-40.

972. _____. "Grief and Grieving," American Journal of Nursing, 64 (Sep., 1964), 93-8.

973. _____. "Is Grief a Disease?" Psychosomatic Medicine, 23 (1961), 18-22.

974. _____. "Sudden and Rapid Death During Psychological Stress: Folklore or Folk Wisdom?" Annals of Internal Medicine, 74 (May, 1971), 771-82.

975. _____. "Sudden Death and the 'Medical Model' in Psychiatry," Canadian Psychiatric Association Journal, 15 (Dec., 1970), 527-38.

976. Engelhardt, H. "Defining Death: Philosophical Problem for Medicine and Law," American Journal of Respiratory Diseases, 112 (1975), 587-90.

977. _____. "Euthanasia and Children: The Injury of Continued Existence," Journal of Pediatrics, 83 (1973), 170-4.

978. _____. "Medicine and the Naturalness of Death: The Counsels of Finitude," Hastings Center Report, 5 (Apr., 1975), 29-36.

979. Englander, O. "Cot Deaths," British Medical Journal, 4 (Dec., 1971), 625-6.

980. Epstein, Charlotte. Nursing the Dying Patient. Reston, VA: Reston Publishing, 1975.

981. Erikson, Erik H. "Identity and the Life Cycle," Psychological Issues, 1 (1959), 1-71.

982. Erickson, Florence. "Stress in the Pediatric Ward," Maternal Child Nursing
       Journal, 1 (Summer, 1972), 113-6.

983. Ermalinski, R. "Questionnaire Responses Regarding Risk-Taking Behavior with
       Death at Stake," Psychological Reports, 31 (Oct., 1972), 435-8.

984. Eron, L. "The Effect of Medical Education on Attitudes: A Follow-Up Study,"
       Journal of Medical Education, 33 (Oct., 1958), 25-33.

985. Eshelman, Byron. Death Row Chaplain. Englewood Cliffs: Prentice Hall, 1962.

986. Ettinger, R.C.W. The Prospect of Immortality. New York: McFadden-Bartell,
       1966.

987. Euler, L. "A General Investigation into the Mortality and Multiplication of
       the Human Species," Theoretical Population Biology, 1 (Nov., 1970),
       307-14.

988. Euthanasia Education Fund, Inc. The Right to Die with Dignity: A Discussion
       of the Medical, Legal, Social and Ethical Aspects of Euthanasia. First
       Euthanasia Conference of the Educational Fund, November 21, 1968.
       New York: Euthanasia Education Fund, 1969.

989. Evans, Audrey E. "If a Child Must Die," New England Journal of Medicine,
       278 (Jan., 1968), 138-42.

990. Evans, Jocelyn. Living with a Man Who Is Dying. New York: Taplinger, 1971.

991. Evans, P.D. "Projected Bereavement and Prognosis in Desensitization," British
       Society of Clinical Psychology, 13 (Feb., 1974), 99-101.

992. Evans, P.R. "The Management of Fatal Illness in Childhood," Proceedings
       of the Royal Society of Medicine, 62 (June, 1969), 549-50.

993. Evans-Pritchard, Edward E. Theories of Primitive Religion. Oxford: Claren-
       don Press, 1965.

994. _____. Witchcraft, Oracles and Magic Among the Azande. New York:
       Oxford University Press, 1937.

995. Evans-Wentz, W.Y., ed. The Tibetan Book of the Dead. New York: Oxford
       University Press, 1960.

996. Evelson, E., R. Granberg. "The Child's Concept of Death," (in Spanish)
       Revista de Psicoanalisis, 19 (1962), 344-50.

997. Everson, R.B., J.F. Fraumeni, Jr. "Mortality Among Medical Students and Young
       Physicians," Journal of Medical Education, 50 (Aug., 1975), 809-11.

998. Exton-Smith, A.N. "Terminal Illness in the Aged," Lancet, 2 (Aug. 5, 1961),
       305-8.

999. Fabian, Johannes. "How Others Die--Reflections on the Anthropology of Death," Social Research, 39 (Autumn, 1972), 543-67.

1000. Facer, W.A.P. et al "Abortion in New Zealand," Journal of Biosocial Science, 5 (Apr., 1973), 151-8.

1001. Faculty of Mathematics, University of Waterloo. Tabulations of Canadian Mortality Data. Waterloo, Ontario: University of Waterloo, 1973.

1002. Fae, F., J. McCall. "Some International Comparisons of Cancer Mortality Rates and Personality--A Brief Note," Journal of Psychology, 85 (Sep., 1973), 87-8.

1003. Fagge, C. Hilton. "On the Different Modes of Dying," Guy's Hospital Reports, 24 (1879), 343-54.

1004. Faigel, H.C. "Ondine's Curse and Sudden Infant Death Syndrome: Teetering on the Brink," Clinical Pediatrics, 13 (July, 1974), 567-8.

1005. Fairbairn, W.R.D. "The Effect of the King's Death Upon Patients Under Analysis," International Journal of Psychoanalysis, 17 (1936), 278-84.

1006. _____. "The War Neuroses--Their Nature and Significance," in Object Relations Theory of the Personality. New York: Basic Books, 1954.

1007. Fairbanks, Rollin J. "Ministering to the Dying," Journal of Pastoral Care, 2 (1948), 6-14.

1008. Farberow, Norman L., ed. Taboo Topics. New York: Atherton Press, 1963.

1009. Fargues, Marie. The Child and the Mystery of Death. Translated by Sister Gertrude. Glen Rock, NJ: Paulist Press, 1966.

1010. Farley, Gail A. "An Investigation of Death Anxiety and the Sense of Competence," Dissertation Abstracts International, 31 (June, 1971), 7595-B.

1011. Farmer, James A., Jr. "Death Education: Adult Education in the Face of a Taboo," Omega, 1 (May, 1970), 109-14.

1012. Farrell, John H. "The Right of a Patient to Die," Journal of the South Carolina Medical Association, 54 (July, 1958), 231-3.

1013. Fast, Irene. "Some Relationships of Infantile Self-Boundary Development to Depression," International Journal of Psychoanalysis, 48 (1967), 259-66.

1014. _____, Albert Cain. "Fears of Death in Bereaved Children and Adults," American Journal of Orthopsychiatry, 34 (1964), 278-9.

1015. _____. "The Stepparent Role: Potential for Disturbances in Family Functioning," American Journal of Orthopsychiatry, 36 (Apr., 1966), 485-91.

1016. Fast, Irene et al. "The Sense of Being Dead and of Dying: Some Perspectives," Journal of Projective Techniques and Personality, 34 (June, 1970), 190-3.

1017. Fatteh, A. "A Lawsuit that Led to a Redefinition of Death," Journal of Legal Medicine, 1 (July-Aug., 1974), 30-4.

1018. Faulkner, William. As I Lay Dying. New York: Random, 1975.

1019. Fauman, S. Joseph, Albert J. Mayer. "Estimation of Jewish Population by the Death Rate Method," Jewish Social Studies, 17 (1955), 315-22.

1020. Faunce, William A., Robert Fulton. "The Sociology of Death: A Neglected Area of Research," Social Forces, 36 (Mar., 1958), 205-9.

1021. Faux, E.J., B. Crawford. "Deaths in a Youth Program," Mental Hygiene, 54 (Oct., 1970), 569-71.

1022. Favarger, C. et al. L'Homme Face a la Mort. Neuchatel: Delachaux and Niestle, 1962.

1023. Fedders, D.L. "Mourning Precipitates Porphyria," Medical Annals of the District of Columbia, 41 (Aug., 1972), 508-9.

1024. Feder, S.L. "Death and Dying: Attitudes of Patient and Doctor, 3: Attitudes of Patients with Advanced Malignancy," Group for the Advancement of Psychiatry, (Symposium #11), 5 (Oct., 1965), 614-22.

1025. Federn, Paul. "The Reality of the Death Instinct, Especially in Melancholia," Psychoanalytic Review, 19 (1932), 129-51.

1026. Fedrick, Jean. "Sudden Unexpected Death in Infants in the Oxford Record Lindage Area," British Journal of Preventive and Social Medicine, 28 (Aug., 1974), 164-71.

1027. Feifel, Herman. "Attitudes of Mentally Ill Patients Toward Death," Journal of Nervous and Mental Disease, 122 (Oct., 1955), 375-80.

1028. _____. "Attitudes Toward Death: A Psychological Perspective," Journal of Consulting and Clinical Psychology, 13 (1969), 292-5.

1029. _____. "Death," in A. Deutsch, ed. The Encyclopedia of Mental Health. New York: Franklin Watts, 1963. Vol. 2.

1030. _____. "Death and Dying: Attitudes of Patient and Doctor, 5: The Function of Attitudes Toward Death," Group for the Advancement of Psychiatry, (Symposium #11), 5 (Oct., 1965), 633-41.

1031. _____. "Death-Relevant Variable in Psychology," in R. May, ed. Existential Psychology. New York: Random House, 1961.

1032. Feifel, Herman. "Discussion of a Symposium on Attitudes Toward Death in Older Persons," Journal of Gerontology, 16 (1961), 44-66.

1033. _____. "The Function of Attitudes Toward Death," in Death and Dying Attitudes of Patient and Doctor. Symposium. New York: Group for the Advancement of Psychiatry, Oct., 1965. 632-41.

1034. _____. "The Meaning of Dying in American Society," Journal of Pastoral Counseling, 9 (Fall-Winter, 1974-5), 53-9.

1035. _____. "Older Persons Look at Death," Geriatrics, 11 (Mar, 1956), 127-30.

1036. _____. "Perception of Death," Annals of the New York Academy of Sciences, 164 (1969), 669-77.

1037. _____. "The Problem of Death," Catholic Psychological Record, 3 (1965), 18-22.

1038. _____. "Psychiatric Patients Look at Old Age: Level of Adjustment and Attitudes Toward Aging," American Journal of Psychiatry, 111 (1954), 459-65.

1039. _____. "Psychology and the Death-Awareness Movement," Journal of Clinical Child Psychology, 3 (Summer, 1974), 6-7.

1040. _____. "Relation of Religious Conviction to Fear of Death in Healthy and Terminally Ill Populations," Journal for the Scientific Study of Religion, 13 (1974), 353-60.

1041. _____. "Scientific Research in Taboo Areas--Death," American Behavioral Scientist, 5 (1962), 28-30.

1042. _____. "The Taboo on Death," The American Behavioral Scientist, 6 (May, 1963), 66-7.

1043. _____, A.B. Branscomb. "Who's Afraid of Death?" Journal of Abnormal Psychology, 81 (June, 1973), 282-8.

1044. _____, Joseph Heller. "Normality, Illness, and Death," Proceedings of the Third World Congress of Psychiatry, 2 (1962), 1252-6.

1045. _____, L.J. Hermann. "Fear of Death in the Mentally Ill," Psychological Reports, 33 (Dec., 1973), 931-8.

1046. _____, R. Jones. "Perception of Death as Related to Nearness to Death," Proceedings of the 76th Annual Convention of the American Psychological Association, 3 (1968), 545-6.

1047. _____, et al. "Death Fear in Dying Heart and Cancer Patients," Journal of Psychosomatic Research, 17 (July, 1973), 161-6.

1048. Feifel, Herman et al. "Physicians Consider Death," Proceedings of the 75th Annual Convention of the American Psychological Association, 3 (1968), 545-6.

1049. _____, ed. The Meaning of Death. New York: McGraw Hill, 1959.

1050. _____, ed. New Meanings of Death. New York: McGraw Hill, 1977.

1051. Feigel, Friedrich K. Das Problem des Todes. Munchen: Reinhardt, 1953.

1052. _____. Tod und Unsterblichkeit im Geistesleben der Menscheit. Gorlitz: Hutten Verlag, 1926.

1053. Feigenberg, Loma. "Care and Understanding of the Dying: A Patient-Centered Approach," Omega, 6 (1975), 81-94.

1054. Feinberg, D. "Preventive Therapy with Siblings of a Dying Child," Journal of the American Academy of Child Psychiatry, 9 (Oct., 1970), 421-5.

1055. Feldman, Marvin J. Fears Related to Death and Suicide. New York: MSS Information, 1974.

1056. _____, Michel Hersia. "Attitudes Toward Death in Nightmare Subjects," Journal of Abnormal Psychology, 72 (Oct., 1967), 421-5

1057. Felner, Robert D. et al. "Crisis Events and School Mental Health Referral Patterns of Young Children," Journal of Consulting and Clinical Psychology, 43 (June, 1975), 305-10.

1058. Fellner, Carl H. "Selections of Living Kidney Donors and the Problem of Informed Consent," Seminars in Psychiatry, 3 (Feb., 1971), 79-85.

1059. _____, J.R. Marshall. "Kidney Donors: The Myth of Informed Consent," American Journal of Psychiatry, 126 (1970), 1245-51.

1060. _____. "Twelve Kidney Donors," Journal of the American Medical Association, 26 (1968), 2703-6.

1061. Fenichel, Otto, "A Critique of the Death Instinct," in The Collected Papers of Otto Fenichel. New York: W.W. Norton and Co., 1953.

1062. Fere, Charles. "L'Etat Mental des Mourants," Revue Philosophique, 45 (1898), 296-302.

1063. Ferenczi, Sandor. The Problem of Acceptance of Unpleasant Ideas: Further Contributions to Theory and Technique of Psychoanalysis. London: Hogarth Press, 1927.

1064. _____. "The Psychological Analysis of Dreams," American Journal of Psychology, 21 (1910), 309-28.

1065. Ferenczi, Sandor. "The Unwelcome Child and His Death-Instinct," _International Journal of Psychoanalysis_, 10 (1929), 125-29.

1066. Fermaglich, J.L. "Determining Cerebral Death," _American Family Physician_, 3 (Mar., 1971), 85-7.

1067. Ferrari, G.C. "La Peur de la Mort," _Revue Scientifique_, 5, Series 4 (1896), 59-60.

1068. Ferrater, Mora Jose. _Being and Death_. Berkeley: University of California Press, 1965.

1069. Ferrero, M. Guillaume. "La Crainte de la Mort," _Revue Scientifique_, 3, Series 4 (Mar. 23, 1895), 361-7.

1070. Ferri, Elsa. "Characteristics of Motherless Families," _British Journal of Social Work_, 3 (Spring, 1973), 91-100.

1071. Ferriar, J. "Of the Treatment of the Dying," in _Medical Histories and Reflections_. Philadelphia: Thomas Dobson, 1816.

1072. Ferris, J.A. "The Cot Death Syndrome," _Journal of the Forensic Science Society_, 12 (Oct., 1972), 575-9.

1073. _____. "The Heart in Sudden Infant Death," _Journal of the Forensic Science Society_, 12 (Oct., 1972), 591-4.

1074. _____. "Hypoxic Changes in Conducting Tissue of the Heart in Sudden Death in Infancy Syndrome," _British Medical Journal_, 2 (Apr. 7, 1973), 23-5.

1075. _____, et al. "Sudden and Unexpected Deaths in Infants: Histology and Virology," _British Medical Journal_, 2 (May 26, 1973), 439-42.

1076. Feuerbach, L. _Tod und Unsterblichkeit_. Stuttgart: Werke, 1903. V. 1.

1077. Ficarra, B.J. "Legal Rights of Sepulcher," _Legal Medicine Annual_, (1974), 137-46.

1078. Fiedler, Leslie A. _Love and Death in the American Novel_. Revised ed. New York: Dell, 1966.

1079. Field, Minna. _Patients are People_. 2d ed. New York: Columbia University Press, 1958.

1080. Filby, E.E. "Some Overtones of Euthanasia," _Hospital Topics_, 43 (Sep, 1965), 55-61.

1081. Fine, M. Ruth. "Psychological Considerations of the Child with a Progressive Terminal Condition in a Residential Setting," _New Outlook for the Blind_, 69 (Mar, 1975), 121-30.

1082. Finesinger, Jacob et al. "Managing the Emotional Problems of the Cancer Patient," CA Bulletin of Cancer Progress, 3 (Jan., 1953), 19-31.

1083. Fischer, Bradley. "Self-Exploration Experiences in Death Encounter," Dissertation Abstracts, 30A2 (1969), 1819.

1084. Fischer, H.K., B.M. Dlin. "Man's Determination of His Time of Illness or Death: Anniversary Reactions and Emotional Deadlines," Geriatrics, 26 (July, 1971), 89-94.

1085. Fishbein, M. "Signs of Death," Medical World News, 12 (Dec. 10, 1971), 80.

1086. _____. "Some International Aspects of Abortion," Medical World News, 12 (Sep. 17, 1971), 68.

1087. Fisher, Gary. "Death, Identity and Creativity," Omega, 2 (Nov., 1971), 303-6.

1088. _____. "Psychotherapy for the Dying: Principles and Illustrative Cases with Special References to the Use of LSD," Omega, 1 (Feb., 1970), 3-15.

1089. Fisher, Jean Ruth. "The Nursing Care of Terminally Ill Patients," Nursing Research, 15 (Winter, 1966), 91-2.

1090. Fitts, William T. "What Philadelphia Physicians Tell Patients with Cancer," Journal of the American Medical Association, 153 (Nov. 7, 1953), 901-4.

1091. Fitzgerald, R.G. "Broken Heart: A Statistical Study of Increased Mortality among Widowers," British Journal of Medicine, 1 (1969), 740.

1092. Fitzgibbons, J.P., Jr. et al. "Sudden Unexpected and Unexplained Death in Infants," Pediatrics, 43 (1969), 980-8.

1093. Flammarion, Camille. Death and Its Mystery Before Death. New York: The Century Co., 1922.

1094. Flannery, R.B., Jr. Behavior Modification of Geriatric Grief: A Transactional Perspective," International Journal of Aging and Human Development, 5 (Spring, 1974), 197-203.

1095. Flatmark, A., H. Bondevik. "The Brain Death Kidney Donor," Scandanvian Journal of Urology and Nephrology, 8 (1974), 235-9.

1096. Fleicher, Peter. Life Without Fear. New York: E.P. Dutton, 1939.

1097. Fleming, Joan, Sol Altschul. "Activation of Mourning and Growth by Psychoanalysis," International Journal of Psychoanalysis, 44 (1963), 419-31.

1098. Fleming, T. et al., eds. Communications and Thanatology. New York: Health Sciences Publishing Corp., 1974.

1099. Flesch, Regina. "A Guide to Interviewing the Bereaved," Journal of Thanatology, 3 (1975), 93-103.

1100. Fletcher, George. "Legal Aspects of the Decision Not to Prolong Life," Journal of the American Medical Association, 203 (Jan. 1, 1968), 65-8.

1101. Fletcher, Joseph. "Abortion, Euthanasia, and Care of Defective Newborns," New England Journal of Medicine, 292 (Jan. 9, 1975), 75-8.

1102. _____. "Ethics and Euthanasia," American Journal of Nursing, 73 (Apr., 1973), 670-5.

1103. _____. "Human Experimentation Ethics in the Consent Situation," Law and Contemporary Problems, 32 (1967), 620-49.

1104. _____. "Indicators of Humanhood: A Tentative Profile of Man," The Hastings Center Report, 2 (1972), 1-4.

1105. _____. Morals and Medicine. Princeton: Princeton University Press, 1954.

1106. _____. "Our Shameful Waste of Human Tissue: An Ethical Problem for the Living and the Dead," in Donald R. Cutler, ed., The Religious Situation 1969. Boston: Beacon Press, 1969.

1107. _____. "Voluntary Euthanasia: The New Shape of Death," Medical Counterpoint, (June, 1970), 13-32.

1108. _____, et al. "When Should Patients Be Allowed to Die? Some Questions of Ethics," Postgraduate Medicine, 43 (Apr., 1968), 197-200.

1109. Flew, Antony, ed. Body, Mind and Death. New York: MacMillan, 1964.

1110. Fliess, Wilhelm. Vom Leben und Tod. Jena: Diederichs, 1919.

1111. Flinchum, G.A. "Death Registration Practices and Problems," North Carolina Medical Journal, 29 (Apr., 1968), 176-7.

1112. Flugel, J.C. "Death Instinct, Homeostasis and Allied Concepts," International Journal of Psychoanalysis, (Supplement), 34 (1953), 43-74.

1113. _____. The Psychoanalytic Study of the Family. London: The Hogarth Press, 1935.

1114. Flumiani, C.M. The Philosophy of Life and the Philosophy of Death. Albuquerque: American Classical College Press, 1974.

1115. Fochtman, Dianne. "A Comparative Study of Pediatric Nurses' Attitudes Toward Death," Life-Threatening Behavior, 4 (Summer, 1974), 107-17.

1116. Fodor, N. "Jung's Sermons to the Dead," Psychoanalytic Review, 51 (1964), 74-8.

1117. Fogelman, William J. "Physicians, Clergymen and the Privileged Communication," Journal of the American Medical Association, 200 (May 8, 1967), 235.

1118. Folck, Marilyn Melcher, Phyllis J. Nie. "Nursing Students Learn to Face Death," Nursing Outlook, 7 (Sep., 1959), 510-13.

1119. Follett, E. "No Time for Fear," Canadian Nursing Journal, 66 (Jan, 1970), 39-40.

1120. Folta, Jeannette F. "The Perception of Death," Nursing Research, 14 (Summer, 1965), 232-5.

1121. _____, Edith Deck. "Social Reconstruction after Death," Tribuna Medica, (Madrid), 10 (Oct. 26, 1972), np.

1122. _____, eds. A Sociological Framework for Patient Care. New York: John Wiley, 1966.

1123. Fond, K.I. "Dealing with Death and Dying through Family-Centered Care," Nursing Clinics of North America, 7 (Mar., 1972), 53-64.

1124. Fontana, Luigi. "Ai Confini tra la Vita e la Morte (Boundaries Between Life and Death)," Minerva Medica, 1 (Mar. 31, 1955), 867-78.

1125. Fontendt, Christine. "The Subject Nobody Teaches," English Journal, 63 (Feb., 1974), 62-3.

1126. Forbes, J.D. Death Warmed Over. Elizabeth, NJ: Pageant-Poseidon, 1975.

1127. Forbes, Thomas R. "Life and Death in Shakespeare's London," American Scientist, 58 (1970), 511-20.

1128. Ford, R.M. "Cot Death Survey: Anaphylaxis and the House Dust Mite," Medical Journal of Australia, 1 (Mar. 31, 1973), 664.

1129. Ford, Robert E. et al. "Fear of Death of Those in a High Stress Occupation," Psychological Reports, 29 (Oct., 1971), 502.

1130. Fordham, Michael. New Developments in Analytical Psychology. London: Routledge and Kegan Paul, 1957.

1131. Forest, Jack D. "The Major Emphasis of the Funeral," Pastoral Psychology, 14 (1963), 19-24.

1132. Forker, Thomas S. "Counseling and the Hospital Chaplain," Guild of Catholic Psychiatrists Bulletin, 11 (1964), 90-101.

1133. Formanek, Ruth. "When Children Ask about Death," Elementary School Journal, 75 (Nov., 1974), 92-7.

1134. Forres, Hildegard. "Emotional Dangers to Children in Hospitals," Mental Health, 2 (1953), 58-62.

1135. Fortier, Millie K. "Dreams and Preparation for Death," Dissetation Abstracts International, 33 (Jan., 1973), 3300-1.

1136. Foss, Martin. Death, Sacrifice and Tragedy. Lincoln: University of Nebraska Press, 1966.

1137. Foster, L.E. et al. "Grief," Pastoral Psychology, 1 (1950), 28-30.

1138. Foster, Zelda P. "How Social Work Can Influence Hospital Management of Fatal Illness," Social Work, 10 (Oct., 1965), 30-5.

1139. Fox, N.L. "A Good Birth, A Good Life, Why Not a Good Death?" Journal of Practical Nursing, 24 (Oct., 1974), 19-20.

1140. Fox, Jean E. "Reflections on Cancer Nursing," American Journal of Nursing, 66 (June, 1966), 1317-9.

1141. Fox, Renee. Experiment Perilous. Glencoe, IL: Free Press, 1959.

1142. _____. "A Sociological Perspective on Organ Transplantation and Hemodialysis," Annals of the New York Academy of Sciences, 169 (Jan. 21, 1970), 406-28.

1143. _____, Judith P. Swazey. The Courage to Fail: A Social View of Organ Transplants and Dialysis. Chicago: University of Chicago Press, 1974.

1144. Fox, S. "The Death of a Child," Nursing Times, 68 (Oct. 19, 1972), 1322-3.

1145. Foxe, Arthur N. "Critique of Freud's Concept of a Death Instinct," Psycho-analytic Review, 30 (1943), 417-27.

1146. _____. "The Life and Death Instincts: Criminological Implications," Journal of Criminal Psychopathology, 4 (1942), 67-91.

1147. Foy, H.M., C.G. Ray. "Epidemiology of Sudden Infant Death Syndrome and Lower Respiratory Tract Disease in Young Children: A Comparison," American Journal of Epidemiology, 89 (Aug., 1973), 69-71.

1148. Fraenkel, Michael. Death is Not Enough: Essays in Active Negation. London: C.W. Daniel, 1939.

1149. Frais, J.A. "Cot Deaths and Hypokalemia," British Medical Journal, 3 (Sep. 9, 1972), 646.

1150. Fraisse, Paul. The Psychology of Time. New York: Harper and Row, 1963.

1151. Francaviglia, Richard V. "The Cemetery as an Evolving Cultural Landscape," Annals of the Association of American Geographers, 61 (Sep., 1971), 501-9

1152. Frankl, Viktor Emil. The Doctor and the Soul. New York: Knopf, 1955.

1153. _____. "Existential Escapism," Omega, 2 (Nov., 1971), 307-12.

1154. _____. From Death Camp to Existentialism. Boston: Beacon Press, 1959.

1155. _____. "Psychiatry and Man's Quest for Meaning," Journal of Religion and Health, 1 (1962), 93-103.

1156. Fransisco, J.T. "Smothering in Infancy: Its Relationship to the Crib Death Syndrome," Southern Medical Journal, 63 (Oct., 1970), 1110-4.

1157. Frazee, H. "Children Who Later Become Schizophrenic," Smith College Studies in Social Work, 23 (1953), 125-49.

1158. Frazer, James G. Belief in Immortality and the Worship of the Dead. London: Macmillan, 1913.

1159. _____. The Fear of the Dead in Primitive Religion. London: Macmillan, 1933. 3 Volumes.

1160. Fredlund, Delphie. "A Nurse Looks at Children's Questions about Death," ANA Clinical Sessions, (1970), 105-12.

1161. Fredrick, Jerome F. "Physiological Reactions Induced by Grief," Omega, 2 (May, 1971), 71-5.

1162. Freedman, A.R. "Interview the Parents of a Dead Child? Absolutely," Clinical Pediatrics, 8 (Oct., 1969), 564-5.

1163. Freedman, Ronald et al. "Social Correlates of Fetal Mortality," Milbank Memorial Fund Quarterly, 44 (July, 1966), 327-44.

1164. Freeman, Elaine. "The 'God Committee'," The New York Times Magazine, (May 21, 1972), 84-90.

1165. Freeman, J.M. "Whose Suffering?" Journal of Pediatrics, 80 (May, 1972), 904-5.

1166. French, Douglas. "The Care of Cancer in Practice," Practitioner, 177 (July, 1956), 78-86.

1167. French, J., D.R. Schwartz. "Terminal Care at Home in Two Cultures," American Journal of Nursing, 73 (Mat., 1973), 502-5.

1168. Fretz, Bruce, Dan Leviton. "Life and Death Attitudes of Parents of Mildly Dysfunctional Children," Omega, 6 (1975), 161-70.

1169. Freud, Anna. "Discussion of 'Grief and Mourning in Infancy and Early Childhood' by Bowlby," The Psychoanalytic Study of the Child, 15 (1960), 53-94.

1170.   Freud, Anna. Normality and Pathology in Childhood. New York: International
        Universities Press, 1965.

1171.   Freud, Anna. "The Role of Bodily Illness in the Mental Life of Children,"
        Psychoanalytic Study of the Child, 7 (1952), 69-81.

1172.   _____, D.T. Burlingham. Infants Without Families. New York: International
        Universities Press, 1944.

1173.   _____. "The Shock of Separation," in War and Children. New York: Inter-
        national Universities Press, 1944.

1174.   _____, Sophie Dann. "An Experiment in Group Upbringing," Psychoanalytic
        Study of the Child, 6 (1951), 127-69.

1175.   Freud, Sigmund. "Beyond the Pleasure Principle," (1920), Standard Edition.
        London: Hogarth, 1955. V. 18.

1176.   _____. "Dostoevsky and Parricide," (1928), Collected Papers. New York:
        Basic Books, 1959. V. 5.

1177.   _____. "Dreams of the Death of Persons of Whom the Dreamer is Fond,"
        (1900), Standard Edition. London: Hogarth, 1953. V. 4.

1178.   _____. "Humour," International Journal of Psychoanalysis, 9 (1928), 1-6.

1179.   _____. "Inhibitions, Symptoms and Anxiety," (1926), Standard Edition.
        London: Hogarth, 1959. V. 4.

1180.   _____. "Mourning and Melancholia," (1917), Collected Papers. New York:
        Basic Books, 1959. V. 4.

1181.   _____. "Our Attitude Toward Death," (1915), Collected Papers. London:
        Hogarth, 1956. V. 4.

1182.   _____. Reflections on War and Death. New York: Moffat, Yard and Co.,
        1918.

1183.   _____. The Standard Edition of the Complete Psychological Works of Sigmund
        Freud. London: Hogarth, 1961.

1184.   _____. "The Theme of the Three Caskets," Collected Papers. New York:
        Basic Books, 1959. V. 4.

1185.   _____. "Thoughts for the Times on War and Death," (1915), Collected Papers.
        New York: Basic Books, 1959. V. 4.

1186.   _____. "The Uncanny," (1919), Collected Papers. New York: Basic Books,
        1959. V. 4.

1187.   Freund, J. "Meaning of Death and Collective Purpose," Archives of Social
        Science and Religion, 20 (1975), 31-44.

1188. Friedlander, Kate. "On the 'Longing to Die'," International Journal of Psychoanalysis.

1189. Friedman, D.B. "Death Anxiety and the Primal Scene," Psychoanalysis, 48 (Winter, 1961-2), 108-18.

1190. Frick, Marlena. All the Days of His Dying. London: Allison and Busby, 1972.

1191. Friedman, Henry J. "Physician Management of Dying Patients: An Exploration," Psychiatry in Medicine, 1 (Oct., 1970), 295-305.

1192. Friedman, Jacob H., David Zaris. "Paradoxical Response to Death of Spouse," Diseases of the Nervous System, 25 (Aug., 1964), 480-3.

1193. Friedman, Judith J. "Structural Constraints on Community Action: The Case of Infant Mortality Rites," Social Problems, 21 (Fall, 1973), 230-45.

1194. Friedman, Stanford B. "Behavioral Observations of Parents Anticipating the Death of a Child," Pediatrics, 32 (Oct., 1963), 610-25.

1195. _____. "Care of the Family of the Child with Cancer," Pediatrics, 40 (Sep., 1967), 498-507.

1196. _____. "Management of Death of a Parent or Sibling," in M. Green and R.J. Haggerty, eds., Ambulatory Pediatrics. Philadelphia: Saunders, 1968.

1197. _____. "Management of Fatal Illness in Children," in M. Green and R.J. Haggerty, eds., Ambulatory Pediatrics. Philadelphia: Saunders, 1968.

1198. _____. "Psychological Aspects of Sudden Unexpected Death in Infants and Children," Pediatric Clinical of North America, 21 (Feb., 1974), 103-11.

1199. _____, et al. Childhood Leukemia--A Pamphlet for Parents. Washington: U.S. Department of Health, Education and Welfare, Public Health Service, 1965.

1200. Friedsam, Hiram J. "The Coming Years: Social Science Perspectives on Aging and Death," Social Science Quarterly, 51 (June, 1970), 120-8.

1201. Friloux, C.A. "Death, When it Does Occur," Baylor Law Review, 27 (1975), 10-21.

1202. Fritz, Mary Appolline. "A Study of Widowhood," Sociology and Social Research, 14 (1930), 553-61.

1203. Froggatt, P., T.N. James. "Sudden Unexpected Death in Infants: Evidence on a Lethal Cardiac Arrhythmia," Ulster Medical Journal, 41 (1973), 136-52.

1204. _____, et al. "Epidemiology of Sudden Unexpected Death in Infants ('Cot Death') in Northern Ireland," British Journal of Preventive Social Medicine, 25 (1971), 119-34.

1205. Frogatt, P. et al. "Sudden Death in Babies: Epdemiology," American Journal
of Cardiology, 22 (Oct., 1968), 457-68.

1206. Frost, M. ". . . . Death," Nursing Mirror, 132 (Jan. 29, 1971), 41-2.

1207. Fuchs, W. "Theorie und Therapie des Sterbens (Theory and Therapy of Dying),"
Psychiatrish Neurologica e Wochenschrift, 39 (1937), 546-52.

1208. Fuller, John L. "Experiential Deprivation and Later Behavior," Science,
158 (1967), 1645-52.

1209. Fulton, Robert, ed. Death and Identity. 2d rev. ed. Bowie, MD: Robert J.
Brady, 1976.

1210. _____, et al. "The Cadaver Donor and the Gift of Life," in R. Simmons,
The Societal Impact of Transplantations. New York: Wiley, 1976.

1211. _____, Robert Bendiksen. "Death and the Child: An Anterospective Test of
the Childhood Bereavement and Later Behavior Disorder Hypothesis,"
Omega, 6 (July, 1975), 45-59.

1212. _____. "Coming to Terms with Death," Omega, 5 (1974), 1-4.

1213. _____. "Some Comments on the Recognition and Resolution of Grief," Proceedings of a National Invitational Conference, College of Human Development, Pennsylvania State University, University Park, Sep. 13-5, 1973, 16-36.

1214. _____. "Widow in America: Some Sociological Observations," Proceedings
from Widow to Widow Program, Laboratory of Community Psychiatry, Department of Psychiatry, Harvard Medical School, Boston, May 23, 1971.
The Director, 2 (Feb., 1973), 2-4.

1215. _____, et al. "The Prospective Organ Transplant Donor: Problems and
Prospects of Medical Innovation," Omega, 3 (Nov., 1972), 319-39.

1216. _____, et al. "Symposium on Death and Attitudes Toward Death," Geriatrics,
27 (Aug., 1972), 52-60.

1217. _____. "Death and Dying: Some Sociological Aspects of Terminal Care,"
Modern Medicine, 40 (May 29, 1972), 74-7.

1218. _____. A Compilation of Studies of Attitudes Toward Death, Funerals,
and Funeral Directors. Minneapolis: Center for Death Education and
Research, University of Minnesota, 1971.

1219. _____. "Contemporary Funeral Practices," in Howard C. Raether, ed.,
Successful Funeral Service Practice. New York: Prentice-Hall, 1971.

1220. _____, Julie Fulton. "A Psychosocial Aspect of Terminal Care: Anticipatory Grief," Omega, 2 (May, 1971), 91-100.

1221. Fulton, Robert, Eric Markusen. "Childhood Bereavement and Behavior Disorders: A Critical Review," Omega, (May, 1971), 107-17.

1222. _____. "Death, Grief and Social Recuperation," Omega, 1 (Feb., 1970), 23-8.

1223. _____, Gilbert Geis. "Social Change and Social Conflict: The Rabbi and the Funeral Director," Sociological Symposium, 1 (Fall, 1968), 1-9.

1224. _____. "On the Dying of Death," in Earl Grollman, ed., Explaining Death to Children. Boston, Beacon Press, 1967.

1225. _____, ed. Death and Identity. New York: Wiley, 1965.

1226. _____. "Death and the Self," Journal of Religion and Health, 3 (1964), 359-68.

1227. _____, Phyllis Langton. "Attitudes Toward Death: An Emerging Mental Health Problem," Nursing Forum, 3 (1964), 104-12.

1228. _____. The Sacred and the Secular: Attitudes of the American Public Toward Death. Milwaukee: Bulfin, 1963.

1229. _____, Gilbert Geis. "Death and Social Values," Indian Journal of Social Research, 3 (1962), 7-14.

1230. _____. "Attitudes Toward Death--A Discussion," Journal of Gerontology, 16 (1961), 63-5.

1231. _____. "The Clergyman and the Funeral Director: A Study in Role Conflict," Social Forces, 39 (May, 1961), 317-23.

1232. _____, William Faunce. "The Sociology of Death: A Neglected Area of Research," Social Forces, 36 (1958), 205-9.

1233. Furman, Erna. A Child's Parent Dies: Studies in Childhood Bereavement. New Haven: Yale University Press, 1974.

1234. Furman, Robert A. "Death and the Young Child: Some Preliminary Considerations," Psychoanalytic Study of the Child, 19 (1964), 321-33.

1235. _____. "Death of a Six-Year-Old's Mother During His Analysis," Psychoanalytic Study of the Child, 19 (1964), 377-97.

1236. Gabel, P. "Freud's Death Instance and Sartre's Fundamental Project," Psycho-analytic Review, 61 (Summer, 1974), 217-27.

1237. Gable, W.D. "Deaths: Usual and Unusual, Associated with Coal Mining Operations in Virginia," Medico-Legal Bulletin, 222 (Oct., 1971), 1-6.

1238. Gabriel, E.A. "Dignity of Dying," Journal of the American Osteopathic Association, 71 (Nov., 1972), 35-40.

1239. Gachs, J. et al. "A Contribution to the Study of Irreversible Coma and Cerebral Death: A Study of 71 Cases," Electroencephalography and Clinical Neurophysiology, 29 (Nov., 1970), 581.

1240. Gajdusek, R.E. "Death, Incest, and the Triple Bond in the Later Plays of Shakespeare," American Imago, 31 (Summer, 1974), 109-58.

1241. Galdston, Iago, "Eros and Thanatos: A Critique and Elaboration of Freud's Death Wish," American Journal of Psychoanalysis, 15 (1955), 123-34.

1242. _____. Medicine and Mankind. New York: D. Appleton-Century, 1936.

1243. Galen, Harlene. "A Matter of Life and Death," Young Children, 27 (Aug., 1972), 351-6.

1244. Gallwitzer, Helmut et al. Dying We Live. New York: Pantheon, 1956.

1245. Gardiner, Alan H. The Attitude of Ancient Egyptians to Death and the Dead. Cambridge: University Press, 1935.

1246. Gardner, L. Pearl. "Attitudes and Activities of the Middle-Aged and Aged," Geriatrics, 1 (Jan.-Feb., 1944), 33-50.

1247. Gardner, M.J. et al. "Patterns of Mortality in Middle and Early Old Age in the County Boroughs of England and Wales," British Journal of Preventive and Social Medicine, 23 (Aug., 1969), 133-40.

1248. Gardner, P.S. "Viruses and the Respiratory Tract in Sudden Infant Deaths," Journal of the Forensic Science Society, 12 (Oct., 1972), 587-9.

1249. Gardner, Richard A. "Guilt Reaction of Parents with a Child with Severe Physical Disease," American Journal of Psychiatry, 126 (1969), 636-44.

1250. Gardner, Russell et al. "The Physician, the Autopsy Request, and the Consent Rate," Journal of Medical Education, 48 (July, 1973), 636-44.

1251. Garfinkel, Harold. "Studies of the Routine Grounds of Everyday Activities," Social Problems, 11 (Winter, 1964), 225-50.

1252. Garma, Aagel. "Within the Realm of the Death Instinct," International Journal of Psychoanalysis, 52 (1971), 145-54.

1253. Garrity, Thomas F. "Psychic Death: Behavioral Types and Physiological Parallels," Omega, 4 (Fall, 1974), 207-15.

1254. Gartley, W., M. Bernasconi. "The Concept of Death in Children," Journal of Genetic Psychology, 110 (Mar., 1967), 71-85.

1255. Garzaaguerrero, A.C. "Culture Shock: Its Mourning and the Vicissitudes of Identity," Journal of the American Psychoanalytic Association, 22 (1974), 408-20.

1256. Gatch, Milton M. Death. New York: Seabury Press, 1969.

1257. Gauchard, P. La Mort. Paris: Presses Universitaires de France, 1951.

1258. Gauthier, Y. "The Mourning Reaction of a Ten-and-a Half-Year-Old Boy," Psychoanalytic Study of the Child, 20 (1965), 481-94.

1259. Gavey, C. The Management of the "Hopeless" Case. London: H.K. Lewis, 1952.

1260. Gay, M.J. et al. "The Late Effects of Loss of Parents in Childhood," British Journal of Psychiatry, 113 (July, 1967), 753-9.

1261. Gaynor, Mildred. "On Facing Death," Nursing Outlook, 7 (Sep., 1959), 509.

1262. _____. "What Man Shall Live and Not See Death?" Nursing Outlook, 12 (Jan., 1964), 23.

1263. Gealy, Fred D. "The Biblical Understanding of Death," Pastoral Psychology, 14 (June, 1963), 33-40.

1264. Geber, M. "The Physician, the Child and Death, 2: the Anguish of Death During Psychotherapy of Children," Revue de Medecine Psychosomatique et de Psychologie Medicale, 10 (Oct.-Dec., 1968), 419-23.

1265. Gebhart, John C. Funeral Costs. New York: G.P. Putnam's Sons, 1928.

1266. _____. "Funerals," Encyclopedia of the Social Sciences, (1931), V. 6, 527-9.

1267. Geenken, Michael, Walter R. Gove. "Race, Sex and Marital Status: Their Effect on Mortality," Social Problems, 21 (Apr., 1974), 567-80.

1268. Geertinger, P. Sudden Death in Infancy. Springfield, IL; C.C. Thomas, 1968.

1269. Geertz, Clifford. "Ritual and Social Change: A Javanese Example," American Anthropologist, 59 (1957), 32-54.

1270. Geiger, A.K. "Childhood Bereavement: Somatic and Behavioral Symptoms of Psychogenic Origin," ACTA Paediatrica Academiae Scientarum Hungaricae, 14 (1973), 159-64.

1271. Geis, D.P. "Mothers' Perceptions of Care Given their Dying Children," American Journal of Nursing, 65 (Feb., 1965), 105-7.

1272. Gerard, H.I. The Relationship Between Religious Belief and Death Affect. Princeton: Princeton University Press, 1958.

1273. Gerber, Irwin. "Bereavement and the Acceptance of Professional Service," Community Mental Health Journal, 5 (1969), 487-96.

1274. _____, et al. "Anticipatory Grief and Aged Widows and Widowers," Journal of Gerontology, 30 (Mar., 1974), 225-9.

1275. Gerchick, E. et al., eds. The Role of the Community Hospital in the Care of the Dying Patient and Bereaved. New York: MSS Information, 1975.

1276. Gertler, R. "The First-Year Resident in Psychiatry: How He Sees the Psychiatric Patient's Attitudes Toward Death and Dying," International Journal of Social Psychiatry, 21 (Winter-Spring, 1974-5), 4-6.

1277. _____, et al. "Attitudes Toward Death and Dying on a Drug Addiction Unit," International Journal of the Addictions, 8 (1973), 265-72.

1278. Gesell, Arnold L. et al. Youth--the Years from Ten to Sixteen. New York: Harper and Brothers, 1956.

1279. Gibson, P.C. "The Dying Patient," Practitioner, 186 (1961), 85-91.

1280. Gibson, R. "Symposium: Care of the Dying: Caring for the Bereaved," Nursing Mirror, 139 (Oct. 10, 1974), 65-6.

1281. Gifford, Sanford. "Freud's Theories of Unconscious Immortality and the Death Instinct: A Reconsideration in the Light of Recent History and Modern Biology," Journal of Thanatology, 1 (Mar.-Apr., 1971), 109.

1282. Gifford, Sanford. "Some Psychoanalytic Theroies about Death: A Selective Historical Review," Annals of the New York Academy of Sciences, 164 (Dec., 1969), 638-68.

1283. Gilbert, Stuart. The Royal Way. New York: H. Smith and R. Hass, 1935.

1284. Gilli, R. et al. "On the Ascertainment of Death and on Freedom to Remove Organs for Transplantation," Minerva Anestesiologica, 34 (Nov., 1968), 1340-51.

1285. Gillon, H. "Defining Death Anew: Brain's Oxygen Use," Science News, 95 (Jan. 11, 1969), 50.

1286. Gilmore, A.J. "The Care and Management of the Dying Patient in General Practice," Practitioner, 213 (Dec., 1974), 833-42.

1287. Gimbel, B. "Editorial--Infanticide: Who Makes the Decision," Wisconsin Medical Journal, 73 (May, 1974), 10-1.

1288. Ginsberg, Raphael. "Should the Elderly Cancer Patient Be Told?" Geriatrics, 4 (Mar.-Apr., 1949), 101-7.

1289. Girdwood, Ronald, Malcolm Ballinger. "The Factors that Commonly Worry the Patient in Hospital," Edinburgh Medical Journal, 56 (1949), 347-52.

1290. Glaister, J. "Phantasies of the Dying," Lancet, 2 (Aug., 1921), 315-17.

1291. Glaser, Barney G. "Disclosure of Terminal Illness," Journal of Health and Human Behavior, 7 (Summer, 1966), 83-91.

1292. _____. "The Social Loss of Aged Dying Patients," The Gerontologist, 6 (June, 1966), 77-80.

1293. _____, Anselm L. Strauss. "Awareness Contexts and Social Interaction," American Sociological Review, 29 (Oct., 1964), 669-79.

1294. _____. Awareness of Dying. Chicago: Aldine Publishing Co., 1965.

1295. _____. "Dying on Time," Trans-Action, 2 (May-June, 1965), 27-31.

1296. _____. "The Social Loss of Dying Patients," American Journal of Nursing, 64 (June, 1964), 119-21.

1297. _____. "Temporal Aspects of Dying as a Non-Scheduled Status Passage," The American Journal of Sociology, 71 (July, 1965), 48-59.

1298. _____. Time for Dying. Chicago: Aldine Publishing Co., 1968.

1299. Glaser, Kurt, Leon Eisenberg. "Maternal Deprivation," Pediatrics, 18 (Oct., 1956), 626-42.

1300. Glass, R.D. "Cot Deaths," Medical Journal of Australia, 2 (July, 1971), 10.

1301. Glasser, Ronald J. Ward 402. New York: George Braziller, 1973.

1302. Glidden, Thomas. "The American Funeral," Pastoral Psychology, 14 (1963), 9-18.

1303. Glick, Ira O. et al. The First Year of Bereavement. New York: Wiley and Sons, 1974.

1304. Gluckman, Max. "Mortuary Customs and the Belief in Survival after Death among the South-Eastern Bantu," Bantu Studies, 11 (1937), 117-36.

1305. _____. "Rituals of Rebellion in South-East Africa," in Rituals of Rebellion. Manchester: Manchester University Press, 1954. 1-36.

1306. _____, ed. Essays on the Ritual of Social Relations. New York: The Humanities Press, 1962.

1307. Godber, G.E. "Abortion Deaths," British Medical Journal, 4 (Nov. 18, 1972), 424.

1308. Godin, Andre, ed. Death and Presence, Studies in the Psychology of Religion. Brussels, Lumen Vitae Press, 1972.

1309. Godwin, J.D., C. Brown. "Magnesium and Sudden Unexpected Infant Death," Lancet, 1 (May 26, 1973), 1176

1310. Goes, Albrecht. Unsere Letzte Stunde (Our Last Hours). Hamburg; Furche Verlag, 1951.

1311. Goette, Alexander W. Uber den Ursprung des Todes. Hamburg and Leipzig: L. Voss, 1883.

1312. Goetz, Harriet. "Needed: A New Approach to the Care of the Dying," Registered Nurse, 25 (Oct., 1962), 60-2.

1313. Goff, W.C. "How Can a Physician Prepare His Patient for Death?" Journal of the American Medical Association, 201 (July 21, 1967), 280.

1314. Goffman, Erving. "On Cooling the Mark Out," Psychiatry, 15 (Nov., 1952), 451-63.

1315. Gold, E. et al. "Viral Infection: A Possible Cause of Sudden Unexpected Death in Infants," New England Journal of Medicine, 264 (1961), 53-60.

1316. Gold, Mark S., Robert H. Ollendorff. "The Unencounter with Death," Humanitas, 10 (Feb., 1974), 43-9.

1317. Goldberg et al., eds. Medical Care of the Dying Patient. New York: Health Sciences Publishing Corp., 1974.

1318. Goldberg, Ivan K. et al., eds. Psychopharmacological Agents for the Terminally Ill and Bereaved. New York: Columbia University Press, 1973.

1319. Goldberg, S.B. "Family Tasks and Reactions in the Crisis of Death," Social Casework, 54 (July, 1973), 398-405.

1320. Goldfarb, A.I. Death and Dying: Attitudes of Patient and Doctor, I: Introduction. Group for the Advancement of Psychiatry. Symposium #11. 5 (Oct., 1965), 591-606.

1321. Goldfogel, L. "Working with the Parent of a Dying Child," American Journal of Nursing, 70 (Aug., 1970), 1675-9.

1322. Golding, Stephen L. et al. "Anxiety and Two Cognitive Forms of Resistance to the Idea of Death," Psychological Reports, 18 (Apr., 1966), 359-64.

1323. Goldman, V. "Death in the Dental Chair," Medical Science and Law, 13 (Jan., 1973), 39-45.

1324. Goldschmidt, Walter. "Freud, Durkheim, and Death among the Sebei," Omega, 3 (Aug., 1972), 227-31.

1325. _____. "Guilt and Pollution in Sebei Mortuary Rituals," Ethos, 1 (Spring, 1973), 75-105.

1326. Goldstein, E.G. "Social Casework and the Dying Person," Social Casework,
          54 (Dec., 1973), 601-8.

1327. Goldstein, S. "Jewish Mortality and Survival Patterns: Providence, Rhode Island,
          1962-1964," Eugenics Quarterly, 13 (Mar., 1966), 48-61.

1328. Goldstein, Sidney. Sudden Death and Coronary Heart Disease. Mt. Kisco, NY:
          Futura Publishing Co., 1974.

1329. Golub, S., M. Reznikoff, "Attitudes Toward Death: A Comparison of Nursing
          Students and Graduate Nurses," Nursing Research, 20 (Nov.-Dec., 1971),
          503-8.

1330. Goode, William J. "A Theory of Role Strain," American Sociological Review,
          25 (Aug., 1960), 483-96.

1331. Goodhart, C.B. "On the Incidence of Illegal Abortion: With a Reply to Dr.
          W.H. James," Population Studies, 27 (July, 1973), 207-33.

1332. Goodman, Paul. "On the Intellectual Inhibition of Explosive Grief and Anger,"
          in Utopian Essays and Practical Proposals. New York: Random House, 1962.

1333. Goodwin, P. "To Be a Strong Hand in the Dark," Nursing Times, 62 (June, 1966),
          10.

1334. Goody, Jack. "Death and Social Control among the Lo Dagaa," Man, 59 (1959b),
          134-8.

1335. _____. Death, Property and the Ancestors: A Study of the Mortuary Customs
          of the Lo Dagaa of West Africa. Palo Alto: Stanford University Press,
          1962.

1336. _____. "Religion and Ritual: the Definitional Problem," British Journal of
          Sociology, 12 (1961), 142-64.

1337. Googe, Mary Catherine Short. "The Death of a Young Man," American Journal of
          Nursing, 64 (Nov., 1964), 133-5.

1338. Gordon, David Cole. Overcoming the Fear of Death. New York: MacMillan, 1970.

1339. Gordon, J.E. et al. "Causes of Death at Different Ages, by Sex, and by
          Season, in a Rural Population of the Punjab," Indian Journal of Medical
          Research, 53 (Sep., 1965), 906-16.

1340. Gordon, Linda. "The Politics of Population: Birth Control and the Eugenics
          Movement," Radical America, 8 (July-Aug., 1974), 61-98.

1341. Gordon, Rosemary. "The Death Instinct and Its Relation to the Self," Journal of
          Analytic Psychology, 6 (July, 1961), 119-35.

1342. Gorer, Geoffrey. Death, Grief, and Mourning. New York: Doubleday, 1965.

1343. Gorer, Geoffrey. "The Pornography of Death," in W. Phillips and P. Rahv, eds., Modern Writing. New York: McGraw-Hill, 1959. 157-88.

1344. Gorostiza, Jose. Death Without End. Austin: University of Texas Press, 1969.

1345. Gorovitz, S. "Editorial: Relating to Dying Patients," American Review of Respiratory Disease, 112 (Aug., 1975), 159-63.

1346. Gotz, Berndt. "Sexualitat, Erkenntnis, Tod," Zeitschrift fur Sexualwissen schaft, 17 (1931), 486-96.

1347. Gough, E.K. "Cults of the Dead among the Nayars," Journal of American Folklore, 71 (1958), 446-78.

1348. Gould, Jonathan, Lord Craigmyle, eds. Your Death Warrant? The Implications of Euthanasia. New Rochelle, NY: Arlington House, 1973.

1349. Gould, R.K., M.B. Rothanberg. "The Chronically Ill Child Facing Death--How Can the Pediatrician Help," Clinical Pediatrics, 12 (July, 1973), 447-9.

1350. Goulooze, William. Pastoral Psychology. Grand Rapids: Baker Book House, 1950.

1351. Gove, W.R. "Sex, Marital Status, and Mortality," American Journal of Sociology, 79 (Summer, 1973), 45-67.

1352. Graber, G.H. "Problem of Death in a Case of Prenatal-Psychoanalytic Treatment: Concept of Dying Patient," Dynamic Psychology, 8 (1975), 290-5.

1353. Grady, M. "Assessment of Behavioral Scientists Role with Dying Patient and Family," Milit Med, 140 (1975), 789-92.

1354. Graham, A.J. "Should the Doctor Play God?" Central African Journal of Medicine 14 (June, 1968), 127-31.

1355. Graham, J.B. "Acceptance of Death: Beginning of Life," North Carolina Medical Journal, 24 (Aug., 1963), 317-9.

1356. Grant, Ian. "Care of the Dying," British Medical Journal, 5060 (Dec. 28, 1957), 1539-40.

1357. Grant, Roald N. "The Child with Leukemia and His Parents," CA Cancer Journal for Clinicians, 14 (March-Apr.,1964), 73-6.

1358. Granville-Grossman, K.L. "Early Bereavement and Schizophrenia," British Journal of Psychiatry, 112 (1966), 1027-34.

1359. Grayson, H. "Grief Reactions to the Relinquishing of Unfulfilled Wishes," American Journal of Psycotherapy, 24 (April, 1970), 287-95.

1360. Green, B.R., D.P. Irish. Death Education: Preparation for Living. Cambridge: Schenkman Publishing, 1971.

1361. Green, J.C. "What Constitutes Legal Death," Journal of the Indiana Medical Association, 61 (Aug., 1968), 1120-4.

1362. Green, J.R. "Brain Death, i.e., Irreversible Coma," Arizona Medical Journal, 31 (Feb., 1974), 101.

1363. Green, Judith Strupp. "The Days of the Dead in Oaxada, Mexico: An Historical Inquiry," Omega, 3 (Aug., 1972), 245-61.

1364. Green, Morris. "Care of the Child with a Long-Term Life-Threatening Illness," Pediatrics, 39 (Mar., 1967), 441-5.

1365. _____. "Care of the Dying Child," Pediatrics, 40 (Sep., 1967), 492-7.

1366. _____. "Psychological Aspects of Sudden Unexpected Death in Infants and Children: Review and Commentary," Pediatric Clinics of North America, 21 (Feb., 1974), 133-4.

1367. _____, A.J. Solnit. "The Pediatric Management of the Dying Child, Part 2: The Child's Reaction (vica) Fear of Dying," in Modern Perspectives in Child Development. New York: International Universities Press, Inc., 1963. 217-28.

1368. _____. "Psychologic Considerations in the Management of Deaths on Pediatric Hospital Services, Part I: The Doctor and the Child's Family," Pediatrics, 24 (1959), 106-12.

1369. _____. "Reactions to the Threatened Loss of a Child; A Vulnerable Child Syndrome: Pediatric Management of the Dying Child, Part III," Pediatrics, 34 (July, 1964), 58-66.

1370. _____, et al. "Something Can Be Done for a Child with Cancer," Hospital Tribune, 1 (July 3, 1967), 8.

1371. Greenacre, Phyllis. Trauma, Growth, and Personality. New York: W.W. Norton, 1952.

1372. Greenberg, Bradley S., Edwin B. Parker, eds. The Kennedy Assassination and the American Public: Social Communication in Crisis. Stanford, CA: Stanford University Press, 1965.

1373. Greenberg, Harvey R., H. Robert Blank. "Dreams of a Dying Patient," British Journal of Medical Psychology, 43 (Dec., 1970), 355-62.

1374. Greenberg, I.M. Death and Dying: Attitudes of Patient and Doctor, 4: Studies on Attitudes Toward Death. Group for the Advancement of Psychiatry. Symposium #11. 5 (Oct., 1965), 623-31.

1375. Greenberg, I.M. "Death in a Lonely Place," Hastings Center Reports, 3 (Dec., 1972), 11-3.

1376. _____, I.E. Alexander. "Some Correlates of Thoughts and Feelings Concerning Death," New York Hillside Hospital Journal, 11 (Apr.-July, 1962), 120-6.

1377. Greenberg, M.A. et al. "A Study of the Relationship Between Sudden Infant Death Syndrome and Environmental Factors," American Journal of Epidemiology, 98 (Dec., 1973), 412-22.

1378. Greenberger, Ellen. "Fantasies of Women Confronting Death," Journal of Consulting Psychology, 29 (June, 1965), 252-60.

1379. Greene, Carlton. Death and Sleep: Their Analogy Illustrated by Examples. London: Elliot Stock, 1904.

1380. Greene, W.A. "The Psychosocial Setting of the Development of Leukemia and Lymphoma," Annals of the New York Academy of Sciences, 125 (1966), 794-801.

1381. _____. "Role of a Vicarious Object in the Adaptation of Object Loss, 1: Use of a Vicarious Object," Psychosomatic Medicine, 20 (1958), 344-50.

1382. _____, et al. "Psychosocial Aspects of Sudden Death: A Preliminary Report," Archives of Internal Medicine, 129 (May, 1972), 725-31.

1383. _____, et al. "Psychological Factors and Reticuloendothelial Disease, 2: Observations on a Group of Women with Lymphomas and Leukemias," Psychosomatic Medicine, 18 (Aug., 1956), 284-303.

1384. _____, Stanley B. Troup, eds. The Patient, Death, and the Family. Conference on the Patient, Death, and the Family. New York: Scribner, 1974.

1385. Greenstock, David L. Death--the Glorious Adventure. Westminster, MD: Newman Press, 1956.

1386. Greer, Steven. "Study of Parental Loss in Neurotics and Sociopaths," Archives of General Psychaitry, 11 (Aug., 1964), 177-80.

1387. Gregory, Ian. "Anterospective Data Following Childhood Loss of a Parent," Archives of General Psychiatry, 13 (Aug., 1965), 99-109.

1388. _____. "Retrospective Estimates of Orphanhood from Generation Life Tables," Milbank Memorial Fund Quarterly, 43 (1965), 323-43.

1389. _____. "Studies of Parental Deprivation in Psychiatric Patients," American Journal of Psychiatry, 115 (1958), 432-42.

1390. Greig, J.Y.T. "Freud's Theory of Wit," British Journal of Medical Psychology, 3 (1923), 51-8.

1391. Greinacher, Norbert, Alois Muller, eds. The Experience of Dying. New York: Herder and Herder, 1974.

1392. Griffin, J.J. "Family Decision: A Crucial Factor in Terminating Life," American Journal of Nursing, 75 (May, 1975), 794-6.

1393. Griffith, J.A. "Three Medical Students Confront Death on a Pediatric Ward: A Case Report," Journal of the American Academy of Child Psychiatry, 13 (Winter, 1974), 72-7.

1394. Griffiths, Ruth. Study of Imagination in Early Childhood and Its Function in Mental Development. London: Routledge, 1935.

1395. Grinberg, L. "Two Kinds of Guilt--Their Relationship with Normal and Patholog-ical Aspects of Mourning," International Journal of Psychoanalysis 45 (Apr.-July, 1964), 366-71.

1396. Grinstein, A. "King Lear's Impending Death," American Imago, 30 (Summer, 1973), 121-41.

1397. Gris, Dorothy P. "Mother's Perceptions of Care Given Their Dying Children," American Journal of Nursing, 65 (Feb., 1965), 105-7.

1398. Grof, S. et al. "LSD-Assisted Psychotherapy in Patients with Terminal Cancer," International Pharmacopsychiatry, 8 (1973), 129-44.

1399. Grohmann, Adolf. "Das Problem von Leben und Tod in der Zeitgenosischen Litera-tur," Zeitschrift fur Deutschkunde, 44 (1930), 449-60.

1400. Grollman, Earl A. Concerning Death: A Practical Guide for the Living. Boston, Beacon Press, 1974.

1401. _____. Talking About Death: A Dialogue Between Parent and Child. Boston: Beacon Press, 1970.

1402. _____, ed. Explaining Death to Children. Boston: Beacon Press, 1967.

1403. Grosse, George et al., eds. The Threat of Impending Disaster. Cambridge: MIT Press, 1964.

1404. Grossman, K.L. "Maternal Age and Parental Loss," British Journal of Psychiatry, 114 (Feb., 1968), 242-3.

1405. Grotjahn, Martin. "About the Representation of Death in the Art of Antiquity and in the Unconscious of Modern Man," in George B. Wilbur and Warner Muensterberger, eds., Psychoanalysis and Culture. New York: International Universities Press, 1951. 410-24.

1406. _____. "Ego Identity and the Fear of Death and Dying," Hillside Hospital Journal, 9 (July, 1960), 147-55.

1407. Grotjahn, Martin. "Some Analytical Observations about the Process of Growing Old," in Psychoanalysis and Social Sciences. New York: International Universities Press, 1950. 3:301-12.

1408. Group for the Adavancement of Psychiatry. Death and Dying: Attitudes of Patient and Doctor. Symposium #11. New York: Group for the Advancement of Psychiatry, 1965/1972.

1409. _____. The Right to Die: Decision and Decision Makers. Symposium #12. New York: Group for the Advancement of Psychiatry, 1973.

1410. Gruber, Otto. When I Die. New York: Vantage Press, 1965.

1411. Gruman Gerald J. "An Historial Introduction to Ideas about Voluntary Euthanasia: With a Bibliographic Survey and Guide for Interdisciplinary Studies," Omega, 4 (1973), 87-138.

1412. Guardini, Romano. The Last Things, Concerning Death, Purification after Death, Resurrection. Translated by Charlotte E. Forsyth and Grace B. Branham. New York: Pantheon Books, 1954.

1413. Gubrium, J.F. "Death Worlds in a Nursing Home," Urban Life, 4 (1975), 317-38.

1414. Guimond, Joyce. "We Knew our Child was Dying," American Journal of Nursing, 74 (Feb., 1974), 248-9.

1415. Gunther, John. Death Be Not Proud. New York: Harper and Brothers, 1950.

1416. Guntheroth, W.G. "The Significance of Pulmonary Petechiae in Crib Death," Pediatrics, 52 (Oct., 1973), 601-3.

1417. Gustafson, Elizabeth. "Dying: The Career of the Nursing Home Patient," Journal of Health and Social Behavior, 13 (Sep., 1972), 226-35.

1418. Gut, Emmy. "Some Aspects of Adult Mourning," Omega, 5 (Winter, 1974), 323-42.

1419. Gutheil, Emil A. Handbook of Dream Analysis. New York: Liveright, 1951.

1420. Gutheil, Thomas G. "A Study of the Image of Death," Harvard Medical Alumni Bulletin, 41 (Winter, 1967), 12-7.

1421. Guthrie, George P. "The Meaning of Death," Omega, 2 (Nov., 1971), 299-302.

1422. Gutmacher, A.F. "Changing Attitudes and Practices Concerning Abortion: A Sociomedical Revolution," Maryland State Medical Journal, 20 (Dec., 1971), 59-63.

1423. Gutmann, David. "Aging Among the Highland Maya: A Comparative Study," Journal of Personality and Social Psychology, 7 (1967), 28-35.

1424. Gutmann, David. "The Country of Old Men: Cross-Cultural Studies in the Psy-
         chology of Later Life," in W. Donahue, ed., Occasional Papers in Geron-
         tology. Ann Arbor: Institute of Gerontology, University of Michigan,
         1969. 1-37.

1425. _____. "An Exploration of Ego Configurations in Middle and Later Life,"
         in B. Neugarten, ed., Personality in Middle and Later Life. New York:
         Atherton, 1964.

1426. _____. "The Hunger of Old Men," Trans-Action, 9 (Nov.-Dec., 1971), 55-66.

1427. _____. "Mayan Aging--A Comparative TAT Study," Psychiatry, 29 (1966),
         246-59.

1428. _____. "The New Mythologies and Premature Aging in the Youth Culture,"
         Journal of Youth and Adolescence, 2 (June, 1973), 139-55.

1429. _____. "The Premature Gerontocracy: Themes of Aging and Death in the Youth
         Culture," Social Research, 39 (Autumn, 1972), 416-48.

1430. Guttentag, Otto E. "The Meaning of Death in Medical Theory," Stanford Medical
         Bulletin, 17 (1959), 165-70.

1431. Guttman, F.M. "On Withholding Treatment," Canadian Medical Association Journal,
         11 (Sep. 21, 1974), 520, 3.

1432. Guyther, J.R. "The Right to Die," Maryland State Medical Journal, 22 (June,
         1973), 44-5.

1433. Gyomroi, Edith Ludowyk. "The Analysis of a Young Concentration Camp Victim,"
         The Psychoanalytic Study of the Child, 18 (1963), 484-510.

1434. Gyulay, J.E. "Forgotten Grievers," American Journal of Nursing, 75 (Sep.,
         1975), 1476-9.

1435. Haas, Michael. "Toward the Study of Biopolitics: A Cross-Sectional Analysis of Mortality Rates," Behavioral Science, 14 (1969), 257-80.

1436. Habenstein, Robert W. "Conflicting Organizational Patterns in Funeral Directing," Human Organization, 22 (Summer, 1963), 126-32.

1437. _____. "The Social Organization of Death," International Encyclopedia of the Social Sciences, (1968), 4:26-8.

1438. _____, William M. Lamers. Funeral Customs the World Over. Milwaukee: Bulfin, 1963.

1439. _____. The History of American Funeral Directing. Milwaukee: Bulfin, 1955.

1440. Haberman, Paul W., Michael M. Baden. "Alcoholism and Violent Death," Quarterly Journal of Statistics on Alcohol, 35 (Mar., 1974), 221-31.

1441. Hackett, Thomas P. "Current Approaches to the Care and Understanding of the Dying Patient," Archives of the Foundation of Thanatology, 1 (1969), 109.

1442. _____, N.H. Cassem. "Patients Facing Sudden Cardiac Death," in B. Schoenberg et al., eds., Psychosocial Aspects of Terminal Care. New York: Columbia University Press, 1972. 47-57.

1443. _____. "Psychological Effects of Acute Coronary Care," in L.E. Maltzer and A.J. Danning, eds., Textbook of Coronary Care. Amsterdam: Excerpta Medica, 1973. 443-52.

1444. _____. "Psychological Reactions to Life Threatening Illness: A Study of Acute Myocardial Infarction," in H.S. Abram, ed., Psychological Aspects of Stress. Springfield: C.C. Thomas, 1970. 29-43.

1445. _____, A.D. Weismann. "Predilection to Death: Death and Dying as a Psychiatric Problem," Psychosomatic Medicine, 23 (May-June, 1961), 232-56.

1446. _____. "The Treatment of the Dying," Current Psychiatric Therapy, 2 (1962), 121-6.

1447. _____, et al. "The Coronary Care Unit: An Appraisal of its Psychological Hazards," New England Journal of Medicine, 279 (Dec. 19, 1968), 1365-70.

1448. Hawden, W.R. Premature Burial. London: Swan Sonnenschein, 1905.

1449. Haering, Bernard. Medical Ethics. Notre Dame: Fides, 1973.

1450. Hagan, J.M. "Infant Death: Nursing Interaction and Intervention with Grieving Families," Nursing Forum, 13 (1974), 371-85.

1451. Hagin, Rosa A., Carol G. Corwin. "Bereaved Children," Journal of Clinical Child Psychology, 3 (Summer, 1974), 39-40.

1452. Haider, Ijaz. "Attitudes Toward Death of Psychiatric Patients," International Journal of Neuropsychiatry, 3 (Feb., 1967), 10-4.

1453. _____, et al. "EEG Signs of Death," British Medical Journal, 3 (Aug. 3, 1968), 314.

1454. Hall, G. Stanley. Adolescence. New York: Appleton, 1917. 1:378-80.

1455. _____. "A Study of Fears," American Journal of Psychology, 8 (Jan., 1897), 147-9.

1456. _____. "Thanatophobia and Immortality," American Journal of Psychology, 26 (1915), 550-613.

1457. Hall, J.H., D.D. Swenson. Psychological and Social Aspects of Human Tissue Transplantation: An Annotated Bibliography. U.S. Department of Health, Education, and Welfare, Public Health Service, National Institute of Mental Health. Washington: USGPO, 1968. Public Health Service Publication #1838.

1458. _____. Psychological and Social Aspects of Human Tissue Transplantation: An Annotated Bibliography, Supplement 1. U.S. Department of Health, Education, and Welfare, Public Health Service, National Institute of Mental Health. Washington: USGPO, 1969. Public Health Service Publication #1838-1.

1459. Halley, M.M., W.F. Harvey. "Medical vs. Legal Definitions of Death," Journal of the American Medical Association, 204 (May 6, 1968), 423-5.

1460. Halley, M.M. et al. "Definitions of Death," Journal of the Kansas Medical Society, 69 (June, 1968), 280-2.

1461. Halluin, Maurice D. La Mort, Cette Inconnue. Paris: Beauchesne, 1952.

1462. Halpern, W.I. "Some Psychiatric Sequelae to Crib Death," American Journal of Psychiatry, 129 (Oct., 1972), 398-402.

1463. Hamburger, Jean. "Medical Ethics and Organ Transplantation," American Medical Women's Association Journal, 23 (Nov., 1968), 981-4.

1464. Hamilton, S.M. "The Dying Patient," Journal of Practical Nursing, 21 (May, 1971), 25.

1465. Hamlin, Hannibal. "Life or Death by EEG," Journal of the American Medical Association, 190 (1964), 112-4.

1466. Hammer, M. "Reflections on One's Own Death as a Peak Experience," Mental Hygiene, 55 (Apr., 1971), 264-5.

1467. Hamner, R.T. "Legal Death: Can It Be Defined?" Journal of the Medical Association of Alabama, 38 (Jan., 1969), 610-4.

1468. Hamovitch, Maurice B. The Parent and the Fatally-Ill Child. Los Angeles:
        Delmar Publishing Co., 1968.

1469. _____. "Research Interviewing in Sensitive Areas, I: Research Interviewing
        in Terminal Illness," Journal of Social Work, 8 (Apr., 1963), 4-9.

1470. Hampe, S.O. "Needs of the Grieving Spouse in a Hospital Setting," Nursing
        Research, 24 (Mar.-Apr., 1975), 113-20.

1471. Hancock, S. "A Death in the Family--A Lay View," British Medical Journal,
        1 (Jan. 6, 1973), 29-30.

1472. Handal, P.J. "Relationship Between Death Anxiety Scale and Repression,"
        Journal of Clinical Psychology, 31 (1975), 675-7.

1473. _____. "The Relationship Between Subjective Life Expectancy, Death Anxiety
        and General Anxiety," Journal of Clinical Psychology, 25 (1969), 39-42.

1474. _____, et al. "Curvilinearity Between Dream Content and Death Anxiety and
        the Relationship of Death Anxiety to Repression-Sensitization," Journal
        of Abnormal Psychology, 77 (Feb., 1971), 11-6.

1475. Haney, C. Allen. "Issues and Considerations in Requesting an Anatomical Gift,"
        Social Science and Medicine, 7 (Aug., 1973), 635-42.

1476. Hansen G. "Diagnosis of Death, Reanimation, Organ Transplantation," Zeitschrift
        fur Aerztliche Fortbildung (Jena), 63 (Feb. 15, 1969), 237-9.

1477. Hansen, Rip (Prepared by Helen Hansen). "Waiting for Wednesday," Omega
        1 (Aug., 1970), 219-33.

1478. Harder, P. "Attitudes Toward Death of Psychiatric Patients," International
        Journal of Neuropsychiatry, 3 (Feb., 1967), 10-4.

1479. Hardgrove, Carol, Louise H. Warrick. "How Shall We Tell the Children?"
        American Journal of Nursing, 74 (Mar., 1974), 448-50.

1480. Hardt, Dale V. "Development of an Investigatory Instrument to Measure Attitudes
        Toward Death," Journal of School Health, 45 (Feb., 1975), 96-9.

1481. Harley, J. "Old Age," Nursing Times, 60 (Oct. 23, 1964), 1401-2.

1482. Harmer, Ruth Mulvey. "Funerals, Fantasy, and Flight," Omega, 2 (Aug., 1971),
        127-35.

1483. _____. The High Cost of Dying. New York: Crowell-Collier Press,
        1963.

1484. _____. "The Place of What Kind of Funeral?" (A response to Howard C. Raether's
        "The Place of the Funeral: The Role of the Funeral Director in Contemp-
        orary America") Omega, 2 (Aug., 1971), 150-4.

1485. Harmon, David K. et al. "The Social Readjustment Rating Scale: A Cross-Cultural Study of Western Europeans and Americans," Journal of Psycho-somatic Research, 14 (Dec., 1970), 391-400.

1486. Harmon, L. "Abortion, Death and the Sanctity of Life," Social Science and Medicine, 5 (1971), 211-8.

1487. Harnes, J.R. "Trash in, Trash Out," New York State Journal of Medicine, 73 (Dec. 15, 1973), 2906-9.

1488. Harnik, J. "One Component of the Fear of Death in Early Infancy," International Journal of Psychoanalysis, 11 (1930), 485-91.

1489. Harp, J.R. "Criteria for the Determination of Death," Anesthesiology, 40 (Apr., 1974), 391-7.

1490. Harper, R.G. et al. "Observations on the Sudden Death of Infants Born to Addicted Mothers," National Conference in Methadone Treatment Proceedings, 2 (1973), 1122-7.

1491. Harrington, Alan. Immortalist: An Approach to the Engineering of Man's Divinity, New York: Random House, 1969.

1492. Harris, Kenneth A. "The Political Meaning of Death: An Existential Overview," Omega, 2 (Nov., 1971), 227-40.

1493. Harris, Raymond I. Outline of Death Investigation. Springfield: C.C. Thomas, 1973.

1494. Harrison, S.I. et al. "Children's Reactions to Bereavement: Adult Confusions and Misperceptions," Archives of General Psychiatry, 17 (Nov., 1967), 593-7.

1495. Harshbarger, Dwight. "Picking up the Pieces: Disaster Intervention and Human Ecology," Omega, 5 (1974), 55-9.

1496. Hartland, E. Sydney. "Death and the Disposal of the Dead," Encyclopaedia of Religion and Ethics, (1912), 4:411-44.

1497. Harvey, Carol D., Howard M. Bahr. "Widowhood, Morale and Affiliation," Journal of Marriage and the Family, 36 (Feb., 1974), 97-106.

1498. Hasselmeyer, E.G. "The Sudden Infant Death Syndrome," Surgery, Gynecology, and Obstetrics, 135 (Dec., 1972), 950.

1499. _____, J.C. Hunter. "The Sudden Infant Death Syndrome," Obstetrics and Gynecology Annual, 4 (1975), 213-36.

1500. Hastings, James, ed. Encyclopedia of Religion and Ethics. New York: Charles Scribner's Sons, 1928.

1501. Havighurst, Robert, Jr., Bernice Neugarten, eds. "Attitudes Toward Death in Older Persons: A Symposium," Journal of Gerontology, 16 (1961), 44-66.

1502. Hawke, Sharryl. Death and Dying: A Living Study. Washington: Department of Health, Education, and Welfare, National Institute of Education, 1974.

1503. Hayano, D.M. "Sorcery Death, Proximity and the Perception of Out-groups: The Tauna Awa of New Guinea," Ethnology, 12 (Apr., 1973), 179-91.

1504. Hays, Joyce Samhammer, "The Night Neil Died," Nursing Outlook, 10 (Dec., 1962), 801-3.

1505. Hazlitt, William. "On the Fear of Death," in Dawson, et al., eds., The Great English Essayist. New York: Harper and Brothers, 1909.

1506. _____. "On the Feeling of Immortality in Youth," in P.P. Hose, ed., Complete Works. London: J.M. Dent and Sons, 1934. XVII.

1507. Hebb, Frank. "The Care of the Dying," Canadian Medical Association Journal, 65 (Sep., 1951), 261-3.

1508. Heckel, R.V. "The Day the President was Assassinated: Patient's Reaction in One Mental Hospital," Mental Hospitals, 15 (1964), 48.

1509. Heffron, Warren A. et al. "Group Discussion with Parents of Leukemic Children," Pediatrics, 52 (Dec., 1973), 831-40.

1510. Heidegger, Martin. Being and Time. Translated by John Macquarrie and Edward Robinson. New York: Harper and Row, 1962.

1511. Heidel, Alexander. Gilgamesh Epic and Old Testament Parallels. Chicago: University of Chicago Press, 1949.

1512. Heifetz, Milton D., Charles Mangel. The Right to Die. New York: Putnam, 1975.

1513. Heilbrunn, Gert. "The Basic Fear," Journal of the American Psychoanalytic Association, 3 (1955), 447-66.

1514. Heim, E. "Psychic Approach to Terminal Illness," Schweizerische Medizinische Wochenschrift, 105 (1975), 321-9.

1515. Heinicke, Christoph M., Ilse Westheimer. Brief Separations. New York: International Universities Press, 1965.

1516. Heller, Joseph. Catch-22. New York: Simon and Schuster, 1961.

1517. Hellman, Ilse. "Hampstead Nursery Follow-Up Studies, I: Sudden Separation and Its Effect Followed Over 20 Years," in Ruth S. Eissler, et al., eds., The Psychoanalytic Study of the Child, 17 (1962), 159-74.

1518. Helpern, Milton. "Death," Encyclopedia Americana, (1972), 8:564.

1519. Helson, G.A. "House Dust Mites and Possible Connection with Sudden Infant
        Death Syndrome," New Zealand Medical Journal, 74 (Sep., 1971), 209.

1520. Hembright, T.Z. "Comparison of Information on Death Certificates and Matching
        1960 Census Records: Age, Marital Status, Race, Nativity and Country
        of Origin," Demography, 6 (1969), 413-23.

1521. Hemmendinger, Miriam. "Admit Parents at All Times," Child Study, 34 (Winter,
        1956-7), 2-9.

1522. Hendal, P.J. "The Relationship Between Subjective Life Expectancy, Death
        Anxiety and General Anxiety," Journal of Clinical Psychology, 25 (1969),
        39-42.

1523. Henderson, Joseph L., Maud Oakes. The Wisdom of the Serpent (The Myths of
        Death, Rebirth and Resurrection). New York: Macmillan, 1971.

1524. Hendin, David. Death as a Fact of Life. New York: W.W. Norton, 1973.

1525. Hendricks, Jon, Carol D. Hendricks. "Defining the Situation: Reflection
        of Life Styles in Funeral Eulogies," Omega, 4 (1973), 57-64.

1526. Hendrix, Robert C. Investigation of Violent and Sudden Death: A Manual for
        Medical Examiners. Springfield: C.C. Thomas, 1972.

1527. Henry, C. "A Time to Live, a Time to Die," Nursing Times, 67 (Aug., 1971),
        1016-8.

1528. Herbert, C. "Life-Influencing Interactions," in A. Simon, et al., eds.,
        The Philosophy of Emotions. Springfield: C.C. Thomas, 1961. 187-209.

1529. Herman, S.J. "Divorce: A Grief Process," Perspectives in Psychiatric Care,
        11 (July-Sep., 1974), 108-12.

1530. Herold, Justin. "Signs and Tests of Death," New Orleans Medical and Surgical
        Journal, 51 (1899), 549-66.

1531. Hershey, N. "On the Question of Prolonging Life," American Journal of Nursing,
        71 (Mar., 1971), 521-2.

1532. _____. "Questions of Life and Death," American Journal of Nursing, 68
        (Sep., 1968), 1910-2.

1533. Hertz, D.G. "Confrontation with Death Effect and Influence of Impending
        Death on Therapeutic Process: Clinical Essay," Dynamic Psychology,
        8 (1975), 197-215.

1534. Hertz, Robert. Death and the Right Hand. Translated by Rodney and Claudia
        Needham. Glencoe, IL: The Free Press, 1960.

1535. Herxheimer, H. "Sudden Death in a Young Asthmatic," British Medical Journal, 2 (Apr. 26, 1969), 246.

1536. Herzog, E. Psyche and Death. Translated by B. Cox and E. Rolfe. London: Hodger and Staughton, Ltd. 1966.

1537. Heuscher, J.E. "Death in the Fairy Tale," Diseases of the Nervous System, 28 (July, 1967), 462-8.

1538. _____. "Existential Crisis, Death and Changing 'World Designs' in Myths and Fairy Tales," Journal of Existentialism, 6 (Fall, 1966), 45-62.

1539. Heuvelmans, Bernard. La Suppression de la Mort. Paris: L'Arche, 1951.

1540. Heuyer, G. et al. "Le Sens de la Mort chez l'Enfant," Revue de Neuropsychiatrie Infantile et d'Hygiene Mentale de l'Enfance, 3 (May-June, 1955), 219-51.

1541. Hewitt, David, Jean Milner. "Drug-Related Deaths in the United States: First Decade of an Epidemic," Health Services Reports, 89 (May, 1974), 211-8.

1542. Heyman, D.K., D.T. Gianturco. "Long-Term Adaptation by the Elderly to Bereavement," Journal of Gerontology, 38 (July, 1973), 359-62.

1543. Heymann, D.A. "Discussions Meet Needs of Dying Patients," Hospitals, 48 (July 16, 1974), 57-62.

1544. Hick, J.F. "Sudden Infant Death Syndrome and Child Abuse," Pediatrics, 52 (July, 1973), 147-8.

1545. Hickerson, Harold. "The Feast of the Dead Among the Seventeenth Century Algonkians of the Upper Great Lakes," American Anthropologist, 62 (1960), 81-107.

1546. Hicks, W., R.S. Daniels. "The Dying Patient, His Physician and the Psychiatric Consultant," Psychosomatics, 9 (Jan.-Feb.,1968), 47-52.

1547. Hildebrand, H.E. "Social Aspects of Sudden Death in Childhood," Medizinische Klinik, 62 (1967), 973-7.

1548. Hilgard, Josephine R. "Anniversary Reactions in Parents Precipitated by Children," Psychiatry, 16 (1953), 73-80.

1549. _____. "Depressive and Psychotic States as Anniversaries to Sibling Death in Childhood," International Psychiatry Clinics, 6 (1969), 197-211.

1550. _____, Fern Fisk. "Disruption of Adult Ego Identity as Related to Childhood Loss of a Mother Through Hospitalization for Psychosis," The Journal of Nervous and Mental Disease, 131 (July, 1960), 47-57.

1551. Hilgard, Josephine R., Fern Fisk. "Stength of Adult Ego Following Childhood Bereavement," American Journal of Orthopsychiatry, 30 (1960), 788-98.

1552. _____, Martha F. Newman. "Anniversaries in Mental Illness," Psychiatry, 22 (1959), 113-21.

1553. _____. "Early Parental Deprivation as a Functional Factor in the Etiology of Schizophrenia and Alcoholism," American Journal of Orthopsychiatry, 33 (1963), 409-20.

1554. _____. "Evidence for Functional Genesis in Mental Illness: Schizophrenia, Depressive Psychoses and Psychoneuroses," The Journal of Nervous and Mental Disease, 132 (Jan., 1961), 3-16.

1555. _____. "Parental Loss by Death in Childhood as an Etiological Factor among Schizophrenic and Alcoholic Patients Compared with a Non-Patient Community Sample," Journal of Nervous and Mental Disease, 137 (July, 1963), 14-28.

1556. Hill, Oscar W. "The Association of Childhood Bereavement with Suicidal Attempt in Depressive Illness," British Journal of Psychiatry, 115 (1969), 301-4.

1557. _____. "Childhood Bereavement and Adult Psychiatric Disturbances," Journal of Psychosomatic Research, 16 (Aug., 1972), 357-60.

1558. _____, J.S. Price. "Childhood Bereavement and Adult Depression," British Journal of Psychiatry, 113 (July, 1967), 743-51.

1559. Hill, Reuben. "Bereavement: A Crisis of Family Dismemberment," in Willard Waller, The Family: A Dynamic Interpretation. New York: The Dryden Press, 1951. 470-99.

1560. _____. Families Under Stress. New York: Harper, 1949.

1561. _____. "Social Stresses on the Family," Social Casework, 39 (1958), 139-50.

1562. Hillegass, L.M. "Magnesium and Sudden Unexpected Death," Lancet, 2 (Oct. 7, 1972), 764.

1563. Hilton, G.W. "The Care of the Dying," Medical Journal of Australia, 2 (July 22, 1972), 177-82.

1564. Hilton, J.M. "Cot Death Syndrome," Australasian Nurses' Journal, 3 (Apr., 1975), 3.

1565. Hingley, Susan. "Today I Saw Death," American Journal of Nursing, 67 (April, 1967), 825.

1566. Hintington, W.R. "Death and the Social Order: Bara Funeral Customs (Madagascar)," African Studies, 32 (1973), 65084.

1567. Hinton, John M. "Assessing the Views of the Dying," Social Science and Medicine, 5 (Feb., 1971), 37-43.

1568. _____. Dying. Baltimore: Penguin, 1972.

1569. _____. "Facing Death," Journal of Psychosomatic Research, 10 (July, 1966), 22-8.

1570. _____. "The Influence of Previous Personality on Reactions to Having Terminal Cancer," Omega, 6 (1975), 95-111.

1571. _____. "Patients' Views on Their Care During Terminal Cancer," Proceedings of the Royal Society of Medicine, 66 (July, 1973), 610.

1572. _____. "The Physical and Mental Distress of the Dying," Quarterly Journal of Medicine, 5 (Jan., 1963), 1-21.

1573. _____. "Problems in the Care of the Dying," Journal of Chronic Diseases, 17 (Mar.,1964), 201-5.

1574. _____. "Psychiatric Consultation in Fatal Illness," Proceedings of the Royal Society of Medicine, 65 (Nov., 1972), 1035-8.

1575. _____. "Talking with People about to Die," British Medical Journal, 2 (July 6, 1974), 25-7.

1576. Hirsh, H.L. "Brain Death," Medical Trial Technique Quarterly, 21 (Spring, 1975), 377-405.

1577. _____. "Death as a Legal Entity," Journal of Forensic Science, 20 (Jan., 1975), 159-68.

1578. Hiscoe, S. "The Awesome Decision," American Journal of Nursing, 73 (Feb., 1973), 291-3.

1579. Hitschmann, Eduard. "Todesangst Durch Totungsdrang--Ein Neurotischer Mechanismus," Zeitschrift fur Kinderpsychiatrie, 3 (1936-8), 165-9.

1580. Hoagland, Hudson. "Mechanisms of Population Control," Daedalus, 93 (Summer, 1964), 812-29.

1581. Hobbins, W.B. "Four Distinctive Views of the Dying Patient: What is a Day of Life Worth?" Registered Nurse, 38 (Apr., 1975), 33-4.

1582. Hoblit, Pamela R. "An Investigation of Changes in Anxiety Level Following consideration of Death in Four Groups," Dissertation Abstracts International, 33 (Nov., 1972), 2346.

1583. Hocart, A.M. "Death Customs," Encyclopedia of the Social Sciences, (1931), 5:21-7.

1584. Hoch, Paul, Joseph Zubin, eds. Depression. New York: Grune and Stratton, 1954.

1585. Hochschild, Arlie Russell. The Unexpected Community. Englewood Cliffs: Prentice-Hall, 1973.

1586. Hocking, W.E. The Meaning of Immortality in Human Experience, Including Thoughts on Life and Death. New York: Harper, 1957.

1587. Hodge, J.R. "Help Your Patients to Mourn Better," Medical Times, 99 (June, 1971), 53-64.

1588. _____. "How to Help your Patients Approach the Inevitable," Medical Times, 102, (Nov., 1974), 123-33.

1589. Hoedt, W., K. Pfeifer. "The Causes of Death in Children Who Suddenly and Unexpectedly Expired (1950-1965)," Deutsche Gesundheitswesen, 21 (1966), 1441-8.

1590. Hoekelman, R.A. "The Physician's Responsibility in the Management of Sudden Infant Death Syndrome," American Journal of Diseases in Childhood, 128 (July, 1974), 16-7.

1591. Hoevet, Sister Martha. "Dying is Also Living," Nursing Care, (July, 1974), 12-5.

1592. Hofer, G. "Death in the Primitive World (On the Question of Death Suggestion in Melanesia)," Confinia Psychiatrica, 9 (1966), 93-114.

1593. Hofer, Myron A. et al. "A Psychoendocrine Study of Bereavement, I: 17-Hydroxycorticosteroid Excretion Rates of Parents Following Death of their Children from Leukemia," Psychosomatic Medicine, 34 (Nov., 1972), 481-91.

1594. _____. "A Psychoendocrine Study of Bereavement, II: Observations on the Process of Mourning in Relation to Adrenocortical Function," Psychosomatic Medicine, 34 (Nov., 1972), 492-504.

1595. Hoffman, Esther. "Don't Give Up on Me," American Journal of Nursing, 71 (Jan., 1971), 60-2.

1596. Hoffman, F.L. Pauper Burials and the Interment of the Dead in Large Cities. Newark: Prudential Press, 1919.

1597. Hoffman, Francis H., Morris W. Brody. "The Symptom: Fear of Death," Psychoanalytic Review, 44 (1957), 433-38.

1598. Hoffman, Frederick J. The Mortal No: Death and the Modern Imagination. Princeton: Princeton University Press, 1964.

1599. Hoffman, Hans. Religion and Mental Health. New York: Harper and Brothers, 1962.

1600. Hoffman, J.W. "When a Loved One is Dying: How to Decide What to Tell Him,"
       Today's Health, 134 (Feb., 1972), 41-3.

1601. Hofling, Charles K. "Terminal Decisions," Medical Opinion and Review,
       2 (Oct., 1966), 40-9.

1602. _____, M. Joy. "Favorable Response to the Loss of a Significant Figure:
       A Preliminary Report," Bulletin of the Menninger Clinic, 38 (Nov., 1974),
       527-37.

1603. Hogan, R.A. "Adolescent Views of Death," Adolescence, 5 (Spring, 1970),
       55-66.

1604. Holck, F.H., ed. Death and Eastern Thought. Nashville: Abingdon Press, 1974.

1605. Holland, Jimmie. "Psychological Response to Death of an Identical Twin by
       the Surviving Twin with the Same Disease," Omega, 2 (Aug., 1971),
       160-7.

1606. Hollender, Marc H. "The Patient with Carcinoma," in The Psychology of Medical
       Practice. Philadelphia: W.B. Saunders, 1958.

1607. _____. "The Physician, the Patient and Cancer," Illinois Medical Journal,
       107(Jan., 1955), 20-3.

1608. Holmes, Joyce. "Teaching About Death: A Review of Selected Materials,"
       Social Studies Journal, 4 (Winter, 1975), 48-50.

1609. Holmes, Thomas H., Minoru Masuda. "Psychosomatic Syndrome," Psychology
       Today, 5 (April, 1972), 71-2ff.

1610. _____, R.H. Rahe. "The Social Readjustment Rating Scale," Journal of
       Psychosomatic Research, 11 (1967), 213-8.

1611. Holsclaw, Pamela A. "Nursing in High Emotional Risk Areas," Nursing Forum,
       4 (1965), 36-45.

1612. Holt, William C. "Death by Suggestion," Canadian Psychiatric Association Journal,
       14 (1969), 81-2.

1613. Hooper, Thornton, Barnard Spilka. "Some Meanings and Correlates of Future
       Time and Death Among College Students," Omega, 1 (Feb., 1970), 49-56.

1614. Hopkins, Lois Jones. "A Basis for Nursing Care of the Terminally Ill Child
       and His Family," Maternal Child Nursing Journal, 2 (Summer, 1973), 93-100.

1615. Hopkinson, G., G.F. Reed. "Bereavement in Childhood and Depressive Psychosis,"
       British Journal of Psychiatry, 112 (1966), 459-63.

1616. Horan, D.J. "Euthanasia, Medical Treatment and Mongoloid Child Death as a
       Treatment of Choice," Baylor Law Review, 27 (1975), 76-85.

1617. Horder, Lord. "Signs and Symptoms of Impending Death," Practitioner, 54 (1948), 1773-9.

1618. Horneman, E. Om Menneskets Tilstand Kort for Doden (About Man's Condition Shortly Before Death). Kjøbenhavn: Lund, 1874.

1619. Horowitz, M.J. Educating Tomorrow's Doctors. New York: Appleton-Century-Crofts, 1964.

1620. Hostler, Phyllis. The Child's World. Harmondsworth, Middlesex, Great Britain: Penguin Books, 1959.

1621. Howard, Alan, Robert A. Scott. "Cultural Values and Attitudes Toward Death," Journal of Existentialism, 6 (Winter, 1965-6), 161-74.

1622. Howard, E. "Effect of Work Experience in a Nursing Home on the Attitudes Toward Death Held by Nurses Aides," Gerontologist, 14 (Fall, 1974), 54-6.

1623. Howard, J.D. "Fear of Death," Journal of the Indiana Medical Association, 54 (Dec., 1961), 1773-9.

1624. Howarth, R.V. "The Psychiatry of Terminal Illness in Children," Proceedings of the Royal Society of Medicine, 65 (Nov., 1972), 1039-50.

1625. Howell, D.A. "A Child Dies," Hospital Topics, 45 (Feb., 1967), 93-6.

1626. Howe, G. Melvyn. "The Geography of Life and Death," Journal of Biosocial Science, 5 (Apr., 1973), 285-305.

1627. Howes, Elizabeth, ed. And a Time to Die. London: Routledge and Kegan Pual, 1961.

1628. Howie, D.L. "Scared to Death," Journal of the Florida Medical Association, 55 (Sep., 1968), 861-2.

1629. Hoyle, Clifford. "The Care of the Dying," Postgraduate Medical Journal, 20 (Apr., 1944), 119-23.

1630. Hsii, Feng Pao. "The Business of Dying," The Nursing Journal of Singapore, 14 (May, 1974), 38-9.

1631. Huang, I. "Children's Conception of Physical Causality: A Critical Summary," Journal of Genetic Psychology, 64 (1943), 71-121.

1632. Huber, Peter B. "Death and Society among the Anggor of New Guinea," Omega, 3 (Aug., 1972), 233-43.

1633. Hughes, Everett Cherrington. Men and Their Work. Glencoe, IL; The Free Press, 1958.

1634. Hughes, Hugh Llewelyn. _Peace at the Last_. London: Calouste Gulbenkian Foundation, 1960.

1635. Huizinga, J. _The Waning of the Middle Ages_. Garden City, NJ: Doubleday, 1924.

1636. Human, M.E. "Death of a Neighbor," _American Journal of Nursing_, 73 (Nov., 1973), 1914-6.

1637. Humphrey, G. Bennet, David A. Vore. "Psychology and the Oncology Team," _Journal of Clinical Child Psychology_, 2 (Summer, 1974), 26-9.

1638. Hunsinger, George. _Kierkegaard, Heidegger and the Concept of Death_. Stanford: Leland Stanford Jr. University, 1969.

1639. Hunt, Leigh. "Deaths of Little Children," in W.J. Dawson and C.W. Dawson, eds., _The Great English Essayists_. New York: Harper and Brothers, 1909. 64-9.

1640. Hunter, Edith F. _The Questioning Child and Religion_. Boston: Beacon Press, 1956.

1641. Hunter, R.C. "On the Experience of Nearly Dying," _American Journal of Psychiatry_, 124 (July, 1967), 84-8.

1642. Huntington, R.W., Jr., J.J. Jarzynka. "Sudden and Unexpected Death in Infancy, with Special Reference to the So-Called Crib Deaths," _American Journal of Clinical Pathology_, 38 (Dec., 1962), 637-8.

1643. Hurlock Elizabeth B. _Child Development_. New York: McGraw-Hill, 1964.

1644. Hurwitz, M.M. "Relieving Pain in the Terminally Ill," _Geriatrics_, 28 (May, 1973), 56, passim.

1645. Hussar, A.E. "Leading Causes of Death in Institutionalized Chronic Schizophrenic Patients: A Study of 1275 Autopsy Protocols," _Journal of Nervous and Mental Disease_, 142 (Jan., 1966), 45-57.

1646. Hussey, H.H. "Editorial: The Cause of Death," _Journal of the American Medical Association_, 229 (July 1, 1974), 75.

1647. Hutschnecker, Arnold A. _The Will to Live_. Englewood Cliffs: Prentice-Hall, 1951.

1648. Hwang, J.C. "The Sudden Infant Death Syndrome," _Archives of Pathology_, 94 (Oct., 1972), 370-1.

1649. Iammarino, N.K. "Relationship Between Death Anxiety and Demographic Variables," Psychological Reports, 37 (Aug., 1975), 262.

1650. Ilg, Frances L., Louise Bates Ames. Child Behavior. New York: Harper and Brothers, 1955.

1651. _____. Development Not Made. Bad Nauheim, Germany: Christian Publishers, 1958.

1652. Imboden, John B. et al. "Separation Experiences and Health Records in a Group of Normal Adults," Psychosomatic Medicine, 25 (1963), 433-40.

1653. Ingelfinger, F.J. "Bedside Ethics for the Hopeless Case," New England Journal of Medicine, 289 (Oct. 25, 1973), 914-5.

1654. Ingles, T. "Death on a Ward," Nursing Outlook, 12 (Jan., 1964), 28.

1655. Ingles, T. "St. Christopher's Hospice," Nursing Outlook, 22 (Dec., 1974), 759-63.

1656. Innes, G. et al. "Mortality Among Psychiatric Patients," Scotland Medical Journal, 15 (Apr., 1970), 143-8.

1657. Institute of Medicine of Chicago, Central Service for the Chronically Ill. Terminal Care for Cancer Patients. Chicago: The Institute of Medicine of Chicago, 1950.

1658. Irion, Clyde. The Profit and Loss of Dying. Santa Monica: DeVorss and Co., 1969.

1659. Irion, Paul. "Death and Contemporary American Man," Theology and Life, 7 (1964), 297-309.

1660. _____. "The Funeral and the Integrity of the Church," Pastoral Psychology, 14 (1963), 25-32.

1661. _____. The Funeral and the Mourners. Nashville: Abingdon Press, 1954.

1662. _____. The Funeral--Vestige or Value? Nashville: Abingdon Press, 1966.

1663. _____. "In the Midst of Life . . . Death!" Pastoral Psychology, 14 (June, 1963), 7ff.

1664. Irish, Donald P., Betty R. Green, eds. Death Education: Preparation for Living. Cambridge: Schenkman, 1971.

1665. Irish, Jerry. A Boy Thirteen (Reflections on Death). Philadelphia: Westminster Press, 1975.

1666. Irle, G. "Attitudes Towards Death in Patients Following Suicide Attempts," Nervenarzt, 39 (June, 1968), 255-60.

1667. Irwin, Robert, Donald L. Weston. "Preschool Child's Response to Death of Infant Sibling," American Journal of Diseases in Childhood, 106 (Dec., 1963), 564-7.

1668. Isaacs, B. "Treatment of the 'Irremediable' Elderly Patient," British Medical Journal, 3 (Sep. 8, 1973), 526-8.

1669. _____, et al. "The Concept of Pre-Death," Lancet, 1 (May 29, 1971), 1115-8.

1670. Isaacs, Nathan. The Growth of Understanding in the Young Child. London: The Education Supply Association, 1961.

1671. Isakower, Otto. "A Contribution to the Patho-Psychology of Phenomena Associated with Falling Asleep," International Journal of Psychoanalysis, 19 (1937), 331-45.

1672. Isambert, F.A. "Transformations in Catholic Ritual for Dying," Archives of Social Science and Religion, 20 (1975), 101-17.

1673. Isham, Lorraine S. Survey of State Laws Governing the Disposal of the Dead and Regulating Those Who Work with the Dead: A Critical Look at the Laws. Hanover, NH: Billings, Lee, 1966.

1674. Ishigaki, Junji. Nasu to Shi (The Nurse and Death). Tokyo: Igaku Shoin, 1951

1675. Isler, Charlotte. "Care of the Pediatric Patient with Leukemia," Registered Nurse, (April, 1972), 30-5.

1676. _____. "Let the Parents Help Care for the Child with Leukemia," Registered Nurse, 25 (June, 1962), 44-57.

1677. Jablon, S. et al. "Studies of the Mortality of A-Bomb Survivors," Radiation Research, 25 (1965), 25-52.

1678. Jackson, Edgar N. The Christian Funeral. New York: Channel Press, 1966.

1679. _____. For the Living. New York: Channel Press, 1963.

1680. _____. "Grief and Guilt," The Pastoral Counselor, 1 (Spring, 1963), 34-8.

1681. _____. "The Law and the Right to Grieve," International Journal of Law and Science, 7 (Jan.-Mar., 1970), 1-10.

1682. _____. Telling a Child about Death. New York: Channel Press, 1965.

1683. _____. Understanding Grief. Nashville: Abingdon Press, 1957.

1684. _____. You and Your Grief. New York: Channel Press, 1961.

1685. Jackson, Maurice. "The Black Experience with Death: A Brief Analysis Through Black Writings," Omega, 3 (Auga., 1972), 203-9.

1686. Jackson, N.A. "A Child's Preoccupation with Death," American Nurse's Association Clinical Sessions, (1968), 172-9.

1687. Jackson, Pat L. "Chronic Grief," American Journal of Nursing, 74 (July, 1974), 1288-91.

1688. _____. "Child's Developing Concept of Death: Implications for Nursing Care of Terminally Ill Child," Nursing Forum, 14 (1975), 204-15.

1689. Jackson, Percival E. "Death (Legal Aspects)," Encyclopaedia Britannica, (1971), 7:132-5.

1690. Jaco, E. Gartly, ed. Patients, Physicians and Illness. Glencoe, IL: Free Press, 1958.

1691. Jacobson, David S. "Death," Universal Jewish Encyclopedia, (1941), 3:503-4.

1692. Jacobson, E. "Introjection in Mourning," International Journal of Psychiatry, 3 (May, 1967), 433-5.

1693. Jaehner, Dors. "Uber Einstellung des Kleinkindes zum Tode (About the Attitude of the Infant to Death)," Zeitschrift fur Angewandte Psychologie, 45-6 (1933-4), 262-88.

1694. Jaglom, Moshe. "Reactions of Three Schizophrenic Patients to their Brother's Death," Israel Annals of Psychiatry and Related Disciplines, 11 (Mar., 1973), 54-65.

1695. Jakobovits, I. "The Dying and their Treatment in Jewish Law," Hebrew Medical Journal, 2 (1961), 242-51.

1696. Jalavisto, E. "Determining Sex Mortality Causes in Adults," Geron: Societas Gerontological Fennica, 16 (1964), 47-57.

1697. James, T.N. "QT Prolongation and Sudden Death," Modern Concepts in Cardiovascular Disease, 38 (July, 1969), 34-7.

1698. _____. "Sudden Death in Babies," American Journal of Cardiology, 22 (1968), 456-506.

1699. Jankelevitch, S. "La Mort et l'Immortalite d'Apres les Donnees de la Biologie," Revue Philosophique, 69 (1910), 358-80

1700. Jankelevitch, Vladimir. La Mort. Paris: Flammarion, 1966.

1701. Jankus, A. "Inflammatory Changes in the Cardiac Conducting System in Sudden Infant Death Syndrome," Medical Journal of Australia, 1 (May 10, 1975), 594-5.

1702. Janzen, E. "Relief of Pain--Prerequisite to the Care and Comfort of the Dying," Nursing Forum, 13 (1974), 48-51.

1703. Jaques, Elliott. "Death and the Mid-Life Crisis," International Journal of Psychoanalysis, 46 (1965), 502-14.

1704. Jarast, Sara G. "El Duelo on Relacion con el Aprendizaje (Mourning in Relation to Learning)," Revista de Psicoanalisis, 15 (Jan.-June, 1958), 31-5.

1705. Jaros, J. "Morbidity and Mortality in the Czechoslovakian S.S.R. in 1963," Ceskoslovenske Zdravotnictvi, 12 (1964), 411-20.

1706. Jatz, Jay, Alexander Morgan Capron. Catastrophic Diseases: Who Decides What? New York: Russell Sage Foundation, 1975.

1707. Jeffers, Frances C., Adriaan Verwoerdt. "Factors Associated with Frequency of Death Thoughts in Elderly Community Volunteers," Proceedings of the 7th International Congress of Gerontology. Vienna, Austria. June 26-July 2, 1966. 149-52.

1708. _____, et al. "Attitudes of Older Persons Toward Death: A Preliminary Study," Journal of Gerontology, 16 (1961), 53-6.

1709. Jelliffe, Smith Ely. "The Death Instinct in Somatic and Psychopathology," Psychoanalytic Review, 20 (Apr., 1933), 121-32.

1710. _____. "Review of the Article 'Thanatophobia and Immortality' by G. Stanley Hall," Journal of Nervous and Mental Disease, 45 (1917), 272-6.

1711. Jensen, Gordon D., John G. Wallace. "Family Mourning Process," Family Process, 6 (1967), 56-66.

1712. Jersild, Arthur T., Frances B. Holmes. Children's Fears. New York: Teachers College, Columbia University, 1935.

1713. _____, et al. Children's Fears, Dreams, Wishes, Daydreams, Likes, Dislikes, Pleasant and Unpleasant Memories. New York: Teachers College, Columbia University, 1933.

1714. Jetter, Lucille E. "Some Emotional Aspects of Prolonged Illness in Children," Survey, 84 (May, 1948), 165.

1715. Jha, M. "Death-Rites among Maithil Brahmans," Man in India, 46 (1966), 241-7.

1716. Johannsen, Dorothea E. "Reactions to the Death of President Roosevelt," Journal of Abnormal and Social Psychology, 41 (1946), 218-22.

1717. Johnson, A.B. "Right to Live or the Right to Die," Nursing Times, 67 (May, 1971), 573-4.

1718. Johnson, Edwin, Charles C. Josey. "A Note on the Development of the Thought Forms of Children as Described by Piaget," Journal of Abnormal and Social Psychology, 26 (1931-1932), 338-9.

1719. Johnson, R.M. "Human Feelings Concerning Approach of Death," Psychopathology of Africa, 10 (1975), 423-9.

1720. Johnson, W.G. "To Die as a Man: Disease, Truth and Christian Ethics," Journal of the Iowa Medical Society, 56 (Aug., 1966), 813-6.

1721. Johnston, E.H. et al. "Investigation of Sudden Death in Addicts, with Emphasis on the Toxicological Findings in Thirty Cases," Medical Annals of the District of Columbia, 38 (July, 1969), 375-80.

1722. Johnston, H.W. "Toward a Phenomenology of Death," Philosophy and Phenomenology, 35 (1975), 396-7.

1723. Jokl E. "Exercise and Cardiac Death," Journal of the American Medical Association, 218 (Dec., 1971), 1707.

1724. Joling, R.J. "The Time of Death," Arizona Medicine, 30 (Mar., 1973), 159-63.

1725. Jones, Barbara. Design for Death. New York: Bobbs-Merrill, 1967.

1726. Jones, C.H. "Four Distinctive Views of the Dying Patient: A Kidney Donor—Providing Life after Death," Registered Nurse, 38 (Apr., 1975), 36-7.

1727. Jones, Ernest. "On Dying Together," in Essays in Applies Psychoanalysis. London: Hogarth, 1951.

1728. _____. "The Psychology of Religion," British Journal of Medical Psychology, 6 (1926), 265-9.

1729. _____, ed. Problems of Human Pleasure and Behavior. London: Hogarth, 1957.

1730. Jones, Ferdinand, David Laskowitz. "Rorschach Study of Adolescent Addicts Who Die of an Overdose: A Sign Approach," Psychiatric Digest, 25 (1964), 21-30.

1731. Jones, J.C. "Premonition of Death," British Medical Journal, 2 (1958), 1051.

1732. Jones, J.J. "The Executive Way to Death," Central African Journal of Medicine, 20 (Nov., 1974), 238-40.

1733. Jones, K.S. "Death and Doctors," Medical Journal of Australia, 49 (1962), 329-34.

1734. Jones, R.G. "A Clinical Perspective on Dying," Canadian Medical Association Journal, 109 (Sep. 9, 1972), 425-7.

1735. Jones, T.T. "Dignity in Death: The Application and Withholding in Interventive Measures," Journal of the Louisiana Medical Society, 13 (May, 1961), 180-3.

1736. Jones, William Tudor. Metaphysics of Life and Death. New York: George H. Doran, 1924.

1737. Jordahl, Edna K. Planning and Paying for Funerals. Minneapolis: University of Minnesota Agricultural Extension Service, 1969.

1738. Jores, A. "Der Tod des Menschen in Psychologischer Sicht (Psychological Aspects of Human Death)," Medizinische Klinik, 54 (Feb. 13, 1959), 237-41.

1739. _____. "Leitsymptom: Angst (Guiding Symptom: Fear)," Munchener Medizinische Wochenschrift, 102 (Apr., 1960), 847-51.

1740. Jorgensen, E.O. "Clinical Note: EEG Without Detectable Cortical Activity and Cranial Nerve Areflexia as Parameters of Brain Death," Electroencephalography and Clinical Neurophysiology, 36 (Jan., 1974), 70-5.

1741. _____. "Technical Contribution: Requirements for Recording the EEG at High Sensitivity in Suspected Brain Death," Electroencephalography and Clinical Neurophysiology, 36 (Jan., 1974), 65-9.

1742. Jorgensen, P.B. et al. "Brain Death Pathogenesis and Diagnosis," ACTA Neurologica Scandanavia, 49 (1973), 355-67.

1743. Joseph, F. "Transference and Countertransference in the Case of a Dying Patient," Psychoanalysis and the Psychoanalytic Review, 49 (1962), 21-34.

1744. Joseph, Harry, Gordon Zern. The Emotional Problems of Children. New York: Crown Publisher, 1954.

1745. Jung, Carl Gustav. The Development of the Personality. New York: Pantheon Books, 1954.

1746. Jung, Carl Gustav. _Wirklichkeit der Seele_. Zurich: Rascher, 1939.

1747. Jung Young Lee. _Death and Beyond in the Eastern Perspective_. New York:
       Gordon and Breach, 1974.

1748. Jungel, Eberhard. _Death: The Riddle and the Mystery_. Philadelphia: West-
       minster Press, 1975.

1749. Kadlub, K.J., K.G. Kadlub. "Crib Death: Disease or Accident?" Michigan Medicine, 73 (Nov., 1974), 663-6.

1750. Kahana, Boaz, Eva Kahana. "Attitudes of Young Men and Women Toward Awareness of Death," Omega, 3 (Feb., 1972), 37-44.

1751. Kahana, R.J. "The Concept and Phenomenology of Depression, with Special Reference to the Aged, Grief and Depression," Journal of Geriatric Psychiatry, 7 (1974), 26-47.

1752. Kahn, Eugen. "Symposium on Anxiety Conditions," Connecticut Medicine, 2 (Jan., 1938), 15-25.

1753. Kaines, Joseph. Last Words of Eminent Persons. London: George Routledge and Sons, 1966.

1754. Kalisch, Philip. "Death Down Below: Coal Mine Disasters in Three Illinois Counties, 1904-62," Journal of the Illinois State Historical Society, 65 (1972), 5-21.

1755. Kalish, Richard A. "The Aged and the Dying Process: The Inevitable Decisions," Journal of Social Issues, 21 (1965), 87-96.

1756. _____. "An Approach to the Study of Death Attitudes," American Behavioral Scientist, 6 (1963), 68-70.

1757. _____. "A Continuum of Subjectively Perceived Death," The Gerontologist, 6 (June, 1966), 73-6.

1758. _____. "Dealing with the Grieving Family," Registered Nurse, 26 (May, 1963), 80-4.

1759. _____. "Death and Bereavement: A Bibliography," Journal of Human Relations, 13 (First Quarter, 1965), 118-41.

1760. _____. "Death and Dying in a Social Context," in R. Binstock and E. Shanas, eds., Handbook of Aging and the Social Sciences. New York: Van Nostrand Reinhold, 1976.

1761. _____. "Death and Responsibility: A Social-Psychological View," Psychiatric Opinion, 3 (Aug., 1966), 14-9.

1762. _____. "The Effects of Death upon the Family," in L. Pearson, ed., Eying and Death. Cleveland: Press of Case Western Reserve University, 1969. 79-107.

1763. _____. "Experiences of Persons Reprieved from Death," in Kutscher, ed., Death and Bereavement. Springfield: C.C. Thomas, 1969. 84-96.

1764. _____. "Life and Death: Dividing the Indivisible," Social Science and Medicine, 2 (Sep., 1968), 249-59.

1765. Kalish, Richard A. "Non-Medical Interventions in Life and Death," Social Science and Medicine, 4 (Dec., 1970), 655-65.

1766. _____. "Of Social Values and the Dying: A Defense of Disengagement," Family Coordinator, 21 (1972), 81-94.

1767. _____. "The Onset of the Dying Process," Omega, 1 (Feb., 1970), 57-69.

1768. _____. "The Practicing Physician and Death Research," Medical Times, 97 (Jan., 1969), 211-20.

1769. _____. "Social Distance and the Dying," Community Mental Health Journal, 12 (Summer, 1966), 152-5.

1770. _____. "Some Variables in Death Attitudes," Journal of Social Psychology, 59 (1963), 137-45.

1771. _____, David K. Reynolds. Death and Ethnicity: A Psychocultural Study. Los Angeles: University of Southern California Press, 1976.

1772. _____. "The Meaning of Death and Dying in the Los Angeles Mexican-American Community," Proceedings of the 6th International Conference for Suicide Prevention, Mexico, D.F., Mexico, Dec. 5-8, 1972. Ann Arbor: Edwards Borthers, 1972. 291-5.

1773. _____. "Phenomenological Reality and Post-Death Contact," Journal for the Scientific Study of Religion, 12 (June, 1973), 209-21.

1774. _____. "Widows View Death: A Brief Report," Omega, 5 (1974), 187-92.

1775. Kalsey, Virginia. "As Life Ebbs," American Journal of Nursing, 48 (Mar., 1948), 170-3.

1776. Kamisar, Yale. "Some Non-Religious Views Against Proposed 'Mercy-Killing' Legislation," Child and Family, 19 (1971), 155-90, 260-88.

1777. Kanders, O. "Der Todesgedanke in der Nervose und in der Psychose," Der Nerven-artz, 6 (1934), 288.

1778. Kane, Fred. "The Development of Concepts of Death," Proceedings of the 6th International Conference for Suicide Prevention, Mexico, D.F., Mexico, Dec. 5-8, 1972. Ann Arbor: Edwards Brothers, 1972. 149-52.

1779. Kane, John. "The Irish Wake: A Sociological Appraisal," Sociological Symposium, 1 (Fall, 1968), 11-6.

1780. Kanof, Abram et al. "The Impact of Infantile Amaurotic Familial Idiocy (Tay-Sachs Disease) on the Family," Pediatrics, 29 (Jan., 1962), 37-45.

1781. Kaplan, David. "Leukemia Strains Emotional Ties," Medical World News, (Apr. 6, 1973), 23.

1782. Kaplan, Joel. "Responses of Mother Squirrel Monkeys to Death of Infants," Primates, 14 (Mar., 1973), 89-91.

1783. Kapleau, Philip. Wheel of Death: A Collection of Writings from Zen Buddhist and Other Sources on Dying-Death-Rebirth. New York: Harper and Row, 1971.

1784. Kar, S.B. "Opinion Towards Induced Abortion among Urban Women in Delhi, India," Social Science and Medicine, 6 (Dec., 1972), 731-6.

1785. Karon, Myron, Joel Vernick. "An Approach to the Emotional Support of Fatally Ill Children," Clinical Pediatrics, 7 (May, 1968), 274-80.

1786. Kass, L.R. "Death as an Event: A Commentary on Robert Morison," Science, 173 (Aug. 20, 1971), 698-702.

1787. _____. "Problems in the Meaning of Death," Science, 170 (Dec. 11, 1970), 1235-6.

1788. Kast, Eric. "LSD and the Dying Patient," Chicago Medical School Quarterly, 26 (Summer, 1966), 82.

1789. Kastenbaum, Robert J. "As the Clock Runs Out," Mental Hygiene, 50 (July, 1966), 332-6.

1790. _____. "Childhood: The Kingdom where Creatures Die," Journal of Clinical Child Psychology, 3 (Summer, 1974), 11-4.

1791. _____. "Death and Responsibility: Introduction and a Critical Review," Psychiatric Opinion, 3 (Aug., 1966), 56, 35-41.

1792. _____. "Death as a Research Problem in Social Gerontology: An Overview," The Gerontologist, 6 (June, 1966), 67-9.

1793. _____. "Disaster, Death, and Human Ecology," Omega, 5 (1974), 65-72.

1794. _____. "The Kingdom Where Nobody Dies," Saturday Review, Science, 55 (Jan., 1973), 33-8.

1795. _____. "Loving, Dying, and other Gerontologic Addenda," in C. Eisdorfer and M.P. Lawton, eds., The Psychology of Adult Development and Aging. Washington: American Psychological Association, 1973.

1796. _____. "The Mental Life of Dying Geriatric Patients," The Gerontologist, 7 (June, 1967), 97-100.

1797. _____. "Multiple Perspectives on a Geriatric 'Death Valley'," Community Mental Health Journal, 3 (Spring, 1967), 21-9.

1798. _____. "On Death and Dying: Should We Have Mixed Feelings about our Ambivalence Toward the Aged?" Journal of Geriatric Psychiatry, 7 (1974), 94-107.

1799. Kastenbaum, Robert. "On the Future of Death: Some Images and Options," Omega, 3 (Nov., 1972), 307-18.

1800. _____. "On the Meaning of Time in Later Life," Journal of Genetic Psychology, 109 (1966), 9-25.

1801. _____. "The Realm of Death: An Emerging Area in Psychology," Journal of Human Relations, 13 (1965), 538-52.

1802. _____, Aisenberg, Ruth. Death in Our Lives and Thoughts. Condensed from The Psychology of Death. New York: Springer, 1975.

1803. _____. The Psychology of Death. New York: Springer, 1972.

1804. _____, Laura Briscoe. "The Street Corner: A Laboratory for the Study of Life-Threatening Behavior," Omega, 6 (1975), 33-44.

1805. _____, Charles E. Goldsmith. "The Funeral Director and the Meaning of Death," American Funeral Director, 86 (Apr., 1963), 35-7; (May, 1963), 47-8; (June, 1963), 45-6.

1806. _____, Ronald Koenig. "Dying, Death, and Lethal Behavior: An Experience in Community Education," Omega, 1 (Feb., 1970), 29-36.

1807. _____, B.L. Mishara. "Premature Death and Self-Injurious Behavior in Old Age," Geriatrics, 26 (July, 1971), 71-81.

1808. Katz, David, Rosa Katz. Conversations with Children. London: Kegan Paul, 1936.

1809. Katz, Jay. Experimentation with Human Beings. New York: Russell Sage Foundation, 1972. Ch 14.

1810. Kaufer, C. et al. "Time of Death Determination Following Dissociated Death of the Brain: Clinical and Electroencephalographic Criteria," Deutsche Medizinische Wochenschrift, 93 (Apr. 5, 1968), 679-84.

1811. Kavanaugh, R.E. Facing Death. Los Angeles: Nash Publishing, 1972.

1812. Kazzaz, David S., Raymond Vickers. "Geriatric Staff Attitudes Toward Death," Journal of the American Geriatric Society, 16 (1968), 1364-71.

1813. Kazamias, T.M. "What Death is Like," American Heart Journal, 78 (July, 1969), 139-40.

1814. Keefe, D.J. "The Life and Death of the Law," Hospital Progress, 53 (Mar., 1972), 64-74.

1815. Keegan, J.J. "Sudden Unexpected Death at All Ages," Nebraska Medical Journal, 58 (Nov., 1973), 393-8.

1816. Keeley, K.A. et al. "Alcohol and Drug Abuse--Causes of Sudden Death," Southern Medical Journal, 67 (Aug., 1974), 970-2.

1817. Keleman, Stanley. Living Your Dying. New York: Random House, 1974.

1818. Keller, Caroline. "Raising the Cancer Patient's Morale," American Journal of Nursing, 49 (Aug., 1949), 508-11.

1819. Kelly, D.T. "Sudden Death," Singapore Medical Journal, 14 (Sep., 1973), 300-1.

1820. Kelly, Gerald. "Care of the Dying," Linacre Quarterly, 19 (Nov., 1952), 109-11.

1821. Kelly, H.J. "Comparability of Infant Death and Birth Certificates and Their Influence on Infant Moratlity: A Study in Minnesota," Public Health Reports, 90 (Mar.-Apr., 1975), 165-7.

1822. Kelly, Orville E. Make Today Count. New York: Delacorte Press, 1975.

1823. Kelly, William H. "Cocopa Attitudes and Practice with Respect to Death and Mourning," Southwestern Journal of Anthropology, 5 (1949), 151-64.

1824. _____, Stanley R. Friesen. "Do Cancer Patients Want to Be Told?" Surgery, 27 (June, 1950, 822-6.

1825. Kelsey, B. "An Interview with Dr. Raymond S. Duff: Which Infants Should Live? Who Should Decide?" Hastings Center Report, 5 (Apr., 1975), 5-8.

1826. Keltinkangas-Jarvinen, L. "Atttiudes Toward Death: An Empirical Study with Normal and Psychiatrically Disturbed Persons," Yearbook of the Psychiatric Clinic of Helsinki University Central Hospital. Helsinki: University Central Hospital, 1971. 161-5.

1827. Kemph, Florence D., Ruth Hill Useem. Dynamics of Behavior in Nursing. Philadelphia: W.B. Saunders, 1964.

1828. Kemph, John P. "Renal Failure, Artificial Kidney and Kidney Transplant," American Journal of Psychiatry, 122 (May, 1966), 1270-4.

1829. Kennard, E.A. "Hope Reactions to Death," American Anthropologist, 29 (1937), 491-4.

1830. Kennedy, B.J. "Letter: Pleasures and Tragedies of Death," Journal of the American Medical Association, 234 (Oct. 6, 1975), 24.

1831. Kennedy, I.M. "The Kansas Statute on Death--An Appraisal," New England Journal of Medicine, 285 (Oct., 1971), 946-50.

1832. _____. "The Legal Definition of Death," Medico Legal Journal, 41 (1973), 36-41.

1833. Kennell, John H. et al. "The Mourning Response of Parents to the Death of a Newborn Infant," New England Journal of Medicine, 283 (Aug. 13, 1970), 344-9.

1834. Kephart, William M. "Status after Death," American Sociological Review, 15 (Oct., 1950), 635-43.

1835. Kerenyi, N.A., J.F. Fekete. "Sudden Unexpected Death in Infancy," Canadian Journal of Public Health, 60 (Sep., 1969), 357-61.

1836. Kerppola-Sirola, I. "The Death of an Old Professor," Journal of the American Medical Association, 232 (May 19, 1975), 278-9.

1837. Kerr, L. "Reflections on Death," Suicide, 5 (1975), 115-20.

1838. Kerstein, M. "Must Medical Progress Leave the Dying Patient Behind?" Geriatrics, 28 (Apr., 1973), 67-8.

1839. Kestenberg, Judith S. "Notes on Ego Development," International Journal of Psychoanalysis, 34 (1953), 111-2.

1840. Kevorkian, J. "The Eye of Death," Clinical Symposia, 13 (1961), 51-62.

1841. Keywood, O. "Care of the Dying in Their Own Home," Nursing Times, 70 (Sep. 16, 1974), 1516-7.

1842. Khan, S.B., V. Zarro. "The Management of the Dying Patient," Seminars on Drug Treatment, 3 (Summer, 1973), 37-44.

1843. Khudr, G.S. "Neonatal Death," Lebanese Medical Journal, 27 (1974), 135-6.

1844. Kidorf, Irwin W. "Jewish Tradition and the Freudian Theory of Mourning," Journal of Religion and Health, 2 (1963), 248-52.

1845. _____. "The Shiva: A Form of Group Psychoatherapy," Journal of Religion and Health, 2 (1963), 248-52.

1846. Kierkegaard, Søren. The Concept of Dread. Translated by Walter Lowrie. Princeton: Princeton University Press, 1944.

1847. _____. Fear and Trembling; and, The Sickness Unto Death. New York: Doubleday, 1954.

1848. Kihn, B. Der Tod als Psychotherapeutsches Problem, Vortrage der Lindauer Psychotherapiewoche. Stuttgart: G. Thieme, 1952.

1849. Killian, Eldon C. "Effect of Geriatric Transfers on Mortality Rates," Social Work, 15 (Jan., 1970), 19-26.

1850. Kimmel, D.C. Adulthood and Aging. New York: Wiley and Sons, 1974.

1851. Kimsey, L.R. et al. "Death, Dying and Denial in the Aged," American Journal of Psychiatry, 129 (Aug., 1972), 161-6.

1852. Kimura, J. et al. "The Isoelectric Electroencephalogram: Significance in Establishing Death in Patients Maintained on Mechanical Respirators," Archives of Internal Medicine, 121 (June, 1968), 511-7.

1853. King, Carole. "A Practical Assessment of Pareto's Theory of Residues and Derivations with Specific Reference to Views on Abortion," Sociological Analysis, 2 (1971-2), 1-12.

1854. King, Donald West. "Death (Biological)," Encyclopaedia Britannica, (1971), 7:129-32.

1855. King, Joan M. "Denial," American Journal of Nursing, 66 (May, 1966), 1010-3.

1856. Kirkpatrick, Jeanne et al. "Bereavement and School Adjustment," Journal of School Psychology, 3 (1965), 58-63.

1857. Kirkpatrick, K. et al. "Dilemma of Trust Relationship Between Medical Care Givers and Parents of Fatally Ill Children," Pediatrics, 54 (Aug., 1974), 169-75.

1858. Kirschner, David. "The Death of a President: Reactions of Psychoanalytic Patients," Behavioral Science, 10 (Jan., 1965), 1-6.

1859. Kirtley, Donald D., Joseph M. Sacks. "Reactions of a Psychotherapy Group to Ambiguous Circumstances Surrounding the Death of a Group Member," Journal of Consulting and Clinical Psychology, 33 (1969), 195-99.

1860. Kitagawa, Evelyn M., Philip Morris Hauser. Differential Mortality in the United States. Cambridge: Harvard University Press, 1973.

1861. Kitay, William. "Let's Retain the Dignity of Dying," Today's Health, 44 (May, 1966), 62-9.

1862. Klausner, Samual. Psychiatry and Religion. New York: Free Press, 1964.

1863. Klebba, A.J. "Mortality Trends in the United States," Vital Health Statistics, 20 (June, 1966), 1-57.

1864. _____, Alice B. Dolman. Comparability of Mortality Statistics for the 7th and 8th Revisions of the International Classification of Diseases. Rockville, MD National Center for Health Statistics, 1975.

1865. _____, et al. Mortality Trends: Age, Color, and Sex, U.S. 1950-69. Rockville, MD: National Center for Health Statistics, 1973.

1866. _____. Mortality Trends for Leading Causes of Death, U.S., 1950-69. Rockville, MD: National Center for Health Statistics, 1974.

1867. Klein, I. "Death in India, 1871-1921," Journal of Asian Studies, 32 (Aug., 1973), 639-59.

1868. Klein, Melanie. "A Contribution to the Theory of Anxiety and Guilt," International Journal of Psychoanalysis, 29 (1948), 114-23.

1869. _____. "Mourning and its Relationship to Manic Depressive States," International Journal of Psychoanalysis, 21 (Apr., 1940), 125-53.

1870. _____. The Psychoanalysis of Children. London: L. and V. Woolf, 1932.

1871. Klein, Stanley. The Final Mystery. Garden City: Doubleday, 1974.

1872. Kleinschmidt, H. "Erziehungsprobleme im Kinderspital VI Inernationaler Kongress," Journal of Pedatrie (Zurich), 3 (1950), 216-7.

1873. Kliman, Gilbert. Preventive Opportunities in Childhood Bereavement (Death of A Parent Study)," White Plains, NY: Center for Preventive Psychiatry, 1964.

1874. _____. Psychological Emergencies of Childhood. New York: Grune and Stratton, 1968.

1875. _____, et al. "Facilitation of Mourning in Childhood," American Journal of Orthopsychiatry, 39 (1969), 247-8.

1876. Kline, Nathan S., Julius Sobin. "The Psychological Management of Cancer Patients," Journal of the American Medical Association, 146 (Aug. 25, 1951), 1547-51.

1877. Klingberg, Gote. "The Distinction Between Living and Not Living Among 7-10 Year Old Children, with Some Remarks Concerning the So-Called Animism Controversy," Journal of Genetic Psychology, 90 (1957), 227-8.

1878. Klingensmith, S.W. "Child Animism: What the Child Means by 'Alive'," Child Development, 24 (Mar., 1953), 51-61.

1879. Kluckhohn, Clyde. "Conceptions of Death among the Southwestern Indians," in R. Kluckhohn, ed., Culture and Behavior. New York: Free Press, 1962. 134-9.

1880. _____. "Myths and Rituals: A General Theory," Harvard Theological Review, 35 (1942), 45-79.

1881. _____, et al. Personality in Nature, Society and Culture. New York: Alfred A. Knopf, 1954.

1882. Kluge, Eike-Henner. The Practice of Death. New Haven: Yale University Press, 1975.

1883. Klute, C.G. "I Can't Quit Now," Canadian Nurse, 71 (Mar., 1975), 38-9.

1884. Knapp, Vrinda S., Howard Hanson. "Helping the Parents of Children with Leukemia," Social Work, 18 (July, 1973), 70-5.

1885. Kneisl, Carol Ren. "Thoughtful Care for the Dying," American Journal of Nursing, 68 (Mar., 1968), 550-3.

1886. Knight, Aldrich C. "Personality Factors and Mortality in the Relocation of the Aged," The Gerontologist, 4 (1964), 92-3.

1887. Knight, B. "Legal and Administrative Problems in the 'Cot Death Syndrome'," Journal of the Forensic Science Society, 12 (Oct., 1972), 581-3.

1888. Knight, James A. "Philosophic Implications of Terminal Illness," North Carolina Medical Journal, 22 (1961), 92-3.

1889. Knipe, M.L. "Serenity for a Terminally Ill Patient," American Journal of Nursing, 66 (Oct., 1966), 493-5.

1890. Knowles, Joseph. "The Role of the Chaplain in Patient Relationships: Care of the Critically Ill," Journal of Pastoral Care, 7 (Summer, 1953), 112-6.

1891. Knudson, Alfred F., Jr, Joseph M. Natterson. "Observations Concerning Fear of Death in Fatally Ill Children and Their Mothers," Psychosomatic Medicine, 22 (Nov.-Dec., 1960), 456-65.

1892. _____. "Participation of parents in the Hospital Care of Fatally Ill Children," Pediatrics, 26 (1960), 482-90.

1893. Kobrzycki, Paula. "Dying with Dignity," American Journal of Nursing, 75 (Aug., 1975), 1312-3.

1894. Koch, Franz. Goethe's Stellung zu Tod und Unsterblichkeit (Goethe's Position on Death and Immortality). Weimar: Verlage der Goethe-Gesellschaft, 1932.

1895. Koenig, Ronald. "Counseling in Catastrophic Illness: A Self-Instructional Unit," Omega, 16 (1975), 227-41.

1896. Koeningsberg, R.A. "F. Scott Fitzgerald: Literature and the Work of Mourning," American Imago, 24 (1967), 248-70.

1897. Koestenbaum, Peter. "The Vitality of Death," Omega, 2 (Nov., 1971), 253-71.

1898. Kofka, Kurt. Die Grundlagen der Psychischen Entwicklung. Osterwieck: A.W. Zickfeldt, 1925.

1899. Kogan, Nathan, Florence Shelton. "Images of 'Old People' and 'People in General' in an Older Sample," Journal of Genetic Psychology, 100 (1962), 3-21.

1900. Kogan, Nathan, Michael Wallach. "Age Changes in Values and Attitudes," Journal of Gerontology, 16 (1961), 272-80.

1901. Kohl, Marvin. The Morality of Killing. New York: Humanities Press, 1974.

1902. _____, ed. Beneficient Euthanasia. Buffalo, NY: Prometheus Books, 1975.

1903. Kohlhaas, M. "On the Determination of the Time of Death," Deutsche Medizinische Wochenschrift, 93 (Mar., 1968), 412-4.

1904. _____. "Once Again: On Determination of the Time of Death," Deutsche Medizinische Wochenschrift, 93 (Aug., 1968), 1575.

1905. Kohn, Lawrence A. "Thoughts on the Care of the Hopelessly Ill," Medical Times, 89 (Nov., 1961), 1177-81.

1906. Koocher, Gerald P. "Childhood, Death, and Cognitive Development," Developmental Psychology, 9 (Nov., 1973), 369-75.

1907. _____. "Conversations with Children about Death: Ethical Considerations in Research," Journal of Clinical Child Psychology, 3 (Summer, 1974), 19-21.

1908. _____. Talking about Death with "Normal" Children: Research Strategies and Issues. Boston: Developmental Evaluation Clinic, The Children's Hospital Medical Center, 1973.

1909. _____. "Talking with Children about Death," American Journal of Orthopsychiatry, 44 (Apr., 1974), 404-11.

1910. _____. "Why Isn't the Gerbil Moving Anymore?" Children Today, 4 (Jan.-Feb., 1975), 18-21.

1911. Koop, C. Everett. "The Death of a Child," Bulletin of the American College of Surgeons, 52 (July-Aug., 1967), 173-4.

1912. _____. "The Seriously Ill or Dying Child: Supporting the Patient and the Family," Pediatric Clinics of North America, 16 (Aug., 1969), 555-64.

1913. Kopel, Kenneth, et al. "A Didactic-Experiential Death and Dying Lab," Newsletter for Research in Mental Health and Behavioral Sciences, 15 (Aug., 1973), 1-2.

1914. _____. "A Human Relations Laboratory Approach to Death and Dying," Omega, 6 (1975), 219-21.

1915. Kosnik, A.R. "Theological Reflections on Criteria for Defining the Moment of Death," Hospital Progress, 54 (Dec., 1973), 64-9.

1916. Kostrubala, T. "Therapy of the Terminally Ill Patient," Illinois Medical Journal, 124 (1963) 545-7.

1917. Kotsovsky, D. "Alter und Todesfurcht (Old Age and the Fear of Death)," Schweizerische Zeitscrift fur Psychologie, 10 (1951), 42-53.

1918. _____. "Die Psychologie der Todesfurcht (The Psychology of the Fear of Death)," Monatsberichte, 1 (1936), 21-40.

1919. Koupernik, C. "A Drama of Our Times: Euthanasia," Concours Medical, 84 (1962), 4687-8.

1920. _____. "Trois Adolescents et la Mort," Concours Medical, 79 (1957), 2567-72.

1921. Kovach-Shand, Nancy. "Psychocultural Integration: A Cross-Cultural Study of Continuities in Artistic Expression, Contact Modalities Throughout the Life Cycle and Institutionalized Responses to Death," Dissertation Abstracts International, 33 (May, 1973), 5106-7.

1922. Kovalev, V. "Dynamics of the Mental Condition of Patients Following Clinical Death of Short Duration," Vestnik Akademii Meditsinskikh Nauk SSR (Moskva), 17 (1962), 17-22.

1923. Krahn, John H. "Pervasive Death: An Avoided Concept," Educational Leadership, 31 (Oct., 1973), 18-20.

1924. Krakowsk, A.J. "Meaning of Death in Psychodynamics of Medical Practice," Dynamic Psychology, 8 (1975), 240-54.

1925. Kram, Charles, John M. Caldwell. "The Dying Patient," Psychosomatics, 10 (Sep.-Oct., 1969), 293-5.

1926. Kram, L. "Closing an Institution--Its Effect on Patients and on Staff," Hospital and Community Psychiatry, 26 (1975), 195.

1927. Krame, M., C. Young. "Administrator Helps Determine the Quality of Dying," Modern Nursing Home, 24 (Apr., 1970), 49ff.

1928. Kramer, Charles H., Hope E. Dunlop. "The Dying Patient," Geriatric Nursing, (Sep.-Oct., 1966), np.

1929. Krant, Melvin J. "A Death in the Family," Journal of the American Medical Association, 231 (Jan. 13, 1975), 195-6.

1930. _____. Dying and Dignity. Springfield: C.C. Thomas.

1931. _____. "Grief and Bereavement: An Unmet Medical Need," Delaware Medical Journal, 45 (Oct., 1973), 282-90.

1932. _____. "Helping Patients Die Well," New England Journal of Medicine, 280 (Jan. 23, 1960), 222.

1933. Krant, Melvin J. "The Organized Care of the Dying Patient," Hospital Practice, 7 (Jan., 1972), 101-8.

1934. _____, Alan Sheldon. "The Dying Patient: Medicine's Responsibility," Journal of Thanatology, 1 (Jan.-Feb., 1971), 1.

1935. Kraus, Arthur S., Abraham M. Lilienfeld. "Some Epidemiologic Aspects of the High Mortality Rate in the Young Widowed Group," Journal of Chronic Diseases, 10 (Sep., 1959), 207-17.

1936. _____, et al. "Further Epidemiologic Observations on Sudden Unexpected Death in Infancy in Ontario," Canadian Journal of Public Health, 62 (May-June, 1971), 210-9.

1937. Kraus, Friedrich. Uber Tod und Sterben (About Death and Dying). Berlin: Urban and Schwarzenberg, 1911.

1938. Kraus, J., N. Borhari. "Post Neonatal Sudden Unexpected Death in California: A Cohort Study," Journal of Epidemiology, 95 (June, 1972), 497-510.

1939. Kravitz, H. et al. "Deaths in Suburbia," Clinical Pediatrics, 5 (May, 1966), 266-7.

1940. Kreis, Bernadine, Alice Pattie. Up From Grief: Patterns of Recovery. New York: Seabury Press, 1969.

1941. Kretschmer, H. "Determination of the Time of Death from the Neurosurgical Viewpoint," Zeitschrift fur Aerztliche Fortbildung, 63 (Aug. 15, 1969), 884-5.

1942. Krippner, Stanley. "The 20-Year Death Cycle of the American Presidency," Research Journal of Philosophy and Social Science, 2 (1965), 65-72.

1943. Kroeber, A.L. "Disposal of the Dead," American Anthropologist, 26 (1927), 308-15.

1944. Krokfors, G. et al. "Parity and Age of Death," Annales Chirurgiae et Gynae-cologiae Fenniae, 53 (1964), 476-9.

1945. Kron, Joan. "Learning to Live with Death," Omega, 5 (1974), 5-24.

1946. Krupp, George R. "The Bereavement Reaction: A Special Case of Separation Anxiety Sociocultural Considerations," The Psychoanalytic Study of Society, 2 (1962), 42-74.

1947. _____. "Maladaptive Reactions to the Death of a Family Member," Social Casework, 53 (July, 1972), 425-34.

1948. _____. "Notes on Identification as a Defense Against Anxiety in Coping with Loss," International Journal of Psychoanalysis, 46 (1965), 303-14.

1949. Krupp, George R., Bernard Kligfeld. "The Bereavement Reaction: A Cross-Cultural Evaluation," Journal of Religion and Health, 1 (1962), 222-46.

1950. Kubler-Ross, Elisabeth. "Anger Before Death," Nursing '71, (Dec., 1971), 12-4.

1951. _____. "The Care of the Dying: Whose Job Is It?" Psychiatry in Medicine, 1 (Apr., 1970), 103-7.

1952. _____. "Coping Patterns of Patients Who Know Their Diagnosis," in Catastrophic Illness in the Seventies: Critical Issues and Complex Decisions. New York: National Cancer Foundation, 1970. 14-9.

1953. _____. "Crisis Management of Dying Persons and Their Families," in Emergency Psychiatric Care: The Management of Mental Health Crises by H.L.P. Resnick and H.L. Ruber. New York: Charles Press, 1974. 143-56.

1954. _____. "Death," Encyclopedia Britannica, 5 (1974), 526-9.

1955. _____. "Death: How Do We Face You?" in John G. Howells, ed., Modern Perspectives in the Psychiatry of Old Age. New York: Brunner/Mazel, 1975.

1956. _____. "Dignity in Death," Medical Bulletin. Naval Regional Medical Center and Naval Hospital, Portsmouth, VA. 6 (Winter, 1971), 76-85.

1957. _____. "Dying from the Patient's Point of View," Triangle, Sandoz Journal of Medical Science, 13 (1974), 25-6.

1958. _____. "The Dying Patient as Teacher: An Experiment and an Experience," The Chicago Theological Seminary Register, 57 (Dec., 1966), 1-14.

1959. _____. "Dying with Dignity," The Canadian Nurse, 67 (Oct., 1971), 31-5.

1960. _____. "The Experience of Death," in Jess E. Weiss, ed., The Vestibule. Port Washington, NY: Ashley Books, Inc., 1972.

1961. _____. "Facing Up to Death," Today's Education, 61 (Jan., 1972), 30-32.

1962. _____. "The Family Physician and the Dying Patient," Canadian Family Physician, (Oct., 1972), 79-83.

1963. _____. "Hope and the Dying Patient," Psychosocial Aspects of Terminal Care, 1972.

1964. _____. "Interview with--Terminal Cancer Patient," Geriatric Focus, 9 (Apr., 1970), 4.

1965. _____. "The Languages of Dying," Journal of Clinical Child Psychology, 3 (Summer, 1974), 22-4.

1966. Kubler-Ross, Elisabeth. "The Languages of the Dying Patients," Humanitas, 10 (Feb., 1974), 5-8.

1967. _____. "Lessons from the Dying," Sociologico de la Muerte, (1974), 15-24.

1968. _____. "Letter to a Nurse about Death," Nursing, 3 (Oct., 1973), np.

1969. _____. On Death and Dying. New York: Macmillan, 1969.

1970. _____. "On Death and Dying," Therapeutic Grand Rounds, No. 36. Journal of the American Medical Association, 221 (July 10, 1972), 174-9.

1971. _____. "On the Use of Psychopharmacologic Agents for the Dying Patient and the Bereaved," Journal of Thanatology, 2 (Winter-Spring, 1972), 563-6.

1972. _____. "Psychotherapy for the Dying Patient," Current Psychiatric Therapies, 10 (1970), 110-7.

1973. _____. Questions and Answers on Death and Dying. New York: Macmillan, 1974.

1974. _____. "The Right to Die with Dignity," Bulletin of the Menninger Foundation, 36 (May, 1972), np.

1975. _____. "A Teaching Approach to the Issues of Death and Dying," Archives of the Foundation of Thanatology, 2 (Fall, 1970), 125-7.

1976. _____. "What Is It Like to Be Dying," American Journal of Nursing, 71 (Jan., 1971), 54-61.

1977. _____, James Anderson. "Psychotherapy with the Least Expected," Rehabilitation Literature, 29 (Mar., 1968), 73-6.

1978. _____, ed. Death--The Final Stage of Growth. Englewood Cliffs: Prentice-Hall, 1975.

1979. Kuller, L. et al. "Sudden and Unexpected Deaths in Young Adults, An Epidemiological Study," Journal of the American Medical Association, 198 (Oct., 1966), 248-52.

1980. Kurtagh, C. "Willie's Drunk and Nellie's Dying: There Ain't Nobody Free," Nursing Forum, 11 (1972), 221-4.

1981. Kurtz, Benjamin. The Pursuit of Death: A Study of Shelley's Poetry. New York: Octagon, 1971.

1982. Lutner, Luis. "Due Process of Euthanasia the Living Will, A Proposal," Indiana Law Journal, 44 (1969), 539-54.

1983. _____. "Living Will: Coping with Historical Event of Death," Baylor Law Review, 27 (1975), 39-53.

1984. Kutscher, Austin H. Communicating Issues in Thanatology. New York: MSS Information Corp., 1975.

1985. _____. "The Foundation of Thantology," Mental Hygiene, 53 (July, 1969), 338-9.

1986. _____, et al. "Death, Grief and the Dental Practitioner: Thanatology as Related to Dentistry," Journal of the American Dental Association, 81 (Dec., 1970), 1373-7.

1987. _____, ed. But Not to Lose. New York: MSS Information, 1975.

1988. _____, ed. Death and Bereavement. Springfield: C.C. Thomas, 1969.

1989. _____, I.K. Goldberg, eds. Oral Care of the Aging and Dying Patient. Springfield: C.C. Thomas, 1973.

1990. _____, M.R. Goldberg, eds. Caring for the Dying Patient and his Family. New York: Health Sciences Publishing, 1973.

1991. _____, A.H. Kutscher, eds. A Bibliography of Books on Death, Bereavement, Loss and Grief Published Since 1935. New York: Health Sciences Publishing, 1970.

1992. _____, L.G. Kutscher, eds. For the Bereaved. New York: Frederick Fell, 1971.

1993. _____, eds. Religion and Bereavement. New York: Health Sciences Publishing, 1972.

1994. _____, et al., eds. Psychopharmacologic Agents in the Care of the Terminally Ill and the Bereaved. New York: Foundation of Thanatology, Columbia University Press, 1973.

1995. _____, eds. The Terminal Patient: Oral Care. New York: Columbia University Press, 1973.

1996. Kutscher, Lillian G., Bernard Schoenberg, eds. Bereavement: Its Psychosocial Aspects. New York: Columbia University Press, 1975.

1997. Kutscher, M.L. et al., eds. Bibliography of the Thanatology Literature. New York: MSS Information, 1975.

1998. Kyle, D. "Terminal Care," Journal of the Royal College of General Practitioners, 21 (July, 1971), 382-6.

1999. Kyle, M. Willa. "The Nurse's Approach to the Patient Attempting to Adjust to Inoperable Cancer," Nursing Research, 14 (Spring, 1965), 178-9.

2000. Labovitz, Sanford. "Control over Death: The Canadian Case," Omega, 4 (Fall, 1974), 217-21.

2001. Lacasse, Christine Mitchell. "A Dying Adolescent," American Journal of Nursing, 75 (Mar., 1975), 433-4.

2002. Lack, Sylvia, Richard Lamerton, eds. The Hour of Death. London: G. Chapman, 1974.

2003. LaDue, John S. "The Management of Terminal Patients with Inoperable Carcinoma," Journal of the Kansas Medical Society, 54 (Jan., 1953), 1-6.

2004. Lafitte, Francois. "Abortion in Britain Today," New Society, 22 (Dec. 14, 1972), 622-6.

2005. Laister, P. "Symposium: Care of the Dying: The Priest's Care of the Terminally Sick," Nursing Mirror, 139 (Oct. 10, 1974), 63-5.

2006. Lambert, E.T. et al. "Sudden Unexpected Death from Cardiovascular Disease in Children: A Cooperative International Study," American Journal of Cardiology, 34 (July, 1974), 189-96.

2007. Lamberto, Vitale. "Le Ultime Parole die Moribondi (The Last Words of the Dying)," Minerva Medica, 49 (Oct. 20, 1950), 256-67.

2008. Lamers, William M., Jr. "Funerals are Good for People--M.D.'s Included," Medical Economics, 46 (June 23, 1969), 104-7.

2009. Lamerton, Richard. Care of the Dying. London: Priory Press, 1973.

2010. _____. "Euthanasia," Nursing Times, 70 (Feb. 21, 1974), 260.

2011. _____. "The Need for Hospices," Nursing Times, 71 (Jan. 23, 1975), 155-7.

2012. _____. "Symposium: Care of the Dying: Ethical Questions in the Care of the Dying," Nursing Mirror, 139 (Oct. 10, 1974), 61-3.

2013. Lamm, Maurice. The Jewish Way in Death and Mourning. New York: Jonathan David, 1969.

2014. _____, Naftali Eskreis. "Viewing the Remains: A New American Custom," Journal of Religion and Health, 5 (1966), 137-43.

2015. Lamm, R.D., S. Davison. "Abortion and Euthanasia," Rocky Mountain Medical Journal, 68 (Fall, 1971), 40-2.

2016. Lamont, Corliss. A Humanist Funeral Service. New York: Horizon Press, 1954.

2017. _____, ed. Man Answers Death. New York: G.P. Putnam's Sons, 1936.

2018. Landsberg, P.L. The Experience of Death: The Moral Problem of Suicide. New York: Philosophical Library, 1953.

2019. Landy, M. "Language and Mourning in 'Lycidas'," American Imago, 30 (Fall, 1973), 294-312.

2020. Lane, W.W. Ritual and the Expression of Emotion in Public Worship. Dissertation Abstracts, 30 (Mar., 1970), 4011A-2A.

2021. Lang, Priscilla, Jeanette Oppenheimer. "The Influence of Social Work When Parents are Faced with the Fatal Illness of a Child," Social Casework, 49 (Mar., 1968), 161-6.

2022. Lange, J. Chris. "Modes of Dying," Pittsburgh Medical Reivew, 3 (1889), 27-34.

2023. Langer, Marion. Learning to Live as a Widow. New York: J. Messner, 1957.

2024. Langer, William I. "The Black Death," Scientific American, 210 (1964), 112-22.

2025. Langford, William S. "Anxiety in Children," American Journal of Orthopsychiatry, 7 (Apr., 1937), 210-8.

2026. _____. "The Child in the Pediatric Hospital: Adaptation to Illness and Hospitalization," American Journal of Orthopsychiatry, 31 (1961), 667-84.

2027. _____. "Psychologic Aspects of Pediatrics (Physical Illness and Convalesence: Their Meaning to the Child)," Journal of Pediatrics, 33 (Aug., 1938), 242-50.

2028. Langone, John. Death is a Noun. Boston: Little, Brown and Co., 1972.

2029. _____. Vital Signs. Boston: Little, Brown, and Co., 1974.

2030. Langsley, Donald G. "Psychology of a Doomed Family," American Journal of Psychotherapy, 15 (1961), 531-8.

2031. _____, et al. "A Family with a Hereditary Fatal Disease," Archives of General Psychiatry, 10 (1964), 647.

2032. Lant, A. "Euthanasia--A Patient's Point of View," Nursing Mirror, 140 (Feb. 6, 1975), 73.

2033. Lappe, Marc et al. "Refinements in Criteria for the Determination of Death: An Appraisal," Journal of the American Medical Association, 221 (July, 1972), 48-53.

2034. Larre, Claude. "La Vie et la Mort dans Tehouang Tseu (Life and Death in Chuang Tzu)," Ethno-Psychologie, 27 (Mar., 1972), 59-78.

2035. Larsen, K.S. et al. "Attitudes Toward Death: A Desensitization Hypothesis," Psychological Reports, 35 (Oct., 1974), 687-90.

2036. Lasagna, Louis. The Doctor's Dilemmas. New York: Harper, 1962.

2037. _____. Life, Death and the Doctor. New York: Knopf, 1968.

2038. Lascari, Andre D. "The Family and the Dying Child: A Compassionate Approach," Medical Times, 97 (May, 1969), 207-15.

2039. _____, James A. Stehbens. "The Reactions of Families to Childhood Leukemia," Clinical Pediatrics, 12 (Apr., 1973), 210-4.

2040. Lasch, C. "Birth, Death and Technology: The Limits of Cultural Laissez-Faire," Inquiry, 2 (June, 1972), 1-4.

2041. Lasker, Arnold A. "Telling Children the Facts of Death," Your Child, (Winter, 1972), 1-6.

2042. Lattes, Leone. "La Buona e la Male Morte (The Good and Bad Death)," Minerva Medica, 1 (Apr. 4, 1953), 847-54.

2043. Laufer, Moses. "Object Loss and Mourning During Adolescence," The Psychoanalytic Study of the Child, 21 (1966), 269-93.

2044. Laurence, G. "Reflexions Devant la Douleur et la Mort (Reflections Before Pain and Death)," Revue du Praticien, 10 (May 21, 1960), 157-8.

2045. Laurie, W. "Athletes' Deaths," British Medical Journal, 4 (Jan. 23, 1971), 233-4.

2046. Laws, E.H. et al. "Views on Euthanasia," Journal of Medical Education, 46 (June, 1971), 540-2.

2047. Lazarus, Herbert, John H. Kosten, Jr. "Psychogenic Hyperventilation and Death Anxiety," Psychosomatics, 10 (1969), 14-22.

2048. Lazarus, Richard S. Psychological Stress and the Coping Process. New York: McGraw-Hill, 1966.

2049. Leahy, M.P. Fear. London: Research Books, 1948.

2050. Leak, W.N. "The Care of the Dying," Practitioner, 161 (Aug., 1948), 80-7.

2051. _____. "Impending Dissolution," Practitioner, 155 (Sep., 1945), 170-5.

2052. Leake, C.D. "The Care of Dying Older Persons," Geriatrics, 22 (Sep., 1967), 91-2.

2053. Lebourdais, E. "The Hospital Inquest: Lessons in Death," Dimensions in Health Service, 51 (Feb., 1974), 12-7.

2054. Lebowitz, M.D. "Influence of Urbanization and Industrialization on Birth and Death Rates," Social Biology, 20 (Mar., 1973), 89-102.

2055. Leclaire, Serge. "La Mort dans la Vie de l'Obsede," Psychoanalyse, 2 (1956), 111-44.

2056. LeComte, E., ed. Dictionary of Last Words. New York: Philosophical Library, 1955.

2057. LeDantec, Felix. "Le Probleme de la Mort," Revue Philosophique, 81 (1916), 105-34.

2058. _____. Le Probleme de la Mort et la Conscience Universelle. Paris: Flammarion, 1917.

2059. Leddon, S.C. "Sleep Paralysis, Psychosis and Death," American Journal of Psychiatry, 126 (Jan., 1970), 1027-31.

2060. Lee, Reuel P. Burial Customs, Ancient and Modern. Minneapolis: The Arya Co., 1929.

2061. Leeds, Morton. "Poems (on Death)," Omega, 3 (Aug., 1972), 175-9.

2062. Lehner, Ernst. Devils, Demons, Death, and Damnation. New York: Dover, 1972.

2063. Lehrman, Samuel R. "Reactions to Untimely Death," Psychiatric Quarterly, 30 (1956), 564-78.

2064. Leibowitz, Sidney. "The Conduct of the Internist Toward the Patient and His Family When a Diagnosis of Malignancy is Established," New York Journal of Medicine, 11 (June 1, 1951), 1421-4.

2065. Lemoine, Jacques. "L'Initiation du Mort chez les Hmong, ii: Les Themes (The Initiation of the Dead among the Hmong, II: The Themes)," l'Homme, 12 (Apr.-June, 1972), 85-125. (July-Sep., 1972), 84-110.

2066. Leng, G.A. "The Problem of Death," Singapore Medical Journal, 10 (June, 1969), 71.

2067. Lennon, J.L. "The God Quad," Rhode Island Medical Journal, 57 (Aug., 1974), 334-7.

2068. Lenz, H. "Zur Bedeutung des Todesangsterlebnisses (Significance of the Experience of the Fear of Death)," Acta Neurovegetativa (Wein), 4 (1952), 534-42.

2069. Lepp, Ignace. Death and Its Mysteries. Translated by Bernard Murchland. New York: Macmillan, 1968.

2070. Lescoe, R.J. "Legislative Proposals for Death with Dignity," Journal of Legal Medicine, 3 (Sep., 1975), 34-5.

2071. LeShan, Lawrence. "Assumptions about War and the Nature of Man," Omega, 1 (Feb., 1970), 17-21.

2072. _____. "A Basic Psychological Orientation Apparently Associated with Malignant Disease," Psychiatric Quarterly, 36 (Apr., 1961), 314-330.

2073. _____. "Mobilizing the Life Force," Annals of the New York Academy of Sciences, 164 (Dec., 1969), 847-61.

2074. _____, E. LeShan. "Psychotherapy and the Patient with a Limited Life Span," Psychiatry, 24 (Nov., 1961), 318-23.

2075. _____, Martha Gassman. "Some Observations on Psychotherapy with Patients Suffering from Neoplastic Disease," American Journal of Psychotherapy, 12 (1958), 723-34.

2076. _____, R.E. Worthington. "Some Psyhchological Correlates of Neoplastic Disease: A Preliminary Report," Journal of Clinical and Experimental Psychopathology and the Quarterly Review of Psychiatric Neurology, 16 (1955), 281-88.

2077. Lessa, William A. "Death Customs and Rites," Collier's Encyclopedia, (1964), 7:757-65.

2078. Lessing, Gotthold Ephraim. Laokoon, and How the Ancients Represented Death, London: G. Bell and Sons, 1914.

2079. Lester, David. "Antecedents of the Fear of the Dead," Psychological Reports, 19 (Dec., 1966), 741-2.

2080. _____. "Attitudes Toward Death and Suicide in a Non-Disturbed Population," Psychological Reports, 29 (Oct., 1971), 368.

2081. _____. "Attitudes Toward Death Held by Staff of a Suicide Prevention Center," Psychological Reports, 28 (Apr., 1971), 650.

2082. _____. "Attitudes Toward Death Today and 35 Years Ago," Omega, 2 (Aug., 1971), 168-73.

2083. _____. "Checking on the Harlequin," Psychological Reports, 19 (Dec., 1966), 984ff.

2084. _____. "Experimental and Correlational Studies of the Fear of Death," Psychological Bulletin, 67 (Jan., 1967), 27-36.

2085. _____. "Fear of Death and Nightmare Experiences," Psychological Reports, 25 (1969), 437-8.

2086. _____. "Fear of Death in Primitive Societies," Behavioral Science Review, 10 (1975), 229-32.

2087. Lester, David. "Fear of Death of Suicidal Persons," Psychological Reports, 20 (1966), 1077.

2088. _____. "The Fear of Death of Those Who Have Nightmares," Journal of Psychology, 69 (July, 1968), 245-7.

2089. _____. "The Fear of the Dead in Non-Literate Societies," Journal of Social Psychology, 77 (Apr., 1969), 283-4.

2090. _____. "Fear of the Death in Nonliterate Societies," Journal of Social Psychology, 90 (Aug., 1973), 329-30.

2091. _____. "The Incidence of Suicide and Fear of the Dead in Non-Literate Societies," Journal of Cross-Cultural Psychology, 2 (June, 1971), 207-8.

2092. _____. "Inconsistency in the Fear of Death of Individuals," Psychological Reports, 20, Supplement (June, 1967), 1084.

2093. _____. "Mortality Rates and Aggression Management," Psychological Reports, 33 (Dec., 1973), 865-6.

2094. _____. "The Need to Achieve and the Fear of Death," Psychological Reports, 27 (Oct., 1970), 516.

2095. _____. "Relation of Fear of Death in Subjects to Fear of Death in their Parents," Psychological Record, 20 (Fall, 1970), 541-3.

2096. _____. "Religious Behavior and the Fear of Death," Omega, 1 (Aug., 1970), 189-200.

2097. _____. "Sex Differences in Attitudes Toward Death: A Replication," Psychological Reports, 28 (June, 1971), 754.

2098. _____. "Studies in Death Attitudes, 2," Psychological Reports, 30 (Apr., 1972), 440.

2099. _____. "Studies on Death-Attitude Scales," Psychological Reports, 24 (Feb., 1969), 182.

2100. _____. "Voodoo Death: Some New Thoughts on an Old Phenomenon," American Anthropologist, 74 (June, 1972), 386-90.

2101. _____, M. Alexander. "More Than One Execution: Who Goes First?" Journal of the American Medical Association, 217 (July 12, 1971), 215.

2102. _____, Elizabeth G. Kam. "Effect of a Friend Dying Upon Attitudes Toward Death," Journal of Social Psychology, 33 (Feb., 1971), 149-50.

2103. _____, D.I. Templer. "Resemblance of Parent-Child Death Anxiety as a Function of Age and Sex of Child," Psychological Reports, 31 (Dec., 1972), 750.

2104. Lester, David, et al. "Attitudes of Nursing Students and Nursing Faculty Toward Death," Nursing Research, (Jan.-Feb., 1974), 50-3.

2105. Lester, Gene, David Lester. "The Fear of Death, the Fear of Dying, and Threshold Differences for Death Words and Neutral Words," Omega, 1 (Aug., 1970), 175-9.

2106. Lester, J. "Voluntary Euthanasia," New England Journal of Medicine, 280 (1969), 1225.

2107. Letourneau, C.U. "Dying with Dignity," Hospital Management, 109 (June, 1970), 27-30.

2108. _____. "A Soliloquy on Death," Hospital Management, 96 (Nov., 1963), 58-60.

2109. Lettieri, Dan J., Michael S. Backenheimer. "Drug-Related Deaths: Theoretical and Methodological Issues," Proceedings of the 81st Annual Convention of the American Psychological Association, Montreal, Canada, 3 (1973), 405-6.

2110. _____, Alexis M. Nehemkis. "A Socio-Clinical Scale for Certifying Mode of Death," in A.T. Beck et al., eds., The Prediction of Suicide. Bowie, MD: Charles Press, 1974.

2111. Levenson, P. "On Sudden Death," Psychiatry, 35 (May, 1972), 160-73.

2112. Leventhal, Brigid G., Stephen Hersh. "Modern Treatment of Childhood Leukemia: The Patient and His Family," Children Today, 3 (May-June, 1974), 2-6.

2113. Leveton, Alan. "Time, Death and Ego-Chill," Journal of Existentialism, 6 (Fall, 1965), 69-80.

2114. Levin, A.J. "The Fiction of the Death Instinct," Psychiatric Quarterly, 25 (Apr., 1951), 257-81.

2115. Levin, Sidney. "The Concept and Phenomenology of Depression, with Special Reference to the Aged: Discussion," Journal of Geriatric Psychiatry, 7 (1974), 48-54.

2116. _____, Ralph Kanaha. Psychodynamic Studies of Aging. New York: International Universities Press, 1967.

2117. Levine, Gene N. "Anxiety about Illness: Psychological and Social Bases," Journal of Health and Human Behavior, 3 (1962), 30-4.

2118. Levine, Seymour. "Stress and Behavior," Scientific American, 224 (Jan., 1971), 26-31.

2119. Levinson, B.M. "The Pet and the Child's Bereavement," Mental Hygiene, 51 (Apr., 1967), 197-200.

2120. Levinson, Peritz. "On Sudden Death," Psychiatry, Washington, D.C., 35 (May, 1972), 160-73.

2121. Levisohn, Arthur. "Voluntary Mercy Deaths," Journal of Forensic Medicine, 8 (1961), np.

2122. Leviton, Dan. "A Course on Death Education and Suicide Prevention: Implications for Health Education," Journal of the American College Health Association, 19 (Apr., 1971), 217-20.

2123. _____. "Death Bereavement, and Suicide Education," in Donald A. Read, New Directions in Health Education. New York: Macmillan, 1971.

2124. _____. "Death Education," in W.R. Johnson, ed., Human Health in Action. New York: Holt, Rinehart & Winston, 1976.

2125. _____. "Education for Death," in H. Feifel, ed., New Meanings of Death. New York: McGraw-Hill, 1977.

2126. _____. "Education for Death, Or Death Becomes Less a Stranger," Omega, 6 (1975) 183-91.

2127. _____. "The Need for Education on Death and Suicide," Journal of School Health, 39 (Apr., 1969), 270-4.

2128. _____. "The Stimulus of Death," Health Education, (Mar.-Apr., 1976), 17.

2129. _____. "A Time to Die," Medical Journal of Australia, 1 (Jan., 1969), 127-8.

2130. _____, Eileen C. Forman. "Death Education for Children and Youth," Journal of Clinical Child Psychology, 3 (Summer, 1974), 8-10.

2131. _____, B. Fretz. "Life and Death Attitudes of Parents of Mildly Dysfunctional Children," Omega, 6 (1975), 161.

2132. Levy, N.B. "Self-Willed Death," Lancet, 2 (Sep. 1, 1973), 496.

2133. Lewak, N. "Sudden Infant Death Syndrome in a Hospitalitzed Infant on an Apnea Monitor," Pediatrics, 56 (Aug., 1975), 296-8.

2134. Lewin, R. "Truth Versus Illusion in Relation to Death," Psychoanalytic Review, 51 (Summer, 1964), 190-200.

2135. Lewis, C.S. A Grief Observed. Greenwich, CT: Seabury Press, 1961.

2136. Lewis, H.P. "Machine Medicine and Its Relation to the Fatally Ill," Journal of the American Medical Association, 206 (Oct. 7, 1968), 387-8.

2137. Lewis, Melvin. "The Management of Parents of Acutely Ill Children in the Hospital," American Journal of Orthopsychiatry, 32 (1962), 60-6.

2138. Lewis, Oscar. _A Death in the Sanchez Family_. New York: Random House, 1969.

2139. Lewis, Thomas H. "A Culturally Patterned Depression in a Mother After Loss of a Child," _Psychiatry_, 38 (Feb., 1975), 92-5.

2140. Lewis, W.R. "A Time to Die," _Nursing Forum_, 4 (1965), 7-26.

2141. Lex, Barbara W. "Voodoo Death: New Thoughts on an Old Explanation," _American Anthropologist_, 76 (Dec., 1974), 818-23.

2142. Lichtenwalner, Muriel E. "Children Ask about Death," _International Journal of Religious Education_, 40 (June, 1964), 14-6.

2143. Lieberman, E. James. "Statement on the Effects of U.S. Casualties in Vietnam on American Families," _Journal of Marriage and the Family_, 32 (May, 1970), 197-9.

2144. Lieberman, Morton A. "Observations on Death and Dying," _The Gerontologist_, 6 (June, 1966), 70-2ff.

2145. _____. "Psychological Correlates of Impending Death: Some Preliminary Observations," _Journal of Gerontology_, 20 (Apr., 1965), 181-90.

2146. _____. "Relationship of Mortality Rates to Entrance to a Home for the Aged," _Geriatrics_, 16 (1961), 515-9.

2147. _____, Annie S. Caplan. "Distance from Death as a Variable in the Study of Aging," _Developemtnal Psychology_, 2 (1970), 71-84.

2148. Liebman, Joshua Loth. _Peace of Mind_. New York: Simon and Schuster, 1946.

2149. Liebman, Samuel. _Stress Situations_. Philadelphia and Montreal: J.P. Lippincott, 1955.

2150. Lief, H.E., N.R. Lief, eds. _The Psychological Basis of Medical Practice_. New York: Hoeber Medical Division, Harper and Row, 1963.

2151. Liegner, L.M. "St. Christopher's Hospice, 1974: Care of Dying Patients," _Journal of the American Medical Association_, 234 (1975), 1047-8.

2152. Lifton, Channing T. "Denial and Mourning," _International Journal of Psychology_, 44 (1963), np.

2153. Lifton, Robert J. "'Death Imprints' on Youth in Vietnam," _Journal of Clinical Child Psychology_, 3 (Summer, 1974), 47-9.

2154. _____. Death in Life: _Survivors of Hiroshima_. New York: Random House, 1967.

2155. _____. _History and Human Survival_. New York: Random House, 1961.

2156. Lifton, Robert J. "On Death and Death Symbolism: The Hiroshima Disaster," Psychiatry, 3 (Aug., 1964), 191-210.

2157. _____. "On Death and the Continuity of Life: A 'New' Pradigm," History of Childhood Quarterly: The Journal of Psychohistory, 1 (Spring, 1974), 681-96.

2158. _____. "On Death and the Continuity of Life: A Psychohistorical Perspective," Omega, 6 (1975), 143-59.

2159. _____. "Psychological Effects of the Atomic Bomb in Hiroshima: The Theme of Death," Daedalus, 92 (1963), 462-97.

2160. _____. "The Sense of Immortality, On Death and the Continuity of Life," American Journal of Psychoanalysis, 33 (1973), 3-15.

2161. _____, Eric Olson. Living and Dying. New York: Bantam, 1975.

2162. Lim, L.E. et al. "Childhood Mortality in the Philippines," Journal of the Philippine Medical Association, 41 (1965), 304-12.

2163. Lindemann, Erich. "Grief," Encyclopedia of Mental Health, (1963), 2:703-6.

2164. _____. "The Medical-Psychological Dynamics of the Normal Individual," Pastoral Psychology, 7 (Mar., 1956), 47-56.

2165. _____. "Psychological Aspects of Mourning," The Director, 31 (1961), 14-7.

2166. _____. "Symptomatology and Management of Acute Grief," American Journal of Psychiatry, 101 (Sep., 1944), 141-8.

2167. _____, Ina May Greer. "A Study of Grief: Emotional Responses to Suicide," Pastoral Psychology, 4 (1953), 9-13.

2168. Lindner, Robert M. "The Equivalents of Matricide," Psychoanalytical Quarterly, 17 (1948), 453.

2169. Linman, A.G. "Concern for Dying Patients," American Journal of Hospital Pharmacy, 32 (1975), 368.

2170. Linn, Louis. "The Role of Perception in the Mechanism of Denial," Journal of the American Psychoanalytic Association, 1 (1953), 690-705.

2171. _____, Leo W. Schwarz. Psychiatry and Religious Experience. New York: Random House, 1958.

2172. Linser, Hans. Tod und Unsterblichkeit (Death and Immortality). Paris: Universitas, 1951.

2173. Lipman, A.G. "Drug Therapy in Terminally Ill Patients," American Journal of Hospital Pharmacy, 32 (Mar., 1975), 270-6.

2174. _____. "Editorial: Concern for Dying Patients," American Journal of Hospital Pharmacy, 32 (Apr., 1975), 368.

2175. _____, P. Marden. "Preparation for Death in Old Age," Journal of Gerontology, 21 (July, 1966), 426-31.

2176. Lipowski, A.J. "Psychosocial Aspects of Disease," Annals of Internal Medicine, 71 (1969), 1197-1206.

2177. Lipsett, D.R. et al. "On Death and Dying: Discussion," Journal of Geriatric Psychiatry, 7 (1974), 108-20.

2178. Lipson, Channing T. "Denial and Mourning," International Journal of Psychoanalysis, 44 (1963), 104-7.

2179. Lirette, W.L. "Management of Patients with Terminal Cancer," Postgraduate Medicine, 46 (Dec., 1969), 145-9.

2180. Liston, Edward H. "Education on Death and Dying: A Neglected Area in the Medical Curriculum," Omega, 6 (1975), 193-8.

2181. _____. "Education on Death and Dying: A Survey of American Medical Schools," Journal of Medical Education, 48 (June, 1973), 577-8.

2182. _____. "Psychiatric Aspects of Life-Threatening Illness: A Course for Medical Students," International Journal of Psychiatry in Medicine, 5 (Winter, 1974), 51-6.

2183. Litin, Edward M. "Should the Cancer Patient Be Told?" Postgraduate Medicine, 28 (Nov., 1960), 470-5.

2184. _____, et al. "Symposium: What Shall We Tell the Cancer Patient?" Proceedings of the Staff Meetings of the Mayo Clinic, 35 (May 11, 1960), 239-57.

2185. Litman, R.E. "Psychological-Psychiatric Aspects in Certifying Modes of Death," Journal of Forensic Sciences, 13 (Jan., 1968), 46-54.

2186. Little, J.C. "Psychiatrists' Attitudes to Abortion," British Medical Journal, 1 (Jan 8, 1972), 110.

2187. Livingston, Peter B., Carl N. Zimet. "Death Anxiety, Authoritarianism and Choice of Specialty in Medical Students," Journal of Nervous and Mental Disease, 140 (Mar., 1965), 222-30.

2188. Loesser, Lewis H., Thea Bry. "The Role of Death Fears in the Etiology of Phobic Anxiety as Reversal in Group Psychotherapy," International Journal of Group Psychotherapy, 10 (July, 1960), 287-97.

2189. Lofland, L.H. "Toward a Sociology of Death and Dying," Urban Life, 4 (1975), 243-9.

2190. Loether, Herman J. Problems of Aging. Encino, CA: Dickenson Publishing, 1975.

2191. Lohman, Keith D. "The Student Mortician: A Study of Occupational Sociali- zation," Colorado Journal of Education Research, 9 (Summer, 1970), 45-50.

2192. Loisy, Alfred. Mort et Vita. Paris: Nourry, 1916.

2193. Lonetto, Richard et al. "The Psychology of Death: A Course Description and Some Student Perceptions," Ontario Psychologist, 7 (June, 1975), 9-14.

2194. Long, Perrin H. "On the Quantity and Quality of Life," Resident Physician, 6 (Apr., 1960), 69-70.

2195. Longmore, D.B., M. Rehahn. "The Cumulative Cost of Death," Lancet, 1 (May 3, 1975), 1023-5.

2196. Lopata, Helena Z. "Grief Work and Identity Reconstruction," Journal of Geriatric Psychology, 8 (1975), 41-55.

2197. _____. "Living Arrangements of American Urban Widows," Sociological Focus, 5 (1971), 41-61.

2198. _____. "Loneliness: Forms and Components," Social Problems, 17 (1969), 248-62.

2199. _____. "The Social Involvement of American Widows," American Behavioral Scientist, 14 (1970), 41-58.

2200. _____. "Social Relations of Widows in Urbanizing Societies," Sociological Quarterly, 13 (1972), 259-71.

2201. _____. Widowhood in an American City. Morristown NJ: General Learning Corporation, 1972.

2202. _____. "Widows as a Minority Group," Gerontologist, 11 (Supplement), (Spring, 1971), 67-77.

2203. Lourie, Reginald S. "Panel Discussion: What to Tell the Parents of a Child With Cancer," Clinical Proceedings of the Children's Hospital (Washington), 17 (Apr., 1961), 91-9.

2204. _____. "The Pediatrician and the Handling of Terminal Illness," Pediatrics, 32 (Oct., 1963), 477-9.

2205. Love, Elizabeth. "Do All Hands Help Ease the Sting of Death by Tact and Kindliness," Hospitals, 18 (Dec., 1944), 47-8.

2206. Loveland, Glen G. "The Effects of Bereavement on Certain Religious Attitudes and Behavior," Sociological Symposium, 1 (Fall, 1968), 17-27.

2207. Lowe, George D., H. Eugene Hodges. "Deaths Associated with Alcohol in George," Quarterly Journal of Statistics on Alcohol, 25 (Mar., 1974), 215-20.

2208. Lowenberg, J.S. "The Coping Behaviors of Fatally Ill Adolescents and Their Parents," Nursing Forum, 9 (1970), 269-87.

2209. Lowenthal, Marjorie Fiske. "Social Isolation and Mental Illness in Old Age," American Sociological Review, 29 (1964), 54-70.

2210. Lowrey, J.J. "Changing Concepts of Death," Hawaii Medical Journal, 30 (July-Aug., 1971), 251-7.

2211. Lowry, Richard J. "Male-Female Differences in Attitudes Toward Death," Dissertation Abstracts, 27 (Nov., 1966), 1607B-8B

2212. Lube, Friedrich. "Vom 'Sterbestubchen in Krankenhausern' und vom Tode Uberhaupt (About the Dying Room in Hospitals)," Muchener Medizinische Wochenschrift, 83 (June 19, 1936), 1019-20.

2213. Lucas, Rex A. "Social Implications of the Immediacy of Death," Canadian Review of Sociology and Anthropology, 5 (Feb., 1968), 1-16.

2214. Lucente, Frank E. "The Dying Patient in Orolaryngology," Laryngoscope, 83 Feb. 24, 1973), 292-8.

2215. _____. "Thanatology: A Study of 100 Deaths on an Otolaryngology Service," Omega, 3 (Aug., 1972), 211-6.

2216. Luchi, R.J. "Diagnosis of Cerebral Death," Journal of the Iowa Medical Society, 61 (May, 1971), 281-84.

2217. Luchina, Isaac, S. Aizemberg. "Una Aguda Amenaza de Merte: 'El Infarto do Miocardio' (An Acute Threat of Death: 'The Myocardic Infarct')," Revista de Psicoanalisis, 19 (Jan.-June, 1962), 103-6.

2218. Ludwik, Krzywicki. Primitive Society and Its Vital Statistic. London: Macmillan, 1934.

2219. Luke, J.L. "Certification of Death by Coroner," New England Journal of Medicine, 280 (June 12, 1969), 1364.

2220. Lund, Charles. "The Doctor, the Patient, and the Truth," Annals of Internal Medicine, 24 (June, 1946), 955-9.

2221. Lund, Doris. Eric. Philadelphia: J.B. Lippincott, 1974.

2222. _____, M. Leming. "Fear of Death Among Cancer Patients," Gerontology, 15 (1975), 72.

2223. Lunt, Lawrence. "Attitudes in Relation to Illness," New England Journal of Medicine, 219 (Oct. 13, 1938), 557-61.

2224. Luntz, A.M. "Uber die Evolution des Todes im Zusammenhand mit der Evolution der Vermehrung," Zhurnal Obschel Biologii (Moskva), 22 (Mar.-Apr., 1961), 95-9.

2225. Luria, S.M. "Average Age at Death of Scientists in Various Specialties," Public Health Reports, 84 (1969), 661-4.

2226. Lutticken, C.A. et al. "Attitudes of Physical Therapists Toward Death and Terminal Illness," Physical Therapy, 54 (Mar., 1974), 226-32.

2227. Luyten, S., K. Barth. Unsterblichkeit (Immortality). Basel: Reinhardt, 1957.

2228. Lyman, Margaret, Joseph Burchenal. "Acute Leukemia," American Journal of Nursing, 63 (Apr., 1963), 82-6.

2229. Lynch, James J., Aaron H. Katcher. "Human Handling and Sudden Death in Laboratory Rats," Journal of Nervous and Mental Disease, 159 (Nov., 1974), 362-5.

2230. Lyons, Catherine. Organ Transplants: The Moral Issues. Philadelphia: The Westminister Press, 1970.

2231. Lyons, Kristin. "Death and the Student Nurse," Tomorrow's Nurse, 4 (Oct.-Nov., 1963), 21-2.

2232. Lyster, William R. "The Altered Seasons of Death in America," Journal of Biosocial Science, 4 (Apr., 1972), 145-51.

2233. Mabuchi, K. N. Maruchi. "The Major Causes of Death in the United States and Japan," Preventive Medicine, 1 (Mar., 1972), 252-4.

2234. McAulay, J.D. "What Understandings Do Second Grade Children Have of Time Relationships?" Journal of Educational Research, 54 (Apr., 1961), 312-4.

2235. McCann, J.C. "Differential Mortality and the Formation of Political Elites-- The Case of the U.S. House of Representatives," American Sociological Review, 37 (Nov., 1972), 689-700.

2236. Mac Carthy, D. "The Repercussions of the Death of a Child," Proceedings of the Royal Society of Medicine, 62 (June, 1969), 553-4.

2237. McCleave, Paul B. "Medicine Seeks the Clergy," Journal of Religion and Health, 2 (Apr., 1963), 239-47.

2238. McClelland, Charles Q. "Relationship of the Physician in Practice to a Children's Cancer Clinic," Pediatrics, (Supplement), 40 (Sep., 1967), 537-9.

2239. McClure, Catherine T. "Guest in the House," American Journal of Nursing, 49 (Dec., 1949), 775-7.

2240. McConville, Brian J. "The Effects of Bereavement on the Child," in A.R. Roberts, ed. Childhood Deprivation. Springfield: C.C. Thomas, 1974.

2241. _____, et al. "Mourning Depressive Responses of Children in Residence Following Sudden Death of Parent," Journal of the American Academy of Child Psychiatry, 11 (Apr., 1972), 361-4.

2242. _____, et al. "Mourning Processes in Children of Varying Ages," Canadian Psychiatric Association Journal, 15 (June, 1970), 252-5.

2243. McCoy, Marjorie C. To Die with Style. Nashville: Abingdon, 1974.

2244. McCracken, Samuel. "The Population Controllers," Commentary, (May, 1972), 45-52.

2245. McCully, Robert S. "Fantasy Productions of Children with a Progressively Crippling and Fatal Illness," The Journal of Genetic Psychology, 102 (June, 1963), 203-16.

2246. MacDonald, Arthur. "Death-Psychology of Historical Personages," American Journal of Psychology, 32 (1921), 552-6.

2247. _____. "Human Death: An Analytical Study," Medical Times, 56 (Aug., 1928), 206-16; 56 (Sep., 1928), 232-41.

2248. _____. "Systematic and Scientific Study of Death in Man," American Journal of Psychology, 38 (1927), 153.

2249. McDonald, Morris J. Farewell to a Friend," American Journal of Nursing, 68 (Apr., 1968), 773.

2250. _____. "The Management of Grief: A Study of Black Funeral Practices," Omega, 4 (1973), 139-48.

2251. McGann, Leona M. "The Cancer Patient's Needs: How Can We Meet Them?" Journal of Rehabilitation, 30 (Nov.-Dec., 1964), 19.

2252. McGrath, Mary J. "The Care of the Patient in Terminal Illness," Canadian Nurse, 57 (June, 1961), 556-71.

2253. McInerny, T.K. et al. "Sudden Unexpected Death," American Journal of Diseases of Children, 120 (Aug., 1970), 167.

2254. McIntyre, Ray. "Voluntary Euthanasia: The Ultimate Perversion," Medical Counterpoint, (June, 1970), 26-9.

2255. Macintyre, S.J. "The Medical Profession and the 1967 Abortion Act in Britain," Social Science and Medicine, 7 (Feb., 1973), 121-34.

2256. Mack, Arien, ed. Death in American Experience. New York: Schocken, 1973.

2257. McKain, W.C. et al. "Effect of Motor Accidents and Other Causes of Death on Work-Life Expectancy in Connecticut," Public Health Report, 79 (1964), 85-6.

2258. MacKenna, Robert W. The Adventure of Death. New York: Putnam, 1917.

2259. MacKinnon, B.L. "Death and the Doctor," Journal of the Maine Medical Association, 63 (Aug., 1972), 169-71.

2260. Mackintosh, H.D. "Sudden Death: A Therapeutic Challenge," Indian Heart Journal, 26 (Supplement), np.

2261. McLaren, H.C. "Abortion Deaths," British Medical Journal, 3 (Sep. 30, 1972),

2262. MacLaurin, Harriet. "In the Hour of Their Going Forth," Social Casework, 40 (Mar., 1959), 136-41.

2263. Maclennan, B.W. "Non-Medical Care of Chronically Ill Children in the Hospital," Lancet, 2 (July 20, 1949), 209-10.

2264. McLure, John W. "Death Education," Phi Delta Kappan, 55 (Mar., 1974), 483-5.

2265. McMahon, J.D. "Death Education--An Independent Study Unit," Journal of School Health, 43 (Oct., 1973), 526-7.

2266. MacMillan, S. "Margaret: A Study in Perception," Nursing Times, 68 (Dec. 28, 1972), 1644-6.

2267. McMurrer, J., F. Clark, Jr. "Psychiatric Intervention in the Case of a
       Terminally Ill College Student," Journal of the American College Health
       Association, 22 (Dec., 1973), 134-7.

2268. MacNamara, Margaret. "Psychosocial Problems in a Renal Unit," British Journal
       of Psychiatry, 113 (1967), 1231-1326.

2269. McNeil, D. "A Death at Home," Canadian Nurse, (Mar., 1974), 17-9.

2270. McNulty, Barbara J. "Care of the Dying," Nursing Times, (Nov. 30, 1972),
       1505-6.

2271. _____. "Continuity of Care," British Medical Journal, 1 (Jan. 6, 1973),
       38-9.

2272. _____. "Discharge of the Terminally Ill Patient," Nursing Times, 66
       (Sep., 1970), 1160-3.

2273. _____. "St. Christopher's Outpatients," American Journal of Nursing,
       71 (Dec., 1971), 2328-30.

2274. _____. "Symposium: Care of the Dying: The Nurse's Contribution in Terminal
       Care," Nursing Mirror, 139 (Oct. 10, 1974), 59-61.

2275. McReacy, L.L. "Warning the Dying of Their Danger," in "Questions and Answers,"
       Clergy Review, 44 (May, 1959), 295-7.

2276. McWeeny, P.M., J.L. Emery. "Unexpected Postneonatal Deaths (Cot Deaths)
       Due to Recognizable Disease," Archives of Disease in Childhood, 50 (Mar.,
       1975), 191-6.

2277. Maddison, D. "The Consequences of Conjugal Bereavement," Nursing Times,
       65 (Jan. 9, 1969), 50-2.

2278. _____. "The Factors Affecting the Outcome of Conjugal Bereavement,"
       British Journal of Psychiatry, 113 (Oct., 1967), 1057-67.

2279. _____. "The Nurse and the Dying Patient," Nursing Times, 65 (Feb. 27,
       1969), 265-6.

2280. _____. "The Relevance of Conjugal Bereavement for Preventive Psychiatry,"
       British Journal of Medical Psychology, 41 (Sep., 1968), 223-33.

2281. _____, A. Viola. "The Health of Widows in the Year Following Bereavement,"
       Journal of Psychosomatic Research, 12 (Dec., 1968), 297-306.

2282. Madow, L., S.E. Hardy. "Incidence and Analysis of the Broken Family in the
       Background of Neurosis," American Journal of Orthopsychiatry, 17 (1946),
       521-8.

2283. Maeterlinck, Maurice. Before the Great Silence. Translated by Bernard Miall. London: Allen and Unwin, 1935.

2284. _____. Death. Translated by A. Teixeria de Mattos. New York: Dodd, Mead, and Co., 1912.

2285. _____. Our Eternity (Extension of Essay on Death). London: Methuen, 1913.

2286. Magni, Klas. "Reactions to Death Stimuli among Theology Students," Journal for the Scientific Study of Religion, 9 (Fall, 1970), 247-8.

2287. Maguire, Daniel C. Death by Choice. New York: Schocken Books, 1975.

2288. Mahler, Margaret S. "Helping Children to Accept Death," Child Study, 27 (1950), 98-9.

2289. _____. "On Sadness and Grief in Infancy and Childhood: Loss and Restoration of the Symbiotic Love Object," The Psychoanalytic Study of the Child, 16 (1960), 332-51.

2290. Mahoney, J. et al. "Anticipation of Death by Violence: Psychological Profile," Suicide, 5 (1975), 86-92.

2291. Maier, C. "SIDS: Death Without Apparent Cause," Life-Threatening Behavior, 3 (Winter, 1973), 298-304.

2292. Maingay, H.C. "Cremation Regulation," British Medical Journal, 3 (Sep., 1971), 770-1.

2293. Makarenko, N.V. "Higher Nervous Activity in Dogs Reanimated after Long Periods of Clinical Death from Drowning and Loss of Blood," Zhurnal Vysshei Nervnoi Deyatel'nosti, 22 (Jan., 1972), 82-8.

2294. Maley, Roger F. "Comments on Conceptual Disasters about Disasters," Omega, 5 (1974), 73-5.

2295. Malino, Jerome R. "Coping with Death in Western Religious Civilization," Zygon: Journal of Religion and Science, 1 (Dec., 1966), 354-65.

2296. Malinowski, Bronislaw. "Baloma: The Spirits of the Dead in the Trobriand Islands," Journal of the Royal Anthropological Institute of Great Britian and Ireland, 46 (1916), 353-430.

2297. _____. "Death and the Reintegration of the Group," in Magic, Science, and Religion. New York: Doubleday, 1954.

2298. Malmquist, Carl P. "Depression and Object Loss in Acute Psychiatric Admissions," American Journal of Psychiatry, 126 (June, 1970), 124-9.

2299. _____. "Depressions in Childhood and Adolescence, Part I," The New England Journal of Medicine, 284 (Apr. 22, 1971), 887-93.

2300. Manabe, H. et al. "Determination of Death of the Heart Donor," Naika, 23 (May, 1969), 854-60.

2301. Manchester, William. The Death of a President. New York: Harper and Row, 1967.

2302. Mandelbaum, David G. "Form, Variation and Meaning of a Ceremony," in Robert Spencer, ed., Method and Perspective in Anthropology: Papers in Honor of Wilson D. Wallis. Minneapolis: University of Minnesota Press, 1954.

2303. Mann, Sylvia A. "Coping with a Child's Fatal Illness," Nursing Clinics of North America, 9 (Mar., 1974), 81-7.

2304. Mannes, Myra. Last Rights. New York: Signet/New American Library, 1975.

2305. Manning, John. "Soviet Funeral Service," The American Funeral Director, 89 (1966), 30.

2306. Mansson, Helge Hilding. "Justifying the Final Solution," Omega, 3 (May, 1972), 79-87.

2307. Mant, A.K. "Sudden and Unexpected Death," Practitioner, 209 (Sep., 1972), 273-8.

2308. Manya, Joan B. La Vida que Pasa. Barcelona: Editorial Atlantide, 1955.

2309. Marberg, Hilde M., Elisheva Susz. "Development of a Kibbutz Girl Who Lost Her Father at the Age of Two Years," ACTA Paedopsychiatrics, 39 (1972), 59-66.

2310. Marchbanks, John B. Your Little One is in Heaven. 2d ed. Neptune, NJ: Loizeax, 1967.

2311. Marcovitz, Eli. "Man in Search of Meaning: Man Looks at Death," Delaware Medical Journal, 44 (Feb., 1972), 38-43.

2312. _____. "Man in Search of Meaning: Hallucinogenic Agents," Delaware Medical Journal, 44 (Mar., 1972), 72-4.

2313. _____. "What is the Meaning of Death to the Dying Person and his Survivors?" Omega, 4 (1973), 13-25.

2314. Marcus, John T. "Death--Consciousness and Civilization," Social Research, 61 (Autumn, 1964), 265-79.

2315. Marek, Z. et al. "The Social and Medico-Legal Aspects of Sudden Death in Children under Three Years of Age," Przeglad Lekarsk, 22 (1966), 593-6.

2316. Margolis, Otto S., ed. Grief and the Meaning of the Funeral. New York: MSS Information, 1975.

2317. Marks, Elaine. Simone de Beauvoir: Encounters with Death. New Brunswick, NJ: Rutgers University Press, 1973.

2318. Markusen, Eric, Robert Fulton. "Childhood Bereavement and Behavioral Disorders: A Critical Review," Omega, 2 (May, 1971), 107-17.

2319. Marmor, Judd. "What Shall We Tell the Cancer Patient," Bulletin of the Los Angeles County Medical Association, 84 (Nov., 1954), 1324ff.

2320. Marriott, Cindy, Dwight Harshbarger. The Hollow Holiday: Christmas, a Time of Death in Appalachia. Rockville, MD: Health Services and Mental Health Administration, Bureau of Community Environmental Management, 1973.

2321. Marris, Peter. Loss and Change. New York: Pantheon Books, 1974.

2322. _____. Widows and Their Families. London: Routledge and Kegan Paul, 1958.

2323. Marshall, A. "Sudden Cot Death Syndrome in Part Melbourne," Medical Journal of Australia, 1 (May 12, 1973), 959.

2324. Marshall, C.E., S.D. Shappell. "Sudden Death and the Ballooning Posterior Leaflet Syndrome: Detailed Anatomic and Histochemical Investigation," Archives of Pathology, 98 (Aug., 1974), 134-9.

2325. Marshall, J.R. "The Geriatric Patient's Fears about Death," Postgraduate Medicine, 57 (Apr., 1975), 144, 147-9.

2326. Marshall, Joanne, Victor Marshall. "The Treatment of Death in Children's Books," Omega, 2 (Feb., 1971), 36-45.

2327. Marshall, John et al. "The Doctor, the Dying Patient and the Bereaved," Annals of Internal Medicine, 70 (Mar., 1969), 615-21.

2328. Marshall, T.K. "Epidemiology of Cot Death: The Northern Ireland Study," Journal of the Forensic Science Society, 12 (Oct., 1972), 575-80;

2329. Marshall, Victor W. "Age and Awareness of Finitude in Developmental Gerontology," Omega, 6 (1975), 113-29.

2330. _____. "Game-Analyzable Dilemmas in a Retirement Village: A Case Study," Aging and Human Development, 4 (Fall, 1973), np.

2331. _____. "The Last Strand: Remnants of Engagment in the Later Years," Omega, 5 (1974), 25-35.

2332. _____. "Socialization for Impending Death in a Retirement Village," American Journal of Sociology, 80 (Mar., 1975), 1124-44.

2333. Martin David. "Existential Approach to Death," Journal of Thanatology, 3 (1975), 105-11.

2334. Martin, David S. "The Role of the Surgeon in the Prospect of Death from Cancer," Cancer Journal for Clinicians, 18 (Sep.-Oct., 1968), 264-7.

2335. _____, Lawrence Wrightsman, "Religion and Fears about Death: A Critical Review of Research," Religious Education, 59 (1964), 174-6.

2336. _____, et al. "The Relationship Between Religious Behavior and Concern about Death," Journal of Social Psychology, 65 (Apr., 1965), 317-23.

2337. Martin, Douglas. "An Existential Approach to Death," Journal of Thanatology, 3 (1975), 105-11.

2338. Martin, Edward. Psychology of Funeral Service. Grand Junction, CO: Sentinel Printers, 1950

2339. Martin, G.M. "Brief Proposal on Immortality: An Interim Solution," Perspectives in Biology and Medicine, 14 (Winter, 1971), 339-40.

2340. Martin, H.L. et al. "The Family of the Fatally Burned Child," Lancet, 2 (Sep. 14, 1968), 628-9.

2341. Margin, L.B., P.A. Collier. "Attitudes Toward Death: A Survey of Nursing Students," Journal of Nursing Education, 14 (Jan., 1975), 28-35.

2342. Martin-Achard, Robert. From Death to Life. Translated by J.P. Smith. Edinburgh: Oliver and Boyd, 1960.

2343. Martinez, N. "Death in Collective Project," Archives of Social Science and Religion, 20 (1975), 159-67.

2344. Martinso, I.M. et al. "Home Care for Dying Child," Pediatric Research, 9 (1975), 389.

2345. Martinson, Ida M. "The Dying Patient Needs Us--Can We Respond to the Challenge?" Cadence, 6 (Jan.-Feb., 1975), 36-9.

2346. _____, et al. Eric. Minneapolis: University of Minnesota, 1973.

2347. Marvin, Frederic Rowland. The Last Words of Distinguished Men and Women. Troy, NY: C.A. Brewster, 1900.

2348. Marx, P. "Death Peddler: War on Unborn," America, 126 (Mar. 19, 1972), 242.

2349. Maslow, A. "The Need to Know and the Fear of Knowing," Journal of Genetic Psychology, 68 (1963), 111-25.

2350. Mason, J.K. et al. "Miltiple Disinterments in Equatorial Africa," Aerospace Medicine, 36 (1965), 636-9.

2351. Masserman, Jules H. "Emotional Reactions to Death and Suicide," American Practitioner and Digest of Treatment, 5 (Nov., 1954), 41-6.

2352. Mastin, B.A. "The Extended Burials at the Mugharet Elwad," Journal of the Royal Anthropological Institute of Great Britain and Ireland, 94 (Jan.-June, 1964), 44-51.

2353. Masuda, M., T.H. Holmes. "Magnitude Estimates of Social Readjustments," Journal of Psychosomatic Research, 11 (Aug., 1967), 219-55.

2354. Matchett, W.F. "Reported Hallucinatory Experiences as a Part of the Mourning Process among Hopi Indian Women," Psychiatry, 35 (May, 1972), 185-94.

2355. Mathieu, Vittorio. "Meditazione sulla Provvidenza: Il Male e la Morte (Meditations on Providence: Evil and Death)," Rivista di Sociologia 11 (Jan.-Dec., 1973), 7-12.

2356. Mathis, James L. "A Sophisticated Version of Voodoo Death," Psychosomatic Medicine, 26 (1964), 104.

2357. Mathison, Jean. "A Cross-Cultural View of Widowhood," Omega, 1 (Aug., 1970), 201-18.

2358. Matse, Jan. "Reactions to Death in Residential Homes for the Aged," Omega, 6 (1975), 21-32.

2359. _____, et al. Bereavement. London: Butterworth Press, 1971.

2360. Matsukura, T. et al. "Symposium: Discussion on the Problems of the Determination of Death," Japanese Journal of Legal Medicine, 23 (July, 1969), 365-9.

2361. Matz, Milton. "Judaism and Bereavement," Journal of Religion and Health, 3 (1964), 345-52.

2362. Maudsley, Henry. "Love of Life," American Journal of Insanity, 18 (Oct., 1861), 138-62.

2363. Maurer, Adah. "Adolescent Attitudes toward Death," Journal of Genetic Psychology, 105 (1964), 75-90.

2364. _____. "The Child's Knowledge of Non-Existence," Journal of Existential Psychiatry, 2 (1961), 193-212.

2365. _____. "Death, Women and History," Omega, 6 (1975), 131-42.

2366. _____. "Fear of Death," Bulletin of the Society for Study of Human Existence, 2 (Feb., 1964), 1-4.

2367. _____. "The Game of Peek-a-Boo," Disease of the Nervous System, 28 (1967), 118-21.

2368. _____. "Intimations of Mortality," Journal of Clinical Child Psychology, 3 (Summer, 1974), 14-7.

2369. Maurer, Adah. "Maturation of Concepts of Death," British Journal of Medical Psychology, 39 (Mar., 1966), 35-41.

2370. _____. "On Bugental's Critique of Koestenbaum's 'The Vitality of Death'," Journal of Existentialism, 6 (Winter, 1965-6), 223-4.

2371. Mauriac, Pierre. "Mourrir en Paix," Presse Medicale, 61 (Oct. 31, 1953), 1413.

2372. Maus, Marcel. "Effect Physique sur L'Individu de L'Idee de Mort Suggeree par la Collectivite," Journal de Psychologie, (1926), 653-69.

2373. Maxwell, I. "When to Turn off the Respirator," Nova Scotia Medical Bulletin, 47 (Dec., 1968), 225-6.

2374. Maxwell, Sister Marie Bernadette. "A Terminally Ill Adolescent and Her Family," American Journal of Nursing, 72 (May, 1962), 925-7.

2375. May, Rollo. "The Daemonic: Love and Death," Psychology Today, 1 (Feb., 1968), 16-25.

2376. _____. The Meaning of Anxiety. New York: Ronald Press, 1950.

2377. _____, ed. Existential Psychology. New York: Random House, 1961.

2378. May, William F. "Attitudes Toward the Newly Dead," The Hastings Center Studies, 1 (1973), 3-14.

2379. _____. "On Not Facing Death Alone: The Trauma of Dying Need Not Mean the Eclipse of the Human," Hastings Center Reports, 9 (June, 1971), 6-7.

2380. _____. "The Sacral Power of Death in Contemporary Experience," Social Research, 39 (Autumn, 1972), 463-88.

2381. Mayer, Milton. "The Theory and Practice of Death," in If Men Were Angels. New York: Atheneum Press, 1972.

2382. Mazlish, B., P. Aries. "Western Attitudes Toward Death--From Middle Ages to Present," Journal of Interdisciplinary History, 5 (1975), 751-2.

2383. Mead, J.M. "It Comes to Us All," Nursing Mirror, 132 (Jan. 29, 1971), 40.

2384. Mead, Margaret. "The Immortality of Man," in Simon Doniger, ed., The Nature of Man. New York: Harper and Row, 1962.

2385. _____. "The Right to Die," Nursing Outlook, 16 (Oct., 1968), 20-1.

2386. Means, Marie Hackl. "Fears of One Thousand College Women," Journal of Abnormal and Social Psychology, 31 (1936), 291-311.

2387. Meerloo, Joost. _Patterns of Panic_. New York: International Universities Press, 1950.

2388. _____. "Psychological Implications of Malignant Growth," _British Journal of Medical Psychology_, 27 (1954), 210-5.

2389. Mehl, Roger. "Evolution of Image of Death in Contemporary Society and Religious Discourse of Church: Reports on 4th Colloquium of Center for Sociology of Protestantism of University of Human Sciences in Strasbourg, Oct. 3-5, 1974," _Archives of Social Science and Religion_, 20 (1975), 3-5.

2390. _____. _Le Vieillissement et La Mort_. Paris: Presses Universitaires de France, 1956.

2391. Meier, Carolyn A. "Sudden Infant Death Syndrome: Death Without Apparent Cause," _Life-Threatening Behavior_, 3 (Winter, 1973), 289-304.

2392. Meisel, A.M. et al. "Reactions to Approaching Death," _Diseases of the Nervous System_, 26 (Jan., 1965), 15-24.

2393. Meiss, M. "The Oedipal Problem of a Fatherless Child," _The Psychoanalytic Study of the Child_, 7 (1952), 216-29.

2394. Meissner, W.W. "Affective Response to Psychoanalytic Death Symbols," _Journal of Abnormal and Social Psychology_, 56 (1958), 295-99.

2395. Melcher, Achim. "Der Tod als Thema der Neuren Medizinischen Literatur," _Jahrbuch fur Psychologie und Psychotherapie_, 3 (1955), 371-83.

2396. Melear, John D. "Children's Conception of Death," _Journal of Genetic Psychology_, 123 (Dec., 1973), 359-60.

2397. Melton, J., III et al. "Sudden and Unexpected Deaths in Infancy," _Virginia Medical Monthly_, 95 (1968), 63-70.

2398. Menaldino, R. "The Cemeteries of Turin from the Hygienico-Sanitary Point of View," _Minerva Medica_, 56 (1965), 907-9.

2399. Mengert, William F. "Terminal Care," _Illinois Medical Journal_, 112 (Sep., 1957), 99-104.

2400. Mennes, Marya. _Last Rights: A Case for the Good Death_. New York: William Morrow and Co., 1974.

2401. Mennichs, J.M. "Death of Man or Development of Taboo," _Gedrag T P_, 3 (1975), 115-34.

2402. Menninger, Karl. "Dr. Karl's Reading Notes," _Menninger Library Journal_, 1 (1956), 15.

2403. Menninger, Karl. "Hope," American Journal of Psychiatry, 116 (1959), 481.

2404. _____. Love Against Hate. New York: Harcourt Brace, 1942.

2405. _____. Man Against Himself. New York: Harcourt, Brace and Co., 1938.

2406. _____, Erich von Lerchenthal. "Death from Psychic Causes," Bulletin of the Menninger Clinic, 12 (1948), 31-6.

2407. Merkely, Donald K. Investigation of Death: An Introduction to the Medico-legal Criminal Investigations for the Police Officer. Springfield: C.C. Thomas, 1957.

2408. Merritt, T.A., B.A. Dudding. "Sudden Infant Death Syndrome: An Approach for Kansas Physicians," Journal of the Kansas Medical Society, 76 (Feb., 1975), 20-33.

2409. Mersey, M.P. "La Tanatophilie dans la Famille des Habsbourg," Revue de Psychiatrie et Psychologie Experimentale, Series 4 (1912), 493-504.

2410. Mervyn, F. "Plight of Dying Patients in Hospitals," American Journal of Nursing, 71 (Oct., 1971), 1988-90.

2411. Mcscrvc, Harry C. Let Children Ask. Boston: Universalist-Unitarian, Inc., 1954.

2412. Metzger, Arnold. Frieheit und Tod. Turingen: M. Neimeyer, 1955.

2413. Meyer, Bernard C. "Should the Patient Know the Truth," Journal of Mount Sinai Hospital (New York), 20 (Mar.-Apr., 1954), 344-50.

2414. Meyer, Joachim E. Death and Neurosis. International Universities Press, 1975.

2415. Meyer, R.J. "Sudden Infant Death Syndrome," New England Journal of Medicine, 288 (Feb. 8, 1973), 324.

2416. Meyers, Mary. "The Effect of Types of Communication on Patients' Reactions to Stress," Nursing Research, 13 (Spring, 1964), 126-31.

2417. Meyerson, Abraham, "Prolonged Cases of Grief Reactions Treated by Electric Shock," New England Journal of Medicine, 230 (1944), 255-6.

2418. Middleton, John. "Death Customs and Rites," Encyclopedia Americana, 8 (1972), 567-8.

2419. Middleton, W.C. "Some Reactions Toward Death Among College Students," Journal of Abnormal and Social Psychology, 31 (1936), 165-73.

2420. Mija, Trudy. "The Child's Perception of Death," Nursing Forum, 11 (1972), 214-20.

2421. Milici, Pompeo S. "The Involutional Death Reaction," Psychiatric Quarterly, 24 (1950), 775-81.

2422. Millard, Charles K. "The Case for Euthanasia," Fortnightly Review, 136 (1931), 239-71.

2423. Miller, A. "The Patients' Right to Know the Truth," Canadian Nurse, 58 (Jan., 1962), 25-9.

2424. Miller, C.R. et al. "Latent Class Analysis and Differential Mortality," Journal of the American Statistical Association, 57 (June, 1962), 430-8.

2425. Miller, J.B. "Children's Reactions to the Death of a Parent: A Review of the Psychoanalytic Literature," Journal of the American Psychoanalytic Association, 19 (Oct., 1971), 697-719.

2426. Miller, Louise B., Edmond Erwin. "A Study of Attitudes and Anxiety in Medical Students," Journal of Medical Education, 34 (1959), 1089-92.

2427. Miller, M.B. "Decision-Making in the Death Process of the Ill Aged," Geriatrics, 26 (May, 1971), 105-16.

2428. Miller, P.G., J. Ozga. "Mommy, What Happens When I Die?" Mental Hygiene, 57 (Spring, 1973), 20-2.

2429. Miller, Paul. "Provenience of the Death Symbolism in Van Gogh's Cornscapes," Psychoanalytic Review, 52 (1965), 60-6.

2430. Miller, R.W. "Childhood Cancer and Congenital Defects: A Study of U.S. Death Certificates During the Period 1960-66," Pediatric Research, 3 (Sep., 1969), 389-97.

2431. Miller, Sheldon, Lawrence Schoenfeld. "Grief in the Navajo--Psychodynamics and Culture," International Journal of Social Psychiatry, 19 (Autumn, 1973), 187-91.

2432. Milligan, H.C. "The Sudden Infant Death Syndrome and its Contribution to Post Neonatal Mortality in Hartlepool, 1960-9," Public Health, 88 (Jan., 1974), 49-61.

2433. Mills, D.H. "Medico-Legal Ramifications of Current Practices and Suggested Changes in Certifying Modes of Death," Journal of Forensic Sciences, 13 (Jan., 1968), 70-5.

2434. _____. "Statutory Brain Death," Journal of the American Medical Association, 229 (Aug. 26, 1974), 1225-6.

2435. Mills, Liston, ed. Perspectives on Death. Nashville: Abingdon Press, 1969.

2436. Milton, G.W. "The Care of the Dying," Medical Journal of Australia, 2 (July 22, 1972), 117-82.

2437. _____. "Self-Willed Death or the Bone-Pointing Syndrome," Lancet, 1 (June 23, 1973), 1435-6.

2438. Minot, Charles. The Problem of Age, Growth and Death. New York: Putnam, 1908.

2439. Mira y Lopez E. "Psychopathology of Anger and Fear Reactions in Wartime," American Clinician, 5 (1943), 98ff.

2440. Mise, J. et al. "Management of Life Prolongation at the Terminal Stage and Its Discontinuation," Naika, 23 (May, 1969), 850-3.

2441. Mishkin, F. "Determination of Cerebral Death by Radionuclide Angiography," Radiology, 115 (Apr., 1975), 135-7.

2442. Mitchell, Marjorie Editha. The Child's Attitude to Death. New York: Schocken, 1967.

2443. Mitchell, Nelle. "The Significance of the Loss of the Father Through Death," American Journal of Orthopsychiatry, 34 (1964), 279-80.

2444. Mitford, Jessica. The American Way of Death. New York: Simon and Schuster, 1963.

2445. Mitra, D.N. "Mourning Customs and Modern Life in Bengal," American Journal of Sociology, 52 (1947), 309-11.

2446. Mitscherlich, Alexander, Fred Mieke. Doctors of Infamy: The Story of the Nazi Medical Crimes. New York: Henry Schuman, 1949.

2447. Miya, T.M. "The Child's Perception of Death," Nursing Forum, 11 (1972), 214-20.

2448. Miyahara, M. "Determination of Death in Heart Transplantation," Naika, 23 (May, 1969), 850-3.

2449. Miyazaki, Y. et al. "Criteria of Cerebral Death," ACTA Radiologica: Diagnosis 13 (1972), 318-28.

2450. Moellenhoff, F. "Ideas of Children about Death," Bulletin of the Menninger Clinic, 3 (1939), 148-56.

2451. Mogar, Mariannina. "Children's Causal Reasoning about Natural Phenomena," Child Development, 31 (1960), 59-65.

2452. Mohandas, A., S.N. Chou. "Brain Death: A Clinical and Pathological Study," Journal of Neurosurgery, 35 (Aug., 1971), 211-8.

2453. Mohr, George J. When Children Face Crises. Chicago: Science Research Associates, Inc., 1952.

2454. Mollo, Suzanna. "Le Theme de la Mort Dans la Litterature Scokire Francaise Contemporaire (The Theme of Death in Contemporary French School Literature)," Ethno-Psychologie, 271 (Mar.,1972), 45-58.

2455. Moloney, James Clark. The Magic Clock. Wakefield, MA: The Montrose Press, 1949.

2456. Momiyama, M. "Seasonal Effects on Human Mortality," Progress in Biometeorology, 1 (1974), 521-48, 709.

2457. Money-Kyrle, R.E. "An Inconclusive Contribution to the 'Theory of the Death Instinct'," in M. Klein, et al., eds., New Directions in Psychoanalysis. London: Tavistock, 1971.

2458. Monsour, Karem J. "Asthma and the Fear of Death," Psychoanalytic Quarterly, 29 (1960), 56-71.

2459. Montague, William P. The Chances of Surviving Death. Ingersall Lecture, 1932. Cambridge: Harvard University Press, 1934.

2460. Montedonico, John S. "Should a Physician Advise the Patient of an Incurable Mortal Malignancy?" Memphis Medical Journal, 32 (Dec., 1957), 403-5.

2461. Montefiore, Canon H. et al. Death Anxiety: Normal and Pathological Aspects. New York: MSS Information, 1973.

2462. Monteiro, Lois. "Disengagment in the Chronically Ill: An Application of Sociological Theory to Nursing Observations," Nursing Research, 14 (Spring, 1965), 175.

2463. Mooney, W.E. "Gustav Mahler: A Note on Life and Death in Music," Psychoanalytic Quarterly, 37 (1968), 80-102.

2464. Moore, F.D. "Medical Responsibility for the Prolongation of Life," Journal of the American Medical Association, 206 (Oct. 7, 1968), 384-6.

2465. Moore, Joan. "The Death Culture of Mexico and Mexican-Americans," Omega, 1 (Nov., 1970), 271-91.

2466. Moore, U.R. "A First Glance at Terminal Care," Journal of the Royal College of Practitioners, 21 (July, 1971), 387-92.

2467. Moore, Virginia. Ho for Heaven! Man's Changing Attitude toward Dying. New York: Dutton, 1956.

2468. Moore, W.R. "Care for the Dying," British Medical Journal, 1 (Feb. 10, 1973), 353-4.

2469. Moore, Wilbert E. "Time: The Ultimate Scarcity," The American Behavioral Scientist, 6 (May, 1963), 58-60.

2470. _____, Melvin Tumin. "Some Social Functions of Ignorance," American Sociological Review, 14 (Dec., 1949), 787-95.

2471. Moran, M.C. "A Student Nurse's Experiences with a Terminal Patient--Grief and Dying," Hospital Progress, 55 (May, 1974), passim.

2472. Moran, P.A.P. "Maternal Age and Parental Loss," British Journal of Psychiatry, 114 (Feb., 1968), 207-14.

2473. _____, K. Abe. "Parental Loss in Homosexuals," British Journal of Psychiatry, 115 (1969), 319-20.

2474. Morduch, A. No Screen for the Dying. London: Regina Press, 1964.

2475. More, Douglas Mills, Allyn Robers. "Societal Variations in Humor Responses to Cartoons," Journal of Social Psychology, 45 (1957), 233-43.

2476. Moreno, J.L. "The Social Atom and Death," Sociometry, 10 (1947), 80-4.

2477. Morgan, Al. "The Bier Barons," Sociological Symposium, 1 (Fall, 1968), 28-35.

2478. Morgan, Ernest. A Manual of Simple Burial. Burnsville, NC: The Celo Press, 1964.

2479. Morgan, L.G. "On Drinking the Hemlock," Hastings Center Reports, 9 (June, 1971), 6-7.

2480. Morgan, R.F. "Note on the Psychopathology of Senility: Senescent Defense Against Threat of Death," Psychological Reports, 16 (Feb., 1965), 305-6.

2481. Morgenson, D.F. "Death and Interpersonal Failure," Canada's Mental Health, 21 (1973), 10-2.

2482. Morgenthau, Hans, J. "Death in the Nuclear Age," Commentary, 32 (1961), 231-4.

2483. Moriarty, David. "Early Loss and the Fear of Mothering," Psychoanalysis and the Psychoanalytic Review, 49 (1962), 63-9.

2484. _____, ed. Loss of Loved Ones: The Effects of a Death in the Family on Personality Development. Springfield: C.C. Thomas, 1967.

2485. Morin, Edgar. L'Homme et La Mort dans L'Histoire. Paris: Correa, 1951.

2486. Morison, Robert S. "Death: Process or Event?" Science, 173 (Aug., 1971), 694-8.

2487. _____. "Dying," Scientific American, 229 (Sep., 1973), 54-62.

2488. Moritz, Alan R. "Sudden Deaths," New England Journal of Medicine, 223 (Nov. 14, 1970), 798-801.

2489. _____, Norman Zamcheck. "Sudden and Unexpected Death of Young Soldiers," Archives of Pathology, 42 (1946), 459-94.

2490. Moriyama, I.M. "The Change in Mortality Trend in the United States," Vital Health Statistics, 3 (1964), 1-43.

2491. Mormont, Marc et al. "Univers Mental et Strategic des Eveques: La Declaration des Eueques de Belgique sur 1'Avortement (Mental Universe and Strategy of the Bishops: The Declaration of the Bishops of Belgium on Abortion)," Social Compass, 20 (1973), 475-96.

2492. Morris, Arval. "Voluntary Euthanasia," Washington Law Review, 45 (1970), 239-71.

2493. Morris, Barbara. "Young Children and Books on Death," Elementary English, 51 (Mar., 1974), 395-8.

2494. Morris, S. Grief and How to Live with It. New York: Grosset and Dunlap, 1972.

2495. Morrissey, James R. "Children's Adaptation to Fatal Illness," American Journal of Psychotherapy, 18 (1964), 606-15.

2496. _____. "Death Anxiety in Children with a Fatal Illness," American Journal of Psychotherapy, 18 (1964), 606-15.

2497. _____. "A Note on Interviews with Children Facing Imminent Death," Social Casework, 44 (June, 1963), 343-45.

2498. Morrow, M. "The Use of Therapeutic Technique in Releasing Old Age Tension," Social Work Technique, 2 (1938), 71.

2499. Morese, Joan. "The Goal of Life Enhancement for a Fatally Ill Child," Children, 17 (Mar.-Apr., 1970), 63-8.

2500. Morse, T.S. "On Talking to Bereaved Burned Children," Journal of Trauma, 7 (Oct., 1971), 894-5.

2501. Mortelmans, Jan. "Etude sur la Nature des Phenomenes de la Vieillesse et de la Mort," Scalpel (Bruxelles), 113 (June, 1960), 471-6.

2502. Mortimer, K.E. "Philosophy of Dying," New Zealand Medical Journal, 81 (1975), 300-2.

2503. Morton, B.G. "Caring for the Dying," Physiotherapy, 58 (Apr., 1972), 124-5.

2504. Moser, R.H. "Editorial: The New Seduction," Journal of the American Medical Association, 230 (Dec. 16, 1974), 1564.

2505. Moss, Sidney Z., Miriam S. Moss. "Separation as a Death Experience," Child Psychiatry and Human Development, 3 (Spring, 1973), 187-94.

2506. Mount, Balfour M. "Improving the Canadian Way of Dying," Ontario Psychologist, 7 (June, 1975), 19-27.

2507. _____, et al. "Death and Dying: Attitudes in a Teaching Hospital," Urology, 4 (Dec., 1974), 741-8.

2508. Moustakas, Clark, ed. Existential Child Therapy. New York: Basic Books, 1966.

2509. Muensterberger, Warner. "Vom Ursprung des Todes (On the Origin of Death: A Psychoanalytic and Ethnological Study on the Fear of Death)," Psyche 17 (1963), 169-84.

2510. Muhsam, H.V. "Differential Mortality in Israel by Socio-Economic Status," Eugenics Quarterly, 12 (Dec., 1965), 227-32.

2511. Muller, Ludwig. "Uber die Seelenverfassung der Sterbenden (About the Mental State of the Dying)," Zeitschrift fur Neurologie und Psychiatrie, 131 (193), 421-44.

2512. _____. Uber die Seelenverfassung der Sterbenden (About the Mental and Emotional States of the Dying)," Berlin: J. Springer, 1931.

2513. Muller, Pierre. "Legal Medicine and the Delimitation of Death," World Medical Journal, 141 (Sep.-Oct., 1967), 140-2.

2514. Mulvey, P.M. "Cot Death Survey: Anaphylaxis and the House Dust Mite," Medical Journal of Australia, 2 (May 25, 1972), 1240-4.

2515. _____. "Cot Deaths," Medical Journal of Australia, 2 (Aug. 7, 1971), 337-8.

2516. Munk, William. Euthanasia: Or Medical Treatment in Aid of an Easy Death. London: Longmans, Green, and Co., 1887.

2517. Munnichs, J.M.A. "Discussion of a Symposium on Attitudes Toward Death in Older Persons," Journal of Gerontology, 16 (1961), 44-66.

2518. _____. Old Age and Finitude. New York: S. Karger, 1966.

2519. Munro, Alistair. "Bereavement as a Psychiatric Emergency," Nursing Times, 66 (July 2, 1970), 841-3.

2520. _____. "Childhood Parent-Loss in a Psychiatrically Normal Population," British Journal of Preventive and Social Medicine, 19 (1965), 69-79.

2521. _____. "Parental Deprivation in Depressive Patients," British Journal of Psychiatry, 112 (1966), 443-57.

2522. Munro, Alistair, A.B. Griffiths. "Further Data on Childhood Parent-Loss in Psychiatric Normals," ACTA Psychiatrica Scandinavica, 44 (1968), 385-400.

2523. _____. "Some Psychiatric Non-Sequelae of Childhood Bereavement," British Journal of Psychiatry, 115 (1969), 305-11.

2524. Munter, Preston K. "Death in the Infirmary: Some Observations about the Dying Patient," Journal of the American College Health Association, 23 (Dec., 1974), 151-3.

2525. Murgoci, A. "Customs Connected with Death and Burial among the Roumanians," Folk-Lore, 30 (1919), 89-102.

2526. Murphey, Bradford. "Psychological Management of the Patient with Incurable Cancer," Geriatrics, 9 (1953), 130-4.

2527. Murphy, B.W. "Creation and Destruction: Notes on Dylan Thomas," British Journal of Medical Psychology, 41 (1968), 15-67.

2528. Murphy, G. "Some Part of Me Will Cheat the Goddess of Death," Nursing Times, 61 (May 21, 1965), 720.

2529. Murphy, J.V., J.A. Perper. "Crib-Death Syndrome," Lancet, 1 (Mar. 17, 1973), 614.

2530. Murray, Henry, Jr. "The Psychology of Humor," Journal of Abnormal Social Psychology, 29 (1934), 66-81.

2531. Murray, J.T. et al. "A Study of the Contribution of the Health Visitor to the Support and Care of Terminally Ill Patients and Their Relatives," Health Bulletin (Edinburgh), 32 (Nov., 1974), 250-2.

2532. Murray, Patricia. "Death Education and its Effect on the Death Anxiety Level of Nurses," Psychological Reports, 35 (Dec., 1974), 1250.

2533. Murrell, A.W. "Long-Term Illness," Nursing Times, 58 (Mar. 23, 1962), 390.

2534. Murstein, Bernard. "The Effect of Long-Term Illness of Children on the Emotional Adjustment of Parents," Child Development, 31 (1960), 157-71.

2535. _____. "Personality and Intellectual Changes in Leukemia: A Case Study," Journal of Projective Techniques and Personality Assessment, 22 (Dec., 1958), 421-6.

2536. Muslin, H.L. et al. "Partners in Dying," American Journal of Psychiatry, 131 (Mar., 1974), 308-10.

2537. Myerowitz, J.H., H.B. Kaplan. "Familial Responses to Stress: The Case of Cystic Fibrosis," Social Science and Medicine, 1 (Sep., 1967), 249-66.

2538. Myers, F.W. Human Personality and Its Survival of Bodily Death. New York: Longmans, Green and Co. 1903.

2539. Myers, S. "Effects of Death on the Living," Journal of Practical Nursing, 25 (Jan., 1975), 31, 6.

2540. Myler, B.B. "Depression and Death in the Aged," Dissertation Abstracts, 28 (Nov., 1967), 2146-B.

2541. Nacht, S. "Instinct de Mort ou Instinct de Vie?" Revue Francaise de Psychanalyse, 20 (1956), 405-16.

2542. Nadelman, M.S. "On the Possible Preconscious Awareness of Impending Death," Bulletin of the Menninger Clinic, 38 (May, 1974), 250-6.

2543. Naeye, R.L. "Pulmonary Arterial Abnormalities in the Sudden Infant Death Syndrome," New England Journal of Medicine, 289 (Nov. 29, 1973), 1167-70.

2544. Nagera, H. "Children's Reactions to the Death of Important Objects: A Developmental Approach," The Psychoanalytic Study of the Child, 25 (1970), 360-400.

2545. Nagi, M.H., E.G. Stockwell. Socioeconomic Differentials in Mortality by Cause of Death," Health Services Report, 88 (May, 1973), 449-56.

2546. Nahum, Louis H. "Dealing with the Last Chapter of Life," Connecticut Medicine 30 (Mar., 1966), 170-4.

2547. Nagy, Maria H. "The Child's Theories Concerning Death," Journal of Genetic Psychology, 73 (1948), 3-27.

2548. Nahum, Louis H. "The Dying Patient's Grief," Connecticut Medicine, 28 (Apr., 1964), 241-5.

2549. _____. "Emotional Stress and Sudden Death," Connecticut Medicine, 35 (Sep., 1971), 558-60.

2550. Nakagawa, Y. "Standards for Determining Death: Philosophy of Death Under Present Standards of Medical Practice," Surgical Therapy, 20 (Apr., 1969), 405-8.

2551. Nass, Martin L. "The Effects of Three Variables on Children's Concepts of Physical Causality," Journal of Abnormal Social Psychology, 53 (1956), 191-6.

2552. Natanson, Maurice. "Death and Situation," American Imago, 4 (1959), 447-57.

2553. Nathan, H. et al. "Death and the Physician in Art," Medizinische Welt, 52 (Dec. 28, 1968), 2845-2852.

2554. Nathan, T.S. et al. "The Psychiatric Pathology of Survivors of the Nazi Holocaust," The Israel Annals of Psychiatry and Related Discliplines, 1 (1963), 113.

2555. _____. "A Psychiatric Study of Survivors of the Nazi Holocaust: A Study in Hospitalized Patients," The Israel Annals of Psychiatry and Related Discliplines, 2 (1964), 47-76.

2556. Nathanson, Morton et al. "Denial of Illness," Archives of Neurology and Psychiatry, 68 (1953), 380-7.

2557. National Association of Social Workers. Helping the Dying Patient and His Family. New York, 1960.

2558. National Institutes of Health. Research Planning Workshops on the Sudden Infant Death Syndrome. Bethesda, MD: National Institutes of Health, 1974.

2559. _____. Sudden Infant Death Syndrome. Bethesda, MD: National Institutes of Health, 1974.

2560. Natterson, J.M., A.G. Knudson. "Observations Concerning Fear of Death in Fatally Ill Children and Their Mothers," Psychosomatic Medicine, 22 (Nov., 1965), 903-6.

2561. Nau, S., E. Pearlman. "Randy--The Silent Teacher," Canadian Nurse, 61 (Nov., 1965), 903-6.

2562. Neal, Robert et al., eds. Death and Ministry. New York: Seabury, 1975.

2563. Neale, A.V. "The Changing Pattern of Death in Childhood: Then and Now," Medical Science Law, 4 (1964), 35-9.

2564. Needleman, Jacob. "Imagining Absence, Non-Existence and Death: A Sketch," Review of Existential Psychology and Psychiatry, 6 (1966), 230-6.

2565. _____. "The Perception of Mortality," Annals of the New York Academy of Sciences, 164 (Dec., 1969), 733-8.

2566. Neilson, C. "The Childhood of Schizophrenics," ACTA Psychiatrica Scandinavica, 29 (1954), 281-9.

2567. Neilson, W.A., C.G. Watkins. Proposals for Legislative Reform Aiding the Consumer of Funeral Industry Products and Services. Burnsville, NC: The Celo Press, 1973.

2568. Nelson, Joan. "As the Patient Sees It: Public Dying," Medical World, 80 (May, 1954), 596-99.

2569. Nelson, K.E. et al. "The Sudden Infant Death Syndrome and Epidemic Viral Disease," American Journal of Epidemiology, 101 (May, 1975), 423-30.

2570. Nelson, L.D., C.C. Nelson. "A Factor Analytic Inquiry into the Multidimensionality of Death Anxiety," Omega, 6 (1975), 171-8.

2571. Nemtzow, Jesse, Stanley R. Lesser. "Reactions of Children and Parents to the Death of President Kennedy," American Journal of Orthopsychiatry, 34 (1964), 280-1.

2572. Nettle, Gwynn. "Review Essay: On Death and Dying," Social Problems, 14 (1967), 335-44.

2573. Neuringer, Charles. "Changes in Attitudes Towards Life and Death During Recovery from a Serious Suicide Attempt," Omega, 1 (Nov., 1970), 301-9.

2574. _____. "Divergencies Between Attitudes Towards Life and Death among Suicidal, Psychosomatic, and Normal Hospitalized Patients," Journal of Consulting Clinical Psychology, 32 (Feb., 1968), 59-63.

2575. _____, R.M. Harris. "The Perception of the Passage of Time among Death-Involved Hospital Patients," Life Threatening Behavior, 4 (Winter, 1974), 250-4.

2576. Newman, John, William L. Graves. "Neo-Natal Mortality and Socio-economic Status in a Metropolitan County," Sociological Symposium, 8 (Spring, 1972), 37-49.

2577. Nichol, Hamish. "The Death of a Parent," Canadian Psychiatric Association Journal, 3 (June, 1964), 262-71.

2578. Nicoulau. "Thanatophobie et Suicide," Annales Medico-Psychologiques, 15 (1892), 189-205.

2579. Niederland, W. "The Problem of the Survivor, Part I: Some Remarks on the Psychiatric Evaluation of Emotional Disorders in Survivors of Nazi Persecution," Journal of Hillside Hospital, 10 (1961), 233-47.

2580. Nighswonger, Carl A. "Ministering to the Dying," Bulletin of the American Protestant Hospital Association, 34 (Nov. 2, 1970), 117-24.

2581. _____. "Ministry to the Dying as a Learning Encounter," Journal of Thanatology, 1 (Mar.-Apr., 1971), 101.

2582. Nix, J.T. "Study of the Relationship of Environmental Factors to the Type and Frequency of Cancer Causing Death in Nuns," Hospital Progress, 45 (1964), 71-4.

2583. Niyogi, A.K. et al. "Diurnal Variations in Death," Indian Journal of Medical Research, 52 (1964), 1092-8.

2584. Nogas, Catherine et al. "An Investigation of Death Anxiety, Sense of Competence, and Need for Achievement," Omega, 4 (Fall, 1974), 245-55.

2585. Nolfi, N.W. "Families in Grief: The Question of Casework Intervention," Social Work, 12 (1967), 40-6.

2586. Noon, John A. "A Preliminary Examination of the Death Concepts of the Ibo," American Anthropologist, 44 (1942), 638-54.

2587. Norbeck, Edward. "Funeral," Encyclopedia Americana, (1972), 12:165.

2588. Norman, M.G. "Sudden Infant Death Syndrome," Canadian Nurse, 70 (July, 1974), 22-3.

2589. Norris, Catherine M. "Comments about the Meaning of Life," Kansas Nurse, 45 (Oct., 1970), 1-3.

2590. _____. "The Nurse and the Dying Patient," American Journal of Nursing, 55 (Oct., 1955), 1214-7.

2591. Northrup, Fran C. "The Dying Child," American Journal of Nursing, (June, 1974), 1066-8.

2592. Norton, Janice. "Treatment of a Dying Female Patient," Psyche, 22 (Feb., 1968), 99-117.

2593. _____. "Treatment of a Dying Patient," The Psychoanalytic Study of the Child, 18 (1963), 541-60.

2594. Noury, Paul. "La Mort et ses Representations," Medecine Internationale, Annee 37 (1929), NLM Microfilm #TS 1862.

2595. Noyes, Russell, Jr. "The Act of Death, The Art of Treatment," Medical Insight, 3 (March, 1971), 22-33.

2596. _____. "The Art of Dying," Perspectives in Biology and Medicine, 14 (Spring, 1971), 432-47.

2597. _____. "The Care and Management of the Dying," Archives of Internal Medicine, 128 (Aug., 1971), 299-303.

2598. _____. "The Experience of Dying," Psychiatry, 35 (May, 1972), 174-84.

2599. _____. "Grief," Journal of the Iowa Medical Society, 59 (1969), 317-23.

2600. _____. "Montaigne on Death," Omega, 1 (Nov., 1970), 311-23.

2601. _____, Roy Klette. "The Experience of Dying from Falls," Omega, 3 (Feb., 1972), 45-52.

2602. _____, T. Travis. "The Care of Terminally Ill Patients," Archives of Internal Medicine, 132 (Oct., 1973), 607-11.

2603. _____, et al. "The Care of Terminal Patients--A Statewide Survey," Journal of the Iowa Medical Association, 63 (Nov., 1973), 527-30.

2604. Nuckols, Robert C. "Widows Study," Catalog of Selected Documents in Psychology, No. 3 (Winter, 1973), 9.

2605. Nye, F. Ivan. "Child Adjustment in Broken and in Unhappy Broken Homes," Marriage and Family Living, 19 (Nov., 1957), 356-61.

2606. Oakden, E.D., Mary Sturt. "The Development of the Knowledge of Time in Children," British Journal of Psychology, 12 (1922), 309-36.

2607. Oakes J. "Pastoral Care of the Dying and the Bereaved," District Nursing, 11 (Mar., 1969), 256-8.

2608. Obridik, Antnonin. "Gallows Humour: A Sociological Phenomenon," American Journal of Sociology, 47 (1942), 709-16.

2609. Ochs, Robert. The Death in Every Now. New York: Sheed and Ward, 1969.

2610. O'Connell, W.E. "Humour and Death," Psychological Reports, 22 (Apr., 1968), 391-402.

2611. O'Connor, Brian et al. The Role of the Minister in Caring for the Dying Patient and the Bereaved. New York: MSS Information Press, 1975.

2612. O'Connor, Mary Catherine. The Art of Dying Well--The Development of Ars Moriendi. New York: Columbia University Press, 1942.

2613. O'Donnell, T.J. "Editorial: To Live--To Die," Journal of the American Medical Association, 228 (Apr. 22, 1974), 501.

2614. Odegard, O. "The Excess Mortality of the Insane," ACTA Psychiatrica Scandinavica, 57 (1952), 353-67.

2615. _____. "Mortality in Norwegian Psychiatric Hospitals," 1950-1962," ACTA Genetica et Statistica Medica (Basel), 17 (1967), 137-53.

2616. Oehmische, W. et al. "The Development of Mortality in the German Democratic Republic from 1953 to 1963," Deutsche Gesundheitswesen, 21 (Jan., 1966), 126-35.

2617. Oelrich, M. "The Patient with a Fatal Illness," American Journal of Occupational Therapy, 28 (Aug., 1974), 429-32.

2618. Oftedal, S.I. et al. "The Use of Evoked Potentials in Evaluation of Brain Death," Electroencephalography and Clinical Neurophysiology, 30 (Mar., 1971), 273.

2619. Ogilvie, Heneage. "Journey's End," Practitioner, 179 (Oct.-Dec.,1957), 584-91.

2620. Oglesby, William B. "Life or Death--Whose Decision: Theological Aspects," Virginia Medical Monthly, 102 (1975), 710-3.

2621. _____, John Barnard. "The Minister and the Physician as Working Partners," Pastoral Psychology, 10 (Sep., 1959), 37-42.

2622. Ogra, P.L. et al. "Secretory Component and Sudden Infant Death Syndrome," Lancet, 2 (Aug. 30, 1975), 387-90.

2623. Oken, Donald. "What to Tell Cancer Patients: A Study of Medical Attitudes," Journal of the American Medical Association, 175 (Apr., 1961), 1120-8.

2624. Okinaka, S. "Internist's View of the Terminal State," Naika, 23 (May, 1969), 804-7.

2625. Olbrycht, J.S. "Contributions on the Theory of Death by Hanging," Deutsche Zeitschrift fur Die Gesamte Gerichtliche Medizin, 54 (Feb., 1964), 407-23.

2626. Oldfield, Josiah. The Mystery of Death. New York: John F. Rider, 1951.

2627. Olin, Harry S. "Failure and Fulfillment: Education in the Use of Psycho-active Drugs in the Dying Patient," Journal of Thanatology, 2 (Winter, 1972), 567-73.

2628. Olinger, S.D. "Medical Death," Baylor Law Review, 27 (1975), 22-6.

2629. Olmsted, R.W. "Care of the Child with a Fatal Illness," Journal of Pediatrics, 76 (May, 1970), 814.

2630. Olson, Robert G. "Death," Omega, 2 (Nov., 1971), 273-86.

2631. Oltman, Jane E., Samual Friedman. "Report on Parental Deprivation in Psychi-atric Disorders," Archives of General Psychiatry, 12 (Jan., 1965), 46-56.

2632. _____, et al. "Parental Deprivation and the Broken Home in Dementia Prae-cox and Other Mental Disorders," American Journal of Psychiatry, 108 (1952), 685-93.

2633. Opler, Morris E. "The Lipan Apache Death Complex and Its Extensions," South-western Journal of Anthropology, 1 (1945), 122-41.

2634. _____. "Reactions to Death among the Mescalero Apache," Southwestern Journal of Anthropology, 2 (1946), 454-67.

2635. _____, William E. Bittle. "The Death Practices and Eschatology of the Kiowa Apache," Southwestern Journal of Anthropology, 17 (1961), 383-94.

2636. Oppenheim, Garrett. "When Patients Ask Tough Questions," Medical Economics, 38 (Jan. 2, 1961), 5408.

2637. Oraftik, N. "Only Time to Touch," Nursing Forum, 11 (1972), 205-13.

2638. Orbach, Charles E. "The Multiple Meanings of the Loss of a Child," American Journal of Psychotherapy, 13 (Oct., 1959), 906-15.

2639. _____, et al. "Psychological Impact of Cancer and Its Treatment, III: The Adaptation of Mothers to the Threatened Loss of their Children through Leukemia, Part II," Cancer, 8 (Jan.-Feb., 1955), 20-33.

2640. O'Reilly, M.J. "Cot Death Survey: Anaphylaxis and the House Dust Mite," Medical Journal of Australia, 1 (Feb. 3, 1973), 262.

2641. Orenstein, H. "Death and Kinship in Hinduism: Structural and Functional Interpretations," American Anthropologist, 72 (Dec., 1970), 1357-77.

2642. Orlansky, Harold. "Reactions to the Death of President Roosevelt," Journal of Social Psychology, 26 (1947), 235-66.

2643. Orth, Joseph. "Legal Aspects Relating to Euthanasia," Maryland Medical Journal, 2 (1953), 28-31.

2644. Orwell, George. "How the Poor Die," in Shooting an Elephant. London: Secker and Warburg, 1950.

2645. Osarchuk, Michael, Sherman J. Tatz. "Effect of Induced Fear of Death on Belief in Afterlife," Journal of Personality and Social Psychology, 27 (Aug., 1973), 256-60.

2646. Osipov, N.E. "Strach ze Smrti (Fear of Death)," Revue v Neurologii a Psychiatrii (Praha), 32 (1935), 17-25.

2647. Osis, Karlis. Deathbed Observations by Physicians and Nurses. Parapsychological Monograph #3. New York: Parapsychology Foundation, 1961.

2648. Osler, William. Counsels and Ideals. Boston: Houghton, Mifflin, 1905.

2649. _____. Science and Immortality: The Ingersoll Lecture, 1904. Boston: Houghton, Mifflin, 1904.

2650. Ostheimer, Nancy C., John M. Ostheimer, eds. Life or Death--Who Controls? New York: Springer, 1975.

2651. Ostow, Mortimer. "The Death Instinct--A Contribution to the Study of Instincts," International Journal of Psychoanalysis, 39 (1958), 5-16.

2652. _____. The Psychology of Melancholy. New York: Harper and Row, 1970.

2653. Osuna, Patricia, David K. Reynolds. "A Funeral in Mexico: Description and Analysis," Omega, 1 (Nov., 1970), 249-69.

2654. Oswald, I. Sleeping and Waking. Amsterdam and New York: Elsevier, 1962.

2655. Ouaknine, G. et al. "Laboratory Criteria of Brain Death," Journal of Neurosurgery, 39 (Oct., 1973), 429-33.

2656. Oxton, Charles. "The Crime of 'Mercy-Killing'," Applied Christianity, (Oct., 1973), 28-31.

2657. Pacyaya, Alfredo G. "Changing Customs of Marriage, Death and Burial among the Sagada," Practical Anthropology, 8 (1961), 125-33.

2658. Pacyna, D.A. "Response to a Dying Child," Nursing Clinics of North America, 5 (Sep., 1970), 421-30.

2659. Page, Irvine H. "On Death," Modern Medicine, 39 (Sep. 20, 1971), 73-5.

2660. Pahnke, Walter N. "The Psychedelic Mystical Experience in the Human Encounter with Death," Psychedelic Review, 11 (Winter, 1970), 3-20.

2661. _____. "Psychedelic Mystical Experiences in Human Encounter with Death," Harvard Theological Review, 62 (Jan., 1969), 1-32.

2662. Palgi, P. "The Socio-Cultural Expressions and Implications of Death, Mourning and Bereavement Arising out of the War Situation in Israel," Israel Annals of Psychiatry, 11 (Dec., 1973), 301-29.

2663. Palmer, John. "Treating Prolonged Mourning in Spanish-Speaking Psychiatric Patients," Hospital and Community Psychiatry, 25 (May, 1973), 337-8.

2664. Palmore, E., F. Jeffers, eds. The Prediction of Life Span: Recent Findings. Lexington, MA: D.C. Heath, 1971.

2665. Pandey, Carol. "The Need for the Psychological Study of Clinical Death," Omega, 1 (Feb., 1971), 1-9.

2666. Pandey, R.E. "The Three-Dimension Factorial Model and Death," Omega, 1 (Nov., 1970), 325-30.

2667. _____. "Vector Analytic Study of Attitudes Toward Death among College Students," International Journal of Social Psychiatry, 21 (Winter-Spring, 1974-5), 7-11.

2668. _____, Donald I. Templer. "Use of the Death Anxiety Scale in an Inter-Racial Setting," Omega, 3 (May, 1972), 127-30.

2669. Papageorgis, D. "On the Ambivalence of Death: The Case of the Missing Harlequin," Psychological Reports, 19 (Aug., 1966), 325-6.

2670. Parad, Howard, Gerald Caplan. "A Framework for Studying Families in Crisis," Social Work, 5 (July, 1960), 3-15.

2671. Paris, J. et al. "Responses to Death and Sex Stimulus Materials as a Function of Repression-Sensitization," Psychological Reports, 19 (Dec., 1966), 1283-91.

2672. Paris, J., J.S.M. Fonblanque. Medical Jurisprudence. London: Phillips, 1823.

2673. Park, Roswell. "Thanatology: A Questionnaire and a Plea for a Neglected Study," Journal of the American Medical Association, 58 (Apr. 27, 1912), 1243-6.

2674. Parker, W.S. "Realities of Responsibility: What Are the Real Priorities in Medical and Nursing Care?" Nursing Times, 67 (Aug. 26, 1971), 1053-4.

2675. Parkes, Colin Murray. "Anticipatory Grief and Widowhood," British Journal of Psychiatry, 122 (May, 1973), 615.

2676. _____. "Bereavement and Mental Illness, Part I: A Clinical Study of the Grief of Bereaved Psychiatric Patients; Part II: A Classification of Bereavement Reactions," British Journal of Medical Psychology, 38 (Mar., 1965), 1-26.

2677. _____. Bereavement: Studies of Grief in Adult Life. New York: International Universities Press, 1973.

2678. _____. "Components of the Reaction to the Loss of a Limb, Spouse, or Home," Journal of Psychosomatic Research, 16 (Aug., 1972), 343-9.

2679. _____. "Determination of Bereavement," Proceedings of the Royal Society of Medicine, 64 (Mar., 1971), 279.

2680. _____. "Effects of Bereavement on Physical and Mental Health--A Study of the Medical Records of Widows," British Medical Journal, 2 (1964), 274-9.

2681. _____. "The First Year of Bereavement: A Longitudinal Study of London Widows to the Death of their Husbands," Psychiatry, 33 (Nov., 1970), 444-67.

2682. _____. "Nature of Grief," International Journal of Psychiatry, 3 (May, 1967), 5-8.

2683. _____. "Recent Bereavement as a Cause of Mental Illness," British Journal of Psychiatry, 110 (1964), 198-204.

2684. _____. "'Seeking' and 'Finding' a Lost Object: Evidence from Recent Studies of the Reaction to Bereavement," Social Science and Medicine, 4 (Aug., 1970), 187-201.

2685. _____, John Birtchnell. "Determination of Outcome Following Bereavement," Proceedings of the Royal Society of Medicine, 64 (Mar., 1971), 279-82.

2686. _____, R.J. Brown. "Health after Bereavement: A Controlled Study of Young Boston Widows and Widowers," Psychosomatic Medicine, 34 (Sep.-Oct., 1972), 449-61.

2687. _____, et al. "Broken Heart: A Statistical Study of Increased Mortality among Widowers," British Journal of Medicine, 1 (Mar. 22, 1969), 740-3.

2688. Parkes, L.C. "Life, Death, Kidney Transplantation and Nursing at the Johns Hopkins Hospital," Alumnae Magazine (Baltimore), 70 (Mar., 1971), 2-6.

2689. Parkhurst, Helen. Exploring the Child's World. New York: Appleton-Century-Crofts, 1951.

2690. _____. "L'Idea che il Bambino ha Della Morete," Scuola e Citta (Pescetto), 5 (1956), 5-16.

2691. Parkinson, D. "Criteria for Death," Journal of Neurosurgery, 38 (Mar., 1973), 399.

2692. Parsons, Henry M. "Life and Death," Human Factors, 12 (1970), 1-6.

2693. Parsons, Talcott. "Death in American Society--A Brief Working Paper," The American Behavioral Scientist, 6 (May, 1963), 61-5.

2694. _____. "Illness and the Role of the Physician: A Sociological Perspective," in C. Kluckhohn, H.A. Murray, and D.M. Schneider, eds., Personality in Nature, Society and Culture. New York: Alfred A. Knopf, 1954. 609-17.

2695. _____, et al. "The 'Gift of Life' and Its Reciprocation," Social Research, 39 (Autumn, 1972), 367-415.

2696. Pasternak, B. "Chinese Tale-Telling Tombs," Ethnology, 12 (July, 1973), 259-73.

2697. Paterson, Ralston, Jean Aitken-Swan. "Public Opinion on Cancer," Lancet, 2 (Oct. 23, 1954), 857-61.

2698. Paton, Alec. "Life and Death: Moral and Ethical Aspects of Transplantation," Seminars in Psychiatry, 3 (Feb., 1971), 161-8.

2699. Paton, Lewis Bayles. Spiritism and the Cult of the Dead in Antiquity. New York: Macmillan, 1921.

2700. Patry, F.L. "A Psychiatric Evaluation of Communicating with the Dying," Diseases of the Nervous System, 26 (Nov., 1965), 715-8.

2701. Patterson, Mary G. "The Care of the Patient with Cancer," Public Health Nursing, 42 (July, 1950), 377-85.

2702. Patterson, R.D. "Grief and Depression in Old People," Maryland Medical Journal, 18 (Sep., 1969), 75-9.

2703. Patterson, R.P. et al., eds. Psychosocial Aspects of Cystic Fibrosis. New York: Columbia University Press, 1973.

2704. Pattison, Charles P., Jr. "Dealing with the Dying Patient," Journal of the Kansas Medical Society, 72 (Aug., 1971), 354-60.

2705. Pattison, E. Mansell. "The Experience of Dying," American Journal of Psychotherapy, 21 (Jan., 1967), 32-43.

2706. _____. "Psychosocial Predictors of Death Prognosis," Omega, 5 (Summer, 1974), 145-60.

2707. Paul, Norman L. "Empathic Excavation of Buried Grief," Roche Report Frontiers of Clinical Psychiatry, 4 (Feb. 15, 1967), 1-2ff.

2708. _____, G.H. Grosser. "Operational Mourning and Its Role in Conjoint Family Therapy," Community Mental Health Journal, 1 (1965), 339-45.

2709. Paulson, G.W. "Who Should Live," Geriatrics, 28 (Mar., 1973), 132-6.

2710. Payne, L.M. "The Moment of Death: An Historical Commentary," Medical and Biological Illustration, 21 (Jan., 1971), 45-51.

2711. Paz, Octavio. "The Day of the Dead," in Labyrinth of Solitude: Life and Thought in Mexico. Translated by Lysander Kemp. New York: Grove Press, 1961. 47-64.

2712. Pearl, Raymond. The Biology of Death. Philadelphia: Lippincott, 1922.

2713. Pearlman, Joel et al. "Attitudes Toward Death among Nursing Home Personnel," Journal of Genetic Psychology, 114 (1969), 63-75.

2714. Pearson, Leonard S., ed. Death and Dying: Current Issues in the Treatment of Dying Persons. New York: Aronson, 1969.

2715. _____. "Medical Certification of Death," Pennsylvania Medicine, 72 (Mar., 1969), 17.

2716. Peck, M. "Notes on Identification in a Case of Depression Reactive to the Death of a Love Object," Psychoanalytic Quarterly, 8 (1939), 1-17.

2717. Pederson, Stefi. "Phallic Fantasies, Fear of Death and Ecstasy," American Imago, 17 (1960), 21-46.

2718. Peery, T.M. "The New and Old Diseases: A Study of Mortality Trends in the United States, 1900-69. Ward Burdick Award Address," American Journal of Clinical Pathology, 63 (Apr., 1975), 453-74.

2719. Pelikan, Jaroslav. The Shape of Death, Life and Immortality in the Early Fathers. Nashville: Abingdon Press, 1961.

2720. Pellegrino, Edmund R. "The Communication Crisis in Nursing and Medical Education," Nursing Forum, 5 (1966), 45-53.

2721. Pells, J. "Prolonging Life, 3: The Hope in Experiment," Nursing Times 70 (Mar. 7, 1974), 352-3.

2722. Pells, J. "Prolonging Life, 4: Nurse's Burden, Doctor's Decision," Nursing Times, 70 (Mar. 14, 1974), 393-4.

2723. _____. "Prolonging Life, 5: Opinions and Guidance," Nursing Times, 70 (Mar. 21, 1974), 440-1.

2724. Pemberton, L.B. "Diagnosis Ca . . . Should We Tell the Truth?" Bulletin of the American College of Surgeons, 56 (Mar., 1971), 7-13.

2725. Peniston, D. Hugh. "The Importance of Death Education in Family Life," Family Life Coordinator, 11 (Jan., 1962), 15-8.

2726. Pentney, Bernard H. "Grief," Nursing Times, 60 (Nov.13, 1964), 1496-8.

2727. _____. "Grief Reaction," District Nursing, 5 (1963), 226-8.

2728. Perelman, R. "Sudden Death in Infants," Concours Medical (Paris), 85 (Jan. 19, 1963), 347-52.

2729. Peretz, D. et al. "A Survey of Physicians' Attitudes Toward Death and Bereavement: A Comparison of Psychiatrists and Non-Psychiatrists," Journal of Thanatology, 1 (Mar.-Apr., 1971), 91.

2730. Pericoli, Ridolfini, F. "The Diagnosis of Death," Policlinico Sezione Pratica, 76 (July 7, 1969), 865-77.

2731. Perske, Robert. "Death and Ministry: Episode and Response," Pastoral Psychology, 15 (Sep., 1964), 25-35.

2732. Perthes, Georg. Uber den Tod (On Death). Stuttgart: F. Enke, 1927.

2733. Pescetto, Guglielmo. "Rapresentazione della Morte nel Bambino," Rassegna de Studi Psichiatrici, 46 (Mar.-Apr., 1957), 165-80.

2734. Pessin, Hoseph. "Self Destructive Tendencies in Adolescence," Bulletin of the Menninger Clinic, 5 (1941), 13ff.

2735. Peterson, B.H. "The Age of Aging," Australian and New Zealand Journal of Psychiatry, 7 (Mar., 1973), 9-15.

2736. Peterson, D.B. et al. "The Sudden Infant Death Syndrome in Hospitalized Babies," Pediatrics, 54 (Nov., 1974), 644-6.

2737. Peterson, D.R. "Sudden, Unexpected Death in Infants," American Journal of Epidemiology, 84 (1966), 478-82.

2738. _____. "Sudden, Unexpected Deaths in Infants: Incidence in Two Climatically Dissimilar Metropolitan Communities," American Journal of Epidemiology, 95 (Feb., 1972), 95-8.

2739. Peterson, D.R., J.B. Beckwith. "Magnesium Deprivation in Sudden Unexpected Infant Death," Lancet, 2 (Aug. 11, 1973), 330.

2740. _____, et al. "A Method for Assessing the Geographic Distribution and Temporal Trends of the Sudden Infant Death Syndrome in the United States from Vital Statistics Data," American Journal of Epidemiology, 100 (Nov., 1974), 373-9.

2741. _____, et al. "Postnatal Growth and the Sudden Infant Death Syndrome," American Journal of Epidemiology, 99 (June, 1974), 389-94.

2742. Peterson, William D., Richard L. Sartore. "Helping Children to Cope with Death," Elementary School Guidance and Counseling, 9 (Mar., 1975), 226-32.

2743. Petersson, P.O., G. Von Sydow. "Letter: Cot Deaths in Sweden," British Medical Journal, 3 (Aug. 23, 1975), 490.

2744. Petherbrigde, Jack. "Darling--! You're Dying--!" Pastoral Psychology, 8 (Apr., 1957), 41-4.

2745. Petri, Harald. "Schmerz und Leid im Sterben," Hippokrates, 24 (July 15, 1953), 394-7.

2746. Petrie, Asenath. Individuality in Pain and Suffering. Chicago: The University of Chicago Press, 1967.

2747. Pfannmuller, D. Gustav. Tod, Jenseits und Unsterblichkeit in der Religion, Literatur und Philosophie der Griechen und Romer. Basel: Ernst Rein-ahrdt, 1953.

2748. Pfeiffer, Mildred, Eloise Lemon. "A Pilot Study in the Home Care of Terminal Cancer Patients," American Journal of Public Health, 43 (1953), 909-14.

2749. Pfister, Oskar. "Schockdenken und Schockphantasien bei Hochster Todesgefahr (Rapid Thoughts in Extreme Dangers of Death)," International Zeitschrift fur Psychoanalyse, 16 (1930), 430-55.

2750. Philiber, M. "Image and Language of Death in Bergman's Cries and Whispers," Archives of Social Science and Religion, 20 (1975), 175-83.

2751. Philip, A.P. "On the Nature of Death," Royal Society of London Philosophical Transactions, 124 (1834), 167-98.

2752. Phillips, David P., Kenneth A. Feldman. "A Dip in Deaths Before Ceremonial Occasions: Some New Relationship Between Social Integration and Mortality," American Sociological Review, 38 (Dec., 1973), 678-96.

2753. Phillips, Donald F. "The Hospital and the Dying Patient," Hospitals, 46 (Feb. 16, 1972), 68.

2754. Phipps, Joyce. Death's Single Privacy. New York: Seabury Press, 1974.

2755. Piaget, Jean. The Child's Conception of Physical Causality. London: Kegan Paul, 1930.

2756. _____. The Child's Conception of the World. London: Kegan Paul, 1929.

2757. _____. The Construction of Reality in the Child. New York: Basic Books, 1954.

2758. _____. The Language and Thought of the Child. London: Routledge, 1952.

2759. Pichon, Edouard. "Mort, Angoisse, Negation (Death, Agony and Negation)," Evolution Psychiatrique (Paris), 1 (1947), 19-46.

2760. Pieper, J. Death and Immortality. New York: Herder and Herder, 1969.

2761. Pieroni, Antoinette. "Role of the Social Worker in a Children's Cancer Clinic," Pediatrics, 40 (Sep., 1967), 534-6.

2762. Pierson, P.S. et al. "Sudden Deaths in Infants Born to Methadone-Maintained Addicts," Journal of the American Medical Association, 220 (June 26, 1972), 1733-4.

2763. Pihlblad, C.T., D.L. Adams. "Widowhood, Social Participation and Life Satisfaction," Aging and Human Development, 3 (1972), 323-30.

2764. _____, et al. "Socio-Economic Adjustment to Widowhood," Omega, 3 (Nov., 1972), 295-305.

2765. Pike L.A. "Comparison of Mortality in the Elderly at Home and in a Welfare Home," Journal of the Royal College of General Practitioners, 22 (Sep., 1972), 649-50.

2766. Pilsecker, Carleton. "Help for the Dying," Social Work, 20 (May, 1975), 190-4.

2767. Pincherle, G. "Mortality of Members of Parliament," British Journal of Preventive and Social Medicine, 23 (1969), 72-6.

2768. Pincus, Lilly. Death and the Family. New York: Pantheon Books, 1974.

2769. Pine, Vanderlyn R. "Comparative Funeral Practices," Practical Anthropology, 16 (Mar.-Apr., 1969), 49-62.

2770. _____. "Social Organization and Death," Omega, 3 (May, 1972), 149-53.

2771. _____, Derek Phillips. "The Cost of Dying: A Sociological Analysis of Funeral Expenditures," Social Problems, 17 (Winter, 1970), 405-17.

2772. Pitts, Ferris N. et al. "Adult Psychiatric Illness Assessed for Childhood Parental Loss, and Psychiatric Illness in Family Members--A Study of 748 Patients and 250 controls," American Journal of Psychiatry, 121 (June, 1965), Supplement, i-x.

2773. Plank, Emma N. "Death on a Children's Ward," Medical Times, 92 (July, 1964), 638-44.

2774. Platt, R. "Reflections on Aging and Death," Lancet, 1 (Jan. 5, 1963), 1-6.

2775. Playfair, Lyon. "On the Dread of Death," British Medical Journal, 1 (Mar. 2, 1889) 489.

2776. Plessner, Helmuth. "On the Relation of Time to Death," in Joseph Campbell, ed., Man and Time. New York: Pantheon Books, 1957. 233-63.

2777. Poelchau, Harold. Die Letzten Stunden (The Last Hours). Berlin: Volk und Welt, 1949.

2778. Pollock, George H. "Bertha Pappenheim's Pathological Mourning: Possible Effects of Childhood Sibling Loss," 20 (July, 1972), 476-93.

2779. _____. "Childhood Parent and Sibling Loss in Adult Patients," Archives of General Psychiatry, 7 (1962), 295-306.

2780. _____. "Mourning and Adaptation," International Journal of Psychoanalysis, 42 (1961), 341-61.

2781. _____. "On Mourning and Anniversaries: The Relationship of Culturally Constituted Defensive Systems to Intra-Psychic Adaptive Processes," Israel Annals of Psychiatry and Related Disciplines, 10 (Mar., 1972), 9-40.

2782. _____. "On Mourning, Immortality, and Utopia," Journal of the American Psychoanalytic Association, 23 (1975), 334-62.

2783. _____. "On Time, Death and Immortality," Psychoanalytic Quarterly, 40 (1971), 425-46.

2784. Polner, Murray, Arthur Barron. The Questions Children Ask. New York: Macmillan, 1964.

2785. Pomedli, Michael M. Heidegger and Freud: Power of Death. Ann Arbor: University Microfilms, 1973.

2786. Pomeroy, M.R. "Sudden Death Syndrome," American Journal of Nursing, 69 (Sep., 1969), 1886-90.

2787. Pompey, H. "Brain Death and Total Death: Moral and Theological Aspects of Heart Transplants," Muchener Medizinische Wochenschrift, 111 (Mar. 28, 1969), 736-41.

2788. Popoff, D., G.R. Funkhouser. "What Are Your Feelings about Death and Dying? Part 3," Nursing (Jenkintown), 5 (Oct., 1975), 39-50.

2789. Porter, K.R. "Four Recurring Themes," British Medical Journal, 1 (Jan. 6, 1973), 40-1.

2790. Porter, William H., Jr. "Some Sociological Notes on a Century of Change in the Funeral Business," Sociological Symposium, 1 (Fall, 1968), 36-46.

2791. Potenca, H., P. Diosi. "Cytomegalovirus Infection and Sudden Death in Infants," Journal of Pediatrics, 85 (Aug., 1974), 281-3.

2792. Potthoff, C.J. "First Aid: Determination of Death," Today's Health, 47 (Sep., 1969), 74.

2793. Pound, Louise, "American Euphemisms for Dying, Death and Burial," American Speech, 11 (Oct., 1936), 195-202.

2794. Poznanski, E.O. "The 'Replacement Child'--A Saga of Unresolved Parental Grief," Journal of Pediatrics, 81 (Dec., 1972), 1190-3.

2795. Prattes, Ora R. "Helping the Family Face an Impending Death," Nursing, '73, (Feb., 1973), 17-20.

2796. Pressey, Sidney L. "Age Counseling: Crises, Services, Potentials," Journal of Counseling Psychology, 20 (July, 1973), 356-60.

2797. Preston, C.E. "Behavior Modification: A Therapeutic Approach to Aging and Dying," Postgraduate Medicine, 54 (Dec., 1973), 64-8.

2798. _____, et al. "Views of the Aged on the Timing of Death," Gerontologist, 11 (Winter, 1971), 300-4.

2799. Preston, S.H. "Demographic and Social Consequences of Various Causes of Death in the United States," Social Biology, 21 (Summer, 1974), 144-62.

2800. _____. "Interrelations Between Death Rates and Birth Rates," Theoretical Population Biology, 3 (June, 1972), 162-85.

2801. _____, et al. Causes of Death. New York: Seminar Press, 1972.

2802. Pretty, L.C. "Ministering to the Bereaved and Dying," Nebraska State Medical Journal, 44 (May, 1959), 243-9.

2803. Prettyman, Barrett. Death and the Supreme Court. New York: Harcourt, Brace, and World, 1961.

2804. Price, Julius J. Rabbinic Conceptions About Death. Chicago: Open Court Press, 1920.

2805. Priest, R.G., A.H. Crisp. "Bereavement and Psychiatric Symptoms--An Item Analysis," Psychotherapy and Psychosomatics, 22 (1973), 166-71.

2806. Pringle-Pattison, Seth A. The Idea of Immortality. New York: Oxford University Press, 1922.

2807. Proctor, R.C. "Psychotheological Treatise on Death," North Carolina Medical Journal, 28 (Nov., 1967), 467-8.

2808. Proulx, J.R. "Ministering to the Dying: A Joint Pastoral and Nursing Effort," Hospital Progress, 56 (Mar., 1975), 62-3.

2809. Provonsha, J.W. "Prolongation of Life," Bulletin of the American Protestant Hospital Assocation, 35 (Spring, 1971), 14-6.

2810. Prugh, Dane G. et al. "A Study of the Emotional Reactions of Children and Families to Hospitalization and Illness," American Journal of Orthopsychiatry, 23 (Jan., 1953), 70-106.

2811. Pruit, Angela, Patricia Rice. "On Death," Tomorrow's Nurse, 4 (Aug.-Sep., 1963), 17-8.

2812. Pruitt, R.D. "Death as an Expression of Functional Disease," Mayo Clinic Proceedings, 49 (Sep., 1974), 627-34.

2813. Puckel, Bertram S. Funeral Customs: Their Origin and Development. London: T.W. Laurie, 1926.

2814. Puffer, Ruth Rice, Carlos V. Serrano. Patterns of Mortality in Childhood. Washington, Pan American Health Organization, 1973.

2815. _____, et al. "Cooperative International Research on Mortality," Boletin de la Oficina Sanitaria Panamericana, 58 (1965), 1-16.

2816. _____. "International Collaborative Research on Mortality," World Health Organization, Public Health Papers, 27 (1965), 113-30.

2817. Purci-Jones, John et al. "Temporal Stability and Change in Attitudes Toward the Kennedy Assassination," Psychological Reports, 23 (1969), 907-13.

2818. Purpura, G. "Civilizations Practicing Interment and Cremation," Annali Della Sanita Publica, 27 (Jan.-Feb., 1966), 188-97.

2819. Purtilo, R.B. "Don't Mention It: The Physical Therapist in a Death Denying Society," Physical Therapy, 52 (Oct., 1972), 1031-5.

2820. Putter, August. "Altern und Sterben (Growing Old and Dying)," Virchows Archiv fur Pathologische Anatomie und Pysiologie und fur Klinische Medizin (Berlin), 261 (1926), 397-424.

2821. Quevauviller, A. "The Public Health Specialist in the Face of Death," Produits et Problemes Pharmaceutiques, 19 (Nov., 1964), 505-18.

2822. Quimby, Freeman Henry et al. Leading Causes of Death in Selected Areas of the World. Washington: USGPO, 1972.

2823. Quinney, Earl Richard. "Mortality Differentials in a Metropolitan Area," Social Forces, 43 (Dec., 1964), 222-30.

2824. Quint, Jeanne D. "Awareness of Death and the Nurse's Composure," Nursing Research, 15 (Winter, 1966), 49-55.

2825. _____. "Communications Problems Affecting Patient Care in Hospitals," Journal of the American Medical Association, 195 (Jan. 3, 1966), 36-7.

2826. _____. "The Dying Patient: A Difficult Nursing Problem," Nursing Clinics of North America, 2 (Dec., 1967), 763-73.

2827. _____. "Hidden Hazards for Nurse Teachers," Nursing Outlook, 15 (Apr., 1967), 34-5.

2828. _____. "Institutional Practices of Information Control," Psychiatry, 28 (May, 1965), 119-32.

2829. _____. "Mastectomy: Signpost in Time," The Journal of Nursing Education, 2 (Sep., 1963), 3ff.

2830. _____. "Mastectomy--Symbol of Cure or Warning Sign?" American Academy of General Practice, 29 (1964), 119-24.

2831. _____. The Nurse and the Dying Patient. New York: Macmillan, 1967.

2832. _____. "Nursing Services and the Care of Dying Patients: Some Speculations," Nursing Science, 2 (Dec., 1964), 432-43.

2833. _____. "Obstacles to Helping the Dying," American Journal of Nursing, 66 (July, 1966), 1568-71.

2834. _____. "Preparing Nurses to Care for the Fatally Ill," International Journal of Nursing Studies, 5 (Mar., 1968), 53-61.

2835. _____. "The Threat of Death: Some Consequences for Patients and Nurses," Nursing Forum, 8 (1969), 286ff.

2836. _____. "When Patients Die: Some Nursing Problems," The Canadian Nurse, 63 (Dec., 1967), 33-6.

2837. _____, Barney Glaser. "Improving Nursing Care of the Dying," Nursing Forum, 6 (Fall, 1967), 368-78.

2838. Quint, Jeanne C., Anselm L. Strauss. "Nursing Students, Assignments and Dying Patients," Nursing Outlook, 12 (Jan., 1964), 24-7.

2839. Racy, J. "Death in an Arab Culture," Annals of the New York Academy of Sciences, 64 (Dec., 1969), 871-80.

2840. Radcliffe-Brown, Alfred Reginald. "Taboo," in Structure and Function in Primitive Society. London: Cohen and West, 1952.

2841. Rado, Sandor. "The Problem of Melancholia," International Journal of Psychoanalysis, 9 (1928), 420-38.

2842. Raether, Howard C. "Comments on Ruth Mulvey Harmer's 'Funerals, Fantasy and Flight'," Omega, 2 (Aug., 1971), 154-8.

2843. _____. "The Place of the Funeral: The Role of the Funeral Director in Contemporary America," Omega, 2 (Aug., 1971), 150-3.

2844. _____. Successful Funeral Service Practice. Englewood Cliffs, NJ: Prentice-Hall, 1971.

2845. Raft, D. "How to Help the Patient Who Is Dying," American Family Physician, 7 (Apr., 1973), 112-5.

2846. Rahe, Richard H. et al. "Social Stress and Illness Onset," Journal of Psychosomatic Research, 8 (1964), 35-44.

2847. _____, Evy Lind. "Psychosocial Factors and Sudden Cardiac Death: A Pilot Study," Journal of Psychosomatic Research, 15 (Mar., 1971), 19-24.

2848. Rahner, Karl. On the Theology of Death. Translated by Charles H. Henkey. New York: Herder and Herder, 1961.

2849. Raimbault, G. et al. "Theme of Death in Children with Chronic Disease," Archives Francaises de Pediatrie, 26 (1969), 1041-53.

2850. Rakoff, Vivian M. "Psychiatric Aspects of Death in America," Social Research, 39 (Autumn, 1972), 515-27.

2851. Ramirez, S. "La Senescincia y la Muerte," Revista de Medicina y Ciencias Afines (Mexico), 4 (Aug., 1945), 5-14.

2852. Ramzy, Ishak, Robert S. Wallerstein. "Pain, Fear and Anxiety," The Psychoanalytic Study of the Child, 13 (1958), 147-89.

2853. Rao, S.L. "On Long-Term Mortality Trends in the United States, 1850-1968," Demography, 10 (Aug., 1973), 405-19.

2854. Rapheal, F. "Representation of Death Among Alsacian Jews," Archives of Social Science and Religion, 29 (1975), 101-17.

2855. Raphael, S.S. "Sudden Death in Infants," Lancet, 1 (Feb. 5, 1972), 325.

2856. Rapoport, J. "A Case of Necrophilia," Journal of Criminal Psychopathology, 4 (1942), 277-89.

2857. Raring, Richard H. Crib Death. Hicksville, NY: Exposition Press, 1975.

2858. Raskind, R. et al. "To Remain Alive with Dignity: A Neurosurgical Viewpoint," Journal of the American Geriatric Society, 20 (Apr., 1972), 170-3.

2859. Ratliff, L.C. "The Physician and Minister Caring for the Terminal Patient," Journal of the Mississippi State Medical Assocation, 13 (May, 1972), 202-7.

2860. Raven, C. "Sudden Infant Death Syndrome--An Epidemiologic Study," Journal of the American Medical Women's Association, 29 (Mar., 1974), passim.

2861. _____. "Why an Obligatory Autopsy in the Sudden Infant Death Syndrome," Forensic Science, 2 (Aug., 1973), 387-9.

2862. Ravitch, M.M. "Let Your Patient Die with Dignity," Medical Times, 93 (June, 1965), 594-6.

2863. Ray, C.D., P. Vogel. "Instrumentation for Deep Brain Implantation for the Diagnosis of Death," Confina Neurologica, 34 (1972), 112-26.

2864. Ray, S.K. et al. "Exhumation," Journal of the Indian Medical Association, 46 (Feb., 1966), 193-7.

2865. Raymond, M.E. et al. "Familial Responses to Mental Illness," Social Casework, 56 (1975), 492-8.

2866. Reboul, H. "Old People and after Death," Archives of Social Science and Religion, 20 (1975), 169-74.

2867. Rector, F.L. "Cancer in Childhood," American Journal of Nursing, 46 (July, 1946), 449-51.

2868. Redl, Fritz. "Strategy and Technique of the Life-Space Interview," American Journal of Orthopsychiatry, 29 (Jan., 1959), 1-18.

2869. Reed, A.W. "Problems of Impending Death: The Concerns of the Dying Patient," Physical Therapy, 48 (July, 1968), 740-3.

2870. Reed, Elizabeth Liggett. Helping Children with the Mystery of Death. Nashville, Abingdon Press, 1970.

2871. Rees, W. Dewi. "The Distress of Dying," Nursing Times, 68 (Nov. 23, 1972), 1479-80.

2872. Rees, W. Dewi. "The Hallucinations and Mortality Following Bereavement," Scientific Proceedings of the Cardiff Medical Society, (1972-3), 1-7.

2873. _____, Sylvia G. Lutkins. "Mortality of Bereavement," British Medical Journal, 4 (Oct. 7, 1967), 13-6.

2874. Reese, William. "The Major Cause of Death," Texas Medicine, 66 (Sep., 1960), 56-61.

2875. Reeves, Robert B., Jr. "A Study of Terminal Cancer Patients," Journal of Pastoral Care, 14 (1960), 218-23.

2876. _____, et al., eds. Pastoral Care of the Dying and Bereaved: Selected Readings. New York: Health Sciences Publications, 1973.

2877. Regan, P.F. "Death and the Dying Patient," Medical Insight, 1 (Dec., 1969), 48ff.

2878. _____. "The Dying Patient and His Family," Journal of the American Medical Association, 192 (May 24, 1965), 666-7.

2879. Reich, Warren T. "Death in Modern Theology," Liturgy, (Nov., 1970), 20-1.

2880. Reid, D.D. et al. "Assessing the Comparability of Mortality Statistics," British Medical Journal, 5422 (1964), 1437-9.

2881. Reik, Theodore. The Search Within. New York: Grove Press, 1956.

2882. Reilly, C.T. "The Diagnosis of Life and Death," Journal of the Medical Society of New Jersey, 66 (Nov., 1969), 601-4.

2883. Reilly, H. Death Demands an Audience. New York: MacFadden-Bartell, 1969.

2884. Reilly, Patricia. "Laura Was Unpleasant and Made us Angry but She Was Dying and that Made us Ashamed," Nursing, '73, (Aug., 1973), 44-6.

2885. Reimanis, Gunars, Russel F. Green. "Imminence of Death and Intellectual Decrement in the Aging," Developmental Psychology, 5 (Sep., 1971), 270-2.

2886. Reimann, Stanley P. "The General Care of the Cancer Patient," Chicago Medical Society Bulletin, 55 (July 12, 1952), 21-6.

2887. Reisner, G.A. The Egyptian Conception of Immortality. Boston: Houghton, Mifflin, 1912.

2888. Reissell, J.K., M.R. Miller. "Care of Women with Terminal Pelvic Cancer," British Medical Journal, 1 (1964), 1214.

2889. Rendoing, J., G.A. Seys. "Psychological Obstacles to Removal of Organs in Cerebral Death," Annals of Anesthesiology, 15 (1974), 147-50.

2890. Renneker, Richard E. "Countertransference Reactions to Cancer," Psychosomatic Medicine, 19 (Sep.-Oct., 1957), 409-18.

2891. Reynolds, David K., Richard A. Kalish. "Anticipation of Futurity as a Function of Ethnicity and Age," Journal of Gerontology, 29 (Mar., 1974), 224-31.

2892. _____. "The Social Ecology of Dying--Observations of Wards for the Terminally Ill," Hospital and Community Psychiatry, 25 (Mar.,1974), 147-52.

2893. _____. "Work Roles in Death-Related Occupations," Journal of Vocational Behavior, 4 (Apr., 1974), 223-5.

2894. Reynolds, Paul Davidson. "On the Protection of Human Subjects and Social Science," International Social Science Journal, 24 (1972), 693-719.

2895. _____, Robert Fulton. Decision for Death: Simulation of a Societal Consensus Group. Minneapolis: University of Minnesota, Center for Death Education and Research, 1973.

2896. Rezek, J.R. "Dying and Death," Journal of Forensic Sciences, 8 (Apr., 1963) 200-8.

2897. Rheingold, Joseph C. The Mother, Anxiety, and Death: The Catastrophic Death Complex. Boston: Little, Brown, 1967.

2898. Rhoads, Paul S. "Management of the Patient with Terminal Illness," Journal of the American Medical Association, 192 (May 24, 1965), 661-5.

2899. Rhudick, Paul J., A.S. Dibner. "Age, Personality and Health Correlates of Death concerns in Normal Aged Individuals," Journal of Gerontology, 16 (Jan., 1961), 44-9.

2900. _____, et al. "Attitudes Toward Death in Older Persons: A Symposium," Journal of Gerontology, 16 (Jan., 1961), 44-66.

2901. Rice, Charles. The Vanishing Right to Live. New York: Doubleday, 1969.

2902. Rich, Theodore. "The Dying Patient," Mind-Psychiatry in General Practice, 1 (Jan., 1973), 15ff.

2903. _____, G.M. Kalmanson. "Attitudes of Medical Residents Toward the Dying Patients in a General Hospital," Postgraduate Medicine, 40 (Oct., 1966), A127-30.

2904. Richards, I.D.G., H. McIntosh. "Confidential Inquiry into 226 Consecutive Cot Deaths," Archives of Diseases in Childhood, 47 (1972), 697-706.

2905. Richardson, Henry B. Patients Have Families. New York: The Commonwealth Fund, 1945.

2906. Richman, J. et al. "A Clinical Study of the Role of Hostility and Death Wishes by the Family and Society in Suicidal Attempts," Israel Annals of Psychiatry and Related Disciplines, 8 (Dec., 1970), 213-31.

2907. Richmond, J.B., H.A. Waisman. "Psychologic Aspects of Management of Children with Malignant Disease," American Journal of the Diseases of Children, 89 (1955), 42-7.

2908. Richmond, Velma B. Laments for the Dead in Medieval Narrative. Atlantic Highlands, NJ: Duquesne University Press, 1966.

2909. Richter, C.P. "On the Phenomenon of Sudden Death in Animals and Man," Psychosomatic Medicine, 19 (1957), 191-8.

2910. Riegel, Klaus F. et al. "A Study of the Dropout Rates in Longitudinal Research on Aging and the Prediction of Death," Journal of Personality and Social Psychology, 5 (1967), 342-8.

2911. Ries, H. "An Unwelcome Child and Her Death Instinct," International Journal of Psychoanalysis, 26 (1945), 153-61.

2912. Riezler, Kurt. "The Social Psychology of Fear," American Journal of Sociology, 49 (May, 1944), 489-98.

2913. Riggins, H.M. et al. "Man, Medicine and the Ministry," Bulletin of the New York Academy of Medicine, 37 (Aug., 1961), 551-79.

2914. Riising, J. "Fagligt og Socialt. Bor VI. Fortaelle vore Doende Patienter Sand-heden (Should our Dying Patients be Told the Truth)?" Ugeskrift for Laeger (Kobenhavn), 96 (Dec. 27, 1934), 1429-32.

2915. Roberts, David E. Existentialism and Religious Belief. New York: Oxford University Press, 1968.

2916. Roberts, Jean L. et al. "How Aged in Nursing Homes View Dying and Death," Geriatrics, 25 (Apr., 1970), 115-9.

2917. Roberts, Robert E. "Modernization and Infant Mortality in Mexico," Economic Development and Cultural Change, 21 (July, 1973), 655-69.

2918. Roberts, W.W. "The Death Instinct in Morbid Anxiety," Journal of the Royal Army Medical Corps, 81 (1943), 61-73.

2919. Robertson, James. Hospitals and Children. London: Victor Gollanca, 1962.

2920. _____. "Some Responses of Young Children to Loss of Maternal Care," Child-Family Digest, 15 (Sep.-Oct., 1956), 7-22.

2921. Robinson, Alice M. "Loss and Grief," The Journal of Practical Nursing, 21 (May, 1971), 18-9ff.

2922. Robinson, George Canby. The Patient as a Person; A Study of the Social Aspects of Illness. New York: The Commonwealth Fund, 1939.

2923. Robinson, Lisa. "We Have No Dying Patients," Nursing Outlook, 22 (Oct., 1974), 651-3.

2924. Robison, R. "Time, Death and the River in Dickens' Novels," English Studies, 53 (Oct., 1972), 436-54.

2925. Robitscher, J.B. "The Right to Die," Hastings Center Reports, 2 (Sep., 1972), 11-4.

2926. Robson, Kenneth S. "Letters to a Dead Husband," Journal of Geriatric Psychiatry, 7 (1974), 208-32.

2927. Rochlin, Gregory. "The Dread of Abandonment," Psychoanalytic Study of the Child, 16 (1961), 451-70.

2928. _____. Griefs and Discontents: The Focus of Change. Boston: Little, Brown, 1965.

2929. _____. "Loss and Restitution," The Psychoanalytic Study of the Child, 8 (1953), 288-309.

2930. _____. "The Loss Complex," Journal of the American Psychoanalytic Association, 7 (1959), 299-316.

2931. Rock, M. "Philosophical View of Dying Basis for Nursing Intervention," Arizona Nurse, 24 (Mar.-Apr., 1971), 6-13.

2932. Rodstein, Manuel, Alfred Bornstein. "Terminal ECG in the Aged," Geriatrics, 25 (Dec., 1970), 91-100.

2933. Rogers, J., M.L. Vachon. "Nurses Can Help the Bereaved," Canadian Nurse, 71 (June, 1975), 16-9.

2934. Rogers, R. "The Influence of Losing One's Parent on Being a Parent," Psychiatry Digest, 29 (May, 1968), 29-36.

2935. Rogerts, William F. "Needs of the Bereaved," Pastoral Psychology, 1 (1950), 17-21.

2936. _____. "The Pastor's Work with Grief," Pastoral Psychology, 14 (Sep., 1963), 24.

2937. _____. Ye Shall Be Comforted. Philadelphia: Westminster Press, 1950.

2938. Rogo, D. Scott. "Parapsychology: Its Contributions to the Study of Death," Omega, 5 (Summer, 1974), 99-113.

2939. Rogot, Eugene. Smoking and General Mortality among U.S. Veterans, 1954-1969. Bethesda, MD: National Heart and Lung Institute, Epidemiology Branch, 1974.

2940. Roheim, Geza. "Animism and Dreams," Psychoanalytic Review, 32 (1945), 62-72.

2941. Roll, S., C.B. Brenneis. "Chicano and Anglo Dreams of Death: Replication," J Cross Cul, 6 (1975), 377-83.

2942. Rom, Paul. "Should I Bequeath My Corpse to a Teaching Hospital?" Omega, 1 (May, 1970), 141-2.

2943. Romains, Jules. The Death of a Nobody. Translated by Desmond MacCarthy and Sidney Waterlow. New York: Alfred A. Knopf, 1944; New American Library, 1961.

2944. Romano, John. "Emotional Components of Illness," Connecticut State Medical Journal, 7 (1943), 22-5.

2945. _____. "On Those Who Care for the Sick," Journal of Chronic Diseases, 1 (1955), 695-7.

2946. Romero, Carol E. The Treatment of Death in Contemporary Children's Literature. New York: Long Island University, 1974.

2947. Roose, Lawrence J. "The Dying Patient," International Journal of Psychoanalysis, 50 (1969), 385-95.

2948. _____. "To Die Alone," Mental Hygiene, 53 (July 1969), 321-6.

2949. Roosevelt, Patricia Peabody. "Eleanor Roosevelt: A Great Lady's Last Brave Days," in I Love a Roosevelt. New York: Doubleday, 1967.

2950. Root, S.A. "Recognition of Chronic Brain Death," New England Journal of Medicine, 288 (Mar. 22, 1973), 636-7.

2951. Rorsman, B. "Mortality Among Psychiatric Patients," ACTA Psychiatrica Scandanavia, 50 (1974), 354-75.

2952. Rose, A.M., W.A. Peterson. Older People and their Social World. Philadelphia: F.A. Davis, 1965.

2953. Rose, Ada Campbell. Acquainted with Grief. Philadelphia: The Westminster Press, 1972.

2954. Rose, M.S. "Who Should Choose," Lancet, 1 (Mar., 1969), 465-6.

2955. Rose, R.J. Maori-European Comparisons in Mortality. Wellington, NZ: National Health Statistics Centre, Department of Health, 1972.

2956. Rosecrans, C.J. "Attitudes Toward Death and Bereavement," Alabama Journal of Medical Science, 8 (Apr., 1971), 242-9.

2957. Rosecrans, C.J. "Is Acceptance of Non-Being Possible?" Alabama Journal of Medical Sciences, 7 (Jan., 1970), 32-7.

2958. Rosen, A. "Lakaren vid den Skukes Dodslager (The Physician at the Death Bed)," Svenska Lakartidningen (Stockholm), 36 (Jan. 13, 1939), 73-101.

2959. Rosen, R.A. et al. "Health Professional's Attitudes Toward Abortion," The Public Opinion Quarterly, 38 (Summer, 1974), 159-73.

2960. Rosen, V.H. "The Role of Denial in Acute Postoperative Affective Reactions Following the Removal of Body Parts," Psychosomatic Medicine, 12 (1950), 354.

2961. Rosenbaum, Ernest H. Living with Cancer. New York: Praeger, 1975.

2962. Rosenbaum, Milton. "Emotional Aspects of Wartime Separations," The Family, 24 (Jan., 1944), 337-41.

2963. Rosenblatt, B. "A Young Boy's Reaction to the Death of his Sister," Journal of the American Academy of Child Psychiatry, 8 (Apr., 1969), 321-35.

2964. Rosenblatt, Paul et al. "Coping with Anger and Aggression in Mourning," Omega 3 (Nov., 1972), 271-84.

2965. Rosenthal, Hattie R. "The Fear of Death as an Indispensable Factor in Psycho-therapy," American Journal of Psychotherapy, 17 (Oct., 1963), 619-30.

2966. _____. "Psychotherapy for the Dying," American Journal of Psychotherapy, 11 (July, 1957), 626-33.

2967. Rosenthal, Pauline. "The Death of the Leader in Group Psychotherapy," American Journal of Orthopsychiatry, 17 (1947), 266-77.

2968. Rosenthal, Ted. How Could I Not Be Among You? New York: Avon Books, 1975.

2969. Rosenwaile, Ira. "Seasonal Variation of Deaths in the United States, 1951-1960," Journal of the American Statistical Association, 61 (Sep., 1966), 706-19.

2970. Rosenzweig, Saul. "Sibling Death as a Psychological Experience with Special Reference to Schizophrenia," Psychoanalytic Review, 30 (Arp., 1943), 177-86.

2971. _____, D. Bray. "Sibling Deaths in Anamnesis of Schizophrenic Patients," Psychoanalytic Review, 30 (1943), 177-86.

2972. Roslansky, John D., George Wald, eds. The End of Life. New York: Fleet Academic Additions, 1973.

2973. Rosner, Albert. "Mourning Before the Fact," Journal of the American Psycho-analytic Association, 10 (July, 1962), 564-70.

2974. Rosner, F. "Emotional Care of Cancer Patients: To Tell or Not to Tell," New York State Journal of Medicine, 74 (July, 1974), 1467-9.

2975. Rosoff, S. et al. "The EEG in Establishing Brain Death: A Ten Year Report with Criteria and Legal Safeguards in the 50 States," Electroencephalography and Clinical Neurophysiology, 24 (Mar., 1968), 283-4.

2976. Ross, Helen. Fears of Children. Chicago: Science Research Associates, 1951.

2977. Ross, Joan M. Post-Mortem Appearances. New York: Oxford University Press, 1963.

2978. Ross, K.K. "The Right to Die with Dignity," Bulletin of the Menninger Clinic, 36 (May, 1972), 302-12.

2979. Rothenberg, Albert. "Psychological Problems in Terminal Cancer Management," Cancer, 14 (Sep.-Oct., 1961), 1063-73.

2980. Rothenberg, Michael B. "Reactions of Those Who Treat Children with Cancer," Pediatrics, 40 (Sep., 1967), 507-12.

2981. Rovasio, A. "L'io dei Morenti (The Ego of the Dying) (The Mental Condition of the Dying)," Rassegna di Studi Psichiatrici (Siena), 22 (1933), 87-106.

2982. Rozovsky, L.E. "The Moment of Death," Canadian Hospital, 49 (Sep., 1972), 24-5.

2983. Rudd, T.N. "Family Doctor at the Death-Bed," Medical World, 85 (July, 1956),

2984. Rueda, Teresa. "The Concept of Death Among French and Mexican Suicidal Persons," Proceedings of the 6th International Conference for Suicide Prevention, Mexico, D.F., Mexico, Dec. 5-8, 1972. Ann Arbor: Edwards Brothers, 1972. 474-9.

2985. Ruesch, Jurgen, A. Rodney Prestwood. "Anxiety," Archives of Neurology and Psychiatry, 62 (1949), 527-50.

2986. Ruitenbeek, Hendrik M. ed. The Interpretation of Death. New York: Aronson, 1973.

2987. Ruff, Frank. "Have We the Right to Prolong Dying?" Medical Economics, 37 (1960), 39-44.

2988. Rupp, J.C. "Sudden Death in the Gay World," Medicine, Science and the Law, 10 (July, 1970), 198-91.

2989. Rush, Alfred Clement. Death and Burial in Christian Antiquity. Washington: The Catholic University of America Press, 1941.

2990. Russell, Bertrand. "Your Child and the Fear of Death," The Forum, 81 (1929), 174-8.

2991. Russell, D.H. Children's Thinking. Boston: Ginn and Co., 1956.

2992. Russell, O. Ruth. Freedom to Die: Moral and Legal Aspects of Euthanasia. New York: Human Science Press, 1975.

2993. Russell, Robert A. Dry Those Tears. Santa Monica: DeVorss and Co., 1975.

2994. Russell, Roger W. "Studies in Animism, II: The Development of Animism," Journal of Genetic Psychology, 56 (1940), 353-66.

2995. _____, Wayne Dennis. "Studies in Animism, I: A Standardized Procedure for the Investigation of Animism," Journal of Genetic Psychology, 55 (1939), 389-400.

2996. Russell, S. "Thoughts on Bereavement," Nursing Times, 61 (Feb. 26, 1965), 285-6.

2997. Rutishauser, H.C. "The Concept of Extra Mortality," South African Medical Journal, 47 (May 26, 1973), 855-8.

2998. _____. "Mortality Tables," South African Medical Journal, 47 (May 26, 1973), 855-8.

2999. Rutter, M.L. "Psychosocial Disorders in Childhood and their Outcome in Adult Life," Journal of the Royal College of Physicians of London, 4 (Apr., 1970), 211-8.

3000. Ryle, John A. "Angor Animi, or the Sense of Dying," Guy Hospital Reports, 78 (July, 1928), 371-6.

3001. _____. "Of Death and Dying," Lancet, 2 (Sep. 28, 1940), 401-2.

3002. Rynearson, Edward H. "You Are Standing at the Bedside of a Patient Dying of Untreatable Cancer," CA Bulletin of Cancer Progress, 9 (1959), 85-7.

3003. Sabatier, Armand. Essai sur la Vie et la Mort. Paris: Babe, 1892.

3004. Sabatini, Paul, R. Kastenbaum. "The Do-It-Yourself Death Certificate as a Research Technique," Life-Threatening Behavior, 2 (1973), 20-32.

3005. Sachs, Hans. "Beauty, Life and Death," American Imago, 1 (1940), 81-133.

3006. _____. "Das Thema--Tod," Imago, 3 (1914), 456-61.

3007. Sackett, W.W. "Death with Dignity: A Legislative Necessity," Journal of the Florida Medical Association, 61 (May, 1974), 366-7.

3008. Saclier, A.L. "Respecting Your Dignity?" Australasian Nurses Journal, 3 (Oct., 1974), 15.

3009. Sadler, Alfred M., Jr., Blair L. Sadler. "Human Experimentation, Transplantation, and the Law," Annals of the New York Academy of Sciences, 169 (Jan. 21, 1970), 546-54.

3010. Sadler, Blair, Alfred Sadler. "Providing Cadaver Organs for Transplantation," The Hastings Center Studies, 1 (1973), 14-26.

3011. Sadwith, J.A. "An Interdisciplinary Approach to Death Education," Journal of School Health, 44 (Oct., 1974), 455-8.

3012. Safier, G. "A Study in Relationships Between Life-Death Concepts in Children," Journal of Genetic Psychology, 105 (Dec., 1964), 283-94.

3013. Saffady, William. "The Effects of Childhood Bereavement and Parental Remarriage in Sixteenth-Century England: The Case of Thomas More," History of Childhood Quarterly, 1 (Fall, 1973), 310-66.

3014. St. John-Stevas, Norman. "Abortion and Euthanasia," Applied Christianity, (Oct., 1973), 10-4.

3015. _____. Life, Death and the Law. Cleveland: World, 1961.

3016. _____. The Right to Life. New York: Rinehart and Winston, 1964.

3017. Salaff, Janet W. "Mortality Decline in the People's Republic of China and the United States," Population Studies, 27 (Nov., 1973), 551-76.

3018. Salk, Lee et al. "Sudden Infant Death: Impact on Family and Physician," Clinical Pediatrics, 10 (May, 1971), 248-50.

3019. _____. "Sudden Infant Death: Normal Cardiac Habituation and Poor Autonomic Control," New England Journal of Medicine, 291 (Aug., 1974), 219-22.

3020. Salomone, Jerome. "An Empirical Report on Some Controversial American Funeral Practices," Sociological Symposium, 1 (Fall, 1968), 47-56.

3021. Salter, C.A., C.D. Salter. "Death Anxiety and Attitudes Toward Aging and Elderly Among Young People," Gerontology, 15 (1975), 89.

3022. Salter, Mary Dinsmore. Deprivation of Maternal Care (with J. Bowlby, Maternal Care and Mental Health) 2 pts. in 1. New York: Schocken, 1966.

3023. Sand, Patricia et al. "Psychological Assessment of Candidates for a Hemodialysis Program," Annals of Internal Medicine, 64 (Mar., 1966), 602-9.

3024. Sanders, J. "Euthanasia: None Dare Call It Murder," Journal of Criminal Law, Criminology and Political Science, 3 (1969), 351-9.

3025. Sandford, B. "Some Notes on a Dying Patient," International Journal of Psychiatry, 38 (1957), np.

3026. Santmeyer, Helen. Ohio Town. Columbus: Ohio State University Press, 1962.

3027. Sanua, Victor D. "A Comparative Study of Schizophrenics of Different Socio-Cultural Backgrounds (Protestant, Irish, Catholic, and Jewish): Parental Loss and Prognosis in Terms of Re-Hospitalization," Revista de Psicologia Normal e Patologica, 11 (1966), 374-85.

3028. Sapwell, J. "Causes of Death in the Elderly," Practitioner, 213 (Sep., 1974), 354.

3029. Sardello, Robert J. "Death and the Imagination," Humanitas, 10 (Feb., 1974), 61-73.

3030. Sarnoff, Irving, Seth M. Corwin. "Castration Anxiety and the Fear of Death," Journal of Personality, 27 (1959), 374-85.

3031. Sarwer-Foner, G.J. "Denial of Death and the Unconscious Longing for Indestructibility and Immortality in the Terminal Phase of Adolescence," Canadian Psychiatric Association Journal, 17, Suppl. 2 (1972), SS51ff.

3032. Sauer, H.I., D.W. Parke. "Counties with Extreme Death Rates and Associated Factors," American Journal of Epidemiology, 99 (Apr., 1974), 258-64.

3033. Saul, L.J "Reactions of a Man to Natural Death," Psychoanalytic Quarterly, 28 (1959), 383-6.

3034. Saul, Sidney R., Shura Saul. "Old People Talk About Death," Omega, 4 (1973), 27-35.

3035. Saunders, Cicely. "And From Sudden Death," Nursing Times, 58 (Aug. 17, 1962), 1045-6.

3036. _____ . Care of the Dying. London: Macmillan, 1960.

3037. _____ . "Death and Responsibility: A Medical Director's View," Psychiatric Opinion, 3 (Aug., 1966), 28-34.

3038. Saunders, Cicely. "A Death in the Family: A Professional View," British Medical Journal, 1 (Jan. 6, 1973), 30-1.

3039. _____. "The Last Stages of Life," American Journal of Nursing, 65 (Mar., 1965), 70-5.

3040. _____. "The Management of Fatal Illness in Childhood," Proceedings of the Royal Society of Medicine, 62 (June, 1969), 550-3.

3041. _____. "The Management of Patients in the Terminal Stage," in R.W. Raven, ed., Cancer. London: Butterworth, 1959.

3042. _____. "The Management of Terminal Illness," Hospital Medicine, Part I: (Dec., 1966), 225-8; Part II: (Jan., 1967), 317-20; Part III: (Feb., 1967), 433-6.

3043. _____. "Mental Distress in the Dying," Nursing Times, 55 (Oct., 30, 1959), 1067-9.

3044. _____. "The Nursing of Patients Dying of Cancer," Nursing Times, 55 (Nov. 6, 1959), 1091-2.

3045. _____. "The Problem of Euthanasia," Nursing Times, 55 (Oct. 9, 1959), 960-1.

3046. _____. "Should a Patient Know . . . . ?" Nursing Times, 55 (Oct. 16, 1959), 994-5.

3047. _____. "When a Patient is Dying," Nursing Times, 55 (Nov. 13, 1959), 1129-30.

3048. Sautler, C. "The Physician, the Child and Death, 3: The Psychoanalytic Approach," Revue de Medecine Psychosomatique et de Psychologie Medicale, 10 (Oct.-Dec., 1968), 425-9.

3049. Savishin, J.S., H. Wimberle. "Living and Dead: Cross Cultural Perspective on Jewish Memorial Observances," Jewish Social Studies, 36 (1974), 281-300.

3050. Schaerer, Rene. "La Philosophie Moderne Devant la Mort," in L'Homme Face a la Mort. Neuchatel: Delachaux and Niestle, 1952.

3051. Scharfetter, F. "The Signs of Irrevocable Death and the Problem When Resuscitation Should be Discontinued as Hopeless," Zeitschrift fur Allegemein-medinizin, 45 (June 20, 1969), 830-4.

3052. Scharl, Adele E. "Regression and Restitution in Object-Loss: Clinical Observations," The Psychoanalytic Study of the Child, 16 (1961), 471-80.

3053. Schatz, I.J. "The Need to Know," Chest, 63 (Jan., 1973), 82-3.

3054. Schein, Edgar. "Reaction Patterns to Severe, Chronic Stress in American Army Prisoners of War of the Chinese," Journal of Social Issues, 13 (1957), 21-30.

3055. Scherlis, L. "Death: The Diagnostic Dilemma," Maryland Medical Journal, 17 (Dec., 1968), 77-8.

3056. Scherzer, Carl J. Ministering to the Dying. Englewood Cliffs: Prentice-Hall, 1963.

3057. Schilder, Paul. "The Attitude of Murderers Toward Death," Journal of Abnormal and Social Psychology, 31 (1936), 348-63.

3058. Schlesinger, B. "The Single Parent Family in Australia: An Overview," Australian Journal of Social Issues, 7 (1972), 151-61.

3059. _____. "The Widowed as a One Parent Family Unit," Social Science, 46 (1971), 26-32.

3060. _____, Alex Macrae. "The Widow and Widower and Remarriage: Selected Findings," Omega, 2 (Feb., 1971), 10-8.

3061. Schleyer, F. "The Value of the Determination of the Time of Death," Beitrage zur Gerichtichen Medizin, 25 (1969), 66-8.

3062. Schmahl, Jane A. "Ritualism in Nursing Practice," Nursing Forum, 3 (1964), 74-84.

3063. Schmale, A.H., Jr. "Psychic Trauma During Bereavement," International Psychiatry Clinics, 8 (1971), 147-68.

3064. _____. "Relationship of Separation and Depression to Disease," Psychosomatic Medicine, 20 (1958), 259-77.

3065. Schmiedeck, Raoul A. "The Funeral of a Psychiatric Aide," Bulletin of the Menninger Clinic, 36 (Nov., 1972), 641-5.

3066. Schmitt, R.C. "Death, Disease, and Property Taxes," Hawaii Medical Journal, 25 (Sep.-Oct., 1965), 34-5.

3067. Schnaper, Nathan. "Care of the Dying Patient," Medical Times, 93 (May, 1965), 537-43.

3068. _____. "Management of the Dying Patient," Modern Treatment, 6 (July, 1963), 746-59.

3069. _____, et al. Management of the Dying Patient and His Family. New York: MSS Information Corp., 1974.

3070. Schneck, J.M. "Unconscious Relationship Between Hypnosis and Death," Psychoanalytic Review, 38 (1951), 271-5.

3071. Schneide, P., R. Schneide. "Young Children's Reaction to Death and Dying," Dynamic Psychology, 94 (1975), 216-33.

3072. Schneider, D.H. "Cancer Patient without Hope," South African Medical Journal, 49 (Mar. 1, 1975), 297-8.

3073. Schneider, H. "Confirmation of Brain Death," Deutsche Medizinische Wochenschrift, 94 (Nov. 14, 1969), 2404-5.

3074. _____. "Criteria of the Beginning of Death," Oeffentliche Gesundheitswesen, 31 (Nov., 1969), 536-41.

3077. Schoenberg, Bernard et al. Physicians and the Bereaved," General Practitioner, 40 (Oct., 1969), 104-8.

3078. _____, eds. Anticipatory Grief. New York: Columbia University Press, 1974.

3079. _____. Bereavement: Its Psychological Aspects. New York: Columbia University Press, 1975.

3080. _____. Loss and Grief. New York: Columbia University Press, 1973.

3081. _____. Psychosocial Aspects of Terminal Care. New York: Columbia University Press, 1972.

3082. Schopenhauer, Arthur. "On the Doctrine of the Indestructibility of Our True Nature by Death," in The Wisdom of Life, and Other Essays by Arthur Schopenhauer. Translated by Bailey Saunders and Ernest Belfort Bax. Washington: M.W. Dunne, 1901.

3083. Schowalter, J.E. et al. "The Adolescent Patient's Decision to Die," Pediatrics, 51 (June, 1973), 97-103.

3084. Schrauzer, G.N. et al. "Sudden Infant Death Syndrome: Plasma Vitamin E Levels and Dietary Factors," Annual Clinical and Laboratory Science, 5 (Jan.-Feb., 1975), 31-7.

3085. Schreiba, D. "Approaches and Developments in Study of Attitudes to Death: Descriptions of Meetings with Physicians and Impressions of their Attitude on this Subject," Israel Annals of Psychology, 13 (1975), 259-69.

3086. Schreiner, George E., John F. Maher. "Hemodialysis of Chronic Renal Failure, III: Medical, Moral and Ethical, and Socio-Economic Problems," Annals of Internal Medicine, 62 (Mar., 1965), 551-6.

3087. Schroeder, Oliver C., Jr. "Death: Legal Aspects," Encylopedia Americana, (1972), 8:565-6.

3088. _____. "Death: A Mystery Becomes an Enigma," Postgraduate Medical Journal, 51 (May, 1972), 57-9.

3089. Schuessler, R.F. "The Deterrent Influence of the Death Penalty," Annals of the American Academy of Political and Social Science, 284 (1952), 54-62.

3090. Schulberg, Herbert C. "Disaster, Crisis Theory, and Intervention Strategies," Omega, 5 (1974), 77-87.

3091. Schulte, W. "Endgultigkeit und Tod als Problem fur die Psychotherapie (Finality and Death as a Problem for Psychotherapy)," Wiener Medizinische Wochen-schrift, 112 (1962), 143-6.

3092. Schulz, Richard, David Aderman. "Clinical Research and the Stages of Dying," Omega, 5 (Summer, 1974), 137-43.

3093. _____. "Effect of Residential Change on the Temporal Distance to Death," Omega, 4 (1973), 157-62.

3094. Schur, Max. "Discussion of Dr. John Bowlby's Paper 'Grief and Mourning in Infancy and Early Childhood'," The Psychoanalytic Study of the Child, 15 (1960), 63-84.

3095. _____. Freud: Living and Dying. New York: International Universities Press, 1973.

3096. Schur, Tomas J. "What Man Has Told Children about Death," Omega, 2 (May, 1971), 84-90.

3097. Schwab, M.L. "The Nurse's Role in Assisting Families of Dying Geriatric Patients to Manage Grief and Guilt," American Nurses Association Clinical Sessions, (1968), 110-6.

3098. Schwarta, Melvin L. "Death: A Neuroscientific Analysis," Omega, 2 (Feb., 1971), 30-5.

3099. Schwarz, Berthold Eric, Bartholomew Ruggieri. Parent-Child Tensions. Phila-delphia: J.B. Lippincott, 1958.

3100. Schwartz, R.S. "On Sudden, Unexpected Death," Medical Trial Technique Quarterly, 2 (Summer, 1974), 49-54.

3101. Scoggins, W.F. "'Growing Old': Death by Installment Plan," Life-Threatening Behavior, 1 (Summer, 1971), 143-7.

3102. Scott, C.A. "Old Age and Death," American Journal of Psychology, 8 (1896), 54-122.

3103. Scott, Frances G., Ruth M. Brewer, eds. Confrontations of Death: A Book of Readings and a Suggested Method of Instruction. Corvallis, Oregon: Continuing Education Publications, 1971.

3104. Scott, Nathan, ed. "Life and Death Among Fellowmen," in The Modern Vision of Death. Richmond: John Knox Press, 1967.

3105. _____. The Modern Vision of Death. Richmond: John Knox Press, 1967.

3106. Scott, W.C. "Mania and Mourning," International Journal of Psychoanalysis, 45 (Apr.-July, 1964), 373-9.

3107. Scoville, A.B., Jr. "The Physician and the Terminal Patient," Journal of the Tennessee Medical Association, 58 (June, 1965), 208-9.

3108. Scripcaru, G. et al. "Attempts of Estimating Risk Ractors in Sudden Death of Children," Revista Medico-Chirurgicala a Societatii di Medici si Naturalisti din Iasi, 16 (July-Sep., 1972), 633-9.

3109. Scwidde, J.T. "On Death and Dying," Rocky Mountain Medical Journal, 70 (Nov., 1973), 23-6.

3110. Searles, H.F. "Schizophrenia and the Inevitability of Death," Psychiatric Quarterly, 35 (Oct., 1961), 631-65.

3111. Seelig, M.G. "Should the Cancer Victim Be Told the Truth?" Missouri Medicine, 40 (Feb., 1943), 33-5.

3112. Segal, Hanna. "Fear of Death: Notes on the Analysis of an Old Man," International Journal of Psychoanalysis, 39 (1958), 178-81.

3113. Seiden, Richard H., Brigette Teitler. "Attitudes Toward Modes of Death," Proceedings of the 6th International Conference for Suicide Prevention, Mexico, D.F. , Mexico, Dec. 5-8, 1972. Ann Arbor: Edwards Borthers, 1972. 171-4.

3114. Seitz, Pauline M., Louise H. Warrick. "Perinatal Death: The Grieving Mother," American Journal of Nursing, 74 (Nov., 1974), 2029-33.

3115. Seligman, Martin E. "Submissive Death: Giving up on Life," Psychology Today, 7 (May, 1974), 80-5.

3116. Seligman, R. et al. "The Effect of Earlier Parental Loss in Adolescence," Archives of General Psychiatry, 31 (Oct., 1974), 475-9.

3117. Seltzer, A.P. "Premonition of Death--A Safeguard from Malpractice," Journal of Legal Medicine, 1 (Sep.-Oct., 1973), 28-9.

3118. Selvey, Carole. "Concerns about Death in Relation to Sex, Dependency, Guilt about Hostility and Feelings of Powerlessness," Dissertation Abstracts Internationale, 31 (Mar., 1971), 5641.

3119. Selvini, A. "Tell the Truth to the Patient," Minerva Medica, 62 (May 16, 1971), 1985-90.

3120. Sepulveda, B. "Concept of Death," Gaceta Medica de Mexico, 99 (July, 1969), 631-3.

3121. Seskin, Jane. Young Widow. New York: Ace Books, 1975.

3122. Secitt, S. "Reflections on Mortality and Causes of Death afer Injury and Burns," Injury, 4 (Nov., 1972), 151-6.

3123. Shaffer, H.B. "Approaches to Death," Editorial Research Reports, 1 (Apr. 21, 1971), 289-306.

3124. Shaffer, John W. et al. "Social Adjustment Profiles of Fatally Injured Drivers: A Replication and Extension," Archives of General Psychiatry, 30 (Apr., 1974), 508-11.

3125. Shaffer, Thomas L. Death, Property and Lawyers: A Behavioral Approach. New York: Dunellen Publishing, 1970.

3126. _____. "The Estate Planning Counsellor and Values Destroyed by Death," Iowa Law Review, 55 (1970), 376.

3127. Shah, B.S. "Death Without Disease," New York State Journal of Medicine, 74 (Oct., 1974), 2153-4.

3128. Shaler, Nathaniel Southgate. The Individual: A Study of Life and Death. New York: D. Appleton and Co., 1901.

3129. Shambaugh, B. "A Study of Loss Reactions in a Seven-Year-Old," The Psychoanalytic Study of the Child, 16 (1961), 510-52.

3130. Shands, Harley C. "Psychological Mechanisms in Cancer Patients," Cancer, 4 (1951), 1159-70.

3131. Shapiro, H.A. "Brain Death and Organ Transplantation," Journal of Forensic Medicine, 15 (July-Sep., 1968), 89-90.

3132. _____. "Criteria for Determining that Death Has Occurred: The Philadelphia Protocol," Journal of Forensic Medicine, 16 (1969), 1-3.

3133. Shapiro, S.I. "Instructional Resources for Teaching the Psychology of Death and Dying," Catalog of Selected Documents in Psychology, 3 (Fall, 1973), 113.

3134. _____. "Teaching the Psychology of Death: Fictional and Nonfictional Resources," Catalog of Selected Documents in Psychology, 4 (Fall, 1974), 108-9.

3135. Shapiro, S.L. "My Death Had Been the Healthiest One in Her Life," Psychiatric Quarterly, 46 (1972), 22-8.

3136. Share, Lynda. "Family Communication in the Crisis of a Child's Fatal Illness: A Literature Review and Analysis," Omega, 3 (Aug., 1972), 187-201.

3137. Sharp, D. "Lessons from a Dying Patient," American Journal of Nursing, 68 (July, 1968), 1517-20.

3138. Sharp, T.H., T.H. Crofts. "Death with Dignity: Physicians Civil Liability," Baylor Law Review, 27 (1975), 86-108.

3139. Shatan, C.F. "The Grief of Soldiers: Vietnam Combat Veterans' Self-Help Movement," American Journal of Orthopsychiatry, 43 (July, 1973), 640-53.

3140. Shaw, E.B. "Sudden Infant Death Syndrome," American Journal of Diseases in Childhood, 124 (Nov., 1972), 787-8.

3141. Shaw, E.B. "Sudden, Unexpected Death in Infancy Syndrome," American Journal of Diseases of Children, 116 (Aug., 1968), 189-215.

3142. Sheatsley, Paul B., Jacob J. Feldman. "The Assassination of President Kennedy: A Preliminary Report on Public Reactions and Behavior," Public Opinion Quarterly, 28 (Summer, 1964), 189-215.

3143. Sheehy, Daniel P. "Rules for Dying: A Study of Alienation and Patient-Spouse Role Expectations During Terminal Illness," Dissertation Abstracts International, 33 (Jan., 1973), 3777.

3144. Sheldon, Alan et al. "An Integrated Family Oriented Cancer Care Program: The Report of a Pilot Project in the Socio-Emotional Management of Chronic Disease," Journal of Chronic Disease, 22 (1970), 743-55.

3145. Shepard, M.W. "This I Believe--About Questioning the Right to Die," Nursing Outlook, 16 (Oct., 1968), 22-5.

3146. Shepherd, J. Barrie. "Ministering to the Dying Patient," The Pulpit, (July-Aug., 1966), 9-12.

3147. Sheps, J. "Management of Fear of Death in Chronic Disease," Journal of the American Geriatric Society, 5 (Sep., 1957), 793-7.

3148. Sher, Byron D. "Funeral Prearrangement: Mitigating the Undertaker's Bargaining Advantage," Stanford Law Review, 15 (May, 1963), 415-79.

3149. Sherlock, William. A Practical Discourse Concerning Death. London: R. Chiswell, 1686.

3150. Sherrill, Helen H., Lews J. Sherrill. "Interpreting Death to Children," International Journal of Religious Education, 28 (Oct., 1951), 4-6.

3151. Shestov, Leon. Les Revelations de la Mort. Paris: Dostoyevsky-Tolstoy, 1923.

3152. Shetrone, H.C. The Mound Builders. New York: D. Appleton and Co., 1930.

3153. Shibles, Warren. Death: An Interdisciplinary Analysis. Whitewater, WI: The Language Press, 1974.

3154. Shiloh, Ailon, Ida C. Selavan. Ethnic Groups of America: Their Mobility, Mortality and Behavior Disorders, I: The Blacks. Springfield: C.C. Thomas, 1974.

3155. Shneidman, Edwin S. Death: Current Perspectives. Palo Alto: Mayfield Publishing, 1976.

3156. _____. Deaths of Man. New York: Penguin, 1974.

3157. _____. "The Enemy," Psychology Today, 4 (Aug., 1970), 37-41ff.

3158. _____. "On the Deromanticization of Death," American Journal of Psychother-apy, 25 (1971), 5-17.

3159. _____. "Orientation Toward Cessation: A Reexamination of Current Modes of Death," Journal of Forensic Sciences, 13 (1968), 33-45.

3160. _____. "Orientations Toward Death," in Robert W. White, ed., The Study of Lives. New York: Atherton Press, 1963. 201-27.

3161. _____. "Postvention: The Care of the Bereaved," in R.O. Pasnau, ed., Consultation-Liaison Psychiatry. New York: Grune and Stratton, 1975.

3162. _____. "Some Reflections on Death and Suicide," Folia Psychiatrica et Neurologica Japnoica, 19 (1965), 317-25.

3163. _____. "Suicide, Sleep and Death: Some Possible Interrelations among Cessation, Interruption and Continuing Phenomena," Journal of Consulting Psychology, 28 (1964), 95-106.

3164. _____. "You and Death," Psychology Today, 5 (June, 1971), 43ff.

3165. _____, ed. Essays in Self-Destruction. New York: Science House, 1967.

3166. Shoben, Edward Joseph, Jr. "Culture, Ego Psychology, and an Image of Man," American Journal of Psychotherapy, 15 (July, 1961), 395-408.

3167. Shontz, Franklin C., Stephen L. Find. "A Psychobiological Analysis of Discom-fort, Pain and Death," Journal of General Psychology, 60 (Apr., 1959), 275-87.

3168. Shoor, Mervyn, Mary H. Speed. "Death, Delinquency, and the Mourning Process," Psychiatry Quarterly, 36 (1963), 540-58.

3169. Shoor, Mervyn, Mary H. Speed. "Delinquency as a Manifestation of the Mourning Process," The Psychiatric Quarterly, 37 (1963), 540-58.

3170. Shor, Ronald E. "A Survey of Representative Literature on Freud's Death-Instinct Hypothesis," Journal of Humanistic Psychology, 1 (1961), 98-110.

3171. Shrut, Samuel D. "Attitudes Toward Old Age and Death," Mental Hygiene, 42 (1958), 259-66.

3172. Shusterman, L.R. "Death and Dying: A Critical Review of the Literature," Nursing Outlook, 21 (July, 1973), 465-71.

3173. _____, L. Sechrist. "Attitudes of Registered Nurses Toward Death in a General Hospital," Psychiatry in Medicine, 4 (Fall, 1973), 411-26.

3174. Sichel, J. "Death Fantasies in a Child," Praxis der Kinderpsychologie und Kinderpsychiatrie (Gottingen), 16 (July, 1967), 172-5.

3175. Siegler, M. "Pascal's Woger and Hanging of Crepe," New England Journal of Medicine, 293 (1975), 853-7.

3176. Sigerist, Henry E. "The Sphere of Life and Death in Early Medieval Manu-scripts," Bulletin of the History of Medicine, 11 (Mar, 1942), 292-303.

3177. Siggins, L.D. "Mourning: A Critical Survey of the Literature," International Journal of Psychoanalysis, 47 (1966), 14-25.

3178. Silberman, H.K. "Appointment with Death: Attitudes and Communications," Missouri Medicine, 70 (Jan., 1973), 37-42.

3179. Silverman, Daniel. "Cerebral Death--The History of the Syndrome and Its Ident-ification," Annals of Internal Medicine, 74 (June, 1971), 1003-5.

3180. _____, et al. "Cerebral Death and the Electroencephalogram," Journal of the American Medical Association, 209 (Sep. 8, 1969), 1505-10.

3181. _____, et al. "Criteria of Brain Death," Science, 170 (Nov 27, 1970), 1000.

3182. Silverman, Phyllis Rolfe. "Factors Involved in Accepting an Offer of Help," Journal of Thanatology, 3 (1971), 161-71.

3183. _____. "Services to the Widowed: First Steps in a Program of Preventive Intervention," Community Mental Health Journal, 3 (Apring, 1967), 37-44.

3184. _____. "The Widow as a Caregiver in a Program of Preventive Intervention with Other Widows," Mental Hygiene, 54 (Oct., 1970), 540-7.

3185. _____. "The Widow-to-Widow Program: An Experiment in Preventive Intervention," Mental Hygiene, 53 (July, 1969), 333-7.

3186. Silverman, Phyllis Rolfe. "Widowhood and Preventive Intervention," The Family Coordinator, 21 (Jan., 1972), 95-102.

3187. _____, Sue Englander. "The Widow's View of Her Dependent Children," Omega, 6 (1975), 3-20.

3188. Silverman, S.M. "Parental Loss in Scientists," Science Studies, 4 (July, 1974), 259-64.

3189. Simko, Annamarie. "Death and the Hereafter: The Structuring of Immaterial Reality," Omega, 1 (May, 1970), 121-36.

3190. Simmel, E. "Self-Preservation and the Death Instinct," Psychoanalytic Quarterly, 13 (1944), 16-85.

3191. Simmons, Leo W., ed. The Role of the Aged in Primitive Society. New Haven: Yale University Press, 1945.

3192. Simmons, Roberta G., Julie Fulton. "Ethical Issues in Kidney Transplantation," Omega, 2 (Aug., 1971), 179-80.

3193. _____, Richard L. Simmons. "Organ Transplantation: A Societal Problem," Social Problems, 19 (Summer, 1971), 36-57.

3194. _____, et al. "Donors and Non-Donors: The Role of the Family and the Physician in Kidney Transplantation," Seminars in Psychiatry, 3 (Feb., 1971), 102-15.

3195. _____, et al. "Family Tension in the Search for a Kidney Donor," Journal of the American Medical Association, 215 (Feb. 8, 1971), 909-12.

3196. _____, et al. "The Prospective Organ Transplant Donor: Problems and Prospects of Medical Innovation," Omega, 3 (Nov., 1972), 391-39.

3197. Simmons, Sandra, Barbara Given. "Nursing Care of the Terminal Patient," Omega, 3 (Aug., 1972), 217-25.

3198. Simon, A.B., A.A. Alonzo. "Sudden Death in Nonhospitalitzed Cardiac Patients: An Epidemiologic Study with Implications for Intervention Techniques," Archives of Internal Medicine, 132 (Aug., 1973), 163-70.

3199. Simon, Nathan M. "A Consideration of Some Problems of the Terminal Phase of Analysis in a Parent-Loss Case," Israel Annals of Psychiatry and Related Disciplines, 10 (June, 1972), 149-63.

3200. Simpson, K. "The Moment of Death: A New Medico-Legal Problem," ACTA Anaesthesiological Scandinavica Supplement, 29 (1968), 361ff.

3201. _____, ed. Taylor's Principles and Practice of Medical Jurisprudence. 12th ed. London: Churchill, 1965.

3202. Simpson, M.A. "Anticipatory Grief," Pharos, 38 (1975), 90-1.

3203. _____. "Brought in Dead," World Medicine, 11 (1975), 91-5.

3204. _____. "Distress of Dying," British Medical Journal, 3 (1972), 231.

3205. _____. "The Do-It-Yourself Death Certificate in Evoking and Estimating Student Attitudes Toward Death," Journal of Medical Education, 50 (May, 1975), 475-8.

3206. _____. "Dying: Why It's Neglected," Social Services, 2 (1973), 1.

3207. _____. "Poetry and Death," in H. Feifel, ed., New Meanings of Death. New York: McGraw-Hill, 1976.

3208. _____. "Teaching about Death and Dying," Nursing Times, 69 (Apr. 5, 1973), 442-3.

3209. _____. "Teaching about Death and Dying: An Interdisciplinary Approach," in R.W. Raven, ed., The Dying Patient. London: Pitmans, 1975.

3210. _____. "What Is Dying Like?" Nursing Times, 69 (Mar. 29, 1973), 405-6.

3211. Sims, A. "Mortality in Neurosis," Lancet, 2 (Nov. 10, 1973), 1072-6.

3212. Sinclair, S. "Vital Statistics--India: Survey of Causes of Death," Indian Pediatrics, 10 (Mar., 1973), 193-8.

3213. Singer, L.J. "The Slowly Dying Child," Clinical Pediatrics, 13 (Oct., 1974), 861-7.

3214. Sinton J. "Another One Gone. Were You on Duty?" Nursing Mirror. 140 (Feb. 6, 1975), 59.

3215. Sire, Glenn. The Deathmaker. New York: Simon and Schuster, 1960.

3216. Sisk, Slenn. "Funeral Customs in the Alabama Black Belt, 1870-1910," Southern Folklore Quarterly, 23 (Sep., 1959), 169-71.

3217. Sivanesan, S., P.C. Sushama. "Cot Deaths in Malaysia," Medical Journal of Malaysia, 29 (Sep., 1974), 29-33.

3218. Skelskie, Barbara E. "An Exploratory Study of Grief in Old Age," Smith College Studies in Social Work, 45 (Feb., 1975), 159-82.

3219. Skillman, J.J. "Ethical Dilemmas in the Care of the Critically Ill," Lancet, 2 (Sep. 14, 1974), 634-7.

3220. Skipper, James K., Jr, Robert C. Leonard, eds. Social Interaction and Patient Care. Philadelphia: J.B. Lippincott, 1965.

3221. Skipper, James K., Jr. et al. "Some Possible Consequences of Limited Communication Between Patients and Hospital Functionaries," Journal of Health
and Human Behavior, 5 (1964), 34-9.

3222. _____. "What Communication Means to Patients," American Journal of Nursing,
64 (Apr., 1964), 101-3.

3223. Skoog, R. "Editorial: Death, and the Problems of Honesty," Wisconsin Medical
Journal, 74 (Feb., 1975), 11-2.

3224. Slater, E. "Case for Voluntary Euthanasia," Contemporary Review, 219 (Aug.,
1971), 84-8.

3225. Slater, Philip E. "Prolegomena to a Psychoanalytic Theory of Aging and Death,"
in R. Kastenbaum, ed., New Thoughts on Old Age. New York: Springer, 1964.
38-55.

3226. Sleeper, Ralph W. "The Resurrection of the Body," Omega, 3 (May, 1972), 139-
48.

3227. Sly, David F., Peter S.K. Chi. "Economic Development, Modernization, and
Demographic Behavior: Longitudinal Analysis of Mortality Change," American
Journal of Economics and Sociology, 31 (Oct., 1972), 373-86.

3228. Smith, A.G. et al. "The Dying Child: Helping the Family Cope with Impending
Death," Clinical Pediatrics, 8 (Mar., 1969), 131-4.

3229. Smith, Andrew J.K., J. Kiffin Penry. Brain Death. Bethesda, MD: National
Institute of Neurological Diseases and Stroke, 1972.

3230. Smith, Bradford. Dear Gift of Life--A Man's Encounter with Death. Wallingford,
PA: Pendle Hill Publishing, 1965.

3231. Smith, Clement, et al. "Help for the Hopeless," Rhode Island Medical Journal,
39 (Sep., 1956), 491-99.

3232. Smith, Curtis A. Help for the Bereaved. Hazel Crest, IL: Educational Development Association, 1972.

3233. Smith, D.H. "Thanatology," West Virginia Medical Journal, 71 (1975), 68.

3234. Smith, H.L. "Abortion, Death and the Sanctity of Life," Social Science and
Medicine, 5 (1971), 211-8.

3235. Smith, JoAnn Kelley. Free Fall. Valley Forge: Judson Press, 1975.

3236. Smith, Harmon. "Ethics and the New Medicine," Nashville: Abingdon Press, 1970.

3237. Smith, Helen C. Care of the Dying Patient: A Comparison of Instructional
Plans. Bloomington, IN: Indiana University Press, 1965.

3238. Smith, R. "The Right to Live or Die," Nursing Mirror, 140 (May 1, 1975), 64.

3239. Smith, S.L. "Care of the Dying," Lancet, 1 (Mar. 10, 1973), 555.

3240. _____. "Right to Die," Lancet, 2 (Nov., 1970), 1088-9.

3241. Smithers, D. "Where to Die," British Medical Journal, 1 (Jan. 6, 1973), 34-5.

3242. Snider, A.J. "Last Rites, Do They Bring Fear or Reassurance?" Science Digest, 65 (June, 1969), 60-1.

3243. _____. "Score Card for Death," Science Digest, 68 (Aug., 1970), 58.

3244. Snow, Lois W. A Death with Dignity. New York: Random, 1975.

3245. Snyder, M. et al. "Changes in Nursing Student's Attitudes Toward Death and Dying: A Measurement of Curriculum Integration Effectiveness," International Journal of Social Psychiatry, 19 (Autumn, 1973), 294-8.

3246. Sobel, B.E. "Reducing the Toll from Sudden Death," California Medicine, 117 (Oct., 1972), 54-5.

3247. Sobel, D.E. "Death and Dying," American Journal of Nursing, 74 (Jan., 1974), 98-9.

3248. Sobosan, Jeffrey G. "Chardin and Death," Journal of Thanatology, 3 (1975) 67-75.

3249. Solitare, G.B. "Sudden Unexpected Death," Lancet, 1 (Mar., 1970), 564.

3250. Sollier, Paul et al. "Observations and Documents 'L'etat Mental des Mourants'," Revue de Philosophie, 41 (1896), 303-13.

3251. Solnit, Albert J. "The Dying Child," Developmental Medicine and Child Neurology, 7 (Dec., 1965), 693-704.

3252. _____. "Emotional Management of Family Stressed in Care of Dying Child," Pediatric Currents, 17 (Sep., 1968), 65.

3253. _____, Morris Green. "The Pediatric Management of the Dying Child, Part II: The Child's Reaction to the Fear of Dying," in Albert J. Solnit and Sally A. Province, eds., Modern Perspectives in Child Development. New York: International Universities Press, 1963. 217-28.

3254. _____. "Psychological Considerations in the Management of Deaths on Pediatric Hospital Services, I: The Doctor and the Child's Famlily," Pediatrics, 24 (July, 1959), 106-12.

3255. _____, Mary Stark. "Mourning and the Birth of a Defective Child," Psychoanalytic Study of the Child, 16 (1961), 523-37.

3256. Soloman, Harry C. "Psychiatric Implications of Cancer," Rocky Mountain Medical Journal, 44 (Oct., 1947), 801-4.

3257. Solzhenitsyn, Alexander. The Cancer Ward. New York: Dial Press, 1969.

3258. Somerville, Rose M. "Death Education as Part of Family Life Education: Using Imaginative Literature for Insights into Family Crises," The Family Coordinator, 20 (July, 1971), 209-24.

3259. _____ . ."Perspective on Death: A Thematic Teaching Unit," Family Coordinator, 23 (Oct., 1974), 421.

3260. Sommer, C. "Four Distinctive Views of the Dying Patient: Managing Terminal Care of Herself," Registered Nurse, 38 (Apr., 1975), 37-8.

3261. Sopher, I.M. "The Pathologist Looks at Death," Maryland State Medical Journal, 23 (June, 1974), 31-2.

3262. Soreff, S.M. "Impact of Staff Suicide on a Psychiatric Inpatient Unit," Journal of Nervous and Mental Disorders, 161 (1975), 130-3.

3263. Soulen, Richard N. Care for the Dying. Atlanta: John Knox Press, 1975.

3264. Spagnolog, S.V. et al. "Medical Intensive Care Unit: Mortality Rate Experience in Large Teaching Hospital," New York State Journal of Medicine, 73 (Mar. 15, 1973), 754-5.

3265. Spalt, Lee. "Death Thoughts in Hysteria, Antisocial Personality, and Anxiety Neurosis," Psychiatric Quarterly, 48 (1974), 441-4.

3266. Spann, W. "Definite Concepts Regarding Legislation on the Actual Time of Death," Munchener Medizinische Wochenschrift, 111 (Oct. 31, 1969), 2253-5.

3267. Spark, Muriel. Memento Mori. New York: Meridian Fiction, 1958.

3268. Spector, Samuel I. "The End of Days," Omega, 4 (Fall, 1974), 267-76.

3269. Spector, W.G. "The Inner North London Survey on Sudden Death in Infancy: A Summary," Public Health, 89 (May, 1975), 157.

3270. _____ . "Sudden Infant Death: The Current Status of the Problem," Austral-asian Nurses Journal, 2 (July, 1974), 3.

3271. Speer, G.M. "Learning about Death," Journal of the American Veterinary Medical Association, 165 (Aug. 15, 1974), 70-3.

3272. Speer, L. "Aborted Crib Death," Journal of the American Medical Association, 223 (Mar. 26, 1973), 1512.

3273. Spencer, Theodore. Death and Elizabethan Tragedy. Cambridge: Harvard University Press, 1936.

3274. Spencer, Thomas E. "Cremation, an Expression of Life Style," Journal of Individual Psychology, 28 (May, 1972), 60-6.

3275. Sperry, Willar L., D. Litt. "Moral Problems in the Practice of Medicine," New England Journal of Medicine, 239 (Dec. 23, 1848), 985-90.

3276. Spiegelman, Mortimer. "The Broken Family--Widowhood and Orphanhood," Annals of the American Academy of Political and Social Science, 188 (Nov., 1936), 117-30.

3277. Spiers, P.S. "Estimated Rates of Concordancy for the Sudden Infant Death Syndrome in Twins," American Journal of Epidemiology, 100 (July, 1974), 1-7.

3278. _____, et al. "Sudden Infant Death Syndrome in the United States: A Study of Geographic and Other Variables," American Journal of Epidemiology, 100 (Nov., 1974), 380-9.

3279. Spilka, Bernard et al. "Religion, American Values and Death Perspectives," Sociological Symposium, 1 (Fall, 1968), 57-66.

3280. Spinetta, John J. "Death Anxiety in Leukemic Children," Dissertation Abstracts International, 33 (Oct., 1972), 1807-8.

3281. _____. "The Dying Child's Awareness of Death--a Review," Psychological Bulletin, 81 (Apr., 1974), 256-60.

3282. _____, et al. "Anxiety in the Dying Child," Pediatrics, 52 (Dec., 1973), 841-5.

3283. _____, et al. "Personal Space as a Measure of a Dying Child's Sense of Isolation," Journal of Consulting and Clinical Psychology, 42 (Dec., 1974), 751-6.

3284. Spiro, Jack D. Time to Mourn: Judaism and the Psychology of Bereavement. New York: Bloch Publishing Co., 1968.

3285. Spitz, Rene. "Hospitalism," Psychoanalytic Study of the Child, 1 (1945), 53-74.

3286. Spitzer, Stephan P., Jeanette R. Folta. "Death in the Hospital: A Problem for Study," Nursing Forum, 3 (1964), 85-92.

3287. Spock, Benjamin. Problems of Parents. Boston: Houghton Mifflin, 1962.

3288. Squillante, A.M. et al. "New Dimensions in the Diagnosis of Death--The Doctor's Liability--A Lawyer's Advice," Journal of the Iowa Medical Society, 61 (May, 1971), 285-8.

3289. Spradley, Barbara W., ed. Contemporary Community Nursing. Boston: Little, Brown, and Co., 1975.

3290. Srivastava, M.L. "Relationship Between the Birth Rate and the Death Rate in Stable Populations with the Same Fertility but Different Mortality Schedules," Eugenics Quarterly, 13 (Sep., 1966), 231-9.

3291. Stacey, C.L., K. Marken. "The Attitudes of College Students and Penitentiary Inmates Toward Death and a Future Life," Psychiatric Quarterly (Supplement), 26 (1952), 27-32.

3292. _____, Marie L. Reichen. "Attitudes Toward Death and Future Life among Normal and Subnormal Adolescent Girls," Exceptional Children, 20 (1954), 259-62.

3293. Staff, Clement. "Death is no Outsider," Psychoanalysis, 2 (1953), 56-70.

3294. Standard, S., Nathan H. Standard, eds. Should the Patient Know the Truth? New York: Springer, 1955.

3295. Staford, G. "Miniguide: A Mini-Course on Death," Scholastic Teacher, (Sep., 1973), 40-4.

3296. Stannard, D.E., ed. Death in America. Philadelphia: University of Pennsylvania Press, 1975.

3297. Starr, S. "I'm Going to Die," Nursing Times, 71 (May 1, 1975), 706-7.

3298. Star, Clarissa. On Becoming a Widow. New York: Family Library, 1973.

3299. Stauder, K.H. et al. "Soll der Arzt dem Kranken die Wahrheit Sagen (Should the Doctor Tell the Patient the Truth)?" Medizinische Klinik, 48 (1953), 403-5.

3300. Stavraky, K. et al. "Psychological Factors in the Outcome of Human Cancer," Journal of Psychosomatic Research, 1 (1968), 251-9.

3301. Steen, John Warren. "Hindrances to the Pastoral Care of the Dying," Pastoral Psychology, 9 (Mar., 1958), 27-32.

3302. Stehbens, J.A., A.D. Lascari. "Psychological Followup of Families with Childhood Leukemia," Journal of Clinical Psychology, 30 (July, 1974), 394-7.

3303. Stein, Arthur. "Resistance to Psychological Prophylaxis in Hospital Pediatrics," Journal of Pediatrics, 55 (1959), 497-503.

3304. Stein, M. et al. Identity and Anxiety. Glencoe, IL: The Free Press, 1960.

3305. Stein, A., M. Susser. "Widowhood and Mental Illness," British Journal of Preventive Social Medicine, 23 (May, 1969), 106-10.

3306. Steincrohn, Peter. How to Master Your Fears. New York: Wilfred Funk, 1952.

3307. Steiner, Gloria L. "Children's Concepts of Life and Death: A Developmental Study," Dissertation Abstracts, 26 (Aug., 1965), 1164.

3308. Steinfels, P., R.M. Veatch, eds. Death Inside Out. New York: Harper and Row, 1975.

3309. Steingiesser, Hildegard. Was die Arzte Aller Zeiten vom Sterben Wussten (What Doctors of All Times Have Known about Death). Greifswald: Arbeiten der Deutschen Nord. Gesellschaft fur Geschichte der Medizin, 1936.

3310. Steinhoff, Patricia G. et al. "Characteristics and Motivations of Women Receiving Abortions," Sociological Symposium, 8 (Spring, 1972), 83-9.

3311. Steinschneider, A. "Prolonged Apnea and the Sudden Infant Death Syndrome: Clinical and Laboratory Observations," Pediatrics, 50 (Oct., 1972), 646-54.

3312. Steinzor, Bernard. "Death and the construction of Reality," in John G. Peatman and Eugene L. Hartley, eds., Festschrift for Gardner Murphy. New York: Harper, 1960. 358-75.

3313. Stekhoven, W. "Professor Van den Berg's Plea for Active Euthanasia," Nederlands Tijdschirft voor Geneeskunde, 113 (Aug. 2, 1969), 1358-60.

3314. Stengle, E. "Attitudes to Death," Journal of Psychosomatic Research, 10 (July, 1966), 21.

3315. Stephens, Simon. Death Comes Home. New York: Morehouse-Barlow, 1973.

3316. Sterba, Richard. "On Halloween," American Imago, 5 (1948), 213-24.

3317. _____. "Report on Some Emotional Reactions to President Roosevelt's Death," Psychoanalytic Review, 33 (Oct., 1946), 393-8.

3318. Stern, Erich. Kind, Krankheit und Tod (Child, Disease and Death). Basel, Seitzerland: Ernst Reinhardt Verlag, 1957.

3319. _____. "Kind und Tod (Child and Death)," Zeitschrift fur Kinderforschung, 41 (1933), 221-40.

3320. _____. "La Psychologie de la Mort," Folia Psychiatrica, Neurological et Neurochirurgica, Neerlandica, 52 (July-Aug., 1949), 227-46.

3321. Stern, Karl. "Death Within Life," Review of Existential Psychology and Psychiatry, 2 (1962), 141-4.

3322. _____. "Observations in an Old Age Counselling Center," Journal of Gerontology, 3 (1948), 48.

3323. _____. "Problems Encountered in an Old Age Counselling Center," in Problems of Aging. New York: Josiah Macy, Jr. Foundation, 1950.

3324. Stern, Karl et al. "Grief Reactions in Later Life," American Journal of Psychiatry, 108 (Oct., 1951), 289-93.

3325. Stern, M.M. "Biotrauma: Fear of Death and Aggression," International Journal of Psychoanalysis, 53 (1972), 291-9.

3326. _____. "Fear of Death and Neurosis," Journal of the American Psychoanalytic Association, 16 (Jan., 1968), 3031.

3327. _____. "Fear of Death and Trauma," Progress in Neurology and Psychiatry, 22 (1967), 457-63.

3328. Sternbac, O. "Death Drive and Problem of Aggression, Sadomasochism: Reinterpretation of Freud's Second Drive Theory," International Journal of Psychology, 56 (1975), 321-33.

3329. Sternberger, A. Der Verstandene Tod. Leipzig: Hirzel, 1934.

3330. Sternglass, E.J. "Infant Mortality and Nuclear Tests," Bulletin of the Atomic Scientists, 25 (Apr., 1969), 18-20.

3331. Stevens, A.C. "Facing Death," Nursing Times, 58 (June 15, 1962), 777-8.

3332. Stewart, A. "Infant Leukaemias and Cot Deaths," British Medical Journal, 2 (June 14, 1975), 605-7.

3333. _____. "Myeloid Leukemia and Cot Deaths," British Medical Journal, 4 (Nov. 18, 1973), 423.

3334. Stewart, Phillis Longton. "Normative Views of Doctors and Nurses an Abortion," Sociological Symposium, 8 (Spring, 1972), 91-9.

3335. Stewart, S.M. "Problem of Prolonged Death--Who Should Decide," Baylor Law Review, 27 (1975), 169-73.

3336. Stickel, Delford L. "Ethical and Moral Aspects of Transplantation," Monographs in the Surgical Sciences, 3 (1966), 267-301.

3337. _____. "Medicolegal and Ethical Aspects of Organ Transplantation," Annals of the New York Academy of Sciences, 169 (Jan 21, 1970), 362-75.

3338. Still, J.W. "The Three Levels of Human Life and Death, the Presumed Location of the Soul, and Some of the Implications for the Social Problems of Abortion, Birth Control and Euthanasia," Medical Annals of the District of Columbia, 37 (June, 1968), 316-8.

3339. _____. "To Be or Not to Be--Alive or Dead?" Journal of the American Geriatrics Society, 17 (May, 1969), 522-4.

3340. Stitt, A. "The Dying Patient and His Family," Emergency Medicine, 2 (May, 1970), 112ff.

3341. Stojic, B. "Is a Man Who is Pulseless and has Stopped Breathing Dead?" Medical Journal of Australia, 2 (Sep. 13, 1969), 571.

3342. Stokes, Adrian. "A Game that Must be Lost," International Journal of Psychoanalysis, 41 (Jan.-Feb., 1960), 70-6.

3343. _____. "On Resignation," International Journal of Psychoanalysis, 43 (Mar.-June, 1962), 75-181.

3344. Stolnitz, G.J. "Recent Mortality Trends in Latin America, Asia and Africa," Population Studies, 19 (Nov., 1965), 117-38.

3345. Stolorow, R.D. "A Note on Death Anxiety as a Developmental Achievement," American Journal of Psychoanalysis, 34 (Winter, 1974), 351-3.

3346. Stone, Gregory P. "Halloween and the Mass Child," American Quarterly, 11 (Fall, 1959), 372-9.

3347. Stoneman, Ethel Turner. Halfway to the Hereafter. Perth, Australia: T.F. Christie, 1935.

3348. Strang, Ruth. "How Children and Adolescents View their World," Mental Hygiene, 38 (1954), 28-33.

3349. _____. Introduction to Child Study. New York: MacMillan, 1959.

3350. Strauss, Anselm L. "Family and Staff During Last Weeks and Days of a Terminal Illness," Annals of the New York Academy of Sciences, 164 (Dec., 1969), 687-95.

3351. _____. "Reforms Needed in Providing Terminal Care and Understanding of Dying Patient," Archives of the Foundation of Thanatology, 1 (1969), 21.

3352. _____. "Sociopsychologic Studies of the Aging Process: Problems of Death and the Dying Patient," Psychiatric Research Reports of the American Psychiatric Association, 23 (Feb., 1968), 198-206.

3353. _____, Barney G. Glaser. Anguish: A Case History of a Dying Trajectory. Mill Valley, CA: Sociology Press, 1970.

3354. _____, Jeanne C. Quint. "The Non-Accountability of Terminal Care," Hospitals, 38 (Jan. 16, 1964), 73-87.

3355. Street, J.R. "A Genetic Study of Immortality," Pedagogical Seminary and Journal of Genetic Psychology, 6 (1899), 267-313.

3356. Strimer, R. et al. "Epidemiologic Features of 1134 Sudden, Unexpected, Infant Deaths," Journal of the American Medical Association, 209 (Sep., 1969), 1493-7.

3357. Stringfellow, W. _Instead of Death_. New York: Seabury Press, 1963.

3358. Strubbe, W. et al. "Children Who Didn't Die: The So-Called 'Vulnerable Child' Syndrome," _Nederlands Tijdschrift voor Geneeskunde_, 116 (Sep. 30, 1972), 1782-6.

3359. Strugnell, Cecile, Phyllis R. Silverman. "The Funeral Director's Wife as Care Giver," _Omega_, 2 (Aug., 1971), 174-8.

3360. Stuart, Friend. _How to Conquer Physical Death_. San Marcos, CA: Dominion Press, 1968.

3361. Stumpf, Samuel Enoch. "Some Moral Dimensions of Medicine," _Annals of Internal Medicine_, 64 (Feb., 1966), 460-70.

3362. Sturges, Stanley. "Understanding Grief," _Menninger Perspective_, 1 (Apr., 1970), 9-12. Also in _Medical Insight_, 1 (Oct., 1969), 12-7.

3363. Sturner, W. "Some Perspectives on 'Cot Death'," _Journal of Forensic Medicine_, 18 (July-Sep., 1971), 96-107.

3364. _____, J.L. Dempsey. "Sudden Infant Death--Chemical Analysis of Vitreous Humor," _Journal of Forensic Science_, 18 (Jan., 1973), 12-9.

3365. Suarez, R.M. et al. "Morbidity and Mortality in Aged Puerto Ricans," _Journal of the American Geriatric Society_, 13 (1965), 805-14.

3366. Sudnow, David. "Dead on Arrival," _Trans-Action_, 5 (Nov., 1967), 36-9.

3367. _____. _Passing On: The Social Organization of Dying_. Englewood Cliffs: Prentice-Hall, 1967.

3368. Sugar, Max. "Adolescent Depression Related to Mourning Processes," _Roche Report: Frontiers of Clinical Psychiatry_, 4 (Feb. 15, 1967), 3.

3369. _____. "Normal Adolescent Mourning," _American Journal of Psychotherapy_, 22 (1968), 258-69.

3370. Sullivan, Harry Stack. _The Meaning of Anxiety in Psychiatry and Life_. New York: William Alanson White Institute of Psychiatry, 1948.,

3371. Sullivan, Jeremiah M. "The Influence of Cause-Specific Mortality Conditions on the Age Pattern of Mortality with Special Reference to Taiwan," _Population Studies_, 27 (Mar., 1973), 135-58.

3372. Sullivan, Joseph. _The Morality of Mercy Killing_. Westminster, MD: Newman Press, 1950.

3373. Sulzberger, Cyrus. _My Brother Death_. New York: Harper and Brothers, 1961.

3374. Sumner, Francis B. "A Biologist Reflects upon Old Age and Death," Scientific Monthly, 61 (Aug., 1945), 143-9.

3375. Sumner, W.G., A.G. Keller. The Science of Society. New Haven: Yale University Press, 1927.

3376. Sunderman, F.W. "A Physician Looks at Death," Annals of Clinical Laboratory Science, 3 (Sep.-Oct., 1973), 393-8.

3377. Surawicz, et al., eds. Sudden Cardiac Death. New York: Grune and Stratton, 1964.

3378. Sutherland, Arthur M. "Psychological Impact of Cancer and Its Therapy," Medical Clinics of North America, 40 (1956), 705-20.

3379. Sutton, R.N.P., J.L. Emery. "Sudden Death in Infancy: A Microbiological and Epidemiological Study," Archives of Diseases in Childhood, 41 (1966), 674-77.

3380. Swenson, Wendell M. "Attitudes Toward Death among the Aged," Minnesota Medicine, 42 (Apr., 1959), 399-402.

3381. _____. "Attitudes Toward Death in an Aged Population," Journal of Gerontology, 16 (Jan., 1961), 49-52.

3382. _____. "A Study of Death Attitudes in the Gerontic Population and their Relationship to Certain Measurable Physical and Social Characteristics," Dissertation Abstracts, 19 (1958), 177.

3383. Swift, P.G., J.L. Emery. "Magnesium and Sudden Unexpected Infant Death," Lancet, 2 (Oct. 21, 1972), 871.

3384. Swift Arrow, Bernadine. "Funeral Rites of the Quechan Tribe," Indian Historian, 7 (Spring, 1974), 22-4.

3385. Switzer, David K. Dynamics of Grief: Its Sources, Pain and Healing. Nashville: Abingdon Press, 1970.

3386. _____. "Repressed Affect and Memory Reactive to Grief: A Case Fragment," Omega, 3 (May, 1972), 121-6.

3387. Symmers, W.S., Sr. "Not Allowed to Die," British Medical Journal, 1 (Feb. 17, 1968), 442.

3388. Symons, N.J. "Does Masochism Necessarily Imply the Existence of a Death-Instinct?" International Journal of Psychoanalysis, 8 (1927), 38-46.

3389. Syun, I. "Loss of Meaning in Death," Japan Interpreter, 9 (1975), 331-43.

3390. Tallmer, Margot et al. "Factors Influencing Children's Concepts of Death," Journal of Clinical Child Psychology, 3 (Summer, 1974), 17-9.

3391. Tanner, A.E. The Child, His Thinking, Feeling and Doing. Chicago: Rand, McNally, 1904.

3392. Tapp, E., B.W. Otridge. "Letter: Myeloid Leukemia and Cot Deaths," British Medical Journal, 2 (Apr. 19, 1975), 140.

3393. Tarnower, W. "The Dying Patient: Psychological Needs of the Patient, His Family and the Physician," Nebraska Medical Journal, 54 (Jan., 1969), 6-10.

3394. Task Force on Death and Dying, Institute of Society, Ethics and the Life Sciences, "Refinements in Criteria for the Determination of Death: An Appraisal," Journal of the American Medical Association, 22 (July 3, 1972), 48-53.

3395. Taves, Isabelle. Love Must not Be Wasted. New York: Thomas Crowell Company, 1975.

3396. Tayback, M. "Death with Dignity," Journal of Gerontologic Nursing, 1 (July-Aug., 1975), 42-4.

3397. Taylor, Jeremy. The Rules and Exercises of Holy Dying. London: Bell and Daldy, 1857.

3398. Taylor, M.P. "A Father Pleads for the Death of His Son," International Journal of Psycho-Analysis, 8 (Jan., 1927), 53-5.

3399. Taylor, P.A. Death Lights a Candle. New York: Norton Press, 1969.

3400. Taylor, Samuel, Danely Sloughter. "The Physician and the Cancer Patient," Journal of the American Medical Association, 150 (1952), 1012-5.

3401. Tebb, Williams et al. Premature Burial. London: Swan Sonnenschein, 1905.

3402. Teicher, J.D. "'Combat Fatigue' or Death Anxiety Neurosis," Journal of Nervous and Mental Disease, 117 (1953), 234-43.

3403. Tejmar, J. "Berlin Wall and Sudden Death," Annals of Internal Medicine, 78 (Apr., 1973), 620.

3404. Teleki, Geza. "Group Response to the Accidental Death of a Chimpanzee in Gombe National Park, Tanzania," Folta Primatologica, 20 (1973), 81-94.

3405. Templer, Donald Irvin. "The Construction and Validation of a Death Anxiety Scale," Journal of General Psychology, 82 (1970), 165-77.

3406. _____. "Death Anxiety as Related to Depression and Health of Retired Persons," Journal of Gerontology, 26 (1971), 521-3.

3407. Templer, Donald Irvin. "Death Anxiety: Extraversion, Neuroticism and Cigarette Smoking," Omega, 3 (Feb., 1972), 361-2.

3408. _____. "Death Anxiety in Religiously Very Involved Persons," Psychological Reports, 31 (Oct., 1972), 361-2.

3409. _____. "The Relationship Between Verbalized and Non-Verbalized Death Anxiety," Journal of Genetic Psychology, 119 (Dec., 1971), 211-4.

3410. _____. "Relatively Non-Technical Description of the Death Anxiety Scale," Archives of the Foundation of Thanatology, 3 (Summer, 1971), 91-3.

3411. _____, D. Lester. "An MMPI Scale for Assessing Death Anxiety," Psychological Reports, 34 (Feb., 1974), 238.

3412. _____, et al. "Alleviation of High Death Anxiety with Symptomatic Treatment of Depression," Psychological Reports, 35 (Aug., 1974), 216.

3413. _____. "Death Anxiety: Age, Sex, and Parental Resemblance in Diverse Populations," Developmental Psychology, 4 (1971), 108.

3414. _____. "Fear of Death and Femininity," Psychological Reports, 35 (Aug., 1974), 530.

3415. _____. "Religious Correlates of Death Anxiety," Psychological Report, 26 (June, 1970), 895-7.

3416. Teraura, T. et al. "Determination of Death: Electrophysiological Background," International Anesthesiology Clinics, 13 (Spring, 1975), 235-44.

3417. Thaler, Otto F. "Grief and Depression," Nursing Forum, 5 (1966), 8-22.

3418. Thauberger, P.C., E.M. Thauberger. "A Consideration of Death and a Sociological Perspective in the Quality of the Dying Patient's Care," Social Science and Medicine, 8 (Aug., 1974), 437-41.

3419. Thielicke, H. Death and Life. Philadlphia: Fortress Press, 1970.

3420. Thomas, B.B. et al. "Learning to Live with Death and Grieving," UNA Nursing Journal, 69 (Apr., 1971), 9-17.

3421. Thomas, C.H. "Last Offices--A Reassessment," Nursing Mirror, 132 (Apr. 9, 1971), 30.

3422. Thomas, Edith. "Terminal Illness," District Nursing, 4 (Oct., 1961), 156-8.

3423. Thomas, Jack Ward and Ronald Dixon. "Cemetery Ecology," Natural History, 82 (Mar., 1973), 60-7.

3424. Thomas, L.V. "Death and Language in West," Archives of Social Science and Religion, 20 (1975), 45-9.

3425. Thomas, L.V. "The Long Habit," New England Journal of Medicine, 286 (1972), 825-6.

3426. _____. "Notes of a Biology-Watcher: Death in the Open," New England Journal of Medicine, 288 (Jan. 11, 1973), 92-3.

3427. _____. "Pour une Semiologie de la Mort Negro-Africane (Toward a Semiology of Negro-African Death)," Ethnopsychologie, 27 (Jun.-Sep., 1972), 157-85.

3428. _____. "Vie et Mort en Afrique: Introduction a l'Ethnothanatologie (Life and Death in Africa: Introduction to Ethnothanatology)," Ethno-Psychologie, 27 (Mar., 1972), 103-23.

3429. Thompson, Edward John. Sutee: A Historical and Philosophical Inquiry into the Hindu Rite of Widow Burning. London: G. Allen and Unwin, 1928.

3430. Thomson, G.P. et al. "Right to Die," Lancet, 2 (Nov., 1970), 1037.

3431. Thorson, James A. "Continuing Education in Death and Dying," Adult Leadership, 23 (Nov., 1974), 141.

3432. Thurmond, Charles. "Last Thoughts Before Drowning," Journal of Abnormal Social Psychology, 38 (1943), 165-84.

3433. Thurston, G. "The Point of Death," Practitioner, 205 (Aug., 1970), 187-90.

3434. Tibbitts, Clark, Wilma Donahue, eds. Social and Psychological Aspects of Aging. New York: Columbia University Press, 1962.

3435. Tichauer, R.W. "Attitudes Toward Death and Dying among the Aymara Indians of Bolivia," Journal of the American Medical Women's Association, 19 (1964), 463-6.

3436. Tierney, E.A. "Accepting Disfigurement when Death is Alternative," American Journal of Nursing, 75 (1975), 2149-50.

3437. Tietz, W. "School Phobia and the Fear of Death," Mental Hygiene, 54 (Oct., 1970), 565-8.

3438. Tietze, C., A.F. Guttmacher. "Deaths after Legal Abortion," Lancet, 1 (Jan. 13, 1973), 105.

3439. Tillich, Paul. The Dynamics of Faith. New York: Harper and Row, 1957.

3440. Tis'Ney, Carol. Mourner Come to My Bosom. Los Angeles: De Vorse, 1933.

3441. Tisza, V.B. "Management of the Parents of the Chronically Ill Child," American Journal of Orthopsychiatry, 32 (1962), 53-9.

3442. Titmuss, Richard. The Gift Relationship: From Human Blood to Social Policy. New York: Pantheon Books, 1971.

3443. Toch, Rudolph. "Management of the Child with a Fatal Disease," Clinical Pediatrics, 3 (July, 1964), 418-27.

3444. Tolor, A., M. Reznikoff. "Relation Between Insight, Repression-Sensitization, Internal-External Control and Death Anxiety," Journal of Abnormal Psychology, 72 (Oct., 1967), 426-30.

3445. Tolma, F.J. "Psychological Disturbances after a Pet Dog's Death," Psychiatrica, Neurologia, Neurochirurgia (Amsterdam), 67 (Sep.-Oct., 1964), 394-405.

3446. Tolstoy, Leo. "The Death of Ivan Ilych," in The Death of Ivan Ilych and Other Stories. Translated by Aylmer Maud. New York: Signet Books, 1960.

3447. Tonkin, S. "Sudden Infant Death Syndrome: Hypothesis of Causation," Pediatrics, 55 (May, 1975), 583-4.

3448. Toole, J.F. "Danger Ahead: Problems in Defining Life and Death," North Carolina Medical Journal, 28 (Nov., 1967), 464-6.

3450. Tooley, Michael. "Abortion and Infanticide," Philosophy and Public Affairs, 2 (Fall, 1972), 37-65.

3451. Torrey, E. Fuller, ed. Ethical Issues in Modern Medicine. Boston: Little, Brown and Co., 1968.

3452. Towbin, A. "Spinal Injury Related to Syndrome of Sudden Death in Infants," American Journal of Clinical Pathology, 19 (1968), 562-7.

3453. _____. "The Respirator Brain Death Syndrome," Human Pathology, 4 (Dec., 1973), 583-94.

3454. Towns, Jim E. Faith Stronger than Death. New York: Pyramid Publications, 1975.

3455. Townsend, Peter. The Family Life of Old People. Baltimore: Penguin Books, 1963.

3456. Toynbee, Arnold et al. Man's Concern with Death. New York: McGraw-Hill, 1969.

3457. _____. Death and Burial in the Roman World. Ithaca, NY: Cornell University Press, 1970.

3458. Travis, T.A. et al. "The Attitudes of Physicians Toward Prolonging Life," Psychiatry in Medicine, 5 (Winter, 1974), 17-26.

3459. Trawick, John D., Jr. "The Psychiatrist and the Cancer Patient," Diseases of the Nervous System, 11 (Sep., 1950), 278-80.

3460. Treaton, Jean-Rene. "Discussion of a Symposium on Attitudes Toward Death in Older Persons," Journal of Gerontology, 16 (1961), 44.

3461. Treffert, D.A. "Dying with their Rights On," American Journal of Psychiatry, 130 (Sep., 1973), 1041.

3462. Troisfontainers, Roger. I Do Not Die. Translated by Francis Albert. New York: Desclee Co., 1963.

3463. Tromp, Nicholas. Primitive Conceptions of Death in the Nether World in the Old Testament. Chicago: Loyola, 1969.

3464. Troup, S.B., W.A. Greene, eds. The Patient, Death, and the Family. New York: Charles Scribner's Sons, 1974.

3465. Trowell, Hugh. The Unfinished Debate on Euthanasia. London: SCM Press, 1973.

3466. Trubo, Richard. An Act of Mercy: Euthanasia Today. Los Angeles: Nash Publishing, 1973.

3467. Trumbo, Dalton. Johnny Got His Gun. New York: Bantam, 1970.

3468. Tuccille, Jerome. Here Comes Immortality. New York: Stein and Day, 1972.

3469. Tuck, William P. Facing Grief and Death. Nashville: Broadman, 1975.

3470. Tuckman, A. "Disaster and Mental Health Intervention," Community Mental Health Journal, 9 (1973), 151-7.

3471. Tunbridge, R.E. "Terminal Care," Practitioner, 196 (Jan., 1966), 110-3.

3472. Turczynowski, R. et al. "Birth and Death Certificates as a Source of Information on the Cause of Death in Past Centuries," Archives of Historial Medicine, 31 (1968), 213-9.

3473. Turner, P.J. "The General Practitioner and the Care of the Dying Patient," South African Medical Journal, 48 (Apr. 6, 1974), 708-10.

3474. Turner, Ron, ed. Anthology of Slow Death. Berkeley: Wingbow Press, 1975.

3475. Twycross, R.G. "The Terminal Care of Patients with Lung Cancer," Postgraduate Medical Journal, 49 (Oct., 1973), 732-7.

3476. Tylor, E.B. Primitive Culture. London: J. Murray, 1913. v. 1.

3477. Ueda, H. et al. "Round Table Discussion: Determination of Death, Information for Clinicians," Naika, 23 (May, 1969), 870-7.

3478. Ujhely, Gertrud B. "Grief and Depression: Implications for Preventive and Therapeutic Nursing Care," Nursing Forum, 5 (1966), 23-5.

3479. _____. The Nurse and Her Problem Patients. New York: Springer, 1963.

3480. Ulanov, Barry. Death--A Book of Preparation and Consolation. New York: Sheed and Ward, 1959.

3481. Unger, J.L. "Sudden Death Syndrome: Recurrent Apnea," Journal of the Kansas Medical Society, 75 (Apr., 1974), 121-2.

3482. U.S. Department of Health, Education, and Welfare. Sudden Infant Death Syndrome: Selected Annotated Bibliography, 1960-71. Washington: USGPO, 1973.

3483. United States Senate. Death with Dignity: An Inquiry into Related Public Issues. Washington: USGPO, 1972.

3484. United States Senate Committe on the Judiciary. Antitrust Aspects of the Funeral Industry--Hearings Before the Subcommittee on Antitrust and Monopoly. Washington: USGPO, 1964

3485. Unwin, D. "But What Kind of Life?" New Zealand Nursing Journal, 68 (Mar., 1975), 19-21.

3486. Urban, Rudolf. Beyond Human Knowledge. New York: Pageant Press, 1958.

3487. Urquhart, G.E.D. et al. "Sudden Unexplained Death in Infancy and Hyper-immunization," Journal of Clinical Pathology, 24 (1971), 736-9.

3488. Vaisrub, S. "Editorial: Dying Is Worked to Death," Journal of the American Medical Association, 229 (Sep. 30, 1974), 1909-10.

3489. _____. "The Fade-Out," Archives of Internal Medicine, 121 (June, 1968), 571.

3490. Vakhovskii, A.I. "Our Experience in the Treatment of Terminal Cases," Klinischeskaia Khirurgiia (Kiev), 4 (Apr., 1965), 41-5.

3491. Valdes, Mario J. Death in the Literature of Unamuno. Urbana: University of Illinois Press, 1966.

3492. Valdes-Dapena, Marie A. "Crib Deaths and Focal Fibrinoid Necrosis of the Infant Larynx," Journal of Forensic Sciences, 3 (1958), 503.

3493. _____. "Sudden and Unexpected Death in Infancy: A Review of the World Literature, 1954-66," Pediatrics, 39 (1967), 123-38.

3494. _____. "Sudden and Unexpected Death in Infants: The Scope of our Ignorance," Pediatric Clinics of North America, 10 (1963), 693.

3495. _____. "Sudden Death in Infancy: A Report for Pathologists," Perspectives in Pediatric Pathology, 2 (1975), 1-14.

3496. _____. "Sudden, Unexpected and Unexplained Death in Infancy--A Status Report, 1973," New England Journal of Medicine, 289 (Nov. 29, 1973), 1195-7.

3497. _____, Rose P. Felipe. "Immunofluorescent Studies in Crib Deaths: Absence of Evidence of Hypersensitivity to Cow's Milk," American Journal of Clinical Pathology, 56 (1971), 412-5.

3498. _____, et al. "The Myocardial Conduction System in Sudden Death in Infancy," New England Journal of Medicine, 289 (Nov. 29, 1973), 1179-80.

3499. _____, et al. "Sudden Unexpected Death in Infancy: A Statistical Analysis of Certain Socio-Economic Factors," Journal of Pediatrics, 73 (Sep., 1968), 386-94.

3500. Vandeman, George E. Papa, Are You Going to Die? Mountain View, CA: Pacific Press, 1970.

3501. van den Aardweg, G.J. "A Grief Theory of Homosexualtiy," American Journal of Psychotherapy, 26 (Jan., 1972), 52-68.

3502. Vanden Bergh, R.L. "Let's Talk about Death to Overcome Inhibiting Emotions," American Journal of Nursing. 66 (Jan., 1966), 71-3.

3503. van Gennep, Arnold. The Rites of Passage. Translated by Monika B. Vizedom and Gabrielle L. Caffe. Chicago: The University of Chicago Press, 1961.

3504. van Leeuwen, W.S. "Symposium on the Significance of EEG for 'Statement on Death,' Introduction," Electroencephalography and Clinical Neurophysiology, 27 (Aug., 1969), 214-5.

3505. Van Zeller, Hubert. Death in Other Words. Springfield: Templegate, 1975.

3506. Vaughan, D.H. "Families Experiencing Sudden, Unexpected Infant Death," Journal of the Royal College of General Practitioners, 16 (1968), 359-67.

3507. Vaughan, G.F. "Children in Hospital," Lancet, 1 (June 1, 1957), 1117-20.

3508. Veatch, R.M. "Brain Death: Welcome Definition--or Dangerous Judgement?" Hastings Center Reports, 2 (Nov., 1972), 10-3.

3509. Vedin, J.A. et al. "Sudden Death: Identification of High Risk Groups," American Heart Journal, 86 (July, 1973), 124-32.

3510. Vernet, Maurice. La Vie et la Mort. Paris: Flammarion, 1952.

3511. Vernick, Joel J. Selected Bibliography on Death and Dying. Washington: National Institutes of Health, USGPO, 1970.

3512. _____, K. Myron. "Who's Afraid of Death on a Leukemia Ward?" American Journal of Diseases of Children, 109 (1965), 393-7.

3513. Vernon, Glenn M. "Death Control," Omega, 3 (May, 1972), 131-8.

3514. _____. "Dying as a Social-Symbolic Process," Humanitas, 10 (Feb., 1974), 21-32.

3515. _____. Sociology of Death: An Analysis of Death-Related Behavior. New York: Ronald Press, 1970.

3516. _____. "Some Questions about the Inevitable-Death Orientation," Sociological Symposium, 1 (Fall, 1968), 82-4.

3517. _____, William D. Payne. "Myth-Conceptions about Death," Journal of Religion and Health, 12 (Jan., 1973), 63-76.

3518. _____, Charles E. Waddell. "Dying as Social Behavior: Mormon Behavior Through Half a Century," Omega, 4 (Fall, 1974), 199-206.

3519. Verwoerdt, Adriaan. "Chronic Ailments: Communication with the Fatally Ill," Chronic Ailments, 15 (May-June, 1965), 105-11.

3520. _____. "Comments On: 'Communication with the Fatally Ill'," Omega, 2 (Mar., 1967), 10-1.

3521. _____. "Communication with the Fatally Ill," Southern Medical Journal, 57 (July, 1964), 787-95.

3522. Verwoerdt, Adriaan. Communication with the Fatally Ill. Springfield: C.C. Thomas, 1966.

3523. _____. "Death and the Family," Medical Opinion and Review, 1 (Sep., 1966), 38-43.

3524. _____. "Informing the Patient with Fatal Illness," Postgraduate Medicine, 40 (Dec., 1966), A95-99.

3525. _____, J.L. Elmore. "Psychological Reactions in Fatal Illness, I: The Prospect of Impending Death," Journal of the American Geriatrics Society 15 (Jan., 1967), 9-19.

3526. _____, R. Wilson. "Communication with Fatally Ill Patients: Tacit or Explicit," American Journal of Nursing, 67 (Nov., 1967), 2307-9.

3527. Vickery, K.O. "Euthanasia, A Medicated Survival--The Press, the Public, the Professions and the Patient," Royal Society of Health Journal, 94 (June, 1974), 118-24.

3528. Viderman, S. "De l'Instinct de la Mort," Revue Francaise de Psychoanalyse, 21 (Jan., 1961), 89-131.

3529. Vincent, G. "Establishments of a New Type of Authority--Sociological Meaning of Preaching and an Ecclesiological Interpretation of Death of Christ in Protestantism," Archives of Social Science and Religion, 20 (1975), 147-58.

3530. Visotsky, H.M. et al. "Coping Behavior Under Extreme Stress," Archives of General Psychiatry, 5 (Nov., 1961), 423-48.

3531. Vitale, Lamberto Dott. "Le Ultime Parole dei Moribondi (The Last Words of the Dying)," Minerva Medica, 49 (Oct. 20, 1950), 256-67.

3532. Vogel, F. "Sudden and Unexplained Death of Two Newborn Siblings," Humangenetik, 22 (Apr. 24, 1974), 89-90.

3533. Vogler, B. "Attitudes Toward Death and Funeral Ceremonies in Rhenish Protestant Churches Around 1600," Archives of Social Science and Religion, 29 (1975), 139-46.

3534. Voigt, J. "The Criteria of Death Particularly in Relation to Transplantaion Surgery," World Medical Journal, 14 (Sep.-Oct., 1967), 143-6.

3535. Voivenel, Paul. Le Medecin Devant la Douleur et la Mort (The Physician Before Pain and Death). Paris: Librarie des Champs-Elysees, 1934.

3536. Volkan, Vamik D. "The Recognition and Prevention of Pathological Grief," Virginia Medical Monthly, 99 (May, 1972), 535-40.

3537. _____. "A Study of a Patient's 'Re-Grief Work': Through Dreams, Psychological Tests and Psychoanalysis," Psychiatric Quarterly, 44 (1970), 231-50.

3538. Volkan, Vamik D. "Typical Findings in Pathological Grief," Psychiatric Quarterly, 44 (1970), 321-50.

3539. _____. "More on 'Re-Grief' Therapy," Journal of Thanatology, 3 (1975), 77-91.

3540. Volkart, Edmund H., Stanley T. Michael. "Bereavement and Mental Health," in A.H. Leighton et al., eds., Explorations in Social Psychology. New York: Basic Books, 1957. 281-307.

3541. Vollman, Rita R. et al. "The Reactions of Family Systems to Sudden and Unexpected Death," Omega, 2 (May, 1971), 101-6.

3542. Von Balthasar, Hans Urs. Der Tod im Heutigen Denken. Olten: Anima, 1956.

3543. Von Ferber, Christian, "Death: An Undigested Problem for the Medical Man and the Sociologist," Koelner Zeitschrift fuer Sociologie und Socialpsychologie, 22 (June, 1970), 237-50.

3544. Von Hentig, Hans. "Pre-Murderous Kindness and Post-Murder Grief," Journal of Criminal Law, Criminology, and Police Science, 48 (1957), 369-77.

3545. Von Hug-hellmuth, Hermine. "The Child's Concept of Death," Psychoanalytic Quarterly, 34 (Oct., 1965), 499-516.

3546. Von Muhlbacher, Walter. "Das Sterbestubchen in Krankenhausern (The Small Dying Room in Hospitals)," Munchener Medizinische Wochenschrift, 83 (May 15, 1936), 797-9.

3547. Von Rechenberg-Linten, Paul. "Unmittelbares Ich-Bewisstsein und Tod (Immediate Ego Consciousness and Death," Archiv fur Systematische Philosophie, 18 (1912), 264-84.

3548. Von Witzleben, Henry. "On Loneliness," Psychiatry, 21 (1958), 37-43.

3549. Vore, David A. "Editorial: A Child's View of Death," Southern Medical Journal, 67 (Apr., 1974), 383-5.

3550. _____, Logan Wright. "Psychological Management of the Family and the Dying Child," in R.E. Hardy and J.G. Cull, eds., Therapeutic Needs of the Family: Problems, Descriptions and Therapeutic Approaches. Springfield: C.C. Thomas, 1974.

3551. Vorreith, M. et al. "Causes of Death in the Army," Vojenske Zdravotnicke Listy, 34 (Dec., 1965), 240-3.

3552. Vovelle, M. "Attitudes Toward Death, Leading Current Theme of History of Mental Habits," Archives of Social Science and Religion, 20 (1975), 17-29.

3553. Vuillemin, Jules. Essai sur la Signification de la Mort. Paris: Presses Universitaires de France, 1948.

3554. Vulliamy, Colwyn Edward. Immortal Man--A Study of Funeral Customs and of
     Beliefs in Regard to the Nature and Fate of the Soul. London: Methuen,
     1926.

3555. Waechter, Eugenia H. "Children's Awareness of Fatal Illness," American Journal of Nursing, 71 (June, 1971), 1168-72.

3556. _____. "Death Anxiety in Children with Fatal Illness," Dissertation Abstracts, 29B (1969), 2505.

3557. Wagner, Berniece M. "Teaching Students to Work with the Dying," American Journal of Nursing, 64 (Nov., 1964), 128-31.

3558. Wagner, F.F. "The Psychiatrist and the Dying Hospital Patient," Mental Hygiene, 51 (Oct., 1967), 486-8.

3559. Wahl, Charles W. "Bolstering the Defenses of Dying Patients," Hospital Physician, 5 (Mar., 1969), 160ff.

3560. _____. "The Differential Diagnosis of Normal and Neurotic Grief Following Bereavement," Psychosomatics, 11 (Mar.-Apr., 1970), 104-6.

3561. _____. "The Fear of Death," Bulletin of the Menninger Clinic, 22 (Nov., 1958), 214-23.

3562. _____. "Helping the Dying Patient and his Family," Journal of Pastoral Care, 26 (June, 1972), 93-8.

3563. _____. "Management of Death and the Dying Patient," in New Dimensions in Psychosomatic Medicine. Boston: Little, Brown, 1964.

3564. _____. "The Physician's Management of the Dying Patient," in J. Masserman, ed., Current Psychiatric Therapies. V. 2. New York: Grune and Stratton, 1962), 127-36.

3565. _____. "Some Antecedent Factors in the Family Histories of 568 Male Schizophrenics in the United States Navy," American Journal of Psychiatry, 113 (1956), 201-9.

3566. _____, et al. Helping the Dying Patient and His Family. New York: National Association of Social Workers, 1960.

3567. Waldo, F.J. "The Ancient Office of Coroner," Coroners' Society Annual Report, 4 (1910), 241-52.

3568. Walkenstein, Eileen. "The Death Experience in Insulin Coma Treatment," American Journal of Psychiatry, 112 (1956), 985-90.

3569. Walker, A.E. "The Death of a Brain," Johns Hopkins Medical Journal, 124 (Apr., 1969), 190-201.

3570. Walker, J.V. "Attitudes to Death," Gerontologia Clinica, 10 (1968), 304-8.

3571. Walker, Kenneth M. The Circle of Life; A Search for an Attitude to Pain, Disease, Old Age and Death. New York: Consortium Press, 1970.

3572. Walker, M. "The Last Hour Before Death," American Journal of Nursing, 73 (Sep., 1973), 1592-3.

3573. Walker, W.J. "Government-Subsidized Death and Disability," Journal of the American Medical Association, 230 (Dec. 16, 1974), 1529-30.

3574. Wallace, E., B.D. Townes. "Dual Role of Comforter and Bereaved: Reactions of Medical Personnel to the Dying Child and His Parents," Mental Hygiene, 53 (July, 1969), 327-32.

3575. Wallace, H.M. et al. "Patterns of Infant and Early Childhood Mortality in the California Project of a Collaborative Inter-American Study," Bulletin of the Pan American Health Organization, 9 (1975), 32-9.

3576. Wallace, L. "Death and the Nurse," Nursing Monthly, 128 (Feb. 28, 1969), 22.

3577. _____. "The Needs of the Dying," Nursing Times, 65 (Nov. 13, 1969), 1450-1.

3578. Wallden, L. "Human Dignity, Healing Art and Care for the Dying," Lakartidnigen, 62 (Sep., 1965), 3113-7.

3579. Walley, K. Warren. "Suicide in Opera: A Brief Analysis," Omega, 2 (Aug., 1971), 191-4.

3580. Walters, Mary Jane. "Psychic Death: Report of a Possible Case," Archives of Neurological Psychiatry, 52 (1944), 84-5.

3581. Waltregny, A. et al. "Cerebral Death and Homotransplants: Criteria Used for Rapid Establishment of the Diagnosis of Irreversible Coma," Electroencephalography and Clinical Neurophysiology, 29 (Nov., 1970), 531.

3582. Walworth, Joy H. "Conceptions of Death and Dying in Personal Poetry," Dissertation Abstracts International, 33 (Jan., 1973), 3327.

3583. Wangensteen, O.H. "Should Patients Be Told They Have Cancer," Surgery, 27 (1950), 944-7.

3584. Warbasse, James Peter. "On Life and Death and Immortality," Zygon--Journal of Religion and Science, 1 (Dec., 1966), 366-72.

3585. _____. "The Ultimate Adventure," Geriatrics, 11 (1956), 468-9.

3586. Ward, Audrey W. "Telling the Patient," Journal of the Royal College of General Practitioners, 42 (July, 1974), 465-8.

3587. _____. "Terminal Care in Malignant Disease," Social Science and Medicine, 8 (July, 1974), 413-20.

3588. Wardle, C.J. "Two Generations of Broken Homes in the Genesis of Conduct and Behavior Disorders in Childhood," British Medical Journal, 2 (Aug. 5, 1961), 349-54.

3589. Warner, W. Lloyd. The Living and the Dead. New Haven: Yale University Press, 1959.

3590. Warren, W.E. "Physical Education and Death," Physical Education, 28 (Oct., 1971), 127-8.

3591. Warthin, A.S. The Physician of the Dance of Death: A Historical Study of the Evolution of the Dance of Death Mythos in Art. New York: Paul B. Hoeber, 1931.

3592. Washburn, Ruth Wendell. Children Have Their Reasons. New York: D. Appleton-Century, 1942.

3593. Wasmuth, Ewalds. Vom Sinn des Todes. Heidelberg, Lambert Schneider, 1959.

3594. Watson, A.A. "Death by Cursing--A Problem for Forensic Psychiatry," Medicine, Science, and the Law, 13 (July, 1973), 192-4.

3595. Watson, E. "A Two-Year Study of Sudden Death in Infancy in Inner North London," Public Health, 89 (May, 1975), 153-5.

3596. Watson, Lyall. The Romeo Error: A Matter of Life and Death. New York: Doubleday, 1975.

3597. Watson, M.J. "Death--A Necessary Concern for Nurses," Nursing Outlook, 16 (Oct., 1968), 22-5.

3598. Watt, Anne S. "Helping Children to Mourn, Part I," Medical Insight, 3 (July, 1971), 29-32ff. Part II, (Aug., 1971), 57-62.

3599. Watt, Jill. Canadian Guide to Death and Dying. Vancouver and Toronto: International Self-Counsel Press, 1974.

3600. Watthana-Kasetr, S.P., P.S. Spiers. "Geographic Mortality Rates and Rates of Aging: A Possible Relationship," Journal of Gerontology, 28 (July, 1973), 374-9.

3601. Watts, Alan. Death. Milbrae, CA: Celestial Arts, 1975.

3602. Watts, Richard G. Straight Talk about Death with Young People. Philadelphia: Westminster Press, 1975.

3603. Waugh, E. The Loved One. Boston: Little, Brown, 1948.

3604. Wacenberg, Sheldon E. "The Importance of the Communication of Feelings about Cancer," Annals of the New York Academy of Science, 125 (1966), 1000-5.

3605. Weber, A. "Zum Erlebnis des Todes bei Kindern (Concerning Children's Experiences with Death)," Monatsschrift fur Psychiatrie und Neurologie, 107 (1943), 192-225.

3606. Weber, Frederick Parkes. Aspects of Death and Correlated Aspects of Life in Art, Epigrams, and Poetry. Washington: Consortium Press, 1970.

3607. Weber, M. "Dealing with Death: Thanatology Looks at the Doctor and the Dying Patient," Medical World News, 12 (May 21, 1971), 30-6.

3608. Webster, F. "Perspectives on Death and the Dying Patient," Hospital Progress, 54 (Dec., 1973), 32-4.

3609. Weidenmann, Jakobus. Furchte dich Nicht! Der Mensch Und der Tod. Zurich: Artemis, 1944.

3610. Weiner, Hannah B. "Living Experiences with Death--A Journeyman's View through Psychodrama," Omega, 6 (1975), 251-74.

3611. Weinstein, Edwin A., Robert L. Kahn. Denial of Illness. Springfield: C.C. Thomas, 1955.

3612. _____. "Personality Factors in Denial of Illness," Archives of Neurology and Psychiatry, 69 (1953), 355-67.

3613. Weisberg, L.M. "Casework with the Terminally Ill," Social Casework, 55 (June, 1974), 337-42.

3614. Weisman, Avery D. "Birth of the Death People," Omega (Newsletter), 1 (1966), 1.

3615. _____. "Coping with Untimely Death," Psychiatry, 36 (Nov., 1973), 366-78.

3616. _____. "Death and Responsibility: A Psychiatrist's View," Psychiatric Opinion, 344 (Aug., 1966), 22-6.

3617. _____. "The Dying Patient," in Pansnau, ed., Consultation-Liaison Psychiatry. New York: Grune and Stratton, Inc., 1975.

3618. _____. The Existential Core of Psychoanalysis. Boston: Little, Brown, 1965.

3619. _____. "How Shall a Physician Learn about Death," Archives of the Foundation of Thanatology, 1 (Apr., 1969), 8-9.

3620. _____. "Is Mourning Necessary?" in B. Shoenberg et al., eds., Anticipatory Grief. New York: Columbia University Press, 1974.

3621. _____. "Misgivings and Misconceptions in the Psychiatric Care of Terminal Patients," Psychiatry, 33 (Feb., 1970), 67-81.

3622. Wesman, Avery D. "On Death and Dying: Does Old Age Make Sense? Decisions and Destiny in Growing Older," Journal of Geriatric Psychiatry, 7 (1974), 84-93.

3623. _____. On Dying and Denying: A Psychiatric Study of Terminality. New York: Behavioral Publications, 1972.

3624. _____. "On the Value of Denying Death," Journal of Pastoral Psychology, 23 (1972), 24-32.

3625. _____. "Psychosocial Considerations in Terminal Care," in B. Schoenberg et al., eds., Psychosocial Aspects of Terminal Care. New York: Columbia University Press, 1972.

3626. _____. "Psychosocial Death," Psychology Today, 6 (Nov., 1972), 77ff.

3627. _____. The Realization of Death: A Guide for the Psychological Autopsy. New York: Aronson, Jason, Inc., 1974.

3628. _____. "Thanatology," in Freedman, A.M. et al., eds., Comprehensive Textbook of Psychiatry. Baltimore: Williams and Wilkins, 1974.

3629. _____, T.P. Hackett. "The Dying Patient," Forest Hospital Publications, 1 (1962), 16-21.

3630. _____. "Predilection to Death: Death and Dying as a Psychiatric Problem," Psychosomatic Medicine, 23 (1961), 232-56.

3631. _____, Robert Kastenbaum. The Psychological Autopsy: A Study of the Terminal Phase of Life. Community Mental Health Journal Monograph #4. New York: Behavioral Publications, 1968.

3632. _____, J. William Worden. "Psychosocial Analysis of Cancer Deaths," Omega, 6 (1975), 61-75.

3633. _____. "The Social Significance of the Danger List," Journal of the American Medical Association, 215 (1972), 1963-6.

3634. Weismann, August. Uber Leben und Tod. Jena: Gustav Fisher, 1892.

3635. Weiss, E. "Todestrib und Masochismus," Imago, 21 (1935), 393-411.

3636. Weiss, J.M.A. "The Gamble with Death in Attempted Suicide," Psychiatry, 20 (1957), 17.

3637. Weiss, Jess. The Vestibule. Port Washington, NY: Ashley Books, 1972.

3638. Weiss, N.S. et al. "Problems in the Use of Death Certificates to Identify Sudden Unexpected Infant Deaths," Health Services Reports, 88 (June-July, 1973), 555-8.

3639. Weissmann, K. "Our Attitude Towards Dead," Revista Brasileira de Medicina (Rio de Janeiro), 25 (Sep., 1968), 623-4.

3640. Wells II, James Ogden. "An Experimental Study of the Assignment of Responsibility for Unintentioned, Subintentioned, and Intentioned Death," Dissertation Abstracts, 31 (Oct., 1970), 2294B

3641. Wenkart, Antonia. "Death in Life," Journal of Existentialism, 8 (Fall, 1967), 75-90.

3642. Weblowsky, R.J. Zwi. "Funerary Rites and Customs," Encyclopedia Britannica, (1971), 9:1011-7.

3643. Werkman, Sidney L. Only a Little Time. Boston: Little, Brown, and Co., 1972.

3644. Wertenbaker, Lael T. Death of a Man. New York: Beacon Press, 1974.

3645. Wertham, Fredric. A Sign for Cain. New York: Paperback Library, 1969.

3646. Wesch, Jerry E. "Self-Actualization and the Fear of Death," Dissertation Abstracts Internationale, 31 (Apr., 1971), 6270-1.

3647. Wessel, M.A. "Death of an Adult and its Impact upon the Child," Clinical Pediatrics, 12 (Jan., 1973), 28-33.

3648. _____. "Death in Family: Impact on Children," Journal of the American Medical Association, 234 (1975), 865-66

3649. West, N.D. "Child's Response to Death Loss," Nebraska Medical Journal, 60 (July, 1975), 228-30.

3650. West, T.S. "Symposium: Care of the Dying: Approach to Death," Nursing Mirror, 139 (Oct. 10, 1974), 56-9.

3651. Westberg, Granger E. "Good Grief," Practical Nursing, 12 (Mar., 1962), 14-5.

3652. _____. Good Grief. Rock Island, IL: Augustana Press, 1962.

3653. _____. Minister and Doctor Meet. New York: Harpers, 1961.

3654. Westerman, Holstijn, Antonie Johan. Leven en Dood. Utrecht, Bijleveli: Medisch-Psychogische Beschouwingen, 1953.

3655. Weston, D., R.C. Irwin. "Preschool Child's Response to Death of Infant Sibling," American Journal of Diseases of Children. 106 (1963), 564-7.

3656. Wetzel, David, Ida M. Martinson. Meri. Minneapolis: University of Minnesota, 1975.

3657. Wheeler, Alban L. "The Dying Person: A Deviant in the Medical Subculture," Dissertation Abstracts International, 33 (June, 1973), 7051.

3658. Whetmore, Robert. "The Role of Grief in Psychoanalysis," International Journal of Psychoanalysis, 44 (1963), 97-103.

3659. Whisman, S. "Four Distinctive Views of the Dying Patient, 'Turn the Respirator Off and Let Danny Die'," Registered Nurse, 38 (Apr., 1975), 34-5.

3660. Whitaker, O'Kelley. Sister Death. New York: Morehouse-Barlow, 1975.

3661. White, David. "Death Control," New Society, 22 (Nov. 30, 1972), 502-5.

3662. White, Douglas K. "An Undergraduate Course in Death," Omega, 1 (Aug., 1970), 167-74.

3663. White, Joanne F. "Yes, I Hear You, Mr. H.," American Journal of Nursing, 75 (Mar., 1975), 411-3.

3664. White, K.L. "Life and Death and Medicine," Scientific American, 229 (1973), 23-175.

3665. White, L.P., ed. "Care of Patients with Fatal Illness," Annals of the New York Academy of Sciences, 162 (1969), 635-96.

3666. White, R.B., L.Y. Gathman. "The Syndrome of Ordinary Grief," American Family Physician, 8 (Aug., 1973), 97-104.

3667. White, R.J. "The Scientific Limitation of Brain Death," Hospital Progress, 53 (Mar., 1972), 48-51.

3668. White, R.W., ed. The Study of Lives. New York: Atherton Press, 1963.

3669. Whitehouse, D. "Johnny, the Little Boy Who Never Smiled," American Journal of Nursing, 55 (Sep., 1955), 110.

3670. Whiting, John W.M. "Sorcery, Sin, and the Superego: A Cross-Cultural Study of Some Mechanisms of Social Control," Nebraska Symposium on Motivation, 7 (1959), 174-95.

3671. Whitman, H.H., S.J. Lukes. "Behavior Modification for Terminally Ill," American Journal of Nursing, 75 (Jan., 1975), 98-101.

3672. Wiener, D.N., W. Simon. "Personality Characteristics of Embalmer Trainees," Journal of Social Issues, 17 (1961), 43-9.

3673. Wiener, I.H. "Death Criteria," Journal of the American Medical Association, 222 (Oct. 2, 1972), 86.

3674. Wilbur, G.B. "Some Problems Presented by Freud's Life-Death Instinct Theory," American Imago, 2 (1941), 134-96, 209-65.

3675. Wilkes, Eric. "How to Provide Effective Home Care for the Terminally Ill," Geriatrics, 28 (Aug., 1973), 93-6.

3676. Wilkes, Eric. "Symposium: Care of the Dying: Relatives, Professional Care, and the Dying Patient," Nursing Mirror, 139 (Oct. 10, 1974), 53-6.

3677. _____. "Terminal Care and the Special Nursing Unit," Nursing Times, 71 (Jan. 9, 1975), 57-9.

3678. _____. "Where to Die," British Medical Journal, 1 (Jan. 6, 1973), 32-3.

3679. Wilkinson, L. "Death is a Family Matter," Registered Nurse, 33 (Sep., 1970), 50ff.

3680. William, J.S., Jr. "Infant and Child Mortality in Burma by Ethnic Group," Eugenics Quarterly, 13 (June, 1966), 128-32.

3681. Willaime, J.P. "God Had Taken unto Himself: Exclusion of Death and Protestant Death in Present Day Society," Archives of Social Science and Religion, 20 (1975), 127-37.

3682. Williams, Glanville. "Euthanasia," Medical Legal Journal, 41 (1973), 14-34.

3683. _____. "Euthanasia and Abortion," Columbia University Law Review, 38 (1971), 178-201.

3684. Williams, H. "On a Teaching Hospital's Responsibility to Counsel Parents Concerning Their Child's Death," Medical Journal of Australia, 2 (Oct., 1963), 643-5.

3685. Williams, M. "Changing Attitudes to Death: A Survey of Contributions in Psychological Abstracts Over a Thiry-Year Period," Human Relations, 19 (Nov., 1966), 405-22.

3686. _____. "The Fear of Death, Part I: The Avoidance of the Fear of Death," Journal of Analytic Psychology, 3 (1958), 157-65.

3687. Williams, Melvin G. The Last Word. Boston: Oldstone Enterprises, 1973.

3688. Williams, Robert H. "The End of Life in the Elderly," Postgraduate Medicine, 54 (Dec., 1973), 55-9.

3689. _____. To Live and to Die--When, Why and How. New York: Springer-Verlag, 1973.

3690. Williams, R.L. et al., eds. Processes of Aging: Social and Psychological Perspectives. New York: Atherton Press, 1963.

3691. _____, et al. "Religiosity, Generalized Anxiety and Apprehension Concerning Death," Journal of Social Psychology, 75 (June, 1968), 111-7.

3692. Williams, Tom A. Dreads and Besetting Fears. Boston: Little, Brown, 1923.

3693. Williams, W. Vail, et al. "Crisis Intervention in Acute Grief," Omega, 3 (Feb., 1972), 67-70.

3694. Williamson, P. "Fear in Elderly People," American Geriatrics Society, 1 (1953), 739-42.

3695. Willing, Martha. Beyond Conception: Our Children's Children. Boston: Gambit, 1971.

3696. Willis, Diane J. "The Families of Terminally Ill Children: Symptomatology and Management," Journal of Clinical Child Psychology, 3 (Summer, 1974), 32-3.

3697. Willis, Paul. "The Triple-X Boys," New Society, 23 (Mar., 1973), 693-5.

3698. Willson, D. "Nursing Care in Leukemia," Canadian Nurse, 59 (Apr., 1963), 345-6.

3699. Wilson, F.G. "Social Isolation and Bereavement," Nursing Times, 67 (1971), 269-70.

3700. Wilson, George R. "The Sense of Danger and the Fear of Death," The Monist, 13 (1902-3), 352-69.

3701. Wilson, Ian C. et al. "Parental Bereavement in Childhood: MMPI Profiles in a Depressed Population," British Journal of Psychiatry, 113 (1967), 761-4.

3702. Wilson, Jerry B. Death by Decision (The Medical, Moral, and Legal Dilemmas of Euthanasia). Philadelphia: Westminster Press, 1975.

3703. Wineman, D. "The Life-Space Interview," Social Work, 4 (Jan., 1959), 3-17.

3704. Wingate, D. "Definition of Death," British Medical Journal, 2 (May 11, 1968), 363.

3705. Winick, Charles. "Personality Characteristics of Embalmers," Personnel and Guidance Journal, 43 (Nov., 1964), 262-66.

3706. Winkelma, F. "Dying Patient and His Family: Balint Groups Experiences," Dynamic Psychology, 8 (1975), 318-27.

3707. Winner, A.L. "Death and Dying," Journal of the Royal College of Physicians of London, 4 (July, 1970), 351-5.

3708. Winter, A. "Death and the Road Back," Journal of the Medical Society of New Jersey, 66 (Dec., 1969), 670-4.

3709. _____, ed. Moment of Death. Springfield: C.C. Thomas, 1969.

3710. Winter, S.T., A. Bloch. "Sudden Infant Deaths in Israel," Forensic Science, 2 (Aug., 1973), 384-6.

3711. _____, N.B. Emetarom. "Sudden Infant Death: A Pilot Inquiry into its Frequency in Israel," Israel Journal of Medical Science, 9 (Apr., 1973), 447-51.

3712. Wise, Carroll A. Religion in Illness and Health. New York: Harper and Brothers, 1942.

3713. Wise, Doreen J. "Learning about Dying," Nursing Outlook, 22 (Jan., 1974), 42-4.

3714. Wittels, I., J. Botwinick. "Survival in Relocation," Journal of Gerontology, 29 (July, 1974), 440-3.

3715. Wittgenstein, G. "Fear of Dying and of Death as a Requirement of the Maturation Process in Man," Hippokrates, 31 (July-Dec., 1960), 765-9.

3716. Wittkewer, E. "Psychological Aspects of Physical Illness," Canadian Medical Association Journal, 66 (1952), 220-4.

3717. Witzel, L. "Behavior of the Dying Patient," British Medical Journal, 2 (Apr. 12, 1975), 81-2.

3718. Wodinsky, Abraham. "Psychiatric   Consultation with Nurses on a Leukemia Service," Mental Hygiene, 48 (1964), 282-7.

3719. Wohlford, Paul. "Extension of Personal Time, Affective States, and Expectation of Personal Death," Journal of Personality and Social Psychology, 3 (May, 1966), 559-66.

3720. Wolf, Anna W.M. Helping Your Child to Understand Death. New York: Child Study Press, 1973.

3721. Wolf, S. "What to Say to the Cancer Suspect," Current Medical Digest, 20 (Apr., 1953), 97-8.

3722. Wolfe, Thomas. From Death to Mourning. New York: C. Scribner and Sons, 1958.

3723. Wolfenstein, Martha. Disaster: A Psychological Essay. New York: Free Press, Macmillan, 1957.

3724. _____. "How is Mourning Possible?" The Psychoanalytic Study of the Child, 21 (1966), 93-123.

3725. _____, Nathan Leites. Movies: A Psychological Study. Glencoe, IL: The Free Press, 1950.

3726. _____, Gilbert Kliman, eds. Children and the Death of a President. New York: Doubleday, 1965.

3727. Wolff, C.T. et al. "Relationship Between Psychological Defenses and Mean Urinary 17-Hydroxycorticoid Excretion, I: A Predictive Study in Parents of Fatally Ill Children," Psychosomatic Medicine, 26 (1964), 576.

3728. Wolff, H. et al., eds. Life Stress and Bodily Disease. Baltimore: The Williams and Wilkins Co., 1950.

3729. Wolff, I. "Am I Going to Die?" Registered Nurse, 25 (Sep., 1962), 91-6.

3730. _____. "When Your Patient Asks: Do I Have Cancer?" Registered Nurse, 23 (May, 1960), 51-2.

3731. Wolff, J.R. et al. "The Emotional Reaction to a Stillbirth," American Journal of Obstetrics and Gynecology, 108 (Sep., 1970), 73-7.

3732. Wolff, Kurt H. The Biological, Sociological and Psychological Aspects of Aging. Springfield, IL: C.C. Thomas, 1959.

3733. _____. Geriatric Psychiatry. Springield, IL: C.C. Thomas, 1963.

3734. _____. "Helping Elderly Patients Face the Fear of Death," Hospital and Community Psychiatry, 18 (May, 1967), 142-4.

3735. _____. "A Partial Analysis of Student Reaction to President Roosevelt's Death," Journal of Social Psychology, 26 (1947), 35-53.

3736. _____. "Personality Type and Reaction Toward Aging and Death," Geriatrics, 21 (Aug., 1966), 189-92.

3737. _____. "The Problem of Death and Dying in the Geriatric Patient," Journal of the American Geriatrics Society, 18 (Dec., 1970), 954-61.

3738. Wolff, Sula. Children Under Stress. London: Allen Lan--The Penguin Press, 1969.

3739. Wolfle, Dael. "Dying with Dignity," Science, 168 (June, 1970), 1403.

3740. Wood, B.G. "Interpersonal Aspects in the Care of Terminally Ill Patients," American Journal of Psychoanalysis, 35 (Spring, 1975), 47-53.

3741. Wood, J. "Structure of Concern: Ministry in Death Related Situations," Urban Life, 4 (1975), 369-84.

3742. Wood, William, John Wharton. Death-Bed Scenes. London: C. and J. Rivington, 1826. 3 V.

3743. Woodruff, M.F. "Ethical Problems in Organ Transplantation," British Medical Journal, 5396 (June 6, 1964), 1457-1460.

3744. Woods, J. "Emotional Problems of the Geriatric Patient and His Family," South Carolina Nurses, 22 (Fall, 1970), 169-70.

3745. Woods, J.E. et al. "Experience with Renal Transplantation in High Risk Patients," Surgery, Gynecology, and Obstetrics, 137 (Sep., 1973), 393-8.

3746. Woodson, L. "We Who Face Death," National Geographic, 147 (1975), 364.

3747. Woodward, W.R. "Scientific Genius and Loss of a Parent," Science Studies, 4 (July, 1974), 265ff.

3748. Woolf, Kurt. "Fear of Death Must be Overcome in Psychotherapy of the Aged," Frontiers of Hospital Psychiatry, (1966), 3.

3749. Woolnough, J. "A Time to Die: Further Reflections," Medical Journal of Australia, 1 (Feb. 22, 1969), 427.

3750. Woon, T. et al. "The Social Readjustment Rating Scale, a Cross-Cultural Study of Malaysians and Americans," Journal of Cross-Cultural Psychology, 2 (Dec., 1971), 373-86.

3751. Worcester, Alfred. The Care of the Aged, the Dying and the Dead. 2d ed. Springfield, IL: C.C. Thomas, 1961.

3752. Worden, J. William. "On Researching Death," Journal of Pastoral Psychology, 23 (1972), 5-8.

3753. _____. "Pastoral Care Workshop," in B. Schoenberg et al., eds., Psychosocial Aspects of Terminal Care. New York: Columbia University Press, 1972.

3754. _____. PDA--Personal Death Awareness. Englewood Cliffs: Prentice-Hall, 1976.

3755. _____. "The Right to Die," Journal of Pastoral Psychology, 23 (1972), 9-14.

3756. _____. "The Theology and Psychology of Death," Journal of Pastoral Psychology, 23 (June, 1972), np.

3757. _____. "Toward an Acceptable Death," Medical Bulletin: Portsmouth, VA Naval Regional Medical Center, 8 (1973), 42-8.

3758. _____, A.D. Weisman. "Psychosocial Components of Lagtime Cancer Diagnosis," Biritsh Journal of Psychosomatic Research, 19 (Feb., 1975), 69-79.

3759. World Health Organization. Manual of the International Statistical Classification of Diseases, Injuries, and Causes of Death: Based on the Recommendations of the 7th Revision Conference, 1955. Geneva: World Health Organization, 1957.

3760. Wrenlewi, J., S. Keleman. "Living Your Dying," Psychology Today, 8 (1975), 14-5.

3761. Wretmark, Gerdt. "A Study in Grief Reactions," ACTA Psychiatrica et Neurologica Scandinavica, 34 (Supplement 136) (1959), 292-9.

3762. Wright, Logan. "An Emotional Support Program for Parents of Dying Children," Journal of Clinical Child Psychology, 3 (Summer, 1974), 37-8.

3763. Wright, Milton. What's Funny and Why. New York: McGraw-Hill, 1939.

3764. Wright, Robert G. et al. "Psychological Stress During Hemodialysis for Chronic Renal Failure," Annals of Internal Medicine, 64 (Mar., 1966), 611-20.

3765. Wygant, W.E., Jr. "Dying, but not Alone," American Journal of Nursing, 67 (Mar., 1967), 574-7.

3766. Wylie, Harold W. et al. "A Dying Patient in a Psychotherapy Group," International Journal of Group Psychotherapy, 14 (1964), 482-90.

3767. Wylie, M. "Living with Grief," Family Health, 2 (Mar., 1970), 28ff.

3768. Wyschogrod, Edith, ed. The Phenomenon of Death. New York: Harper and Row, 1973.

3769. Yalon, I. "Observations on Mourning," New Physician, 13 (Mar., 1964), 80-1.

3770. Yamamoto, J. "Cultural Factors in Loneliness, Death and Separation," Medical Times, 98 (July, 1970), 177-83.

3771. _____, et al. "Mourning in Japan," American Journal of Psychiatry, 125 (1969), 1660-5.

3772. Yamazaki, S. "The Physical Attitudes of Youths Toward Death," Japanese Journal of Psychology, 15 (1940), 469-75.

3773. Yanovski, A. "Pseudo-Orientation in Time and Anticipated Parental Death," American Journal of Clinical Hypnosis, 14 (Jan., 1972), 156-66.

3774. Yarrow, H.C. "A Further Contribution to the Study of the Mortuary Customs of the North American Indians," First Annual Report, Bureau of American Ethnology, 1 (1879-80), 87-203.

3775. Yarrow, Leon J. "Maternal Deprivation: Toward an Empirical and Conceptual Re-Evaluation," Psychological Bulletin, 58 (1961), 459-90.

3776. _____. "Separation from Parents During Early Childhood," in Martin L. Hoffman and Lois W. Hoffman, eds., Review of Child Development in Research, V. 1. New York: Russell Sage Foundation, 1964.

3777. Yeaworth, R.C. et al. "Attitudes of Nursing Students Toward the Dying Patient," Nursing Research, 23 (Jan.-Feb., 1974), 20-4.

3778. Yinger, J. Milton. "The Influence of Anthropology on Sociological Theories of Religion," American Anthropologist, 60 (1958), 487-95.

3779. Yoeli, M. "Death and Compassion in Medicine and Literature," American Journal of Medical Science, 263 (June, 1972), 437-43.

3780. Yorukoglu, A. "Children's Immediate Reactions to Death in the Family," Turkish Journal of Pediatrics, 13 (Apr.,1971), 72-84.

3781. Young, Frank W. "Graveyards and Social Structure," Rural Sociology, 25 (Dec., 1960), 446-50.

3782. Young, Michael et al. "The Mortality of Widowers," Lancet, 2 (Aug. 31, 1963), 454-6.

3783. Young, William H. "Death of a Patient During Psychotherapy," Psychiatry, 23 (Feb., 1960), 103-8.

3784. _____. "The Question of Honesty," Pastoral Care, 14 (Summer, 1960), 65-77.

3785. Yudkin, S. "Children and Death," Lancet, 1 (Jan. 7, 1967), 37-41.

3786. Zaehner, R.C. Mysticism, Sacred and Profane. New York: Oxford University Press, 1967.

3787. Zahn, Margaret A. Mark Bancivegno. "Violent Death: A Comparison Between Drug Users and Nondrug Users," Addictive Diseases: An International Journal, 1 (1974), 283-96.

3788. Zahourek, R., J.S. Jensen. "Grieving and the Loss of the Newborn," American Journal of Nursing, 73 (May, 1973), 836-9.

3789. Zator, S. "Molly," Registered Nurse, 34 (Nov., 1971), 51-2.

3790. Zazzaro, Joanne. "Death be not Distorted," Nation's Schools, 91 (May, 1973), 39-42, 102.

3791. Zeligs, Rose. "Children's Attitudes Toward Death," Mental Hygiene, 51 (July, 1967), 393-6.

3792. _____. Children's Experience with Death. Springfield: C.C. Thomas, 1974.

3793. _____. "Children's New Year's Resolutions," Childhood Education, 40 (Jan., 1964), 244-6.

3794. _____. "Death Casts its Shadow on a Child," Mental Hygiene, 51 (Jan., 1967), 9-20.

3795. _____. "Death is a Part of Life," California Parent-Teacher, 36 (1959), 7.

3796. _____. "Judy Learns about Death," California Parent-Teacher, 41 (1964), 6-7.

3797. Zhiani-Rezai, A. "Doctors and Death," Dissertation Abstracts, 30 (Aug., 1969), 839B.

3798. Zidowecki, H.M. "Sudden Infant Death Program in Maine," Journal of the Maine Medical Association, 65 (Apr., 1974), 93-5.

3799. Zilboorg, Gregory. "Fear of Death," Psychoanalytic Quarterly, 12 (1943), 465-75.

3800. _____. "The Sense of Immortality," Psychoanalytic Quarterly, 7 (1938), 171-99.

3801. Zimring, J.G. "The Right to Die with Dignity," New York State Journal of Medicine, 73 (July 1, 1973), 1815-6.

3802. Zinker, Joseph C., Stephen L. Find. "The Possibility for Psychological Growth in a Dying Person," The Journal of General Psychology, 74 (Apr., 1966), 185-99.

3803. Zinner, Ellen S. "A Proposal: Developing the Role of the Clinical Associate in the Field of Terminal Patient Care," Journal of Thanatology, 1 (May-June, 1971), 156.

3804. Ziskind, Eugene. "Isolation Stress in Medical and Mental Illness," Journal of the American Medical Association, 168 (Nov. 15, 1968), 1427-30.

3805. Zopf, D. "The Dying Patient: Meeting His Needs Could Be Easier than You Think," Nursing (Jenkintown), 5 (Mar.,1975), 16.

3806. Zuehlke, T.E., J.T. Watkins. 'Use of Psychotherapy with Dying Patients: Exploratory Study," Journal of Clinical Psychology, 31 (1975), 729-32.

INDEX

Note: The numbers following each entry correspond to the items as numbered in the bibliography.

References greater than 3806 are cited in the Addendum, following the Index.

ABORTION
       23, 75, 82, 171, 173, 183, 370, 380, 381, 414, 506, 519, 561, 693, 741,
       802, 834, 867, 874, 1000, 1086, 1307, 1331, 1422, 1486, 1784, 1853,
       2004, 2015, 2185, 2255, 2261, 2348, 2491, 2959, 3014, 3234, 3310,
       3334, 3438, 3450, 3683.

AGING
       31, 32, 222, 324, 492, 510, 557, 575, 607, 641, 751, 776, 781, 814,
       844, 857, 916, 1038, 1094, 1246, 1407, 1423, 1424, 1425, 1426, 1427,
       1428, 1481, 1542, 1585, 1668, 1703, 1751, 1795, 1798, 1800, 1850,
       1899, 1900, 1989, 2115, 2116, 2177, 2190, 2209, 2325, 2329, 2331, 2332,
       2480, 2498, 2592, 2709, 2735, 2765, 2796, 2797, 2866, 2891, 3021, 3028,
       3101, 3171, 3322, 3396, 3434, 3455, 3622, 3690, 3699, 3714, 3732, 3733,
       3744.
   death and
       45, 47, 48, 118, 200, 219, 255, 275, 341, 364, 575, 739, 783, 939,
       998, 1084, 1200, 1269, 1292, 1413, 1622, 1755, 1760, 1796, 1797, 1849,
       1850, 1917, 2052, 2147, 2175, 2190, 2329, 2390, 2438, 2501, 2518, 2536,
       2540, 2613, 2702, 2713, 2763, 2774, 2796, 2798, 2820, 2851, 2885,
       2932, 3034, 3102, 3112, 3218, 3225, 3324, 3352, 3365, 3382, 3406,
       3688, 3734, 3736, 3748, 3809, 3817.
   See also "Attitudes toward death--of the elderly."

ALCOHOL AND DRUGS
       1277, 1440, 1541, 1553, 1721, 1730, 2109, 2110, 2207, 2312, 2627,
       2762, 3787.
   For drug use in terminal care see "Psychotherapy--for the dying" and
   "Terminal care."

ANTHROPOLOGY
       206, 311, 411, 420, 430, 433, 513, 574, 585, 605, 821, 852, 869, 993,
       994, 999, 1305, 1325, 1336, 1423, 1424, 1427, 1503, 1523, 1566, 1626,
       2065, 2162, 2384, 2696, 2955, 3384, 3503, 3750, 3778.
   attitudes toward death in other cultures
       33, 64, 368, 433, 481, 482, 594, 596, 605, 620, 811, 852, 870, 899,
       917, 962, 1000, 1158, 1159, 1209, 1245, 1304, 1324, 1331, 1334, 1335,
       1347, 1363, 1405, 1485, 1545, 1592, 1604, 1621, 1632, 1695, 1715,
       1747, 1771, 1772, 1783, 1784, 1829, 1867, 1871, 1879, 1921, 2013, 2034,
       2077, 2078, 2086, 2089, 2090, 2091, 2100, 2255, 2256, 2296, 2297,
       2314, 2418, 2431, 2454, 2465, 2586, 2633, 2634, 2635, 2641, 2699,
       2711, 2747, 2818, 2839, 2840, 2854, 2887, 2941, 2984, 2989, 3005,
       3049, 3166, 3191, 3216, 3279, 3284, 3296, 3316, 3389, 3428, 3429,
       3435, 3457, 3463, 3471, 3491, 3503, 3533, 3554, 3639, 3750, 3751,
       3823, 3827, 3837.

   mourning customs
       5, 69, 198, 223, 258, 318, 380, 381, 420, 521, 850, 883, 1304, 1325,
       1438, 1583, 1779, 1823, 1844, 1880, 1949, 2013, 2060, 2077, 2302, 2305,
       2352, 2354, 2431, 2445, 2525, 2653, 2647, 2818, 3152, 3216, 3397, 3428,
       3429, 3457, 3554, 3642, 3771, 3774.

ANXIETY
   2, 278, 3]2, 325, 459, 474, 491, 832, 853, 861, 1010, 1179, 1473,
   1752, 1846, 1847, 1948, 2103, 2117, 2376, 3487, 2388, 2570, 2584,
   2912, 2985, 3030, 3167, 3289, 3304, 3370, 3410, 3571, 3962.
and guilt
   14, 524, 1249, 1868.
and pain
   651, 2852.

ATTITUDES TOWARD DEATH
   52, 184, 205, 206, 207, 208, 209, 212, 298, 326, 375, 380, 381, 384,
   387, 393, 410, 415, 426, 538, 660, 661, 719, 757, 774, 803, 822,
   860, 863, 875, 963, 983, 1028, 1033, 1036, 1056, 1168, 1181, 1209,
   1227, 1355, 1374, 1400, 1408, 1421, 1466, 1480, 1491, 1522, 1631,
   1719, 1747, 1750, 1756, 1766, 1770, 1794, 1806, 1811, 1826, 1930,
   2035, 2080, 2082, 2083, 2095, 2097, 2098, 2099, 2101, 2102, 2131,
   2170, 2178, 2211, 2246, 2378, 2381, 2382, 2383, 2394, 2419, 2454,
   2467, 2486, 2571, 2667, 2669, 2673, 2956, 3033, 3050, 3118, 3154,
   3157, 3158, 3159, 3160, 3164, 3171, 3291, 3314, 3427, 3428, 3516,
   3517, 3552, 3570, 3571, 3685, 3757, 3586.
of adolescents
   51, 597, 713, 730, 1428, 1603, 1908, 1920, 2208, 2363, 2374, 3031,
   3021, 3116, 3292, 3697, 3772.
of children
   29, 51, 213, 276, 374, 534, 667, 730, 750, 840, 996, 1009, 1133,
   1160, 1254, 1468, 1488, 1540, 1686, 1693, 1804, 2364, 2420, 2442,
   2450, 2547, 2571, 2784, 2990, 3012, 3013, 3174, 3213, 3289, 3545,
   3605, 3785, 3791.
contemporary American
   105, 207, 294, 314, 326, 342, 589, 672, 673, 774, 909, 1008, 1029,
   1040, 1041, 1042, 1044, 1230, 1218, 1228, 1216, 1343, 1524, 1659,
   1947, 2256, 2380, 2382, 2482, 2693, 2793, 2850, 2946, 3075, 3104,
   3105, 3296
in other cultures
   See "Anthropology--Attitudes toward death in other cultures."
of the dying
   12, 13, 14, 26, 39, 46, 57, 108, 127, 138, 236, 312, 362, 386, 462,
   478, 484, 501, 504, 522, 589, 619, 638, 788, 845, 853, 1024, 1040,
   1043, 1045, 1047, 1062, 1290, 1373, 1378, 1408, 1567, 1822, 1855,
   1889, 1950, 1976, 1978, 2044, 2072, 2074, 2075, 2208, 2563, 2511,
   2512, 2598, 2961, 2968, 2981, 3044, 3083, 3235, 3250, 3353, 3525,
   3632.
of the elderly
   6, 118, 166, 200, 558, 641, 674, 739, 751, 939, 1032, 1035, 1246,
   1269, 1501, 1703, 1707, 1708, 1755, 1796, 1807, 1851, 1917, 2147,
   2427, 2517, 2798, 2900, 2910, 2916, 3380, 3381, 3382, 3406, 3460.
of the mentally ill
   6, 28, 348, 418, 429, 499, 508, 615, 574, 707, 727, 1005, 1025,
   1027, 1038, 1452, 1478, 1508, 1552, 1694, 1826, 1858, 1859, 2298,
   1573, 2574, 2716, 3262.

ATTITUDES TOWARD DEATH (cont.)
    of professionals
        91, 108, 135, 136, 154, 259, 277, 389, 331, 446, 462, 577, 616, 719,
        754, 988, 1115, 1231, 1445, 1329, 1408, 1630, 1798, 1811, 1812, 1986,
        2081, 2186, 2226, 2255, 2286, 2341, 2358, 2386, 2713, 2884, 2819,
        2821, 2893, 2923, 3085, 3334, 3359, 3374, 3543, 3640, 3832.
        (See also "Nurses--Attitudes toward death" and "Physicians--Attitudes
        toward death.")
    of the social deviant
        1146, 1277, 1306, 1730, 3057, 3291, 3544, 3697.

BEHAVIOR
    children and infants
        320, 321, 325, 340, 965, 1428, 1650, 3013.
    concepts of death and
        206, 652, 983, 1133, 2157.

BEREAVEMENT
        5, 69, 76, 88, 128, 225, 263, 297, 317, 394, 395, 396, 398, 400,
        460, 499, 541, 542, 543, 686, 687, 689, 752, 770, 772, 944, 946,
        947, 948, 949, 951, 949, 964, 991, 1014, 1275, 1280, 1318, 1434,
        1471, 1494, 1542, 1559, 1593, 1602, 1711, 1856, 1831, 1946, 1949,
        1988, 1992, 1993, 1994, 1996, 2063, 2351, 2359, 2505, 2512, 2539,
        1577, 2611, 2662, 2676, 2677, 2679, 2680, 2681, 2685, 2716, 2933,
        2956, 2996, 3038, 3063, 3079, 3080, 3188, 3386, 3445, 3540, 3699,
        3647, 3747.
    abnormal response to
        4, 70, 203, 261, 262, 263, 264, 265, 266, 323, 348, 397, 402, 403,
        404, 405, 406, 441, 450, 464, 465, 468, 514, 515, 541, 542, 564,
        566, 567, 568, 686, 847, 920, 1023, 1057, 1192, 1196, 1303, 1332,
        1386, 1389, 1549, 1553, 1555, 1556, 1557, 1615, 1692, 1781, 1850,
        1947, 2421, 2676, 2677, 2683, 2716, 2805, 2872, 3168, 3169, 3218,
        3386.
    childhood
        203, 316, 257, 261, 262, 264, 275, 266, 291, 293, 305, 323, 345,
        391, 395, 396, 397, 398, 399, 400, 401, 402, 403, 404, 405, 406,
        436, 441, 463, 464, 465, 468, 472, 514, 515, 516, 543, 544, 566,
        567, 568, 682, 730, 767, 807, 839, 858, 866, 1014, 1057, 1070,
        1169, 1172, 1173, 1221, 1233, 1235, 1258, 1260, 1270, 1358, 1387,
        1404, 1451, 1494, 1549, 1551, 1553, 1555, 1556, 1557, 1558, 1615,
        1873, 1875, 1971, 2240, 2241, 2242, 2289, 2309, 2318, 2443, 2472,
        2500, 2520, 2523, 2544, 2772, 2999, 3013, 3094, 3116, 3168, 3169,
        3187, 3276, 3598, 3701, 3649, 3773, 3780.
        (See also "Children--Reactions to the death of parents, --Reactions
        to the death of pets, --Reactions to the death of siblings," and
        "Separation and loss.")
    conjugal
        239, 261, 451, 564, 689, 927, 952, 1192, 1303, 2277, 2278, 2280,
        2675, 3368, 3417, 3478.

DEATH
42, 63, 76, 77, 86, 103, 120, 157, 175, 271, 279, 288, 319, 369,
373, 384, 421, 422, 449, 452, 509, 511, 531, 547, 601, 606, 614,
644, 651, 681, 708, 786, 817, 821, 822, 854, 855, 900, 903, 904,
1050, 1051, 1093, 1098, 1126, 1182, 1185, 1190, 1201, 1209, 1212,
1222, 1277, 1342, 1344, 1461, 1471, 1487, 1493, 1518, 1636, 1691,
1699, 1791, 1830, 1836, 1882, 1937, 1954, 1960, 1969, 1973, 1984,
1997, 2002, 2028, 2067, 2103, 2190, 2269, 2304, 2459, 2504, 2507,
2539, 2542, 2594, 2613, 2662, 2760, 2768, 2785, 2789, 2972, 2977,
2986, 3007, 3029, 3038, 3076, 3109, 3135, 3151, 3153, 3155, 3172,
3223, 3247, 3261, 3376, 3403, 3418, 3426, 3464, 3488, 3505, 3608,
3627, 3643, 3647, 3707, 3768, 3821, 3823, 3841.
anxiety
294, 313, 365, 522, 529, 538, 809, 861, 862, 1189, 1255, 1322, 1367,
1472, 1473, 1474, 1522, 1579, 1582, 1649, 1719, 1804, 1811, 1978,
2047, 2152, 2153, 2188, 2355, 2414, 2461, 2532, 2570, 2584, 2645,
2668, 2941, 3021, 3075, 3265, 3280, 3289, 3345, 3402, 3405, 2406,
3407, 3408, 3409, 3410, 3411, 3412, 3413, 3415, 3444.
and the arts
1081, 1405, 1725, 1978, 2429, 2463, 2553, 3579, 3591, 3606, 3725.
disasters and megadeath
392, 680, 722, 829, 495, 1793, 2157, 2161, 2294, 3090, 3156, 3470,
3723, 3842, 3844, 3846, 3850.
fear of
3, 53, 118, 135, 174, 198, 214, 250, 298, 325, 365, 367, 390, 474,
.595, 615, 646, 648, 708, 712, 904, 908, 909, 930, 1014, 1040, 1055,
1067, 1069, 1129, 1338, 1406, 1455, 1456, 1488, 1505, 1513, 1597,
1623, 1710, 1891, 1918, 1978, 2062, 2068, 2084, 2085, 2086, 2087,
2088, 2089, 2090, 2092, 2094, 2095, 2096, 2105, 2222, 2325, 2355,
2378, 2409, 2458, 2509, 2560, 2578, 2646, 2717, 2775, 2965, 3030,
3147, 3325, 3326, 3414, 3437, 3561, 3646, 3686, 3700, 3715, 3799, 3853.
historical view of
20, 79, 125, 205, 207, 230, 431, 523, 524, 706, 803, 833, 901, 905,
943, 1051, 1635, 1871, 2158, 2365, 2381, 2401, 2485, 2719, 2908,
3013, 3176, 3216, 3226, 3309, 3456, 3457, 3552, 3567, 3664, 3827, 3837.
impending
See "Death--Threat of."
of leaders
215, 879, 1005, 1372, 1508, 1753, 1858, 1942, 2000, 2301, 2571,
2642, 2767, 2817, 2949, 2967, 3142, 3317, 3726, 3735.
and life concepts
89, 104, 206, 230, 231, 244, 389, 410, 434, 485, 538, 540, 708,
757, 778, 787, 799, 898, 909, 1050, 1104, 1110, 1168, 1316, 1783,
1795, 1804, 1817, 1837, 1924, 1945, 2131, 2196, 2290, 2329, 2337,
2368, 2481, 2692, 2891, 2994, 2995, 3029, 3124, 3248, 3265, 3312,
3389, 3390, 3427, 3436, 3474, 3517, 3596, 3601, 3624, 3746, 3754,
3757, 3809, 3852.

DEATH (cont.)
  in literature
    8, 12, 16, 32, 58, 202, 424, 612, 639, 732, 743, 759, 812, 825,
    826, 829, 277, 905, 906, 985, 1018, 1078, 1127, 1176, 1240, 1301,
    1396, 1399, 1415, 1505, 1506, 1516, 1538, 1598, 1639, 1674, 1674,
    1685, 1896, 1981, 2002, 2061, 2138, 2317, 2326, 2454, 2493, 2527,
    2600, 2644, 2711, 2747, 2750, 2908, 2924, 2946, 2968, 3075, 3153,
    3248, 3273, 3296, 3446, 3463, 3467, 3491, 3505, 3603, 3606, 3676,
    3779, 3582, 3645.
  psychological autopsy
    3156, 3627, 3631.
  and the self
    19, 108, 925, 926, 1068, 1087, 1097, 1210, 1226, 1341, 1371, 1955,
    1956, 2311, 2317, 2408, 2481, 2868, 3029, 3115, 3128, 3283, 3312,
    3436, 3609, 3601, 3754.
  and sexuality
    280, 437, 497, 1346, 2473, 2671, 2717, 2856, 2988.
  and social structure
    23, 215, 235, 314, 411, 416, 722, 765, 814, 851, 930, 943, 987,
    1121, 1187, 1193, 1223, 1229, 1267, 1330, 1340, 1488, 1566, 1649,
    1834, 1921, 2034, 2153, 2157, 2195, 2256, 2295, 2297, 2321, 2332,
    2353, 2545, 2576, 2644, 2706, 2752, 2770, 2799, 2893, 2917, 3026,
    3093, 3187, 3227, 3286, 3366, 3389, 3514, 3573, 3632, 3781, 3822, 3845.
  sudden or unexplained
    50, 83, 170, 178, 246, 250, 324. 585, 588, 734, 746, 974, 975, 1323,
    1328, 1351, 1382, 1442, 1526, 1535, 1547, 1589, 1697, 1815, 1816,
    1819, 1979, 2063, 2111, 2120, 2229, 2253, 2307, 2315, 2406, 2407,
    2488, 2489, 2549, 2786, 2847, 2909, 2988, 3035, 3090, 3108, 3115,
    3198, 3246, 3249, 3377, 3403, 3509, 3541, 3568, 3615, 3723.
    (See also "Sudden death of infants.")
  threat of
    118, 200, 522, 579, 798, 1403, 1444, 1763, 1922, 2145, 2217, 2392,
    2401, 2489, 2554, 2555, 2579, 2749, 2869, 3432, 3474, 3723.
    (See also "Children--Reaction and/or adaptation to stress")

DEATH EDUCATION
    213, 271, 272, 273, 277, 327, 342, 343, 374, 415, 423, 425, 628,
    656, 663, 719, 787, 831, 837, 1011, 1064, 1125, 903, 1360, 1393,
    1400, 1502, 1608, 1908, 1913, 1923, 1961, 1973, 1975, 1984, 1985,
    2122, 2123, 2124, 2125, 2126, 2127, 2128, 2130, 2180, 2181, 2182,
    2193. 2264. 2265, 2532, 2666, 2667, 2673, 2725. 3011, 3076. 3096.
    3103, 3133, 3134, 3150, 3172, 3178, 3205, 3208, 3245, 3258, 3259,
    3271, 3295, 3431, 3599, 3514, 3662, 3684, 3713, 3762, 3790.
  and children
    16, 202, 213, 374, 612, 730, 837, 1243, 1401, 1402, 1479, 1682, 1910,
    2041, 2130, 2142, 2288, 2326, 2411, 2428, 2493, 2742, 2870, 2946,
    3295, 3602, 3720, 3795, 3796.

ETHICAL ISSUES

23, 40, 54, 74, 81, 110, 123, 153, 158, 160, 186, 187, 189, 201, 204, 227, 300, 310, 389, 443, 484, 487, 500, 518, 519, 561, 562, 599, 611, 618, 632, 647, 664, 668, 714, 827, 872, 886, 902, 931, 953, 1101, 1103, 1105, 1111, 1164, 1210, 1287, 1340, 1348, 1354, 1431, 1432, 1449, 1463, 1486, 1500, 1512, 1616, 1543, 1717, 1720, 1735, 1776, 1798, 1809, 1882, 1888, 1901, 1907, 1913, 1930, 1956, 1974, 1982, 1983, 2004, 2012, 2036, 2040, 2067, 2121, 2183, 2184, 2185, 2244, 2254, 2287, 2304, 2319, 2413, 2423, 2460, 2482, 2620, 2650, 2655, 2656, 2672, 2714, 2803, 2889, 2894, 2895, 2901, 2913, 2914, 3007, 3009, 3014, 3015, 3016, 3046, 3075, 3083, 3086, 3098, 3111', 3119, 3125, 3155, 3201, 3219, 3236, 3244, 3275, 3294, 3299, 3335, 3369, 3372, 3450, 3451, 3461, 3465, 3466, 3508, 3583, 3622, 3661, 3683, 3684, 3702, 3743, 3755, 3817, 3822, 3825, 3839.

prolongation of life

10, 11, 37, 101, 186, 187, 631, 717, 766, 838, 957, 1100, 1531, 2287, 2240, 2464, 2721, 2723, 2809, 2987, 3051, 3083, 3458, 3467, 3485. (See also "Abortion; Definition of Death; Euthanasia; Organ donation and transplantation," and "Right to die.")

EUTHANASIA

84, 87, 130, 131, 132, 133, 193, 228, 290, 310, 519, 631, 694, 733, 846, 890, 945, 977, 988, 1080, 1101, 1102, 1107, 1287, 1348, 1392, 1409, 1411, 1431, 1616, 1776, 1825, 1901, 1902, 1919, 1982, 1983, 2010, 2015, 2032, 2046, 2106, 2121, 2254, 2287, 2386, 2400, 2422, 2492, 2516, 2643, 2656, 2901, 2992, 3014, 3024, 3045, 3224, 3438, 3244, 3313, 3335, 3338, 3372, 3465, 3466, 3527, 3649, 3661, 3682, 3683, 3702, 3831.

FAMILY

22, 32, 308, 420, 455, 640, 745, 891, 922, 1113, 1267, 1351, 1384, 2725, 2962, 3099.

crisis in the

75, 213, 367, 385, 386, 475, 483, 588, 700, 813, 885, 1015, 1192, 1319, 1357, 1468, 1560, 1561, 1676, 1780, 1892, 1912, 2030, 2137, 2203, 2208, 2282, 2303, 2340, 2505, 2534, 2537, 2557, 2560, 2585, 2605, 2639, 2795, 2865, 2897, 2934, 3058, 3059, 3114, 3136, 3143, 3144, 3228, 3289, 3393, 3441, 3506, 3541, 3566, 3727, 3731.

death and the

107, 213, 305, 323, 331, 367, 545, 685, 813, 885, 915, 968, 1054, 1132, 1194, 1199, 1271, 1319, 1321, 1340, 1351, 3169, 1392, 1404, 1509, 1559, 1711, 1762, 1781, 1893, 1929, 1947, 1990, 2071, 2031, 2038, 2484, 2768, 2878, 3069, 3289, 3464, 3523, 3550, 3648, 3676, 3679, 3696, 3706, 3762, 3813, 3820.

the grieving

285, 292, 293, 305, 376, 475, 700, 944, 946, 948, 952, 968, 1121, 1162, 1194, 1559, 1758, 2039, 2143, 2505, 2708, 3501.

FUNERAL DIRECTING
    283, 407, 621, 1231, 1224, 1436, 1805, 2191, 3359, 3672, 3705, 3835,
        3838, 3840, 3844, 3848.
FUNERALS
    217, 368, 376, 377, 378, 407, 411, 412, 473, 539, 560, 740, 887,
    1077, 1131, 1218, 1219, 1222, 1265, 1266, 1302, 1325, 1482, 1483,
    1484, 1525, 1566, 1660, 1661, 1662, 1672, 1678, 1679, 1737, 1978,
    2008, 2014, 2016, 2020, 2250, 2304, 2316, 2444, 2477, 2478, 2567,
    2587, 2769, 2771, 2790, 2813, 2842, 2843, 2844, 3020, 3065, 3148,
    3274, 3384, 3484, 3599, 3835, 3838, 3840, 3844, 3848, 3849.

GHOSTS
    298, 498, 840, 1773, 2296.

GRIEF
    46, 226, 279, 296, 317, 480, 494, 513, 559, 610, 687, 716, 741,
    797, 798, 847, 972, 973, 1137, 1209, 1332, 1359, 1529, 1680, 1681,
    1811, 1931, 2103, 2135, 2163, 2166, 2167, 2196, 2313, 2316, 2431,
    1471, 2599, 2662, 2682, 2726, 2953, 3080, 3139, 3188, 3313, 3315,
    3362, 3385, 3386, 3417, 3469, 3478, 3537, 3560, 3649, 3652, 3658,
    3761, 3767.
  anticipatory
    46, 341, 386, 475, 545, 559, 662, 688, 1194, 1220, 1274, 1602, 1884,
    2462, 2675, 2973, 3078, 3620, 3773, 3810.
  management
    83, 185, 229, 281, 507, 548, 656, 676, 713, 716, 742, 768, 817, 915,
    941, 1094, 1099, 1213, 1273, 1280, 1434, 1470, 1495, 1610, 1683,
    1781, 1684, 1940, 1953, 1990, 1994, 2250, 2303, 2494, 2707, 2993,
    3065, 3075, 3161, 3232, 3289, 3420, 3550, 3615, 3693, 3696, 3812, 3842.
  and mourning
    229, 234, 259, 281, 329, 341, 450, 492, 680, 797, 831, 914, 1091,
    1213, 1233, 1593, 1594, 1665, 1751, 1947, 1987, 2303, 2794, 3065,
    3106, 3114, 3218, 3315.
  normal
    252, 1211, 1395, 1873, 3666.
  pathological
    70, 267, 323, 348, 468, 564, 676, 702, 847, 1395, 1687, 1694,
    2417, 2777, 3536, 3538, 3560, 3829, 3830, 3842, 3854.
  psychophysiology of
    252, 973, 1023, 1161, 2281, 2680, 2686, 2657, 2873, 3727, 3829, 3830.
    (See also "Bereavement" and "Mourning.")

HOMICIDE
    433, 697, 794, 2446, 3544.

HUMOR
    1178, 1390, 2475, 2530, 2608, 2610, 3763.

MORTALITY (cont.)
  statistics
      47, 48, 111, 142, 150, 151, 167, 176, 408, 493, 580, 623, 658, 937,
      1002, 1019, 1111, 1193, 1247, 1267, 1327, 1339, 1351, 1395, 1436,
      1520, 1626, 1656, 1863, 1867, 1935, 2004, 2054, 2093, 2146, 2162,
      2224, 2225, 2232, 2257, 2424, 2430, 2456, 2490, 2510, 2545, 2567,
      2582, 2583, 2614, 1615, 2664, 2718, 1752, 2799, 2800, 2815, 2816,
      2823, 2880, 2917, 2951, 2969, 2997, 2998, 3017, 3154, 3212, 3227,
      3290, 3330, 3344, 3365, 3371, 3472, 3600, 3855.

MORTICIANS
  See "Funeral Directing."

MOURNING
      251, 411, 492, 691, 801, 971, 1023, 1097, 1180, 1233, 1255, 1342,
      1395, 1587, 1661, 1692, 1869, 2019, 2043, 2152, 2165, 2178, 2662,
      2663, 2708, 2768, 2780, 2781, 2782, 2926, 2964, 3106, 3177, 3369,
      3440, 3620, 3769.
  process of
      469, 691, 894, 1418, 1594, 1875, 1896, 2152, 2431, 2768, 3368, 3404, 3810.
      (See also "Bereavement, Grief," and "Grief--and mourning.")

NURSES
      211, 372, 373, 432, 489, 519, 525, 546, 842, 873, 876, 889, 915,
      1139, 1578, 1581, 1636, 1726, 2270, 2647, 2681, 3062, 3247, 3264,
      3297, 3659.
  attitudes toward death
      108, 155, 192, 439, 445, 496, 501, 526, 551, 619, 841, 892, 934,
      1113, 1329, 1611, 1674, 1769, 2104, 2266, 2341, 2358, 2471, 2532,
      2788, 2811, 2824, 3173, 3574, 3576, 3597, 3718, 3777.
  education and training
      330, 344, 815, 897, 1115, 1118, 1611, 1827, 2104, 2231, 2341, 2345,
      2471, 2507, 2532, 2674, 2720, 2827, 2834, 2838, 2923, 3172, 3245,
      3289, 3420, 2502, 3557, 3713, 3777, 3814, 3815.
  nurse-patient relationship
      2, 9, 89, 248, 290, 331, 445, 456, 815, 873, 941, 1079, 1122, 1144,
      1958, 1968, 2001, 2303, 2346, 2374, 2471, 2591, 2637, 2825, 2837,
      2884, 2923, 2933, 2974, 2980, 3137, 3222, 3479, 3730, 3811.
  role in the care of the dying
      9, 78, 98, 134, 290, 331, 332, 333, 334, 483, 496, 517, 556, 619,
      623, 679, 726, 784, 806, 810, 815, 902, 940, 980k 1089, 1140, 1144,
      1312, 1321, 1333, 1397, 1414, 1464, 1591, 1614, 1630, 1675, 1818,
      1841, 1883, 1885, 1893, 1966, 1968, 1999, 2001, 2012, 2205, 2252,
      2269, 2274, 2279, 2303, 2345, 2346, 2536, 2590, 2591, 2658, 2722,
      2795, 2808, 2826, 2831, 2832, 2833, 2835, 2836, 2871, 2884, 2931,
      3008, 3039, 3043, 3044, 3069, 3083, 3097, 3197, 3214, 3238, 3350,
      3396, 3447, 3357, 3572, 3576, 3650, 3656, 3663, 3665, 3676, 3677,
      3698, 3713, 3765, 3789, 3805, 3811, 3812, 3814, 3815, 3816, 3818.

PHYSICIANS (cont.)
   doctor-patient relationship
      68, 194, 240, 371, 486, 530, 537, 636, 714, 715, 735, 1053, 816,
      1079, 1117, 1122, 1301, 1343, 1345, 1546, 1587, 1607, 1653, 1690,
      1931, 1958, 1970, 2039, 2064, 2220, 2636, 2694, 2825, 2845, 2905,
      2922, 2974, 2980, 3220, 3221, 3223, 3400, 3721, 3808, 3824.
   education and training
      270, 273, 295, 330, 344, 371, 423, 765, 984, 1191, 1276, 1393, 1475,
      1619, 2150, 2180, 2181, 2182, 2187, 2507, 2674, 2720, 2903, 3175,
      3264, 3619, 3664.
   role in the care of the dying
      68, 83, 102, 115, 190, 194, 196, 237, 385, 331, 341, 371, 486,
      545, 556, 570, 571, 623, 636, 657, 670, 675, 765, 768, 820, 830,
      902, 915, 936, 992, 1053, 1082, 1090, 1196, 1197, 1210, 1279, 1286,
      1301, 1313, 1349, 1364, 1365, 1370, 1546, 1575, 1588, 1601, 1630,
      1702, 1706, 1824, 1857, 1930, 1932, 1933, 1934, 1962, 1966, 1970,
      2009, 2039, 2112, 2204, 2205, 2327, 2334, 2460, 2536, 2621, 2722,
      2802, 2859, 2914, 2958, 2983, 3037, 3069, 3083, 3107, 3138, 3233,
      3254, 3350, 3425, 3458, 3473, 3559, 3564, 3586, 3607, 3665, 3808, 3824.

PSYCHIATRY
      10, 11, 267, 268, 271, 322, 460, 479, 629, 670, 767, 707, 708, 771,
      772, 878, 879, 959, 975, 1045, 1155, 1276, 1445, 1574, 1624, 1761,
      1791, 1862, 2139, 2267, 2532, 2536, 2662, 2663, 2805, 2872, 2951,
      3065, 3139, 3156, 3211, 3328, 3615, 3616, 3616, 3617, 3621, 3623,
      3627, 3630, 3740, 3854.

PSYCHOANALYSIS
   current perspectives
      3, 242, 325, 335, 390, 436, 437, 438, 491, 505, 509, 528, 554, 555,
      1063, 1116, 1175, 1176, 1177, 1179, 1180, 1183, 1184, 1188, 1281,
      1282, 1341, 1389, 1390, 1405, 1433, 1671, 1743, 1745, 1871, 2059,
      2158, 2168, 2394, 2414, 2509, 2652, 2785, 2812, 2881, 2911, 2948,
      3048, 3052, 3070, 3095, 3166, 3199, 3328.
   death instinct
      49, 703, 1025, 1661, 1065, 1112, 1146, 1236, 1252, 1281, 1341, 1709,
      2114, 2457, 2541, 2651, 2911, 2918, 3170, 3190, 3328, 3388, 3528,
      3674.
   death wish
      50, 604, 935, 1188, 1241, 2906, 3635.
   dreams
      1064, 1135, 1177, 1373, 1419, 1474, 3537.
   therapy
      1063, 1097.
   (See also "Therapy techniques and methods.")

PSYCHOLOGY
      214, 274, 387, 708, 862, 937, 991, 1002, 1047, 1055, 1130, 1255,
      1277, 1480, 1637, 1649, 2035, 2093, 2161, 2171, 2414, 2542, 2575,
      2604, 2788, 2797, 2891, 3173, 3211, 3345, 3411, 3414, 3427, 3671,
      3740.

PSYCHOLOGY (cont.)
  adolescent
      413, 1045, 1278, 2299, 2734, 3199, 3348.
  child
      256, 320, 321, 340, 360, 361, 457, 467, 472, 476, 895, 1170, 1171,
      1174, 1620, 1643, 1670, 1712, 1713, 1744, 1790, 1906, 2025, 2299,
      2393, 2451, 2755, 2756, 2757, 2758, 3013, 3287, 3348, 3349, 3391.
  of death
      8, 18, 206, 274, 365, 390, 527, 592, 593, 596, 600, 761, 845, 935,
      1039, 1135, 1443, 1444, 1472, 1771, 1801, 1802, 1803, 2157, 2193,
      2290, 2372, 2752, 2889, 3079, 3130, 3134, 3320, 3626, 3631, 3756.
  existential
      See "Philosophy--Existentialism."
  pastoral
      See "Religion."

PSYCHOTHERAPY
      935, 1094, 2414, 3412.
  current perspectives
      1856, 1924, 1977, 2965, 2967, 3539, 3610, 3748, 3806.
  death and
      251, 1235, 1264, 1352, 1533, 1645, 1924, 1977, 2309, 2414, 3091,
      3265, 3539, 3806.
  for the dying
      795, 1088, 1318, 1398, 1446, 1546, 1788, 1972, 2074, 2075, 2660,
      2661, 2797, 2966, 3459, 3558, 3621, 3740, 3766.

PUBLIC HEALTH
      607, 752, 1841, 2821, 3017, 3371.

RELATED BIBLIOGRAPHIES
      1991, 1997, 3482.

RELIGION
      17, 241, 242, 442, 481, 482, 523, 574, 584, 616, 724, 869, 870, 899,
      907, 962, 993, 1052, 1500, 1599, 1640, 1660, 1728, 1747, 1862, 2171,
      2389, 2562, 3439, 3529, 3712.
  death and
      30, 79, 200, 365, 613, 632, 634, 693, 695, 819, 880, 881, 919, 942,
      961, 995, 1158, 1159, 1187, 1263, 1272, 1511, 1672, 1695, 1748,
      1844, 1915, 1978, 1993, 2013, 2206, 2295, 2335, 2336, 2343, 2361,
      2389, 2435, 2620, 2656, 2781, 2804, 2848, 2854, 2866, 2879, 3014,
      3146, 3189, 3242, 3268, 3279, 3284, 3397, 3424, 3454, 3463, 3518,
      3533, 3584, 3637, 3660, 3681, 3741, 3752, 3756.
  individual and his
      445, 751, 2807, 3189, 3268, 3454, 3518.

RELIGION (cont.)
  pastoral care of the dying and bereaved
    200, 229, 289, 442, 446, 593, 616, 642, 663, 729, 775, 785, 985,
    1007, 1034, 1117, 1132, 1231, 1224, 1350, 1680, 1873, 1890, 2005,
    2237, 2275, 2562, 2580, 2581, 2607, 2611, 2621, 2731, 2808, 2859,
    2975, 2876, 2913, 2935, 2936, 2937, 2993, 3146, 3301, 3562, 3741,
    3753.
  religiosity and anxiety
    365, 600, 1040, 1043, 2096, 2645, 3408, 3415, 3691.
    (See also "Anxiety.")

RESEARCH TECHNIQUES AND METHODS
    200, 313, 365, 387, 527, 600, 862, 909, 1043, 1472, 1480, 1502, 1649,
    1821, 1893, 1907, 1908, 1914, 2035, 2110, 2265, 2320, 2332, 2570,
    2603, 2667, 2788, 3004, 3205, 3411, 3627, 3631, 3752, 3828.

RIGHT TO DIE
    10, 11, 37, 41, 172, 81, 193, 210, 249, 310, 443, 643, 733, 890,
    1012, 1108, 1348, 1409, 1432, 1512, 1717, 1735, 1930, 2287, 2304,
    2385, 2925, 2978, 3016, 3138, 3145, 3240, 3266, 3339, 3372, 3430,
    3461, 3483, 3661, 3702, 3755, 3839.

SEPARATION AND LOSS
    4, 36, 211, 251, 261, 264, 461, 463, 467, 470, 471, 472, 495, 499,
    503, 550, 551, 565, 665, 832, 848, 866, 911, 921, 927, 965, 1208,
    1299, 1381, 1386, 1515, 1517, 1521, 1550, 1553, 1652, 1782, 1926,
    1946, 1948, 2043, 2289, 2298, 2321, 2393, 2483, 2521, 2522, 2539,
    2544, 2631, 2632, 2678, 2684, 2716, 2765, 2919, 2920, 2927, 2929,
    2930, 2962, 3022, 3027, 3052, 3058, 3064, 3129, 3445, 3588, 3701,
    3714, 3770, 3775, 3776.
    (See also "Bereavement" and "Bereavement--Childhood.")

SOCIAL CASEWORK
    227, 342, 446, 754, 793, 1138, 1319, 1326, 1884, 1947, 2071, 2262,
    2531, 2557, 2585, 2742, 2761, 3613, 3703, 2766, 2933.

SOCIOLOGY OF DEATH
    735, 1020, 1143, 1187, 1224, 1228, 1231, 1232, 1437, 1485, 1525,
    1626, 1722, 1751, 1760, 1853, 1996, 2054, 2189, 2256, 2321, 2330,
    2603, 2752, 2782, 2895, 3093, 3143, 3227, 3310, 3367, 3418, 3514,
    3515, 3529, 3633, 3836, 3847, 3849.
    (See also "Death and social structure.")

STAGES OF DYING
  See "Dying--Stages of."

STATISTICS
  See "Mortality--Statistics."

STRESS
34, 53, 129, 235, 250, 276, 278, 284, 385, 522, 529, 530, 622, 960,
1129, 1179, 1182, 1185, 1403, 1516, 1723, 1754, 1947, 2048, 2071,
2118, 2143, 2149, 2154, 2156, 2159, 2414, 2416, 2439, 2549, 2554,
2555, 2579, 2962, 3402, 3530, 3728.
    reaction to extreme
7, 129, 428, 588, 600, 974, 1006, 1433, 3054, 3115, 3289, 3728.
(See also "Anxiety" and "Children--Reaction and/or adaptation to
stress.")

SUDDEN DEATH OF INFANTS
24, 25, 99, 100, 177, 179, 180, 181, 188, 254, 287, 300, 301, 303,
352, 353, 357, 358, 448, 502, 576, 578, 581, 583, 721, 808, 967, 1072,
1092, 1268, 1300, 1498, 1499, 1642, 1698, 1815, 1835, 1843, 2291,
2323, 2391, 2397, 2408, 2415, 2515, 2529, 2559, 2588, 2728, 2736,
2743, 3855, 2904, 3100, 3140, 3141, 3217, 3270, 3272, 3363, 3482,
3493, 3494, 3496, 3807.
    determination of
35, 146, 966, 969, 1544, 1648, 1887, 2324, 2543, 2861, 3364, 3492,
3495, 3638, 3710.
    etiology and epidemiology
55, 74, 161, 218, 238, 286, 299, 302, 356, 366, 408, 417, 418, 549,
649, 684, 773, 970, 1004, 1026, 1073, 1074, 1075, 1128, 1147, 1149,
1156, 1203, 1204, 1205, 1208, 1248, 1309, 1315, 1377, 1416, 1490,
1519, 1562, 1564, 1701, 1749, 1821, 1936, 1938, 2006, 2229, 2276,
2328, 2432, 2514, 2558, 2569, 2622, 2640, 2737, 2738, 2739, 2740,
2741, 2762, 2791, 2860, 3019, 3084, 3269, 3277, 3278, 3311, 3332,
3333, 3356, 3379, 3383, 3392, 3447, 3452, 3481, 3487, 3497, 3498,
3499, 3532, 3575, 3595, 3711, 3798.
    impact on survivors
349, 350, 355, 582, 588, 968, 1198, 1366, 1450, 1462, 1590, 1667,
1833, 2260, 3018, 3114, 3506, 3731, 3788, 3834.
    prevention of
66, 73, 354, 609, 2133.

SUICIDE, ATTEMPTED SUICIDE, AND SELF-DESTRUCTIVE BEHAVIOR
58, 405, 433, 541, 542, 543, 544, 564, 566, 620, 753, 771, 789, 1055,
1480, 1556, 1666, 1778, 1804, 1806, 1807, 1837, 1838, 2018, 2080,
2087, 2091, 2122, 2123, 2132, 2167, 2290, 2351, 2437, 2479, 2573,
2574, 2578, 2734, 2906, 2984, 3113, 3159, 3162, 3163, 3165, 3262,
3636, 3820.

TERMINAL CARE

59, 62, 78, 91, 92, 93, 94, 117, 122, 134, 144, 162, 169, 219, 312, 488, 501, 525, 571, 572, 577, 630, 635, 806, 820, 823, 868, 876, 889, 980, 1071, 1217, 1220, 1259, 1286, 1312, 1317, 1326, 1345, 1356, 1417, 1507, 1514, 1563, 1572, 1573, 1575, 1588, 1591, 1629, 1630, 1644, 1702, 1726, 1811, 1820, 1842, 1883, 1885, 1905, 1916, 1925, 1957, 1934, 1971, 1976, 1990, 1998, 2005, 1009, 1050, 2136, 2169, 2173, 2174, 2177, 2195, 2266, 2270, 2271, 2274, 2345, 2399, 2436, 2466, 2468, 2487, 2503, 2504, 2592, 2602, 2603, 2611, 2617, 2704, 2714, 2766, 2789, 2802, 2808, 2837, 2848, 2869, 2871, 2884, 2898, 3036, 3067, 3068, 3081, 3109, 3127, 3210, 3214, 3239, 3236, 3418, 3471, 3474, 3488, 3490, 3563, 3573, 3577, 3663, 3608, 3650, 3677, 3678, 3717, 3805, 3808, 3826.
(See also "Attitudes toward death--of the dying; Children--Reaction and/or adaptation to stress; Dying--Communicating with the; Illness--Terminal" and "Illness--Terminal--cancer.")

of cancer patients

15, 573, 705, 738, 795, 1166, 1288, 1370, 1398, 1571, 1637, 1657, 1824, 1876, 2003, 2179, 2251, 2526, 2701, 2748, 2875, 2888, 2961, 1974, 2979, 3002, 3040, 3072, 3378, 3475, 3587, 3632.

of children

331, 386, 496, 535, 545, 556, 895, 912, 1081, 1172, 1271, 1349, 1364, 1365, 1370, 1397, 1414, 1509, 1614, 1624, 1637, 1675, 1076, 1688, 1785, 1825, 1847, 1892, 2001, 2039, 2112, 2303, 2344, 2346, 2374, 2499, 2591, 2593, 2629, 2907, 3040, 3083, 3213, 3282, 3283, 3302, 3443, 3574, 3656, 3659, 3819.

of the elderly

31, 607, 1288, 1417, 1668, 1798, 1989, 2052, 2177, 2358, 3622, 3675.

ethics

81, 162, 169, 227, 237, 484, 562, 577, 631, 632, 705, 714, 715, 795, 889, 893, 1102, 1312, 1375, 1392, 1431, 1441, 1578, 1581, 1601, 1824, 1825, 1857, 1893, 1951, 1952, 2012, 2070, 2379, 2479, 2506, 2721, 2722, 2974, 3008, 3053, 3083, 3117, 3219, 3223, 3351, 3354, 3578, 3586, 3622, 3659, 3801, 3803.

and the family

253, 483, 891, 1172, 1220, 1271, 1280, 1318, 1384, 1392, 1397, 1414, 1470, 1509, 1614, 1953, 1971, 1990, 1994, 2112, 2374, 2531, 2611, 2766, 3069, 3302, 3566, 3574, 3676.

home care

38, 1081, 1167, 1676, 1841, 2344, 2748, 3656, 3675.

institutional care

81, 137, 195, 546, 747, 748, 888, 1089, 1138, 1217, 1275, 1470, 1543, 1581, 1933, 2011, 2151, 2272, 2273, 2358, 2410, 2524, 2753, 2892, 2923, 3037, 3072, 3241, 3367, 3558.
(See also "Physicians--Role in the care of the dying" and "Nurses--Role in the care of the dying.")

of leukemia

331, 545, 1509, 1675, 1676, 2039, 2112, 3446, 3302.

TERMINAL CARE (cont.)
    psychological approaches
        346, 479, 592, 637, 738, 761, 895, 1053, 1081, 1441, 1546, 1574,
        1624, 2637, 1743, 1842, 1895, 1951, 1953, 1977, 1994, 2173, 2267,
        2499, 2526, 2627, 2902, 2907, 3283, 3302, 3378, 3558, 3615, 3621,
        3625, 3671, 3740.
        (See also "Psychotherapy.")

THERAPY TECHNIQUES AND METHODS
        600, 691, 1099, 1352, 1353, 1398, 1523, 1702, 1995, 2160, 2182,
        2617, 1627, 3090, 3232, 3470, 3539, 3671, 3696, 3748, 3762, 3806.

TIME
        438, 476, 1150, 1800, 2234, 2469, 2575, 2606, 2776, 2783, 3719.

TRANSPLANTATION
    See "Organ donation and transplantation."

WIDOWS AND WIDOWERS
        163, 222, 292, 337, 338, 339, 451, 453, 569, 666, 688, 689, 690,
        699, 704, 736, 745, 756, 938, 1091, 1202, 1214, 1274, 1303, 1351,
        1935, 2023, 2190, 2197, 2199, 2200, 2201, 2202, 2281, 2321, 2322,
        2357, 2494, 2604, 2675, 2680, 2681, 2686, 2687, 2754, 2763, 2764,
        2926, 3059, 3060, 3121, 3182, 3183, 3184, 3185, 3186, 3187, 3218,
        3276, 3298, 3305, 3395, 3429, 3782.

ADDENDUM

3807-3856

3807. Anonymous. "Cot Deaths," British Medical Journal, 2 (Mar., 1974), np.

3808. _____. "The Paradox of Death and the 'Omnipotent' Family Doctor," Patient Care: Management Concepts, 4 (May 31, 1970), passim.

3809. Benoliel, Jeanne Quint. "The Aging Process and the Meaning of Death," Imprint, 20 (Feb., 1973), 10-1.

3810. _____. "Anticipatory Grief in Physicians and Nurses," in B. Schoenberg et al., eds., Anticipatory Grief. New York: Columbia University Press, 1974. 218-28.

3811. _____. "Conversations with Dying Patients," in M.Z. Davis et al., eds., Nurses in Practice--A Perspective on Work Environments. St. Louis: C.V. Mosby, 1975. 25-48.

3812. _____. "The Dying Patient: A Difficult Nursing Problem," in Management of the Dying Patient and His Family. New York: MSS Information, 1974. 111-7.

3813. _____. "The Dying Patient and the Family," in Stanley B. Troup and William A. Green, eds., The Patient, Death, and the Family. New York: Charles Scribner's Sons, 1974. 111-23.

3814. _____. "Four Commentaries," in Loretta Bermosk and Raymond Corsini, eds., Critical Incidents in Nursing. Philadelphia: W.B. Saunders, 1973.

3815. _____. "Loss," in Ann L. Clark and Dyanne D. Affonso, eds., Childbearing: A Nursing Perspective. Philadelphia: F.A. Davis, 1976. 87-94.

3816. _____. "Nursing Care for the Terminal Patient: A Psychosocial Approach," in Bernard Schoenberg et al., eds., Psychosocial Aspects of Terminal Care. New York: Columbia University Press, 1972.

3817. _____. "The Practitioners' Dilemma: Problems and Priorities," in Dealing with Death. Los Angeles: Ethel Percy Andrus Gerontology Center, University of Southern California, 1973. 33-45.

3818. _____. "Research Related to Death and the Dying Patient," in Phyllis Verhonick, ed., Nursing Research I. Boston: Little, Brown, and Co., 1975. 189-227.

3819. _____. "The Terminally Ill Child," in Gladys Scipien et al., eds., Comprehensive Pediatric Nursing. New York: McGraw-Hill, 1975.

3820. Cain, Albert, ed. Survivors of Suicide. Springfield: C.C. Thomas, 1972.

3821. Cook, Stephani. "I'll Say This for Death," Journal of Current Social Issues, 12 (Fall, 1975), 38-42.

3822. Feigenberg, Loma. "Death and Death Problems: Reflections on Death in Society and in Medical Care," Larkartidningen, 71 (1974), 3766-70.

3823. _____. "Death and Dying," Lakartindningen, 68 (1971), 5811-21.

3824. _____. "The Doctor and Death," Lakartidningen, 68 (1971), 6103-12.

3825. _____. "Humane Death," Lakartidningen, 68 (1971), 5965-75.

3826. _____, Robert Fulton. "Care of the Dying," Lakartidningen, 73 (1976), 2253-8.

3827. _____. "Death in Sweden Then and Now," Lakartidningen, 73 (1976), 2179-82.

3828. Flesch, Regina. "A Guide to Interviewing the Bereaved, Part II: The Focused Interview Schedule," Journal of Thanatology, 3 (1975), 143-60.

3829. Fredrick, Jerome. "Grief and Cancer," The Dodge Magazine, 68 (Mar., 1976), 4-5, 28.

3830. _____. "Grief as a Disease Process: A Physiological-Endocrine Model," Omega, 6 (1975), np.

3831. Fourth Euthanasia Conference, New York Academy of Medicine. Dilemmas of Euthanasia. New York: The Euthanasia Educational Council, Inc., 1971.

3832. Geizhals, Judith Susan. "Attitudes Toward Death and Dying: A Study of Occupational Therapists," Journal of Thanatology, 3 (1975), 243-68.

3833. Gillon, Edmund V., Jr. Victorian Cemetery Art. New York: Dover, 1972.

3834. Lewak, N, R. Vail. "Letter: SIDS: Problem of the Parents," Journal of the American Medical Association, 230 (Nov. 4, 1974), 671.

3835. McPherson, Thomas A. American Funeral Cars and Ambulances Since 1900. Glen Ellyn, IL: Crestline Publishing, 1973.

3836. Mechanic, D. Medical Sociology. New York: Free Press, 1968.

3837. Moser, Michael J. "Death in Chinese: A Two-Dimensional Analysis," Journal of Thanatology, 3 (1975), 169-86.

3838. Mossman, B.C., M.W. Stark. The Last Salute: Civil and Military Funerals, 1921-1969. Washington: Department of the Army, 1971.

3839. Nelson, William. "Mr. Smith Wants to Die," Journal of Current Social Issues, 12 (Fall, 1975), 36-7.

3840. Pine, Vanderlyn R. Caretaker of the Dead: The American Funeral Director. New York: Irvington, 1975.

3841. Pine, Vanderlyn R. "Dying, Death, and Social Behavior," in Ivan K. Goldberg et al., eds., Psychosocial Aspects of Anticipatory Grief. New York: Columbia University Press, 1974. 31-47.

3842. _____. "Grief Work and Dirty Work: The Aftermath of an Aircrash," Omega, 5 (1974), 281-6.

3843. _____. "Institutionalized Communication about Dying and Death," Journal of Thanatology, 3 (1975), 1012.

3844. _____. "The Role of the Funeral Director in Disaster," The Director, 39 (Aug., 1969), 11-3.

3845. _____. "Social Organization and Death," Omega, 3 (May, 1972), 149-53.

3846. _____. "Social Organization in Disaster," The Director, 29 (July, 1969), 3-5.

3847. _____. "The Sociology of Death," The American Funeral Director, (June, 1969), 29-30, 44.

3848. _____. Statistical Abstract of Funeral Service Facts and Figures of the United States 1975 Edition. Milwaukee: National Funeral Directors Association, 1974.

3849. _____, Derek Phillips. "The Cost of Dying: A Sociological Analysis of Funeral Expenditures," Social Problems, 17 (Winter, 1970), 405-17.

3850. _____, ed. Responding to Disaster. Milwaukee: Bulfin, 1974.

3851. Rosner, Fred. "Organ Transplants: The Jewish Viewpoint," Journal of Thanatology, 3 (1975), 233-42.

3852. Scientific American. Life and Death and Medicine. San Fransisco: W.H. Freeman, 1973.

3853. Stewart, David W. "Religious Correlates of the Fear of Death," Journal of Thanatology, 3 (1975), 161-4.

3854. Stone, Michael H. "The Role of Loss in Borderline and Psychotic Conditions," Journal of Thanatology, 3 (1975), 207-22.

3855. United States Department of Health, Education, and Welfare, Public Health Service. The Facts of Life and Death: Selected Statistics on the Nation's Health and People. Washington: National Center for Health Statistics, 1965.

3856. _____. Leading Components of Upturn in Mortality for Men: United States-- 1952-67. Rockville, MD: National Center for Health Statistics, 1971.

THE LITERATURE OF
DEATH AND DYING

Abrahamsson, Hans. **The Origin of Death:** Studies in African Mythology. 1951

Alden, Timothy. **A Collection of American Epitaphs and Inscriptions with Occasional Notes.** Five vols. in two. 1814

Austin, Mary. **Experiences Facing Death.** 1931

Bacon, Francis. **The Historie of Life and Death with Observations Naturall and Experimentall for the Prolongation of Life.** 1638

Barth, Karl. **The Resurrection of the Dead.** 1933

Bataille, Georges. **Death and Sensuality:** A Study of Eroticism and the Taboo. 1962

Bichat, [Marie François] Xavier. **Physiological Researches on Life and Death.** 1827

Browne, Thomas. **Hydriotaphia.** 1927

Carrington, Hereward. **Death:** Its Causes and Phenomena with Special Reference to Immortality. 1921

Comper, Frances M. M., editor. **The Book of the Craft of Dying and Other Early English Tracts Concerning Death.** 1917

Death and the Visual Arts. 1976

Death as a Speculative Theme in Religious, Scientific, and Social Thought. 1976

Donne, John. **Biathanatos.** 1930

Farber, Maurice L. **Theory of Suicide.** 1968

Fechner, Gustav Theodor. **The Little Book of Life After Death.** 1904

Frazer, James George. **The Fear of the Dead in Primitive Religion.** Three vols. in one. 1933/1934/1936

Fulton, Robert. **A Bibliography on Death, Grief and Bereavement:** 1845-1975. 1976

Gorer, Geoffrey. **Death, Grief, and Mourning.** 1965

Gruman, Gerald J. **A History of Ideas About the Prolongation of Life.** 1966

Henry, Andrew F. and James F. Short, Jr. **Suicide and Homicide.** 1954

Howells, W[illiam] D[ean], et al. **In After Days;** Thoughts on the Future Life. 1910

Irion, Paul E. **The Funeral:** Vestige or Value? 1966

Landsberg, Paul-Louis. **The Experience of Death:** The Moral Problem of Suicide. 1953

Maeterlinck, Maurice. **Before the Great Silence.** 1937

Maeterlinck, Maurice. **Death.** 1912

Metchnikoff, Élie. **The Nature of Man:** Studies in Optimistic Philosophy. 1910

Metchnikoff, Élie. **The Prolongation of Life:** Optimistic Studies. 1908

Munk, William. **Euthanasia.** 1887

Osler, William. **Science and Immortality.** 1904

Return to Life: Two Imaginings of the Lazarus Theme. 1976

Stephens, C[harles] A[sbury]. **Natural Salvation:** The Message of Science. 1905

Sulzberger, Cyrus. **My Brother Death.** 1961

Taylor, Jeremy. **The Rule and Exercises of Holy Dying.** 1819

Walker, G[eorge] A[lfred]. **Gatherings from Graveyards.** 1839

Warthin, Aldred Scott. **The Physician of the Dance of Death.** 1931

Whiter, Walter. **Dissertation on the Disorder of Death.** 1819

Whyte, Florence. **The Dance of Death in Spain and Catalonia.** 1931

Wolfenstein, Martha. **Disaster:** A Psychological Essay. 1957

Worcester, Alfred. **The Care of the Aged, the Dying, and the Dead.** 1950

Zandee, J[an]. **Death as an Enemy According to Ancient Egyptian Conceptions.** 1960